Thomas Aquinas Library

Companion to the

Summa Theologica

Volume 3

Revelation Insight Publishing Co. 2010

Dear Reader

1 Corinthians 2, 7-15: We speak the hidden mystical wisdom of God, which God ordained before the world unto our Glory; which none of the princes of this world knew, for had they known it, they would not have crucified the Lord of Glory. However, as it is written, eye has not seen, nor ear heard, neither has it entered into the Heart of man to conceive the things which God has prepared for them that Love him. However, God has revealed them unto us by His Spirit: For the Spirit searches all things, yes, and the deep things of God. For what man knows the things of a man, save the spirit o a man, which is in him? Even so, the thing of God knows no man, but the Spirit of God. Now we have received, not the Spirit of this world, but the Spirit, which is of God; that we might know the things that are freely given us of God. Which things also we speak, not in the words which man's wisdom teaches, but which the Holy Spirit teaches, comparing spiritual things with Spiritual. However, the natural man receives not the things of the Spirit of God. For they are foolishness unto him, neither can he know them, because they are spiritually discerned. Nevertheless, he that is spiritual judges or discerns all things.

Companion to the
Summa Theologica
by
Walter Farrell O.P.

The Complete Unabridged Texts

Re-edited for Today's Reader

Behold I stand at the door and knock, if anyone hears my voice and opens the door; I will come in and dine with him, and he with Me. He who overcomes, I will grant to sit down with Me on My throne, as I also overcame and with My Father on His throne. "Rev 3: 20-21

ISBN # 978-1-936392-09-4

Library of Congress Cataloging in Publication Data.

2009927245

BASAIC # REL 006000

Printed and bound in the USA

© 2011 Revelation Insight Publishing Co.

E-Mail: Mystic@Orthodox.com

Aquinas Library Series Forward

The staff at "Revelation-Insight" presents this series. The objective of this particular series is to provide the focused reader, student, and others who have a need to go beyond the fundamental basics and achieve something more. This series was designed to provide you with the necessary tools by Thomas Aquinas to have a ready answer to foundational subject matter and answers to key and essential portions of various philosophical and theological works.

These tools will come in the form of apologies, a historical reference, systematic theology and various dissertations. This particular work, which is more than an overview of the accumulative life's effort and its varied formularies; it is an insightful guide. Presenting you with the essential and fundamental key elements required in answering a bevy of questions and perhaps summarizing the information with a need for a deeper explanation.

Throughout this series, there will be additions, which could be considered not simply a reference work but much more, and indeed that is our aim. By, providing you with much more than you intended upon receiving and yet not to the point of becoming overwhelmed. This is our pledge to you the consumer, to always bring to you in a palatable formula and format. To the student, a ready reference, to the reader, to educate through pertinent information, to the educator an essential reference tool for all avenues and venues. This is what we inspire to become for you the consumer. Many times libraries have bits and pieces spread across numerous volumes, requiring numerous hours to comb through. This series is designed and produced to provide you with the correct and proper information you need to come to grasp and obtain a sure foundation in your understanding your history belief events, leading up to its current formulary. Since history is what it is, and the facts remain self evident, in this series, we will not subscribe nor slant our presentations, following particular denominations. We will present these as straightforward as numbers are in a math equation. The rational is the numbers and the equation is what it is. There is no need to interpret. There is only one way to solve, one way to proceed, and only one correct answer to grasp.

Editor's Notes

Rational, Method and Aim of This Modernization

The intention of this book is not for the scholar. Instead, it is for the pilgrim who does not have access, to such works. It is for such individuals, that this edition has been prepared. My aim has been to make Aquinas's meaning clear to the modern reader with as little alteration of the available texts as possible. I have modernized the spelling, have simplified long and involved constructions, and have tried to illuminate the meaning by careful punctuation. I have dealt sparingly with the vocabulary, striving to keep some of the words likely to be understood.

I am aware that by my modernization, I have laid myself open to criticism in many directions. I strove for consistency, and tried solely to retain as far as possible the simplicity and charm of the original spirit and intent

I could not, nor will I attempt to alter this authors' works. I concur in my small effort, which is based upon his efforts. I will however add that the majority of this work has some editorial alterations solely for readability purposes. My intention is to solidify the meaning. As many will attest, this composition and some of its siblings are quite intense and are neither easily understood nor digested in their original. Therefore, I have only added a select number of footnotes I trust this will enhance the readability of this monumental masterpiece.

<u>This text is presented in its entirety. It remains unabridged.</u>

This text carries it a style quite similar in grammar, expression, and phraseology that many early writers used. The complexity and other factors hint of this particular flavor. This effort follows Aristotle's, a.k.a. the philosopher's, format Nevertheless, I cannot begin to express what an impact this has had on me as I begin to edit this material. I am only a quarter of the way through this work and I feel and see such insight and reverence, which I have rarely seen before on such a minute and focused topic.

Aquinas is one who regardless of your placement on your spiritual journey. Aquinas is the basis for so much of what we have come to regard as dogma. This work is essential to not only understanding Aquinas's other works, but also our own journey. These issues, which he presents are not only fundamental, for many they are stumbling blocks, for others, they tend to be work around issues. These writings are the basics and yet essential works out of the plethora of works Aquinas has written. These are by no means the end all of him. They are merely the tip of a large glacier, which seems to forever be moving us forward.

A Locksmith

In time, much of this topic, enquiry and understanding will be relegated to the immortals as we plunged into the Dark Ages. It will not reemerge into the fore front until the likes of an equal intellectual Titan begins to bellow. This is none other than Thomas Aquinas, a prodigy, under the tutelage of Albert Magnus, a.k.a. Albert the Great, of the Cologne University. Aquinas is one of the few, who not only undertake this extraordinary issue to task, but will also bear fruit in this endeavor.

A Cipher and Mirror

a) The statement, "Reason is the handmaid of enlightenment."
b) "After what I have experienced, all that I have written are as straw."

The first comes to us from the Leviathan "Summa Theologica." [Aquinas 1.79.2] The second is just a few months prior to his death, it was not written, but intimately shared with a traveling monk. What is left in between has caused me to vacillate between the two and find the center portal, by which I may enter and ascend and pass on a discourse.

First, to dismiss Thomas Aquinas, is to dismiss the existence of the Empire State building when visiting, passing through or merely flying over NYC, you cannot mistake, nor fail to perceive its eminent presence among its contemporizes scraping against the skyline, more importantly, nor can you ignore its landmark heritage. The same applies to Thomas, his written efforts, and his rightful place among the School of Titans.

In this initial effort it is debuted by Walter Farrell's colossal undertaking of Synthesizing Thomas's Summa Theologica into a modern variation, making it relative to our world, environment and issues.

Peace be with you.

Brother Smith SGS 2011'

Introduction

Who is he?   Walter Farrell was a Dominican Theologian who, like Thomas in addressing his colleagues, attempted to provide a thorough understanding of this leviathan for the laity in a modern perspective of the original work coming into print by 1938.

What is objective? *Walter* attempts in these four books to treat and address the fundamentals of interpretation, using classic avenues of rhetoric and its siblings. He then applies this to understanding some of the fundamental issues, which continue to plaque many even today. This work has broad implications regarding man in his relationship with God. This effort, like its true narrative remains unrivaled.

The benefits of the work: This is a multifaceted response. Each of the above themes resonates in any scriptural interpreter. The lay out, progression is a three part progression of general overview, "Quid Pro Quo" format. The idea is to have you come to a quick overview of rhetoric and interpretation and then present you with a paper to skim through and find your way with supportive measures. Aquinas's work however, is not one to be taken lightly which you will see as you delve deeper into this matrix. In this presentation, it takes on a much more personal and manifested performance and experience, which I have not found, evidenced within another writer.

I am not sure of any other collection of his, which has such an underlying motive and yet, addresses the subject with the intensity as these four accomplish. We believe as you begin your journey beyond the neighborhood, and venture out, you will find this work indeed an essential work and a masterpiece in itself. In the last work presented here, Walter, using Thomas's work, addresses and hammers away at supporting and defining God's will and our will, righteousness and evil.

This works is of such great importance to our relationship with God. Our understanding of how God works and allows certain, events to transpire. To date, there is no other work assemblage as there is within this volume, which you are holding. To deny Aquinas, is to dismiss so much of what we have come to believe. Regardless of what faith denomination you are affiliated with, his works are the foundation of many seminaries and universities. This phase begins a bit stronger and tougher elements for the pilgrim. This phase will bring the pilgrim into the path and provide nourishment, rest, and shelter on their spiritual journey through these works.

Once again, I would like to caution you in this assembled work. In keeping as close to his style, it is problematic to edit. He is quite skillful in rhetoric, his points are quite accurate. While working through this arrangement, you will discover, uncover, and become face to face with many issues, which perhaps were inadequately assumed, presented, and believed. Aquinas/ Farrell will call you in for questioning and seek a resolution to your ideas.

A COMPANION TO THE SUMMA

VOLUME III -- THE FULLNESS OF LIFE

(Corresponding to the *Summa Theologica IIa Iiae*)

By
Walter Farrell

CONTENTS

I. FREEDOM FOR THE MIND q. 1-9

II. FREEDOM FOR THE WILL q. 10-22

III. SHARING THE DIVINE LIFE q. 23-26

IV. THE FULLNESS OF LOVE q. 27-36

V. THE EMPTINESS OF STRIFE q. 37-46

VI. THE FULLNESS OF ACTION q. 47-56

VII. THE FULLNESS OF SOCIAL LIFE q. 57-62

VIII. THE ESSENCE OF ANARCHY - I q. 63-71

IX. THE ESSENCE OF ANARCHY - II q. 72-80

X. THE FULLNESS OF RELIGION q. 81-87

XI. THE BARRENNESS OF IRRELIGION q. 88-100

XII. SOCIETY'S DEBTOR q. 101-110

XIII. ROOTS OF RUDENESS q. 111-122

XIV. THE FULLNESS OF COURAGE q. 123-127

XV. GREATNESS OF SOUL q. 128-140

XVI. THE HUMAN ANIMAL q. 141-145

XVII. THE FREEDOM OF PURITY q. 146-154

XVIII. THE FULLNESS OF TRUTH q. 155-165

XIX. MODESTY AND MIRACLES q. 166-178

XX. THE FULLNESS OF LIFE q. 179-189

CHAPTER I -- FREEDOM FOR THE MIND
(Q. 1-9)

1. Limitation and imperfection.

2. The limitless freedom of faith, from its object:
   (a) The object of faith -- the Supreme Truth.
   (b) The authority of faith -- a guarantee.
   (c) The obscurity of faith -- a promise.
   (d) Faith fitted to human stature -- the creeds.

3. The acts of a mind freed by faith:
   (a) Internal act -- belief, a contrast to natural belief.
        (1) Distinct from all other acts of the mind: knowledge,
             doubt, suspicion, opinion.
        (2) The merit of belief.
        (3) Necessity of belief:
             a. Concerning implicit belief.
             b. Regarding explicit belief.
   (b) External act -- confession of faith.

4. The habit of faith:
   (a) Its definition.
   (b) Its intellectuality.
   (c) Living and dead faith.
   (d) Its place among the virtues.
   (e) Its certitude.

5. The possessors of the freedom of faith:
   (a) Slaves of disbelief: the damned, devils, heretics.
   (b) Freemen of faith: angels, men, souls in Purgatory.

6. Sole cause of faith, living or dead.

7. Effects of faith: fear and purity.

8. Gifts of the Holy Spirit perfecting faith:
    (a) Understanding:
        (1) Its relation to faith and distinction from other gifts.
        (2) Its practicality.
        (3) Possessors of understanding.
        (4) Its beatitude and fruit.
    (b) Knowledge -- its nature and beatitude.

Conclusion:
1. Modern intellectual slavery:
    (a) Modern notions of faith.
    (b) Modern limitations of intellect:
        (1) To the tangible.
        (2) To the demonstrable.
        (3) To the fictitious.

2. Faith and intellect -- a perfection not a substitution.

3. Freedom for the mind:
    (a) The courage of faith.
    (b) The fullness of faith.
    (c) The practicality of faith.
    (d) The future of faith.

◫CHAPTER I ◫
FREEDOM FOR THE MIND
(Q. 1-9)

The spectacle of a wild bird beating out its life against the windows of a desolate house into which it has wandered awakens pity within us. This creature was made for long, swift, free flights. Yet this picture cannot compare with that of the misery of a man beating out his life against the prison walls of sense, or indeed, with the innate tragedy of human nature which must always beat out its energy against the prison walls of the universe itself. It is true that while a dog chained up becomes irritable and eventually savage, a man might accept and even relish a narrow, confining room; accepting it as a challenge to be met by the power of his mind to wander outside its walls, outside the limits of time and space. He exults in the knowledge that nothing material can really confine him.

Limitation and imperfection.

Nevertheless, in the human mind itself there is a limitation, a confinement. It can reach outside the day or the hour, it can reach back into the past or ahead into the future; it can reach up even to God. Yet only to God as the author of nature, only to a partial view of divinity. However, long the labors of a man, however keen his intellect, however earnest his efforts, man must always come up short against the barriers of the natural universe. The nature of man does not surpass the powers of nature.

Man, left to himself, is essentially a prisoner; a prisoner of his own nature. At the same time, that nature is crying out for freedom, crying out for a fuller and fuller vision of the things that remain to be seen. The prison walls that limit his freedom can be penetrated by only one force. Those walls are the walls of nature; only the supernatural can tear them down, only an agent above nature can give man the vast freedom of infinity, of eternity, can permit him to grasp the things that are too bright for his eyes -- only God Himself through the gift known as the virtue of faith.

The limitless freedom of faith, from its object

It is essential that we see faith in the guise of a liberator, if we are to see it at all. To see it as a limitation, a suppression of, or a substitute for, man's intellect is to lose completely the essential notion of faith. Let us look at it this way: man has a journey to make: to take one step on this journey he must know his destination. To give that knowledge is the work of faith. It is the starting gun in the race of life; by faith, man is set free to rush to the goal of faith, which is the goal of life. Since the goal is no less than the essence of God Himself, we can see immediately that faith sets a man free to rush beyond the uttermost limits of the universe.

The object of faith -- the Supreme Truth

Some men have described faith as an exaggerated optimism, a kind of super-confidence; but that was because they did not know the purpose of faith. Others have reduced faith to emotion; and that was because they did not know what faith was. Still others have cynically put under faith every bit of our rational knowledge of God; and that was because they did not know what man was. Faith is something bigger than all this. In fact it is so big we can walk by and never see it; it is not to be caught in the corner of the eye, it demands the whole of a man's eye, the whole of his mind. Its bigness can be appreciated only by concentrating on the goal to which it goes and the means by which it reaches that goal. Seen in this light it towers over us frighteningly, for it aims at supreme Truth and so at the supreme perfection of the intellect of man. How can we know the First Truth unless we be told by the one Being Who can know it, knowing Himself? Faith has rightly been called a theological, a divine virtue; it looks to the very essence of God Himself, and attains to its sublime object through the action of God Himself, through the supreme Truth's gracious stooping to tell us about Himself. It is saturated with divinity though it is made for man.

Because faith is so wrapped up in divinity, it brings to the human mind mystery piled on mystery. Nor is the element of mystery confined to the ineffable secrets of divinity which faith brings to man; the very revelation by which these secrets are made known is itself mysterious. It is the strong light, which brings out in the dim sharpness of a silhouette the lineaments of the face of God. Of course this light does not need, indeed cannot have, another light by which it itself is seen; in other words, the very revelation itself is not only the means, it is also an object of faith. The divine message cannot be made known by natural means; its contents surpasses all of nature. Miracles may be worked by way of confirmation of it or as evidence of its credibility but it can be surely known only by faith itself.

Faith then is a giant cannon which hurls man out beyond the boundaries of the universe into the world of the infinite It is not to be conceived of as something mild, sweetly enfeebling. Rather it must be thought of in terms of strength, of an explosion, which has broken down the walls of the world, of a storming of nature by the hosts of heaven that man might be released from the limitations of his humanity. It grants to man the freedom by which he can surpass not only the limits of the present, of the past, of space, of material things, but even the limits of all nature. By it, his mind walks into the limitlessness of God.

The attitude of the modern world to faith is as unreasonable, and in its own way as comic, as the attitude of the man who dislikes only one thing about collars -- that they go around his neck. In the face of faith, we feel an irritation at its darkness, its obscurity. Of course, faith is obscure. The whole point of faith is precisely that it gives us a truth we cannot see of ourselves. Because we are using the eyes of God, in the darkness we can know the incredible truths that only God can see. To demand clear brightness in matters of faith and at the same time to expect to win to the freedom of faith is like wishing the sun would disappear forever from the heavens that we might the more comfortably enjoy the summer.

The young lady who attempts to enhance her charm by using baby-talk presents as distastefully incongruous a picture as a child swearing like a trooper. Adulthood and infancy are not thus intermingled. Yet it is something like this we insist on in demanding that we see the things of faith. When it comes to the inner life of God Himself, God is the teacher and we are the children gathered at His feet; we do not, cannot see the things of which He tells us, for vision is the work of the adult, even of our Father God. Our part is the part of children, to believe, not to see, until one day when we are supernaturally grown up, possessed of our own mansion in heaven.

The authority of faith -- a guarantee

There are some truths, which a man may first believe and later see, truths that are within the reach of reason but which the circumstances of life do not allow to be scientifically investigated by everyone Even such as these are guaranteed by the gracious authority of God. Now the primary truths of faith, supernatural truths, are beyond the fingertips of our minds.

In fact, we make ourselves ridiculous when we mistake the reasons offered by saints or by theologians for proofs of such truths as the Trinity or the Incarnation. They are never proofs: persuasions perhaps, evidences that these truths are not impossible, facilitating the bending of our stubborn wills and petty intellects, but no more. The reason, the only reason, for our acceptance of supernatural truth is the authority of God Himself. It is always a solid, safe thing to accept truth from the Supreme Truth.

We are not only irritated at faith's darkness; we too often resent the very authority upon which faith rests. Behind this irritation, there is a fear of error if a truth is not subjected to the judgment of our mind that is not unlike the uneasiness of a woman who is quite sure the house will not be cleaned properly unless she cleans it herself. Acceptance of truth on faith seems somehow to be a reflection on ourselves, to be an indignity to the nature of man. However, the whole point of faith is that it gives us truths we cannot possibly reach of ourselves. If we do not take these truths on some one's authority we cannot have them at all; and we must have them for the living of life.

The obscurity of faith -- a promise

The obscurity of faith gives us a promise that here and now in this darkness we will hear of unutterable things, things that only God has a right to see. More than that, it is a promise that when this present darkness cowers and flies before an eternal sun, these incredible truths will remain for us to see with our own eyes. Indeed this obscurity is a beginning of a future life, the beginning of that vision of God, which will reach its full clarity only when life is over and we have attained our goal. The authority to which we must submit is not an insult; it is a guarantee, a guarantee that trusting ourselves to God in this darkness, nothing of injury shall come to us. We shall not be misled, not be tricked; but rather we shall be shown the riches, the beauty, the goodness of divinity.

It is rare that a girl finds her prince charming in the lad who lives next door. Either he is a complete stranger, or he is so well known as to be taken for granted, which means that he is never seen at all. Somewhat the same thing is true of faith in the modern world. It may be taken for granted by those to whom it has been so freely given, or ignored by those to whom it is a stranger. Now, it demands a peculiar blindness to miss the charm of faith. There is obviously about faith the charm of tenderness, of whispered details between lovers as God shares the intimate secrets of His divine light with his friends. Even more touching perhaps is faith's charm of thoughtfulness. The Infinite Being stoops to the level of our childish minds, putting into the short, simple, straightforward language of the creed the ineffable truths of His divinity in order that the simplest of the faithful might easily and securely hold to truths that surpass the highest of created minds.

Faith fitted to human stature -- the creeds

There is, in fact, a divine ingenuity about the formulation of the creed. What could be more divinely simple than the limitation of the creed to the end or goal of man -- God and the things of God -- and the way by which man reaches that goal -- the humanity of Christ and the things that pertain to that humanity? Yet that is precisely the make-up of the symbols of the faith. On God's side, faith has the unity of divinity itself. On our side, the individual articles of faith are distinguished in order that what might represent a special difficulty for our belief might not in any way confuse us as to what is to be believed.

In this connection, men too often make the mistake of seeing the Church as an imperious mother regulating the last details of the lives of her children long after they are well able to take care of themselves. It is true that ecclesiastical authority determines the form in which these articles of faith shall be proposed; but it is not ecclesiastical authority that reveals the truths, which are to be believed. The Church tells us, not that these things are true, but that they are truly revealed. Their truth rests on God and on God alone.

Faith's story is not a bit of gossip started by a whisper from God and bandied about down through the ages, becoming richer, more spicy with the telling, until finally it becomes a story so tall that it would astonish God Himself. It is not a primitive discovery of truth that has been enriched through the thought, the experiments, the imaginations of men. The Church has made no substantial increase in matters of faith. Let us put it this way. The articles of faith are the first principles of supernatural knowledge; every supernatural truth must be traced back to the first principles and is, in fact, contained in those first principles. Of these first principles, the absolutely first are the truths of God's existence as author of the supernatural and God's providence by which men are led to their end. Perhaps St. Gregory had it right when he said that those who were very close to Christ did not need so much explanation, so much explicit statement of those first principles. They saw in them all the other truths, much as the angels see all other truths in the first principles of natural thought.

Now, that is hardly so of the rest of us. From Adam to Christ the story of faith was slowly being told; after the death of John the Evangelist, faith was a story completely told. From then on, it was a matter of repeating repeatedly an old, loved tale, savoring it, caressing it, allowing its perfume to permeate the remotest corners of our souls. All this involved no substantial increase, but it did demand what might be called an accidental increase; that is an unfolding, an uncovering of truths contained in these first truths. On the other hand, in one word, a penetration of the truths that had been given us.

There have been, for example, explicit propositions of implicit truths such as the Immaculate Conception; scientific expositions of such truths as the Trinity -- through the distinction of nature and person; express propositions of truths formerly proposed only passingly or by practice, or truths that had been called into doubt such as the validity of baptism by heretics.

Indeed, it would have been most strange if there had been no such increase. The Church would have been a most unkind mother to ignore the threat of confusion to her children made by heresies when a clear definition would have protected them. Her love of truth could not ignore the opportunities offered for illustration and further exposition by the progress of philosophical and scientific thought. Surely the love and thoughtfulness of the Holy Spirit, the long investigations of theologians, the sincere and profound devotion of the faithful should not have failed to uncover more and more of the profound beauties, the hidden truths contained in these first principles of all supernatural truth.

The acts of a mind freed by faith
Internal act -- belief, a contrast to natural belief

Faith's object, the Supreme Truth, is reached by the act of faith, an act which is first internal -- belief -- and then external -- confession of that belief. In the order of human faith, the internal act is completed when the gullible victim believes the soothing story of the confidence man. The external act is the eager purchase of a gold brick. The comparison of human and supernatural faith is not without purpose. Human faith has considerable discredit attached to it, and rightly so. It is not a virtue perfecting the intellect of man; much more frequently, it is a means of emptying his pockets or betraying his mind for it contains too many possibilities of error and mistake even when the human authority upon which it rests is most sincere. In history, for example, based as it is on human faith, we have uncovered serious mistakes, which have endured for centuries. No such thing can happen in supernatural faith. It is an infallible source of truth; it rests not on the mind and veracity of man, but on the mind and the veracity of God.

Distinct from all other acts of the mind: knowledge, doubt, suspicion, opinion

To describe the act of supernatural belief we could do no better than to define it as "the act of pondering with assent". It is, of course, paradoxical that our intellect should be restless, pondering, in the face of a truth, yet at the same time assent to that truth firmly. Actually this definition brings out the full nature of the act of faith We do not suspect this truth, as a man might suspect the presence of burglars from the uneasiness of his dog; we are not doubting it; we have not merely an opinion of it, such as we might gather from the hasty accounts in a morning newspaper; we do not see it clearly, as we might the results of a scientific experiment. We believe it. Additionally, we thereby produce an act distinct from all other acts of the mind.

The merit of belief

Faith is like a jack-in-the-box: the spring is the intellect; the lid, holding down the spring, is the will. The intellect is straining against the obscurity of faith. With the weakening of the will, through moral degeneration, the power to hold down the intellect becomes less and less until finally, with sufficient weakening of the will, the spring pop, out -- faith is lost. With the loss of faith man becomes a rebel against God, for the act of belief completes man's subjection to God, a subjection which perfects his will in its loving, the intellect in its belief. Indeed, that paradoxical pondering with assent is the secret of the great merit of faith for it means that every act of faith must come from our free will, not at all forced upon us by our intellect faced with indisputable evidence.

It is not intellectual progress, then, but moral decay which represents a threat to faith. The cardinal of the Catholic Church has learned much since, as a tot, he stumbled over his catechism. Undoubtedly now he can prove to his own satisfaction many of those preliminary truths he formerly accepted by faith. However, obviously his intellectual progress has not equipped him to grapple with truths that are above all natural powers. Just as obviously, his present abilities have done no injury to his faith. If you like, the extent of his faith has decreased but not its intensity; for now, as in the beginning of his rational life, the cardinal has that same deep respect for and ready acceptance of the authority of God. Additionally, it is this, which provides the merit of faith.

Whatever his genius, this cardinal, all through life, will constantly face the thoughtfully humiliating gesture of God by which He assures men that spirit of humble inquiry which is the root of knowledge. It was kind of God to toss before our minds truths which those minds can never possibly absorb; to give us something to think about that no amount of thinking can possibly unravel. Now we shall be slow indeed to cherish any illusions about the supreme powers of our minds.

Necessity of belief

Now all this was more than kind, it was necessary. It is only by such humble belief that we can possibly know of the supernatural end which constitutes our happiness, and it is only by knowing of it that we can take any steps towards it. Faith ordains us directly to God; and by that, ordination both unites us to the rest of the universe and at the same time cuts us off distinctly from every other creature. Every creature in the universe is moved by a superior, ordered to an end above itself, though in achieving that end it is itself destroyed. Man alone has no immediate superior in the universe by whom and to whom he can be moved. The plant can exist for the animal to feed upon it, the animal for man. Animals can be moved by men and elevated to the plane of man, sustaining him; they can even participate in the very reason of man by the training he gives them. Yet man is a solitary creature, a lonely sovereign in the universe. He is at the top, and the top is too often an empty, desolate place. For his movement, for his perfecting termination and ordination, for his final end, man must look to God Himself. Achieving that infinitely superior plane, he is not destroyed but perfected.

To our modern generation, one of the most annoying characteristics of faith is its absolute character. It permits of no compromise; you must take all of it or have none of it. How much nicer it would be if we could shop around among the wares of faith, accepting heaven but rejecting hell, embracing the Savior and snubbing the Judge, sighing over love and ignoring justice. Just so, a woman might stroll out in the early afternoon to buy asparagus but shudder at carrots and, perhaps, be insulted at the butcher's suggestion of stew for supper. It would be so much nicer -- if we were not looking for faith! However pleased we might be with our selections, when the package was untied we would find any number of things there, but not faith. For faith accepts truths because of the infallible authority of the one revealing, not because of the palatability of those truths to jaded appetites. To reject any one truth is to reject the authority, which offers all of these truths, to accuse God of having been fooled Himself, or of trying to fool us.

Concerning implicit belief

In matters of faith we cannot pick and choose; we must take all or nothing. Of course, much may be taken implicitly; but some at least must be believed explicitly -- at the very least the existence of God our supernatural end, and His providence. It is the opinion of St. Thomas that the Trinity and Incarnation must also be explicitly believed, that they too are truths absolutely necessary for salvation. His reasoning is clear and compelling. Man must believe the truths without which he cannot reach his end. Since the Incarnate God is the way of salvation, the Incarnation surely must be believed; and to believe the Incarnation is to believe that the Son of God was conceived by the Virgin through the power of the Holy Spirit. In other words, the proposition of the truth of the Incarnation necessarily involves the declaration of the truth of the Trinity. However, this opinion of St. Thomas is not a blanket condemnation of infidels as will be made evident in the next chapter. Other truths must, of course, be explicitly believed; but not because of their absolutely essential connection with our last end, rather because of the solemn nature of the assurance given that these truths are indeed revealed by God. Such, for example, are the articles of faith contained in the creed and the sacraments necessary for salvation.

Regarding explicit belief

No one expects an unlettered washwoman to have the same explicit faith as has a bishop. Perhaps the woman has never heard of transubstantiation, though she knows with the sure knowledge of faith that she receives her Lord and her God in Holy Communion; but may God help the bishop if he has never heard of transubstantiation. In the orderly divine plane of the universe, inferior creatures are moved to their ends by their superiors. Nor is the divine order different in the world of men. High positions, rare gifts, are not merely assets or privileges; they are much more responsibilities, and in a sense debts in reference to those in inferior positions or of inferior gifts. In the ecclesiastical world, those in authority by their very office are obliged to have a much more explicit faith than their subjects that they might more surely guide those over whom they are placed. However, of course every Catholic is obliged, by the very notion of faith, to believe, at least implicitly, absolutely every truth God has revealed. Anything less than this is a rejection of the basis on which every truth of faith rests.

External act -- confession of faith

We can ponder without grunting, we can assent without shouting hallelujah; for active belief is something entirely within us. The external expression of the act of belief is called confession of faith. In a negative sense we are all obliged to confess our faith always; i.e., there is never a time when it is legitimate to deny the faith, for there is never a time when we may deny God and the truth of God. However, in a positive sense, the confession of faith is quite another story.

The drunkard who solemnly recites the Hail Mary as he staggers down the street is doing himself no good, and is certainly doing the Church no good. He is surely not fulfilling a precept commanding him to confess his faith. A Catholic is not obliged to jump up in a meeting of Orangemen and shout out his Catholicity. Riot is not necessary for the confession of faith; common sense is. Some courage is necessary; cowardice is never wholly excusable. The simple norms by which our obligation to confess our faith can be determined are: the honor of God, and the good of our neighbor. We are obliged to confess our faith when our silence would do great injury to the honor of God or fail to win a great honor for God. As far as our neighbor is concerned, when our silence drives some one away from the faith or seriously holds back some person from approaching to that faith, we fail at a time when we should confess our faith. Or when a great spiritual advantage is lost to our neighbor by our failure to confess our faith if that advantage cannot be given effectively in any other way or any other time and place except here and now by our confession of faith, then we have failed not only our neighbor but we have failed God. Yet the obligation to confess the faith does not mean that we must walk up to a persecutor and demand that he shoot us. Indeed the Catholic in full flight from an enemy of the faith is confessing his faith though in a different fashion than his fellows who face a firing squad in defense of the faith. He flees precisely that he may not run the risk of failing to confess his faith; for surely there would be no need of flight if he were to disown the faith that is being persecuted. Up to this point, we have been dealing with faith as though we were tracing the trajectory of a heavy shell from the hole it has made, trying to determine the angle that we might come back to the big gun from which it was hurled. We began by examining the object of faith, the final goal which faith hits. From that goal, we saw the long arch of the act of faith by which men come to that last goal. Now we come to the source, the gun from which that act of faith is projected. We have come to the habit of faith.

The habit of faith: Its definition

Thomas' definition of it, "a habit of mind by which eternal life is begun in us, making our intellect assent to unseen truths", is worthy of his metaphysician's mind and his poet's heart. However, dark or obscure that beginning may be, faith is a beginning of that vision of Supreme Truth, which will make up the essence of eternal life. Into those few words, Thomas has packed the supernatural character of faith, its celestial beauty, and the work of intellect and will in the habit of faith. Let us look at these last two more closely.

Its intellectuality

In his insistence on faith as a "habit of mind", St. Thomas stresses the intellectual character of faith. It was almost a prophetic emphasis Thomas made, for about this very point revolve two of the most serious errors against faith since the time of St. Thomas. As an intellectual virtue -- a good operative habit -- faith perfects the intellect in order to its proper object of truth; indeed faith equips the intellect to know the Supreme Truth Additionally, this is in flat opposition to the sentimentalists and irrationalists from Feuerbach down who have made faith a matter of feeling or emotion. However great the perfection conferred on the intellect by faith, as a virtue it must always limp simply because it is an intellectual virtue. Its super-naturality does not excuse it from the common fault of intellectual virtues, i.e., the fault of limitation of perfection. Excellence in the science of chemistry does not make a man good, but rather makes him a good chemist; for these intellectual virtues, of their very nature, seek not the good of man, but the good of his intellect only. It was ignorance of this fundamental philosophical truth that was at the root of the exaggerated optimism of Luther and the reformers relative to Faith.

Living and dead faith

The fact remains that faith, of itself, must always stop short at its proper intellectual goal; giving a man knowledge of sublime truths, but no more. The elimination of this imperfection of faith must come from outside itself, from another virtue that will order it beyond its own proper object to the goal of the whole man. It is in this way that faith is changed from a dead to a living faith, from faith unformed to formed faith, when charity, coming with sanctifying grace, orders it to the end of the will, the end of charity, which is the goal of man.

In the sense that this further ordination does not come from faith itself, it is accidental to faith. Yet, it is by no means unimportant to faith. Yet this accidental character of faith's perfection must not be forgotten; it means that God in His goodness, does not give the sinner a full foretaste of hell. While serious sin, other than infidelity, destroys grace, charity, and most of the infused virtues, it still leaves the foundation stone of supernatural life, the basis of hope -- a firm belief in the supreme Truth and the infallible authority of that supreme Truth telling us the details of His personal life.

Its place among the virtues

For faith is fundamental, and therefore first. Not of course in the sense of the winner of a six-day bicycle race being first. All the infused virtues are given simultaneously; but in the order in which we must think of these things, the theological virtues dealing with the end of man come before the moral virtues dealing with the means to the end and the end must be known (by faith) before it can be striven for (by hope) or embraced (by charity). There may, of course, be some accidental virtues preceding faith such as a kind of fortitude or humility to deal with the fundamental impediments to faith. Whether we are looking at the case of the Anglican minister who hesitates to embrace the faith because of the family dependent on him, or of the university professor who hesitates to sacrifice the self-sufficiency of his intellect to belief in the First Intellect, these fundamental impediments to which all others are reduced are always fear and pride.

The part of the will in faith, which is to bring about assent to unseen truths, far outweighs the part of the intellect. Normally one sick and one healthy parent generate a sickly child, one good and one bad football team produce a miserable game; it is expecting too much to demand that the effect be more perfect than the principles which produce it. Now, although faith proceeds from both intellect and will, its vigor depends little on the intellect, desperately on the will. After all the truths of faith do not depend on the acuity, vitality or energy of the human intellect, these truths are above all created intellect. Now, as the will is less strong, there is inevitably a loss to the strength and vigor of faith.

Its certitude

For all the restlessness of the intellect, the house of faith is a serene, peaceful home. Certainly, there is in it none of the bickering always to be found in the mansions of art and prudence, which deal only with contingent things. Indeed, in its cause, the certitude of faith exceeds even the certitude of the speculative virtues, knowledge, wisdom and understanding; it is, in fact, as much more certain as the intellect of God is more perfect than the intellect of man. It is true that subjectively we might feel more secure holding to the first principles seen by the intellect than to the truths believed by faith. Yet, so too might a man feel much more sure that he has seen a ghost than that two and two are four, although certainly the simple sum of addition rests upon a much greater metaphysical certitude than does the wandering ghost. Still, faith is not a question of feeling, it is not a question of intellectual rest, it is not a question of stubborn adherence. It is a matter of complete, absolute infallibility that can come from only the one source, the First, Supreme Truth. Even the angelically operating intellectual gifts of the Holy Spirit must make their obeisance to faith as their superior, as the mistress, they work to beautify and adorn.

The possessors of the freedom of faith: Slaves of disbelief: the damned, devils, heretics

The modern pagan businessman shrugs off faith as contemptuously as a football star might shrug off the rubbers sent out to him on a rainy day by an over-solicitous coach. After all, he is doing very well without faith; obviously, he can get along without it. Let the women, children and weaklings have it. In fact, the only man who does not need faith is a dead man; it is only in heaven or hell that there is no room for faith. What need have angels or the saints in heaven for faith when they are seeing God face to face? What need have devils for the foundation of hope, who are without hope? What right has the damned souls of men to a supernatural gift where there is nothing of the supernatural but punishment? The devils may have their suspicions of opinions on matters of faith, the damned may have poignant memories of the acts of faith they have made in life; but the faith that gives infallible knowledge of the intimate details of the life of divinity -- no, there is none of that in hell.

What of those who have "lost the faith?" Their eyes remain the same color, their walk has the same aggressiveness, their smile the same attraction; but then we did not expect an exterior change. What if they had lost only one truth, say the truth of papal infallibility; do they not hold as firmly as ever to all the rest? Indeed, they do not. So long as faith remains, nothing pertaining to faith can be denied; when anything of faith is lost, all is lost.

The heretic has been too often painted in heroic colors, as a strong man who stood up in defiance of the lightnings of ecclesiastical, and often civil, authority. Actually, the heretic is a weakling. The faith is for the strong, for those who are willing to go all the way; there is no room here for mediocrity, for compromising. We must take all or take nothing. Faith demands a boldness, a storming of the walls of heaven with all bridges burnt behind us, a courage that must always make the weakling of the world shiver.

Sole cause of faith, living or dead

The heretic is a weakling, but a weakling who has suffered a tragic loss. How can he regain his faith? Faith is not to be bought or sold; it cannot be stolen, or wheedled out of some one. If Christ working miracles, preaching divinely wise sermons, making prophecies and fulfilling them, giving up His very life, left many astonished and struck with fear but only a few believing, it is clear that no external cause can bring us faith. Nothing within us can give us something above all nature. Faith must always remain a gift of God; a story told by the only One Who knows it. Now -- and this is supremely important -- it is a gift offered to every man who comes into the world; withheld from a man only because he has placed an impediment to its reception. Once we have tossed the inestimable gift away through pride or sensuality, it is only the benevolence of God that can return the lost gift to us.

The child, who does not think about so serious a thing as health, dreams of meals that are made up of desserts. Men and women, who do not think about so serious a thing as living, dream of a life that consists only of sweetness, soft music and rest to the echo of applause and gently sympathetic understanding. Meals are never like that; neither is life. In the same vein, our modern men and women dream of God as a being of whom no one could ever be afraid, a gentle, stupid god who would allow men and women to ruin themselves and then admire them for the work they had done in destroying his masterpiece. You see they never really think about God, for God is not like that.

Effects of faith: fear and purity

One of the very first effects of faith is fear. It is hard to see how it could be otherwise. For one of the disconcerting things about faith is that it tells us not only of heaven but also of hell; it not only speaks of the true but it also warns of the false end of man; it insists, not only that God is worth having, but also that the loss of Him is the supreme tragedy. To really know God means that we must know Him also as the judge of men, the punisher of evil; and we are afraid of His punishments. This is what the theologians call the "fear of a slave". Understand it is not that hypocritical fear that holds back a man's hands or feet from sin, leaving his heart free to embrace the evil action. It is rather a solid, honest, thoroughly understandable fear, a supernatural fear that is the product of unformed or dead faith.

When charity breathes the breath of life into faith, the fear engendered by faith is the fear of a loving child faced with the possibility of becoming separated from its parents; for by this live faith we not only know God, He is the most desirable thing in our life. As this "fear of a child", this reverential fear increases with the increase of charity, the fear of punishment decreases because the very grounds for fearing punishment -- the temptation to separate from that desirable good -- becomes less and less. In a word, we think less of self and more of God. An interesting corollary of this fear inspired by faith is that there is really more hope for the salvation of those who frankly fight God than for those who are indifferent to Him; for this battle against divinity springs from fear, a fear that should lead to hope but which can be made to end in despair.

If we recognize the fact that the farther a man gets from mud the less likely he is to pick up mud on his clothing, or the further we remove gold from its alloys the purer it gets, we are in a fair way to see that purity is a second effect of faith. This purity is, of course, primarily intellectual purity, freedom from error; but it is at the same time the foundation and the goal of purity of the affections, moral purity. For moral purity is a means to an end, a step taken toward a goal, it is asking too much to demand it when there is no goal in sight. Moral impurity in a world that has pushed aside the intellect, denied the goal, or smiled at the possibility of approaching a Supreme Truth which would give infallible knowledge is not surprising, however pained the classroom philosopher may be by its appearance on his campus.

By the gift of faith we stand outside the walls of the natural world, free and thoroughly bewildered, We are as much puzzled by our freedom as we were resentful at our limitations. In a world that is native to God, we are immigrants, awkward, strange, ill at ease, for we are not gods. We need something more than faith to give us that flexibility, familiarity and suavity that belong to a citizen of this world; and that something more comes to us by the gifts of the Holy Spirit.

Gifts of the Holy Spirit perfecting faith: Understanding

In the natural order, when we see that turnips do not agree with us, we do more than assent to that truth; we penetrate it to some extent, it becomes a part of our equipment and enters into our judgments. We may take turnips again, but only because our passion for turnips has rushed us into action against our better judgment. Such a truth is natural to us. Now the truths of faith are above us, assenting to them by faith, we do not penetrate them; have them enter into our judgments. Rather we handle them somewhat as a foreigner handles our language. However, we must penetrate these truths, seize on them, experience them, intimately apply them in all our judgments; they must become a part of our point of view. This is the work of the gifts of the Holy Spirit, supplementing and perfecting faith.

Its relation to faith and distinction from other gifts

The first of these gifts, the gift of understanding, has for its special work precisely that penetration of faith. It goes beyond assent to a kind of probing of these truths, but in a way as different from our natural operation as an angel's mind is different from a man's. It makes the truths of faith con natural to us. We plunge into their depths with the speed of an angelic mind, probing them to their core, not with effort, slowly, step by step, stumbling from principle to conclusion, but intuitively, immediately, con-naturally.

We get some notion of the work of this gift when we realize that its perfection is no less than a clear vision of the essence of God. It is then impossible to have the full perfection of the gift of understanding in this life. Indeed, it is difficult to describe the effect of that share of the gift possible in this life. Perhaps we can say best that it deepens the darkness of faith. That is, it allows us to see intimately what this particular truth is by seeing what it is not and, consequently how far above anything natural, above all the capacities of our intellect, this truth is. The gift allows us to appreciate the sublimity of the truths that faith has given us.

Its practicality

Remember now, the gift of understanding is not an exotic thing reserved for the higher levels of sanctity. It is absolutely necessary for everyone if life is to be lived successfully. It is by no means a spiritual luxury, for it has that eminent practicality of the truths of faith themselves, the practicality of the fundamental rule of life and action. Our actions, all of them, must be steeped in divine truth, dyed with the divinity, which is their end; otherwise, they are disastrously against all we are living for. There are, of course, different grades of perfection of this gift of understanding; but at least the lowest grade must be had by everyone who is to win to the goal of life.

Possessors of understanding

This will be immediately clear when we understand this first or lowest grade is that which is sufficient for fulfilling our obligations, the grade of penetration of the truths of faith by which we resist all objections, all difficulties. Up a step higher, we are enabled to see more profoundly into the perfection of God and, by contrast, into the miseries of man; this is the grade of perfection of the gift necessary for the observance of the counsels of Christ. Finally, the sublime grade of understanding in this life, the heroic grade, pertains to the mystical life and is a principle of infused contemplation. It is what the saints have tried to describe vaguely as a mystical marriage to the spouse of the soul; it is, somehow, an intimate knowledge of the presence of divinity.

Its beatitude and fruit

Earlier in this chapter, we have said that moral purity while an effect of the intellectual purity of faith was in a larger sense a beginning of an intellectual purity that ultimately will be the essential happiness of man. It is in the light of this truth that St. Thomas points out the beatitude, "Blessed are the clean of heart for they shall see God," as corresponding to the sharply intellectual gift of understanding, cleanness of heart as the element of merit, vision of God as the reward. Indeed this growth to a greater and greater intellectual purity is stated in the very terms traditionally used to describe the progress of spiritual life -- the purgative, illuminative and unitive way; for it is by his intellect that man receives light and ultimately is united to God. The supreme effect, the ultimate ripe fruit of this gift of understanding is an eminent certitude, which is, indeed. Common to the three intellectual gifts of knowledge, understanding and wisdom, for all work to the perfection of faith and faith itself is given to us that we might certainly know God.

Knowledge -- its nature and beatitude

We are released from the prison of the universe by faith. Understanding allows us to enter intimately into the divine world. The gift of knowledge enables us to see the world from which we have escaped in the light of the world to which faith has brought us. It is seen in a high degree of perfection in the life of St. Francis of Assisi where, obviously, its work was neither assent, nor penetration, but judgment of created things in the light of divine truths. We might say that it makes the knowledge of faith a personal knowledge. By it, we are enabled to see God in the dust, as the good thief saw a king in the criminal dying on a cross. Strictly speaking, there is no beatitude corresponding to this gift for it deals with the created world, which contains no final resting place for the soul of man; it is always a step, a means to beatitude, not a place of ultimately desirable things. However on its less practical side, speaking in our clumsy sense of practicality, it might be said that the beatitude, "Blessed are they that mourn, for they shall be comforted," does correspond to the gift of knowledge.

A not uncommon error sees in this beatitude a justification of the whiners of the world. At the mere mention of "this vale of tears", the weepers heave a sigh that has about it the suspicious perfection of a publicity department, and indulge in another fit of tears of self-pity. The truth of the matter is that beatitude and self-pity are not even distant relations, however comforting self-pity may be. By valley of tears, we really mean valley of mistakes. We have no grounds for tears that we are abused, misunderstood, suffer, have accidents happen to us; in fact we do not have nearly as much misfortune as we deserve for our ingratitude to God. Our real grounds for tears are to be found in our own mistakes, in the intimate knowledge of the damage we have done to ourselves by our inordinate affection for and use of creatures. On the other hand, the knowledge of the good that has come to us from orderly affection for and use of creatures is a source of solid comfort.

To put all this more plainly, this gift of knowledge lights up the path by which we can avoid Puritanism and at the same time escape the absurdities of plunging into the world of creatures. This gift, like all the gifts, not only leads us securely to God, its operation is evident in the heights of mystical life; in other words, this gift insists upon the advantages of an orderly affection for and use of creatures all along the long road to God, indeed not only advantages, positive necessities of such an orderly affection.

Conclusion: Modern intellectual slavery

To say that the modern world has condemned itself to intellectual slavery, or to say that the modern world knows nothing of supernatural faith is really to say the same thing. We can approach this conclusion from either of two angles: either by looking at modern notions of faith, or at the actual limitations placed upon the intellect by the modern world.

Modern notions of faith

From the first point of view, it is clear that practically from the time of the Reformation faith has been relegated to the realm of the emotional. In our own times this tendency has reached what must be a climax when the neo-super naturalists, the very champions of faith, reject intellect as a constant source of error; ethical intuitionists and aesthetic naturalists make faith an irrational thing in no way connected with the rational; while the philosophers rooted in the tradition of naturalism -- by far the greater part of vocal American philosophers -- chuckle cynically at all this and put faith aside as unworthy of man, particularly of a man of science accustomed to investigating evidence and arriving at logical conclusions.

Today faith is a hypothesis, a postulate, a mere wish or will to believe, perhaps an emotional affair that is entirely individual and personal. Certainly then our modern world will condemn the intellect, at the very least, to its own limitations, to the limitations of the world of creatures.

Modern limitations of intellect:

To the tangible; to the demonstrable; to the fictitious

Yet viewing the modern position from the angle of the actual limitation placed upon the intellect by philosophers, we see the incredible picture of a man who not only insists upon his own confinement, he refuses to take advantage of the prison courtyard for his exercise, indeed refuses even to move in the narrow corridors between the cells. He insists that he be kept rigidly in his cell bound hand and foot because there is nothing beyond his chains. This may sound incredible, but it is not nearly as incredible as our modern philosophers limiting the mind of man to tangible things, or going further and limiting the mind of man to those things that can be demonstrated, or even, in these latter days, limiting the intellect to the purely fictitious, as a purveyor of error for practical purposes. The future will have a hard time indeed, if it is to surpass this as a climax of absurdity; for never in the history of the world has there been anything as impractical as error.

Faith and intellect -- a perfection not a substitution

All of this is intellectual slavery; all of it implies an abysmal ignorance of the very nature of supernatural faith. Faith is not an opponent of intellect; it is not a substitute for intellectual operations. It is a perfection of intellect. It carries the intellect far beyond anything it could reach of itself; surely, it in no way makes intellectual activity useless, suspicious or positively vicious. Faith and natural intellect operate on different planes. Our minds can go just so far, as far as the limits of the universe; and that would seem to be far enough for many men. Faith allows us to go as far as the essence of God. The whole purpose of faith is to allow the intellect to step beyond itself, as the telephone allows our voice to stretch beyond itself, or the telescope extends the vision of our eyes. Yet no one considers a telephone or a telescope an insult to a man, nor a substitution for his voice or his eyes. Faith is not an enemy of the intellect; rather it is intellect's liberator.

Freedom for the mind: The courage of faith

Because it gives freedom, faith demands courage. It takes courage to see God not only as the ultimate reward to be gained, but also as a reward that may be eternally lost. It takes courage to see in every one of our actions a deliberate choice of eternity, of heaven or of hell; to kneel before the gentle Christ and tell Him with complete frankness how completely we have betrayed Him; to pick oneself up again and again and again, with the grim determination to continue to pick oneself up, to continue to try no matter how often we may fail. It takes courage to be a man; it takes much greater courage to be a Christian man, a friend of Christ. It takes the kind of courage that carried Christ through the last moments on the Cross -- but beyond that to the morning of the resurrection.

The fullness of faith

The fullness of faith, comparable only to the limitless fullness of infinity, makes our natural life seem a narrow, dark, blind corridor. Faith opens up eternity itself to us and allows our spirit to stretch itself to the limits of its great possibilities. While giving us intimate details of divinity, it also gives the only solid ground of hope and of love, furnishing a measuring-rod for both.

The practicality of faith

Additionally, considering the part that hope and love play in human life, faith is surely possessed of a practicality more than sufficient to satisfy the most practical-minded age. Only the dead can dispense with faith. To the sinner it gives a reason for hope and the means of attaining that hope; to the saint it gives the reason for love and the means to perfect that love. To the layman it is a short cut to necessary knowledge; to the religious it is the very basis of his life. To the successful it teaches moderation and corrects easily mistaken values; to the mediocre, the elimination of dullness, of drudgery in a divinely high romance; to failures in our human sense it gives happiness and a knowledge of the real difference between eternal and ephemeral success. To the laborer it gives consecration, courage, and an unshakeable basis of justice; to the employer it teaches the limitations of power, the deep roots of justice, the pettiness of the great things of this world. Additionally, so we might go on and on through men, women and children, the sick, the healthy, the young, the old, the apostle, the scholar, domestic society, political society and so on. The universal practicality of faith is bound up intimately with the absolutely universal practicality of the one and only goal of human life, plus the infallible authority of the word of God.

The future of faith

Perhaps the most inspiring thing to remember about faith is that it is only a beginning. It starts a life that goes on for all eternity. As such, it carries with it in this world the joy that can be fully appreciated only by God and those to whom He has opened up the secrets of his divinity. There is an obscurity about faith now; there is an intellectual restlessness at its darkness; in it, there is a rigid dependence on the moral strength of our human will. Still, like every beginning, it is a promise. Additionally, the promise faith holds out to us is not one of increased obscurity, or even of decreased obscurity, but of brilliant light, the promise of the light of glory by which we shall see God as He is and in that vision attain the goal of human living, which is the happiness of man.

CHAPTER II

FREEDOM FOR THE WILL
(Q. 10-22)

1. The symbol of slavery:
   (a) External and internal liberty.
   (b) Hope and internal liberty.

2. Optimistic pessimism:
   (a) The fact.
   (b) The explanation
      (1) Natural and supernatural hope.
      (2) The basis of hope – faith.

3. Demolisher of hope's foundation -- infidelity.
   (a) In general:
      (1) Negative, positive and contrary infidelity.
      (2) Malice and extent of the corruption of
infidelity.
   (b) In particular:
      (1) Comparative malice of infidelity of pagans,
Jews and heretics.
      (2) Treatment of infidels:
         a. In their persons:
            1. Disputation.
            2. Compulsion.
         b. In their rites.
         c. In their children.

4. Further attacks on the foundation of hope:
   (a) Blasphemy.
   (b) Sins against the Holy Spirit.
   (c) Spiritual blindness and sluggishness.

5. The virtue of hope:

(a) The essence of hope, its object and subject.

(b) Place of hope among the virtues.

6. The perfection of hope:
   (a) The gift of fear.
      (1) Varieties of fear.
      (2) The gift of the Holy Spirit.
   (b) Corresponding beatitude: Blessed are the poor in spirit.

7. Annihilator of hope:
   (a) Presumption.
   (b) Despair.

Conclusion

1. The enslaved will:
   (a) Desire of the slave.
   (b) Love of the slave.
   (c) Despair of the slave.

2. A Contrast: the cross and the throne.

3. Hope and life:
   (a) Hope and faith.
   (b) Hope and action.
   (c) Hope and love.
   (d) Hope and courage.

CHAPTER II
FREEDOM FOR THE WILL
(Q. 10-22)

The symbol of slavery: External and internal liberty

The cold shivers that runs up our spine as we pass the dull walls of a prison or hear the clank of chains in a ghost story is our nature's recognition of accurate symbols of slavery. The walls and the chains are instruments of imprisonment. For, essentially, our notion of liberty is the ability to go somewhere, the capacity to choose a path to a goal and to take, or refuse to take, some steps along that path. The limitations of a man's physical ability to move about touch our spirit with the cold finger of fear, in spite of the fact that we know in our hearts that there are no walls, no chains, which can restrain the mind and the heart of a man.

Hope and internal liberty

As long as the mind of man knows a goal, as long as his heart can soar on the wings of hope and love following the directions of his mind, a man is essentially free. He is still a man; he still has reason for living. There is no display of a dictator's power, no lash of a whip, no smile of scorn, indeed no power on earth, which can stop the mind and the heart of a man from rushing to its goal. When you have seen the light of that goal die out of the face of a man, when you have seen him surrender hope of choosing a path to somewhere and of stepping along that path, when you have seen the death of hope, you have seen the death of man and the birth of a slave. This is true no matter how free a man may be to move about this physical world of ours; he is a slave, for his mind and his heart have no place to go.

Optimistic pessimism: The fact

This slave may be optimistic about his slavery. He may go at his living as enthusiastically as a dog digs for a nonexistent bone -- and with just as much grounds for his optimism. He may admit the existence of the goal but deny that he has any power to reach that goal, and so place himself in the position of a starving paralytic staring hopelessly at a full meal. Alternatively, he may whine to the universe that no adequate means of reaching the goal is offered to him and sulk like a movie fan in love with a star he will never see.

These are not amusing fictions; they are the possibilities held out to man by modern philosophy. These modern philosophers may sound bright, cheery, and completely optimistic about man and the universe but the invitation they issue is to absolute pessimism. The fact is that we cannot be free without hope; and a slave has no grounds for optimism. We must have hope, hope of getting to a place that is worthwhile, that is, hope in a personal goal and the means to that goal.

The explanation: Natural and supernatural hope

There is an unconscious realization of this in the tribute we pay to hope, even on the natural scale. To us, it smacks of the heroic, of courage and magnanimity; there is a young beauty about it, a sense of strong endeavor and great accomplishment. The tragedy of this natural hope is that it is built upon so utterly frail a basis, like a financial empire reared upon baseless credit or the reputation of a man depending on the breath of a whisper. For this natural hope depends on human faith; that is to say, it rests on no more than a strong opinion. Hope must always rest on faith and, if it is a human hope, it must rest on human faith.

The basis of hope -- faith

St. Thomas compares supernatural hope to an anchor holding the soul firm. What is there in this life that can secure a soul? Can we think of the mind of man as secure when we see the learned men of the ages making mistakes as ridiculous as those of a schoolboy? Who will say that the love of man gives us absolute security? Will we place our security in the feelings and sense of a man that change with every breath of wind? In a political organization? In a military power? Will we even dare to place our security in nature itself knowing it is not a goal but merely a beginning? We cannot sink the anchor of our hope in the depths; paradoxically we must fix it to the heights, even to

God Himself. That is what supernatural hope does. It gives us confidence of eternal life through the promises of help of Almighty God Himself. While there are no human-made bars that can imprison the mind of man, no jail that can hold his heart, the hope of that heart and mind can be demolished by the destruction of the foundation of hope; by taking away from man his faith in the existence of a God Who is faithful to His promises and powerful enough to help man win through to divinity itself.

Demolisher of hope's foundation -- infidelity
Negative, positive and contrary infidelity

Infidelity -- the contrary of faith -- is, then, the greatest tragedy, which can enter into human life for it blasts out the foundation of that hope which is the starting point of our activity. This infidelity may be that of the pagan who has never heard of the faith, or that of the man who, having heard of the faith persistently refuses it much as a man might refuse olives at dinner, without rancor. On the other hand, it may be the militant infidelity, which attacks the faith as an enemy of humanity. Remembering that faith is the basis of hope, it seems difficult to believe that there are those who thus fight the faith; but there are such men and women, and plenty of them. Objectively, at least, they commit a sin much greater than murder, adultery, theft or any of the sins against the moral virtues; their sin is directly against God, these others are only indirectly against Him. Indeed, their sin so completely separates man from God as to leave him, not only spiritually dead, but completely off the supernatural plane. Notice, however, that we say "objectively", for no man can judge of the subjective guilt of another. Who can say that this infidel, viciously attacking all that the Church stands for, commits a graver sin than the backbiting housewife? That is known only to God.

Malice and extent of the corruption of infidelity

The "broad-minded" man, rejecting the faith politely and without rancor, commits the same sin; he too has that contempt for God so tragically exemplified by William James when he said, "The truth or falsehood of the theistic proofs makes little difference, for such a god is of no use to men." Now if there could be such a thing as the purely negative infidelity of the pagan, it would involve no formal sin; sin, you know, does not happen by accident through no fault of our own. However, Thomas rightly denies that such negative infidelity is possible. If a man does not place one of the fundamental impediments to faith -- pride or fear -- God will, if necessary, reveal to him directly what is to be believed or even, miraculously, send him a preacher to announce to him the good tidings of faith.

There is a fiction, current in intellectual circles today; to the effect, that Christianity maintains man is totally corrupt, that all of his acts are sinful, even mortally sinful. If we identify Christianity with the religion of Luther and the reformers, this ceases to be fiction and becomes fact; but if we suppose this absurd statement is a corollary of the great sinfulness of infidelity we are calling for our fiction straight, with no slightest admixture of fact. Catholicism vehemently denies any such corruption in man, not only in Christian man but in any man. Of course, an infidel can build a house, bake a good pie, give alms to the poor or sympathy and encouragement to one in suffering; all of these are certainly not sins. They are good works, possessed of real value. However. supernaturally they are dead works. They are not coin of the realm of Christ precisely because of the infidelity and consequent lack of charity: they have no value for eternal life.

Fiction such as this, which springs from a lumping together of all that lays claim to the name Christian, is responsible for much of the indifference and even hostility to Christianity among men and women today, particularly among learned men and women. They know that men and women, whatever their faith, are not utterly vicious, not totally corrupt. Nowhere will they find a more whole-hearted support of that knowledge than in the Church. In fact it can be taken as a general rule that in any attack on humanity, whether in the name of religion, politics, militarism or anything else, the Church will always be found on the side of the defense. Additionally, its defense of humanity will not be a gentle, timid disagreement, a polite remonstrance, nor a neutrality that stands aghast but does nothing. It will be a thundering condemnation such as was hurled against Luther, Calvin, Jansenius and Baius on this precise point.

Comparative malice of infidelity of pagans, Jews and heretics

Every type of infidelity rules out the possibility of faith in a man's mind and consequently destroys the basis of hope. It makes no difference whether the infidelity be that of the pagan who has never heard of faith, the Jew who has accepted it only in its prefigures and prophecies, the heretic rejecting his faith, or the apostate turning his back on the truths that were once his. This is obvious in what Thomas considers the purely hypothetical case of the pagan's negative infidelity. Concerning the others, a distinction must be made between material and formal infidelity. By the first, a man holds fast to the formal reason of faith -- the authority of God revealing the truths of faith; what he rejects, he turns aside from precisely on the grounds that it is not revealed by God. By the second, formal infidelity, a man pits his mind against the mind of God and rejects this or that supernatural truth, or all supernatural truths, precisely as such. On the other hand, to put the same truth in another way, the material infidel's doubts fall on the declaration of the revealed character of certain truths; the formal infidel doubts the truths themselves.

In this connection, it is well to remember that the testimony of the Church is not a formal motive of faith, but a condition of faith. The infallibility of the Church's declarations is itself a revealed truth and an object of faith. However, a revealed truth is not lost inculpably and accidentally. Material infidelity is understandable because of corrupt teaching or of no teaching at all, consequently in a second or third generation of heretics or, in simple souls, in a first generation following the teaching of its formally corrupt leaders. It is difficult to conceive of it in other circumstances.

In one sense these formal infidelities are all equal for all completely destroy faith, rejecting its formal reason -- the authority of God revealing these truths. Yet, from another angle, there is no equality among them, i.e., from the angle of the truths which are still accepted. Obviously, the Jew has more of these truths than the pagan, and the heretic has more than the Jew; yet the order of malice is just the reverse. We might say that in the argument with God over the truths of faith, the heretic shouts out insults at the top of his voice; the Jew's is a conversational disagreement; while the pagan stands stubbornly silent, refusing to admit anything.

Treatment of infidels: In their persons: Disputation

It sounds strange to us today that between Catholics and infidels, whatever their type, some norm of action must be laid down. After all, Republicans and Democrats flare up at each other only once in four years, while Rotarians and Elks have no trouble avoiding ill feeling. Perhaps this impatience with religious quarrels comes from the idea that religion is not worth fighting about; or, more probably, it may be based on ignorance of the terribly destructive force of infidelity. In a Catholic, such ignorance is hardly excusable. It is not only that his appreciation of the inestimable value of the faith should give him an insight into the tragedy of infidelity: there is also the glaring fact of the comparative zeal of the enemies of the faith and his own zeal. A thoughtful consideration of that fact gives us the key to the tremendous power for destruction in infidelity. The Catholic's zeal springs from love of neighbor and love of God; it is always a rather serene thing, for the false gods and false goals of others do not threaten the security of his own soul, of his own life. Additionally, this very serenity and security too often make it a mild, tepid thing. The infidel's zeal, on the contrary, is inspired by desperate, bitter self-defense. Supernatural faith itself, God, the final goal of life are all devastating accusations which strike at the roots of his philosophy, at the basis upon which he has built his life; in order to protect himself in his own eyes, he must destroy these things, or do his utmost to effect their destruction. Something, then, must be done about infidelity. What? What is Catholicism's mode of procedure in the face of infidelity? Well, the obvious thing that Catholics, at one time or another, must do with infidels is argue. Certainly, it is going to be necessary to protect the faith of the simple faithful, to confute error and reply to accusations leveled against the faith. St. Dominic, and all his disputatious sons after him, recognized the necessity of argument for the return of the infidel to the faith, although not many can successfully emulate Dominic's example of arguing all night with a heretic. boredom and conversion are poles apart and only a saint or a genius can preserve an all-night argument from boredom.

This arguing in favor of the faith is not to be confused with the fruit of an unpleasant disposition or a poor night's sleep. Not anyone who feels in the mood for argument is justified in arguing about the faith. It would seem that almost anyone can argue, any time, about a sporting event, politics or international policies with no appreciable effect on sport, politics or internationalism. However, the same cannot be said of arguments about the faith. The fact that we have picked up a smattering of theology, know something of the difficulties against this or that truth of faith, does not give us a right to parade our knowledge before simple people who are perfectly content in their faith. Our Catholicism does not give us the right to stand up before any audience and take on any adversary in our defense of the faith, as a wrestler might challenge anyone in the audience to grapple with him. This is not a game. We shall probably do the faith much more good by keeping a discreet silence and letting it be known that we are not fitted for an argument with this adversary, or under these circumstances, and insisting that it be done by one who is so equipped.

The right of disputation is questioned by no one in America today. Its limitations are dictated by common sense. Now beyond that -- well the world used to tell us to be very tolerant. That was some time ago. That was before the floods of vicious intolerance were let loose, not against error, but against truth. Today the world at large is a decidedly intolerant world; it is only of us that tolerance is still expected. Yet there is something to be said for intolerance of error, nothing for intolerance of truth. The very word tolerance indicates that we are putting up with an evil. We do not tolerate a good; we embrace it, enthusiastically encourage it and do all in our power to promote it. However, we do tolerate the noise of the little boy next door, the snorings in a Pullman, the eccentricities of a statesman, graft in public administration, and so on. We do not question the unpleasantness or positive evil of these things. Certainly, we are not enthusiastic about them; we put up with them and none too cheerfully, because that is all we can do without causing greater unpleasantness or greater evil. If it were otherwise we would be enjoying these things or cowardly about them; either way we would have little to be proud of. The Church in this matter has much to be proud of, and she is neither a gourmand of evil nor a coward.

The tolerance of infidels on the part of the Church is not, then, to be mistaken for approbation. Indeed even that tolerance, to be well understood, must be seen in its causes. It is quite impossible for the Church to force infidels to believe. Not only has she absolutely no jurisdiction over the Jew or the pagan, the very act of belief enjoys all the inviolability of an act of free will; no force on earth, in hell or in heaven can possibly force the free will of man. The Church has her hands full dealing with her own obstreperous brood; she has no time to attempt the impossible.

However, she is a mother. She can and does force others to cease persecuting the faith, injuring it by their blasphemy, undermining the faith of the simple faithful by clever argumentation. In other words, she demands, forcefully if necessary, that the faith be left alone. The Church has the serious obligation, imposed by Christ Himself, to preach the gospel to all nations. Surely then she has the right to fulfill that obligation; and others have the obligation to respect that right of the Church.

Compulsion

There can never be question of forcing a man to believe, to accept the faith. Yet, to force those who were baptized and who deserted the faith, to fulfill that which had been promised in faith's acceptance -- that is another story. It can be done, and historically it has been done, not only by spiritual penalties, but also by the much less serious corporal penances. It is this compulsion of heretics that goes against the grain of our modern world; let us look at it a little more closely.

In this case, the Church is not a busybody slipping into a neighbor's house to spank children who are nothing to her but nuisances. These heretics are her own children; by baptism, they entered the Church, and by that sacrament, the Church has over them the same power it has over all the rest of its subjects. Moreover, these heretics are committing moral suicide; they are doing tremendous, eternal damage to themselves and to others in blasting out the one foundation of hope, the faith. No one seriously questions the sensibleness of compulsion, even physical compulsion, against a man plotting the overthrow of a legally constituted and properly functioning government; against the man who undermines the health of the community by spreading a dangerous disease; or against the traitor in war who attempts to betray his country. The social and physical life of man are concrete, tangible goods. Perhaps this is the clue to the root of our difficulty: we cannot realize the enormity of the damage accomplished by the heretic because we value so slightly the spiritual life of men. Let us put the same thing in terms of physical health. Let us suppose a man were to go from city to city deliberately spreading the germ of a fatal disease. What limitation would we place on the physical coercion, which might be inflicted on him? Would there be any question in our minds However that these activities should be stopped no matter what the physical damage necessary to stop that campaign immediately? Now look at heresy objectively, considering the seriousness of it in itself. Has the Church the right to protect its own and to warn the heretic by excommunicating him from all participation in sacramental life? Indeed, looked at objectively, the reasonableness even of the execution of that heretic to preserve the common good of the spiritual life is not hard to see. Actually, the procedure of the Church has never been immediate execution; rather it has always been a slow, infinitely patient attempt to protect all of her children, the attacking heretic as well as the faithful ones. Her gestures were not those of exasperation, of frightened weakness, of ruthless power. Even in the middle ages, when the death penalty for heresy, while not universal, was not uncommonly inflicted by the state, the Church's corrections proceeded with that same slow, unruffled pace. The heretic was warned; then he was warned a second time; if he still held stubbornly to his error, the Church not hoping very stoutly for his conversion, provided for the salvation of others by excommunicating him. Finally, when all hope of his conversion was abandoned, the Church turned him over to the secular arm for the infliction of the death penalty; and she stood beside him to the very last, offering the divine forgiveness that would assure her wayward son of eternal life. Her love for her children, in other words, has never been a weak, timid, sentimental thing, too selfish to be severe; her sense of values was serene, absolute; she knew there was no answer to the question, "What shall a man give in exchange for his soul?" -- surely, the answer was not physical life.

In their rites

Today we accept this version of strong love with a cynical smile. The argument is that such a course of action violates the conscience of heretics who, very often, are in good faith. Yet our newspapers week after week, tell us of police thwarting attempted suicides, snatching people from ledges of high buildings, grabbing the poison from their hands, pumping out their stomachs, searching prisoners lest they conceal instruments of self-destruction. Doesn't the consciences of these people tell them that suicide is the thing for them to do? Of course, but their consciences are erroneous, they are wrong. So also, is that of the heretic; just as men of sane conscience are obliged to correct and prevent the attempted suicides, so also is the Church. The hero who drags a woman from the river and forces her to continue to live, against her conscience, is not forcing her to commit sin. Sin is not in the material act, but in the will; and the will cannot be forced. In the same way, a heretic forced to conform to the rites of the faith is not forced to commit sin. Rather he is protected from pursuing a way of sin, a road away from the end of life; he is kept in a position to attain the supreme goal when and if he returns to spiritual sanity.

In their children

Another modern argument is drawn from the infringement on the liberty of infants who were baptized without having anything to say, at least intelligibly, about it. Nevertheless, after all liberty is a choice of means to an end. The Church, insisting that the child, baptized as an infant, live up to his faith, is insisting that a person under the jurisdiction of the Church hold fast to the means to the one end of life. That is not an interference with but a guarantee of the material of liberty.

Why should the child be obliged to what he did not personally promise? Well, why not? It was necessary at that time, i.e., the earliest possible moment that the step be taken; the elevation of man to the supernatural plane upon which he must move is not something that can be put off. The child could not act of itself, so others acted for him on the presumption -- a most reasonable presumption -- that if the child knew the truth and were capable of action, this is what he would do. The crux of the whole question is, of course, that this act is one that cannot be taken back; it impresses the indelible character of baptism on the soul. The absurdity that children must be allowed to grow up like animals until such a time as they should choose their religion for themselves was formally condemned by the Council of Trent. There is still no exchange a man can make for his soul. We instill habits of personal hygiene, even though the child vociferously protests at the very sight of a bathtub or a toothbrush. Usually it is not the age of reason but his first girl that inspires a boy to wash behind his ears freely, industriously, without compulsion. Certainly, the bathtub and toothbrush have done the child no injury. Perhaps some day our moderns will become convinced that there are things even more important than personal hygiene, such things for example as the supernatural habits that make possible the success of human living.

With a clear realization of the malice of infidelity in men, it is not difficult to understand why the Church, at one time or another forbade Catholics to have business or social relations with infidels. The thing could not be done, of course, the other way around; the Church, you will remember, has no jurisdiction over the unbaptized. Nor was this prohibition of the Church a merely arbitrary procedure, a flight from the shadow of a ghost, as we can see faintly here in America today. It would be strange indeed, if a corrupt but almost universal view on marriage in itself, divorce and remarriage, or on business, political and medical ethics had not had some effect on the simple Catholic living in such an atmosphere.

When we turn to a consideration of the Church's attitude towards the services of heretics and infidels, we must keep in mind that toleration is not approbation. That these church rites can be tolerated either because of some good in them or to avoid some greater evil is evident; indeed, it may be obligatory to tolerate them. Even God Himself tolerates some evil; no human regime, even an ecclesiastical regime, can hope to effect a government more perfect than the divine.

To come down to particulars, the rites of the Jewish religion can be tolerated of themselves; there is always some good coming from them. In fact, they are a constant witness to the faith, for they give the testimony of the prefigures and of the prophets. The rites of pagans and heretics, on the contrary, have nothing in themselves to recommend their toleration: they are always a danger to the faith; at least materially, they are sins. Now there are strong reasons for toleration of these rites, for example: to avoid spiritual damage, either to the faithful or to the infidels themselves, to avoid riots and bloodshed, because any other mode of procedure would be a serious impediment to the eternal salvation of these infidels. Being tolerated, the infidels might gradually, little by little, turn to the faith. How essential this toleration is may be gathered from the fact of the great multitude of men who are infidels, and the memory that, in the eyes of God, the soul of just one man is well worth the last drop of blood, even of the God-man. This truth, so completely overlooked in any discussion of the tolerance of the Church, cannot be emphasized too strongly: the secret of the assured tolerance of Catholicism is not a continued lack of opportunity, but a divinely guaranteed appreciation of the value of the soul of man; the Church will be tolerant, persistently, patiently, to the very end, because of her divine love for the souls of those who know not Christ.

Perhaps all this could be said briefly by pointing out that just as faith does not enslave but rather frees the mind of man with a divine freedom, so does the guardian of the faith hold her place in the world not as the enemy of the freedom of man but the staunchest champion of that freedom. She will always be the object of attack, as will the faith, for freedom demands both courage and respect for others; and always in the world, there will be cowards and tyrants. Nowhere does this championship of the rights of men appear more evident than in relation to the children of infidels.

In the mind of St. Thomas, there was no doubt but that the rights of the parents were supreme. It was not merely that the baptism of infidel children against the wishes of their parents would do great damage to the faith, since these children normally have very little chance of being educated in that faith; it would be a serious injury to natural justice. Thomas is quite clear in asserting the foundation of his argument: the inviolability of the children of infidels rests on the natural right of the parent. The child, until he has the use of reason, until he is able to care for himself, is under the care, indeed a part of the parents. His salvation is the responsibility of the parents; nor do these parents lose their rights by contact with Divine law, which does not destroy but perfects the law of nature. Both the law of grace and the law of nature have come from the mind of the same supreme Lawgiver and work harmoniously to bring men back to that supreme Truth.

Further attacks on the foundation of hope: Blasphemy

The angry man who spouts blasphemies is not necessarily guilty of sin; ordinarily he is only the victim of a limited vocabulary. Though she is struggling for emphasis, not expletive, the vivacious young lady swaying on the subway strap, and shouting the name of God above all the roar of the train is suffering from the same limitation. These two are not at all in the same class as the university professor who calmly assures us that God is a symbol. His is a sin, but a dry, dusty, languid sin, with little heart in it. The complete blasphemer is seen in the atheist who viciously attacks the notion that God is good, that God is omnipotent, that He is the provider of His children in this world. Here we have the sin, which stands at the peak of all the sins of infidelity, a sin that consists in verbally insulting God.

By it, we attribute to God something, which does not belong to Him, or deny Him something that is His divine prerogative. In its full stupidity, it outstrips all sins against the moral virtues, even sins of despair and presumption against the virtue of hope; it gives place, reluctantly, only to that supreme sin which is hatred of God. When blasphemy proceeds from hatred of God itself, then blasphemy is the supreme sin.

However brief it be, however softly whispered, there is nothing small about the smallest of blasphemies; for just one, any one, destroys our union with God. In the human order, an insulting word or a moment of infidelity does not necessarily destroy the love that binds a man and woman together; but then that love is a natural thing, with roots deep in nature. The love that binds us to God is not at all natural; its roots are not in nature. From our side it must always be a frail, engrafted thing; in cherishing our union with God, we must tread fearfully, carefully with the fear and caution looking out, not towards God, but towards ourselves.

An eavesdropper at the keyhole of the gate of heaven would listen in vain for God and His friends to hurl insults. Blasphemy has no place in heaven, and no place among the friends of God on earth. Men do of course blaspheme. The devils too blaspheme, not with lips but with their affections. Once the damned souls in hell are reunited to their bodies the uproar in hell will really commence, and one of the constant activities in the social life of hell will be blasphemy. There is a terrible significance to this truth, for it indicates that there is no limit to the sins and wickedness of hell; in fact, that very wickedness is a part of the punishment of hell. If nothing else would, this truth shows us that there is no Joy in sin for if there were; the devils could have none of it.

Sins against the Holy Spirit

To most of us, there is more viciousness in the contempt of a snub than there is in the attack of open insult: the latter at least does us the honor of opposition. Some such subtle contempt is involved in the blasphemies, which have come to be known as the sins against the Holy Spirit. Their cold arrogance is the ultimate in snobbery. They are the characteristic gestures of those who are too good for God; at least these sins always imply contempt for God's goodness for they proceed, not from ignorance, not from weakness nor passion, but from deliberate malice, from a rejection of the protection offered to us against the choice of sin.

By these sins against the Holy Spirit, we slam the door of our mind against the brightness of God, which drives out the darkness of sin. We prefer the dust, the dampness the dirt and cobwebs, the hidden ugliness of sin; an ugliness that is so revolting that, were it shown in bright light, it would be too much even for us. So we hurl shut the door of our mind against all consideration of the divine judgment, lest its justice and mercy hold us back from presumption and despair. We turn away from the consideration of the gifts of God, lest the knowledge of His truth halt our attacks on divine revelation at the very start. We refuse to consider the help of interior grace, that our enmity for the grace of others might be unrestrained. We refuse to look at sin honestly, lest its disorder and foulness should move us to amendment and penance. We blind ourselves to the pettiness of the apparent good of sin, that our obstinacy might be undisturbed.

Obviously, such a sinner is really in a bad way. His sin has no excuse; it is a sin of malice. These sins directly exclude the very things, which might bring us to our knees before the gentle Christ. Only the omnipotence of God makes it possible for these sins to be forgiven up until the very moment of death. However, as far as the sinner himself is concerned, he has already signed his own death warrant with a ghastly flourish.

The variety of these sins may be frightening: presumption, despair, attack on divine truth, envy of the grace of others, impenitence and obstinacy. Fortunately, they are not starting points; rather they are climaxes of evil. Human nature, ordinarily, does not reach any heights or depths in one jump. Normally it takes some little effort to be thoroughly bad. Usually the sinner starts with sins that have some excuse in ignorance or passion that is with sins that leave at least a few tatters to cover his self-respect. It is only later that it is possible for him to abandon self- respect in his mad passion for sin, to plunge into the depths of contempt for the goodness of God.

Spiritual blindness and sluggishness

The virtue of faith, perfected by the gift of understanding, is the clear eye of a pilot spotting a landing field in the dusk, a landing field to which the heart rushes on the wings of hope. Blindness of the pilot means the end of hope and the crash of the flight of the heart, indeed, sleepiness, heaviness, sluggishness are almost as surely fatal. That is exactly the attack made on the gift of understanding by spiritual blindness and spiritual sluggishness. Both are sins against the Holy Spirit by attacking His gifts; and the attack is an odd, indirect thing. It consists in a voluntary non-consideration of spiritual goods. Understand in this case a man does not refuse to consider this or that particular aid to this or that particular action; he is attacking in a much more sweeping fashion, attacking the root principles, if you like, of the enlightenment of man.

He is blind to the things of the spirit because the world has got into his eyes; for this blindness is traceable primarily to lust, the sluggishness to gluttony. This is not to be misunderstood; it is not a matter of the rush of blood to the stomach after a heavy meal, crippling our thinking power. It is a question here of the concentration of our attention, of our hearts, upon these things of the flesh. The world is in our eyes; we will not see, and so we cannot see. Time only adds to our blindness until, after a while, we convince ourselves that we are not blind, that these things we cannot see no longer exist. Then indeed is hope definitely dead.

The virtue of hope: The essence of hope, its object and subject

The man whose hope is dead no longer confidently expects everlasting life and the means to attain it because of the omnipotence, mercy and fidelity of God. He no longer possesses that theological virtue of hope which makes a man look to God as to a good to be possessed, that makes a man stand awe-struck at the spectacle of divine omnipotence, determined by divine mercy and divine fidelity, making of his weak hands, of his stumbling feet, the instruments by which he constructs an eternal habitation inside the walls of heaven itself.

Moreover, there is little that anyone else can do for him. Just as no one can walk, or sleep, or digest for me, so no man can hope for me. The act of hope cannot be carried through by a substitute; it is an intimately personal thing, the act of the appetite of man desiring God. No man can hope for another unless somehow these two be one, unless they be cemented in that bond of unity, which is the love of God. One Christian, united to others by charity, can hope for the ultimate happiness of these others with whom he is one, just as he can hope for himself; for in truth, these to whom he is united are other selves.

It is true that many a man has been brought to heaven by the prayers of a mother, a wife or a child. It is true that many a man may escape the trap of despair because of someone's great love for him and the help they give him. Now that does not mean that we can hope *in* other men, except, as they are instruments of God. No man, no woman, no prayer, no sacrifice can bring us to the possession of God; only the Omnipotent Himself can do that for us. Just as the authority of God is the solid basis of faith, so the omnipotence of God is the solid basis of hope, upon that foundation alone can operate safely rear the high towers of his hopes.

Place of hope among the virtues

There is something youthful about hope; it puts a spring into our step, a lilt into our heart. To understand something of that eternal youthfulness of hope and the young eyes it puts into the faces of the saints, it is only necessary to compare it with the other theological virtues. Charity looks to God as to an end to be serenely possessed; its outlook then is one of serene wisdom. Faith looks to God as a principle, a fountain from which pours truth; its eagerness is tempered by an abashed humility staring at unutterable truths. Hope looks to God as a principle, a beginning, a source of successful action; its eyes sweep youth's glorious world of long futures, of things, great things, still to be done.

Hope presupposes faith. It follows on the heels of faith as the heart follows in the steps of the mind, or hope springs from our will: and the will, the appetite of man, cannot, will not, plunge blindly about in the dark. It follows only so far as the intellect can lead; it takes only those steps that are possible because faith, knowledge, has gone before hacking out foot holes. Hope comes from Faith; it leads to love, to charity. With the increase of charity there is also an increase of hope; of course we expect much more, and more confidently, from our friends. Additionally, charity means that God is our friend. The difference between the hope that walks arm and arm with charity and the hope that walks alone is the difference between the living and the dead. For charity is the soul of hope, as it is the soul of faith, as it is the soul of all the virtues. It alone gives them life.

When we say that the wish is the father to the thought, we are flattering ourselves. Now if the alleged thought proceeds from emotion, rather than emotion proceeding from thought, the result is not thought at all. If it is anything, it is an emotional prejudice. In other words, it is important to remember that hope is in the will of man, not in his intellect. Consequently, hope is not a foundation of knowledge or conviction, much less can it be the foundation of all religion, as much modern Protestantism and modernism suppose.

It is true enough that there is a certitude in hope. After all, anything based solidly on God has certitude about it. However, the certitude of the mercy and the omnipotence of God towards us, the certitude of the possibility of our happiness, is a certitude that comes from faith. Understand well that it is not a certitude, which establishes the absolute success of our own life. It by no means assures us that now we need not give the matter of salvation a thought; that we are saved; that we have religion and now all that is necessary is to sit back and wait, smilingly, for the crown to be placed on our head, meanwhile, perhaps whiling away the time by tick, ticking at those who are not as holy as we are. That smugness is even a little too much for God to swallow. It is always certain that God is merciful and omnipotent, that beatitude is possible to us; but it is not certain in this life that we ourselves will acquire that eternal happiness. It may seem, from a superficial glance, that the Reformers were doing a sweet, kind thing in extending the certitude of hope to the lengths of a personal guarantee. In fact, their attempt was cloying, saccharine; it reduced the religious tribute we pay to God to a gust of emotionalism without foundation.

The perfection of hope: The gift of fear · Varieties of fear

The ordinary human being is an easy victim of drama. A brief sentence, a picture, a passing portrayal of emotion, even though none of these ring quite true, will close our threats, wet our eyes, bow down our hearts. We are fearfully impressed, not merely fearful, when we read an immortal poet's dramatic line, "Abandon all hope, ye who enter here", as written over the gates of hell. The same thing might just as well have been written above the gates of heaven, for it is just as true that there is no hope in heaven, as it is that there is no hope in hell; although of course for a different reason. In heaven, there is no need for hope because what was once hoped for is now possessed; but in hell, there is no possibility of hope because that which was once hoped for can now never be possessed.

That chord of fear, struck in our hearts at the thought of abandoning all hope, is a reasonable thing. Yet even the greatest hope, in full stride to the accomplishment of high, hard things, must have some solid fear in its make-up. We make a serious mistake today in supposing that all fear is opposed to courage. It is not. There can be great courage present with extremely great fear. After all, we have seen that there is a fear produced by faith, and faith is possible only to one of great courage. Indeed the fearless man, who has no fear of God, man or the devil, is undoubtedly a fool; there are many things of which we can, even must be, reasonably afraid. Certainly, we must fear the Lord; not, you understand, as we fear death, disease or accident; rather we fear Him as a judge, evaluating our actions and giving them their just due. Only a fool would not fear strict justice.

The gift of the Holy Spirit

Nevertheless, there is another sense of fear in which it is a sublime gift of the Holy Spirit. This fear is not a cowardly embracing of sin to escape temporal evil; it is not that honest, supernatural fear which is the effect of faith and which drives us from sin through the threat of punishment; rather it is the child's fear of separation from one who is desirable above all else. It is the fear that makes us easily moved by the breath of God towards God Himself by placing within us the first condition of easy mobility, that is, a complete, willing subjection to and reverence for God. It removes all sulkiness from our response to the inspirations of the Holy Spirit. In a sense, it makes us grow up; though it is a child's fear, by it we are no longer children stamping the floor and pouting because we cannot have our own way. We grow up, we bow down before the supreme wisdom of God and, in ourselves, the beginnings of wisdom appear.

For fear is really the beginning of wisdom. It is not the first principle of wisdom; that privilege belongs to faith's first long view of the goal. Fear is the beginning of wisdom in the sense of being the first concept of wisdom from which wisdom itself begins to operate. Indirectly the fear produced by faith begins wisdom through its expulsion of attachment to sin, for such an attachment makes wise direction impossible. Yet directly wisdom is begun by the child's fear, the gift of the Holy Spirit, which implants in our souls the conditions necessary for all direction, for all regulation, for all progress towards God -- reverence and subjection.

You will have noticed that in this fear of God there was a double element: a fear of separation from our divine Friend, and a note of reverence and subjection to God. It is in that double sense that we fear the Lord in this life. As we approach more closely to God, we revere Him more deeply and are more thoroughly subject to Him, while the idea of being separated from Him, even for an instant, becomes more and more intolerable. When we reach the perfect union with God that is proper to heaven, the fear of separation disappears altogether; but our reverence and subjection reach their peak. In other words, in heaven our fear will be perfect because we will be fully grown up. Perhaps another way of saying this is that complete independence belongs to God alone. When we attempt to climb into the clothes of God, we look as pathetic as the child thrashing about in her mother's shoes, playing that she is grown up. Our perfection consists, not in greater independence, but in being perfectly subject to God and in giving Him the reverence due to the Creator from the creature.

Corresponding beatitude: Blessed are the poor in spirit

The highest reaches of the gift of fear, its supreme and ultimate acts, are those of poverty of spirit. This does not mean that such perfection is reserved for those who can present a union card; this gift can be, must be, had by all classes for it is necessary for salvation. For the rich as well as for the poor, the ultimate perfection of fear of the Lord is poverty; and it is strictly true that in this sense of poverty, the richest of men can be poorer than the most abandoned dweller in the slums. St. Augustine described poverty of spirit as "the emptying out of a proud, inflated spirit." The phrase gives us a picture of a pinprick deflating a balloon. It really means that, with this perfect fear of the Lord, we no longer seek our greatness in any other but God. We no longer have to bolster the frail structure of our souls with riches and honors; we do not have to magnify ourselves by pride; we do not have to protect our weakness by a bulwark of external, temporal things. The very fact that we are so perfectly subject to God, that we have such deep reverence for Him that we no longer seek outside of Him a source of greatness for ourselves -- this is the height of hope. It is this that frees the rich man from the tentacles of his riches, takes the bitterness out of the smile of poverty, and sends both rich and poor rushing on eager feet to the embrace of God.

Annihilator of hope: Presumption; Despair

Earlier in this chapter, we have seen that infidelity indirectly destroys hope by blasting away its foundations. Two other sins train their guns directly upon hope and destroy it by blowing it apart. These are presumption and despair; and both of them are the result of a mistake. Despair judges eternal happiness to be impossible. It decides that God denies pardon here and now to this penitent sinner, it looks at an impossible good and so it quits. Presumption fixes its eyes upon an irresistible personality -- the personality of the sinner himself. The presumptuous man decides that he is so important that God cannot condemn him; he will be given heaven without good works, pardon for his sins without any sorrow.

The one gives up the search for heaven; the other gives up the avoidance of hell. Both place the sinner in exactly the same place. Both are lesser sins than infidelity and hatred of God for, while all are directly against God, presumption and despair are less so. A moment's consideration will make this clear: infidelity opposes the supreme Truth: hatred of God opposes the supreme Good; but despair and presumption go against our supreme happiness, i.e., against God inasmuch as He is participated by us. Nevertheless, these two sins, precisely because they have God for their object, are greater than any sins against any or all of the moral virtues.

If we compare the two we see that despair ranks above presumption in its gravity. It denies to God His perfection of mercy, a perfection which belongs to Him by His very nature, while presumption denies to Him things that pertain to God in reference to our actions, namely, His punishment and reward.

Make no mistake about this. Because despair and presumption rank third and fourth among all the sins man can commit, they are not to be dismissed lightly. Despair is, in fact, a sin of very, very serious danger. In a sense, it is a climax of sin, a height of evil; in another sense, it is the beginning of sin, and this is a horrible truth. The despairing man is stripped of everything that might have held him back from sin. Now he is a vicious, wild animal, cut loose from all curb on his madness. Indeed the presumptuous man is in much the same position. His insolent assurance of God's overlooking his sin strips him of all that might restrain his appetites. Both are high points of evil, normally reached after a long hard journey through sin; but both are the beginning of new horrors whose end can be seen only in a hell without end.

The despairing man is convinced that absolutely no means of remedy is of use to him; the presumptuous man is convinced that no means is necessary for him. How can they be helped? Only by the omnipotence of God, His relentless love and floods of His grace can turn the life of the presumptuous or despairing man from failure to high success. Now if man is so helpless in the grip of these sins at least he can, while still free of them, see clearly, what brings them on and so protect himself from their extremely serious dangers. Despair is a lazy sin. It springs from spiritual sloth, which runs away from spiritual good because it involves too much labor. It is bored with spiritual activity; things of God and the soul are distasteful to it. St. Thomas puts it briefly when he describes despair as "a sorrow of spirit casting us down." Dejection makes things look much harder, even as hard as the impossible. This particular dejection, springing principally from sins of the flesh, inverses the values of the spiritual and the carnal; the spiritual goods seem smaller and smaller, less and less worthwhile when seen in the light of the labor they demand and the easy richness of the goods of the flesh. Presumption, on the other hand. is an elation of spirit that exceeds all reason: it expects things, which are impossible even to the ordinary power of God. Plainly, it is the fruit of pride.

In its eyes the practice of virtue, the doing of penance are grubbing in the earth. This sort of thing is petty, venal work far beneath the presumptuous man. A person as important as he is in the eyes of God does not need such things. He is the perfect picture of the utterly fearless man; and so he is a perfect portrait of the utter fool.

The enslaved will: Desire of the slave

Infidelity, despair and presumption -- these are the chains and the grim walls that have succeeded in doing what nothing else in the world could do, for they have imprisoned the heart of man, they have destroyed hope. No matter how much the modern man talks of freedom, no matter what his championship of democracy, no matter how freely he walks the street, flies the skies or rushes over the ocean, he cannot get away from that bondage within his own heart. He is a slave. His desire, his love are the desire and love of a slave. When he looks at the end of it all, as he must sometime, his despair is the despair of the slave; not of the physical slave, not of the political slave, not of the economic slave, but of the moral slave whose heart has no place to go.

Love of the slave

This is the hopeless man whose desires are limited to a few hours, a few months, a few years; to the things he can see and touch; to narrow limits: of natural life, of personal accomplishment, of human faith, of the security to be had in this present world. This is the hopeless man whose love has been limited, as has his desire. It is the love of a machine, of an animal, or, at best, the love of a man. At its best, it is doomed to frustration from the very start; it grows in perfection only to lose the thing it loved; it stops at the walls of the world, shrinks in horror from sickness, brings up short before the barrier of death. It is the love of the slave; the love of the hour that dare not look ahead because of what the future holds for it.

Despair of the slave

For to the heart that has no place to go, there is nothing open but despair. Nothing within the heart of man can satisfy that heart; nothing within the natural universe is worthy of the yearnings of that heart. It has no place to go; yet it was made to go to sublime places, even into the hearts of other men and other women, even info the heart of God. Now, without hope, it is chained down. On its short chain it becomes sullen, vicious, savage, consumed with a violent hate -- all of which are only the outer signs of inner despair.

A Contrast: the cross and the throne

It is an astonishing thing that, with all our love for liberty, we have not seen the innate liberty of a Man nailed to a cross as contrasted with the innate slavery of a man chained to a throne. The Man on the cross was there as the fulfillment of a long hope. He died in hope to give birth to hope. He was there because the human heart had wandered so far; because it still had gone so far, it could go, because that road must be left open to all human hearts that were to come after His. The man on the throne of power today is there because of despair. He is not reigning in hope because his heart has so much further to go; it has already reached its goal. What road is he opening to the hearts of his followers but the narrow, short road he has already trod to its end? He holds out to men the prospect of merging themselves into a political machine, into a social process or into a cosmological process. Yet with all this power, he cannot make one small hole in the walls of the world for the escape of the human heart.

Hope and life: faith, action, and love

Supernatural faith frees the mind of man. It breaks a breach in the walls of the world; through the breach, hope follows. Faith has freed man's mind; hope frees his heart. With heart and mind free, man has limitless things to do, limitless love to give and to take, limitless courage with which to do these things, with which to prove that love. Because that goal beyond the world is so clearly and surely, before us, because it can be accomplished by our own acts, and we know this securely because of the omnipotence and mercy of God, we can take steps towards that goal, we can get something done. There is no moment of life, nor smallest action of life that cannot be bent toward that supreme task.

Hope and courage

Life is not a dull, plodding affair; life is not the fruitless labor of a slave. Life is the swift action of a free man rushing to an end worthy of his freedom. Because his heart is free by hope, man's love is not balked at death, not hindered by sickness; it is not even held back by the limits of the world. The hearts of other men and women are thrown open to him, not for a day, not for an hour, not for a month, not for years, but forever. Additionally, the heart of God is just as wide open and for just as long a time. Of course, this free man can sacrifice in the name of love; of course, he can face terrific difficulties driven on by that love; of course, he can fail and pick himself up repeatedly and again, and never be beaten. For always freedom and hope burn in his heart. This man can face the fearful things of hell because he can hope for the divine things of heaven.

CHAPTER III

SHARING THE DIVINE LIFE
(Q. 23-26)

1. The nature of friendship:
   (a) Mutual benevolent love.
   (b) On a common ground.

2. The friendship of men:
   (a) Its strength.
   (b) Its frailty

3. The friendship of God:
   (a) Its benevolent love: affective and effective.
   (b) Its common ground -- the life of God:
       (1) Its strength -- a habit.
       (2) Its excellence -- a virtue:
           a. Its unity.
           b. Its relations to other virtues:
               1. The supreme virtue.
               2. The condition for perfection in every
virtue.
               3. The form of all the virtues.

4. Charity and the soul of man:
   (a) Its object and origin.
   (b) Its increase.
   (c) Its boundless perfection.
   (d) Its decrease and loss.

5. Love in the soul of man as wide as the love of
God:
   (a) Goods about us: neighbors, irrational
creation.
   (b) Ourselves.

(c) Evils about us: sinners, enemies.

(d) Good and evil above us angels, saints, devils.

6. Friendship's preferences:

    (a) The place of God.

    (b) The place of ourselves.

    (c) The place of neighbor:

        (1) Inequality.

        (2) Double foundation: goodness and bonds of union.

Conclusion:

1. The norm of friendship -- generosity.

2. Friendship and the nature of man.

3. The limits of friendship.

4. Friends of God:

    (a) Living the life of God.

    (b) Loving with the love of God.

    (c) Embrace as wide as the arms of God.

5. Charity and the modern world:

    (a) Doctrines of hate.

    (b) Doctrines of selfishness.

    (c) The narrow love of men

    (d) The death of love.

CHAPTER III
SHARING THE DIVINE LIFE
(Q. 23-26)

The unquestionably accepted axiom, "friendship is rare," would be a terrible indictment of the human race, if it were true. Of course, it is not. Friendship is not nearly so rare as is appreciation of it. These gloomy axioms furnish us with fine excuses when we run short of material for self-pity, especially at times when our mouth is watering for a dreary session with ourselves. Friendship is not rare among human beings because unselfishness is not rare among them; and unselfish love is the one fundamental for true friendship that might be come at with difficulty.

The nature of friendship

Surely, the amateur burglar, striking up an acquaintance with an expert in his line, cannot be said to have true friendship. He hopes to get something out of it, at least some expertness in burglary. The girl who is an official fascinator, looking out for material comfort for the future, is certainly not a true friend of her men friends. Neither of these is true friendship because neither of them is based on unselfish love.

Mutual benevolent love, on a common ground

Unselfish love means no more than the constant, effective desire to do good to another. Briefly, it means that we have identified ourselves with another; his will is our will so that his good is our good, his happiness our happiness. Now unselfish love is not necessarily a guarantee of friendship, it is not the whole story. The charming girl student may feel ever so kindly towards her professor of Ancient History and still fail resoundingly whenever he has anything to do with her examinations. For friendship, there must also be a common ground upon which two can walk a requirement not at all difficult to meet. We have common ground enough with men and women about us: we also worry about bills at the first of the month, we too are thrilled at football games; we have our secret, unrealized hopes, our sorrows, sacrifices, little triumphs. In any one of these fields, we can meet countless other men and women. The difficulty is can we meet them unselfishly? Can we see in them our other selves? Can we attain to that mutual, benevolent, unselfish love on this common ground and so be assured of real friendship?

The friendship of men: Its strength

Friendship would certainly seem to be worth having. It means, at the very least, that through it we live, not one narrow life, rather we live two lives. A door is thrown open and we are admitted to regions that are proper to God alone, for by friendship we stroll into the soul of another. It offers us completion for our incomplete, lonely human hearts, a fulfillment that is sought by every man from the beginning of his existence. If friendship brought no more than this to a man, it might quite reasonably be foregone. An unlimited amount of cosmetics will not beautify an ugly face, it will merely hide its ugliness; nor will a football suit change the puny physique of a man. These additions are extrinsic to the face and the physique; and it is always true that only the intrinsic additions to man really perfect him. In other words, the important thing about friendship is what it does to the individuals involved. It brings out the best in every man; rather paradoxically, it is true, by making him forget himself. It opens up to him possibilities of sacrifice that he has formerly associated with heroism, with the sublime in the efforts of man. Understand; now, by friendship is meant all human love: whether between man and man, woman and woman, man and woman -- indeed all human love that escapes the taint of selfishness.

While friendship is a great comfort, it is not to be pictured in terms of dim lights, quiet corners and intimate whispers. Rather it scans wide horizons with deep wisdom and is a source of enormous strength. It shows us, for example, the stupidity of gloomy sacrifice; it tears away the veil of mystery from the cheerfulness, even eagerness, of love's embrace of hardships. Perhaps when we say that friendship is rare, we are really apologizing for ourselves, explaining that we are not strong. At least, as soon as we make self-basic, we have begun to corrupt sacrifice and coddle cowardice; we have begun to tear out the foundations of friendship. More than that, we have begun to tear out something from the depths of the human heart; for men have always looked, perhaps at times only wistfully, to sacrifice as the fullest expression of a generous heart.

Its frailty

For all its strength, comfort, sublimity, human friendship has about it the frail delicacy of old lace. It is frail because its truth can never be clearly seen but must always be taken on faith, and because its task of surrender can never be fully accomplished. In a word, human friendship is never a rugged thing because of our inability to share our inner self. The closest we come to sharing the truth of friendship is in our clumsy symbols of it; perhaps the closest we come to accomplishing its task is in the physical generation of children. In neither case can we give ourselves utterly to another. Fundamentally, the reason is obvious: we cannot give ourselves away utterly because we do not belong completely to ourselves.

The friendship of God

Friendship's loss can be as unobtrusively quiet a thing as the death of a rose. It has none of the hard durability of a virtue, for it is rather an outgrowth of virtue; it pre-supposes a goodness in us that others can love. This is an unflattering answer to the tight-lipped, bitter-faced individual's complaint that he has no friends; if he realized the full implication of that complaint, undoubtedly he would squeeze the fact into the narrow confines of his petty soul and bind it hand and foot On the other hand, this truth explains the vitality and universality of God's love, stressing its distinction from human love. We must discover the good we love; God does not discover it, He creates it. We can, and do plant the flag of discovery and chant our *Te Deum* too soon; for us, friendship holds extreme possibilities of evil, as well as extreme possibilities of good, for we can make the mistake of throwing open the doors of our soul to a marauder.

To an honest human heart, the sublime experience of human love is a joyful humiliation. There is nothing contradictory in the office boy's lofty gesture as he tells the newspaper carrier to keep the change, and the panicky haste with which he responds to his beloved's slightest wish. He is at the same time a lord and a slave. To him, as to everyone, love is humiliating because of his intimate knowledge of his own imperfection. We are ashamed because we fall so far short of the opinion our friends have of us. Yet we expand with an odd, exuberant joy. It seems so impossible that someone can value us so highly, can put us above everything else, even above themselves. That very joy and humiliation spur us on to heights we could never reach without love. In fact, unselfish human love is always a kind of miracle. It is as incredible to an honest mind as the works of God; yet there is a friendship much more incredible even than this supreme effort of the human heart -- the friendship with God, which is called charity.

Its benevolent love: affective and effective

We would never have dared to use the word friendship in relation to God if He Himself had not done so first, if He had not come among us and lived familiarly with us. Now we are friends of God in the strictest sense of the word. There is between God and us a mutual, unselfish love. It is to be understood, however, that God does not putter about the wreckage of human nature looking for something of good to love, as an ambulance-chasing lawyer might scan an automobile crash in search of a client. God's love does not discover good, as ours does; it creates the good it loves. In other words, on God's side, this friendship is effective, creative; He loves us that He might make us good. On our side, the friendship is not effective but affective; it confronts us with all that is desirable. We love Him because in Him we see, in its full perfection, all that we have seen merely mirrored, imaged, in the world about us, even in the world of men and women. It is not too difficult to see the unselfish love on broth sides of this friendship between God and man.

Its common ground -- the life of God

What is much more difficult to see is the common ground upon which we can walk with God. It is not a matter of a super-highway. Plastic surgery will not make us look any more like God; nor can a Paris designer make a modern hat god-like. We cannot pull ourselves up to His level; nor could we -- nor would we want to if we could -- pull Him down to our level. He can, and He does, lift us up to the level of Divinity. This is the incredible thing in the friendship of God: the common ground upon which that friendship strolls is the life of God Himself. Men and women are upraised to the point where they can, and do, live the life of God. Additionally, the medium by which that miracle of divine generosity is accomplished is His divine grace.

No lengthy argument is necessary to prove that this life of God within us is imperfect now. Nevertheless, this divine life is a reality here and now, it will be perfected in us only in heaven. Here and now, far as we are from heaven. we know God as God knows Himself, for He has given us that intimate knowledge in telling us the truths of faith. We love Him as He loves Himself, because of His supreme goodness. We live on the divine plane; our acts, dimly like His, are of eternal significance within the family of God. This, then, is our friendship with God: a mutual, benevolent love, based on the mysterious common ground of divine life.

Its strength -- a habit

This friendship is not a half-hearted affair of suspicion and secrets withheld; it does not wait on a mood for intimacy. God shares His inner life with us and our souls are naked and open to His divine eye. There are no depths of affections which, because they cannot be done up in the clumsy wrappings of words, must depend for their expression on a pressure of the hand, a caressing glance, the quick welling of tears. Our souls are thrown open to God; God has thrown Himself open to us. More than that, the love of God has put something positive within that soul of ours, His is a creative love; and the creation of His Love within us is called the habit of charity.

In other words, this love of ours for God is not the empty echo of a ventriloquist's vanity. Our will does not put forth this love as a mere instrument responding helplessly to a musician's touch, even though the musician be a Divine Artist. We produce acts that are our very own; and, as we saw in the second volume of this work, our intellects and wills can produce acts only when those tremendous reservoirs of power have been tapped by the pipelines of habit, when they have been determined to a course of action by habit. It is the habit of charity, which is the immediate principle, the determining factor, in our acts of love of God. There is a profound significance in the fact that the effect of God's creative caress is a habit. This means that what is natural to God has now become second nature for us; charity is con natural to a human heart. It is a strong, free, joyous thing. For habit, if it does anything, produces its acts ever more perfectly, more easily, more joyfully, more efficaciously. The brave man *enjoys* his courage; the temperate man *enjoys* his moderation. To put the same truth in another way, stingy, begrudging, laborious or even bitter charity is a mockery. Thomas says rightly: "There is no virtue, no habit that has so much of an inclination to its own action as has charity. There is no habit that acts with so much joy." Fuller reasons for this will be given in the course of this chapter as it becomes clearer that charity is the supreme habit, that it is moved by no other but moves all others, in a word that it enjoys the fullest freedom.

Its excellence -- a virtue

It will, perhaps, be better to concentrate on this habit of charity within us in treating of divine friendship; after all, that is our side of this friendship and, as in all friendships, the one side which is under our control. As a good habit, charity is a virtue. In fact it is a kind of super-virtue; a giant that stands head and shoulders above the rest of the crowd. Its great strength is impatient of the limitations imposed on other virtues; to attempt to confine it to those rules would be like condemning Dante or Shakespeare to oblivion on grounds of punctuation. Temperance, for example, is a virtue insofar as it measures up to the rule of human reason, which is the rule of human action; the same is true of justice and fortitude. Now charity does not stop at the rule of human reason. It plunges beyond that to attain the rule, which is behind the rule of human reason, the supreme rule of human action, the supreme guide to successful living -- God Himself. Charity can by no means be mistaken for a moral virtue for it does not even seek the good of reason. It is not faith, whose object is God as supremely credible; nor is it hope, whose object is God as attainable through the help of His omnipotence. Charity is a distinct, a special virtue whose object is God as the supremely Lovable Being.

Its unity

Charity moves through the world with a lover's smile on its face and a lover's gentleness in its hands. Strangely enough, the world she sees is a lover's world, giving her back smile for smile. It is as though the simplicity of love's concentration gave the entire world a simple unity that made it take on something of the splendor of divinity. Certain it is that everything with which our heart makes contact through charity glows with the lustrous beauty of divinity. For by charity we love everything and everyone because we love God.

Human love has a variety that charity totally lacks. We might love a wise man for the wisdom we might share, a good conversationalist for the entertainment he gives wife, children and us for their very selves; there is no such distinction in the love of charity. For charity, you see, is not a partial but a total love. It has no end but the end of utter unselfishness, the end of the divine good; its common ground does not vary according to nationality, interests, relationship, but is always the same unvarying share in divine life. This is an extremely important truth, which will be brought out more fully as this chapter unfolds: it will be sufficient to point out here that this means that love of neighbor is not the teetering chair upon which we stand precariously reaching for God. We do not reach God through our neighbor; rather we reach our neighbor through God. We love our neighbor because in some way, he belongs to our Friend, Who is God, or because he participates with us in that common ground, by which we are friends of God, the common ground of divine life. There are no short cuts to altruism; we must go the long, triangular way around, through God to neighbor.

Its relations to other virtues: The supreme virtue

In the preceding volume of this work, we saw that virtue was not a dull, routine thing, but the condition for all progress, the basis for extraordinary action, the groundwork for heroism. If this be true of all the virtues, the good habits, we can expect extraordinary things to be almost ordinary when we come to the habit of charity. For charity is the supreme principle of sublime human action in this life, it is the peak of all the virtues. Beside the achievements of charity, the accomplishments of intellectual and moral habits are the precocious drawings of a child contrasted with the work of a master. The intellectual and moral habits are clumsy, humble servants who know well that they are not equipped to serve the master directly; charity walks straight into the presence of God. The object of faith compares with that of charity as a photograph compares with the living presence of a friend; while hope's object, in a like comparison, is a medal from a king compared to a warm welcome into the royal family life. Charity seeks only God and loves Him for Himself.

There is an unconscious humor in the way we ordinarily phrase that truth: charity seeks *only* God. It is something like the shrewdness in Thomas' answer when, having submitted his manuscript on the Blessed Sacrament to the crucifix, the voice of the Lord asked him what reward he would have for writing so well of Him. Thomas said: "Nothing but You, O Lord." Nothing else! No partial reward, no image of the divinity, only the divinity itself would satisfy Thomas. That is what charity wants: only God; in other words, everything.

When a miser rushes into his burning house to save his money at the cost of his life, the bystanders may pity his foolishness; they will not admire him as a brave man. This is an exhibition of the virtue of fortitude. He is not practicing the virtue of temperance when he abstains because it costs money to buy drinks. These are not virtues; they have the wrong goal, they do not bring a man to his end. Yet we do sometimes make the mistake of thinking a man without charity can have perfect virtue.

The form of all the virtues

It simply cannot be done. Charity, in the order of virtue, is the breath of life. Without it, other virtues drag themselves along dispiritedly to a halfway mark, and then fall down exhausted. The other virtues without charity are like men who do not know God; they have a life of their own, but a disappointingly incomplete life. We might say that charity enables the virtues to lead double lives, just as grace enables us to lead two lives. The soul of man gives him natural life; but with no more than this, men must stop at the borders of nature. Grace, perfecting the soul, allows man to lead a divine life; in other words, it goes beyond the natural stopping place of the soul and pushes on to the ultimate goal of the vision of God. So the virtues direct a man to their own proper object, they live their own proper lives; charity comes along and pushes them far beyond that halfway place to the end of ends. Just as prudence is absolutely necessary if there are to be any virtues at all, so charity is necessary if there are to be any perfect virtues. Without prudence, there is no virtue; without charity, there is no perfect virtue, but only that imperfect virtue that bogs down far short of God. That end of ends is proper only to charity.

Charity and the soul of man: Its object and origin

It might be well, here, to rule out the modern confusion of love with mere sentiment. Long, happy sighs, a dazed expression, or copious tears shed at a movie may mean no more than a low, an exceedingly low I.Q. Love, if it be worthy of a human being, must have something rational in it; after all, it proceeds from man's rational appetite, his will. Yet charity is often far from reasonable. A cursory reading of the lives of the saints will impress us immediately with their divine madness, their attempts at impossible things, which nevertheless they accomplished. To say that charity is rational is like saying a mathematical genius is good at arithmetic. Reason is not the rule of charity as it is of the human virtues. Charity is regulated only by the wisdom of God Himself. For charity exceeds all nature, aiming at God Himself; so, of course, it exceeds all reason. It is not to be explained by natural principles, nor by constantly placed human acts. True enough, God is the most lovable thing there is; but it is also true that God is the most knowable thing there is, and yet to us, He is the least known. So also, He is the least loved. In our choice of things to love, we must furnish the angels with much material for kindly amusement. We are like children who much prefer toys to warm clothes as Christmas gifts. If the house were burning down, the child would be quite satisfied if he could grab all his toys and carry them to safety; certainly, he would not shed tears over the loss of his galoshes. A child must be poured into warm clothes; charity must be poured into us. Nor is this gift necessarily given according to our natural capacity for love. A great lover is not necessarily a great saint, although a great saint is always a very great lover.

Surely one of the secondary joys of heaven will be the discovery of the ranking stars in the game of love; imagine the buzz that will run through the heavenly ranks when Don Juan and Thomas Aquinas come up for a comparison of their averages! For charity, like all the theological virtues, is above nature. Our very preparation for it is itself a supernatural preparation; we can be very sure that curly hair, a flashing smile or soulful eyes have nothing whatever to do with the amount of charity we receive from God.

Its increase

However, this truth must be well understood. The fact that charity is not from nature, nor doled out in proportion to natural capacity for love, does not mean that there is nothing for us to do about it. A man cannot sit back and wait for something to happen, half-expecting, perhaps, that some morning he will wake up and, to the astonishment of his wife, suddenly be a saint. There is a great deal we can do about charity, for it is beyond all doubt true that charity can be increased. This means no more than that we can constantly come closer to God, for the approach to God is not by a lunge of the body, but by a lunge of the heart. Our life has rightly been called a "way"; it is a way to an end, to a goal, to God. We can always move towards that goal as long as we have life. We approach God by love, by charity.

More concretely, we can do in this thing of charity, what we can do in any friendship. The busy young man who is furious because his beloved is not waiting beside the telephone for his call, the young lady who pouts because her friend is not attentive enough or who scans every inch of a gift in search of a price tag will soon be looking for other partners. We know from experience how surely friendship can be killed by attempting to increase it through pressure, not upon ourselves, but upon the other party. Our love does not reform our friends, it re-forms us. At least the one thing we can do about friendship is to work on our side of it, to deepen the common ground, within ourselves, upon which that friendship is based. We get nowhere by insisting on thoughtfulness, attention, caresses; for all that comes from the other side, the side that is beyond our control.

In this divine friendship, the common ground is the divine life. We can increase that friendship in only one way: by deepening that common ground, by increasing the life of God within our soul. Certainly, we cannot increase divine love, any more than we can increase human love, by a kind of promiscuity. It is useless to look around for more things to love by charity, for with the tiniest amount of charity all things that can be loved by charity, are so loved. If we except any of them, we have already destroyed charity. An increase in weight may make us bigger lovers, but not greater ones. We cannot search around eagerly for some new, improved kind of charity, there is no new kind. There is only one kind, the kind that loves God for Himself. We increase charity by digging it deeper into our souls, and in no other way.

To say that a man has become great through the years does not mean that he has developed extraordinary muscles or increased his vegetative powers tremendously. It means that he has become more of a man. He has done more of the things that are proper to humanity: more thinking, deeper loving, more orderly action. Increase, in anything, must be judged according to the nature of that thing. Therefore, charity, which is a habit, must increase the way habits increase. It is the nature of every habit to be in a faculty; its increase, then, means that it is more deeply in that faculty, it is greater because it has penetrated more deeply into its subject. Alternatively, very briefly, the increase of charity can never be by extension; it is never quantitative but always a matter of intensity. It has been said that in the spiritual life, to stand still is to go backward. You may be able to detect a bit of the brogue in that. Yet it is true if properly understood; that is, if we understand that the very dispositions for progress are themselves a kind of progress. The very use of a habit, any habit, is a disposition for a better use of that habit; but actually, the habit will not increase until we have produced an act more intense than the habit itself. For example, if our habit of charity is, say, of the power of five, and for a period of a year we have produced only acts of the power of four, then during all that year we have not actually increased our charity. Still, we have, during all of that year, piled up dispositions for better acts of charity. Actual increase of charity is only by more intense acts; but dispositive increase is brought about by every one of our acts.

All this would be true of any habit. However, of this supernatural habit of charity, it is also true that we can merit an increase. Let us put it this way: by every act of charity, we merit eternal life, but that eternal life is given to us only at the proper time -- the moment of death. So, also, by every act of charity we merit an increase in the habit of charity, but that increase is to be given only at its proper time -- when we produce a more intense act of charity.

Its boundless perfection

When a father asks his little girl how much she loves her daddy, he is taking a loving revenge for all the unanswerable questions she has showered upon him; he knows the question is very difficult to answer. Later on in life, the answer will be so much easier. By then we know that the measure of love is sacrifice; but we never know any definite limit to the possibilities of the human heart for love. Yet there are limits. This is only a human heart and the object of its human love is only a human being, possessed of only a limited goodness, along with many defects and shortcomings. If we find it difficult to place a limit to human friendship, we find it impossible to place a limit to divine friendship. There is simply nothing to limit it but the human heart itself. God is always, eminently, infinitely desirable; the constant flood of His grace makes more and more intense acts of charity always possible to us. Additionally, even that finite heart, which must harbor all this love, increases its capacity for love by loving.

All this is not discouraging, in the sense that the work of loving is an impossible job, never to be finished; rather it is encouraging in the sense of assuring us that we shall never be satiated with divine love. It does not mean that we are condemned to failure, never reaching perfection in divine love. In one sense, that divine friendship, that charity, is always perfect -- in the sense that we always love God, above all things because He Himself is so supremely good, in another sense, it is always imperfect, for certainly we can never love God as much as He deserves to be loved -- that would demand an infinite act. Now there is another sense in which charity is progressively more and more perfect.

Obviously, it is in heaven, not in this life, that we are free constantly to praise and love God without interruption. In this life, the best we can do is to refuse to trifle with His rivals. It may be our vocation to make a sweeping denunciation of all impediments to love, *actually* excluding, as religious do, even necessary things of life that we may be free for God. Or it may be that we can exclude these impediments only *habitually*, as do all the faithful when they place their hearts in God habitually so that they refuse to think or to will anything contrary to that divine love; that is, when they keep the Ten Commandments. From yet another angle, the angle of emphasis of the act of charity, the progressive perfection of charity is easily seen.

Almost every Christian is familiar with this division on the grounds of emphasis, a division often stated as the three grades of spiritual life: the purgative, the illuminative and the unitive way. St. Thomas phrases it more simply, calling it the state of the beginner, of one progressing and of the perfect. Perhaps all this can be made clear by an example. In our settlement of the West, the first pioneers went out with guns in their hands to explore the country, defending their lives every instant. They were followed by the settlers and the railroad builders, who still had their guns at hand ready to protect their lives every moment. Finally, the farmers came, established their farms and lived in a degree of peace, but still under the necessity of protecting themselves. In the spiritual life, in the first stages of charity, our chief preoccupation is to protect ourselves from the enemy, sin. In the second stage, our interest is principally progress in charity, penetrating the country of God, but we are still in danger, constant danger. Finally, in the third stage, our principal task is an experience and enjoyment of God. Yet in all these stages, there must be a constant alertness to any incursion of sin. In more simple terms, we might say that the purgative state is our period of infancy, when we are in greatest danger of disease or death; the illuminative state is one of adolescence, where we are more fully developing our powers; finally, the unitive state is a state of spiritual adulthood.

Its decrease and loss

Now not even an adult can, successfully, dispute the right of way with an express train, nor frown typhoid out of the room. However perfect our charity in this life it can always be lost. In fact, it can be lost in one crashing instant through a single mortal sin. These two, charity and mortal sin, are mutually exclusives: one is a total surrender to God; the other is a complete rebellion against God. One places God above all things, the other places man himself above all things; one is light, the other darkness. Additionally, sin is always possible to our human will as long as God is not seen face to face.

While this is always possible, it is not usual; in fact, it is quite extraordinary. Normally we do not pass from depths to heights, or heights to depths, in one jump; we are cautious even in our sins. Charity is ordinarily lost through a previous diminution of it. Not that we can cut down charity as we slice down a loaf of bread. We must wear charity down by shadow boxing it, for there is no means of getting at it directly. Like all love, this love too was made to last forever; an element of temporality, of caution, some means of escape is a frank statement of the absence of love. Charity itself cannot fail. Look at it closely: God cannot become less lovable; the flood of His grace will not desert us; this habit of charity is not a human habit; built up by human acts and to be torn down by human acts. It comes directly from God. There is absolutely no creative agency that can act upon it directly. This is a love that is secure. Nevertheless, it can be indirectly limited; that is, its increase can be stopped effectively in two ways. either by ceasing all acts of charity -- the fruit of boredom with God -- which means that we are not getting up any steam for that further, more intense act of charity which would increase the habit; or, secondly, by venial sin.

Mrs. O'Malley may send words of love from her lips while her eyes are twin vultures circling the church for signs of weakness in her prey. It is true that venial sin is not opposed to the *habit* of charity; but it is impossible for us, at the same time, to make an act of love and commit a venial sin. Venial sin is opposed to the *act* of charity. It effectively bars the increase of charity by disposing us to the opposite of charity, to mortal sin. An honest glance at any venial sin will make this clear. It caters to our depraved tastes, increasing them; it develops our love for temporal things, petty, secondary things in comparison with the divine friendship; and it gives us the habit of transgressing the law. We are like a child who, because he has escaped unscathed when he tossed a cup on the floor, decided it would be great fun to crash all the china in one quick tug at the tablecloth. We get used to breaking the law in smaller things; the bigger things seem much less big than formerly and we are much less careful of keeping them intact. We might call venial sin a kind of spiritual polygamy. At least it scatters the forces of our will, cutting down the intensity of our love for any one object and thus assuring us of no further progress in charity. At the same time, it feeds our natural appetite in a disorderly fashion, a fashion whose normal climax is mortal sin.

Love in the soul of man as wide as the love of God: Good's about us: neighbors, irrational creation

As the novel opens, Father Malachy (the miracle-worker) is sitting in a third-class railroad carriage meditating on the love of God, when suddenly two utterly unprepossessing persons come in and sit opposite him. Father Malachy's eyes closed with a snap that almost awoke an echo, as he reflected that if, loving God, he must love his neighbors, at least he did not have to love them with his eyes open. There is something in this, at least the truth that we do not love our neighbors supernaturally because of their personal charm. However, it would be truer to say that charity turns an x-ray on our neighbors uncovering hidden goodness, rather than forcing us to love them blindly.

Not even a saint would attempt to deny that this individual has a face like a horse; nor pretend that a public enemy was a kindly, misunderstood boy. The point is that even if the horse-face never wins a beauty contest and the public enemy never gets to be president, both have a solid, unfailing claim to our love. We love them because they belong to God. We can, we must, find love for them no matter what they are, just as a husband, because he loves his wife, can find some love for her relatives. These neighbors belong to our Friend. Not only that, but as long as they are in this life, they possess, or can possess, that same common ground of divine life upon which our own friendship with God is based. Really, they are united to us in God. This is not to say that charity does not extend to all human loves that arc not founded in sin. It does. Now, it consecrates them, lifts them up to higher ground. Christ did not demand the impossible in commanding us to love our neighbors; He asked that our love embrace them as belonging to God and as, at least potentially, friends of God and so our friends.

Charity, in other words, is not a sentimental hypocrite; nor is it a sob-sister, sick with the passion of pity. By it, we do not weep over the discouragement, sickness or loneliness of our neighbors as though these were the supreme tragedies of life. The good we wish them by our mutually benevolent love is that good which belongs to charity -- a share in divine life. In addition, we do what we can to make that wish effective.

Thomas, overall, was an easy-going man, not easily aroused; he was particularly considerate of the opinions of others. It comes as somewhat of a shock to hear him answer the question, "Can irrational creation be loved from charity, be a friend of man?" with an explosive "Ridiculous!" One wonders if medieval Paris, about eleven o'clock at night, had the equivalent of Park Avenue's disgusted servants and self-conscious dogs. It is, of course, ridiculous to expect benevolent love from a creature that is driven, that cannot give and take that cannot surrender as love demands. Irrational creatures can be loved as belonging to our divine Friend.

Ourselves

Still the fact that irrational creatures can, in some way, be loved, makes it clear that there is little to which charity does not extend. Certainly, we must love ourselves; fortunately, this is not too difficult, no matter what ravages nature and the wear and tear of life have effected. Moreover, we must love ourselves, from charity, second only to God. The objection that a man can hardly be united to himself, yet charity, as friendship, demands union, overlooks a profound truth. That truth is that union demands unity as its root; and we, ourselves, are the units of that union which is our friendship with God. The love by which we love ourselves is the form, the basis, of the friendship, which we have for others.

This truth has been misconstrued by opponents of St. Thomas to mean that we must love ourselves even above God, because we are the unit of that friendship with God. True, we are a unit in that friendship, but not the primary or principal unit; we are a secondary unit, God is the primary. Of these two, God and ourselves, is built the bridge by which we cross the gap separating us from our neighbor. We cannot love ourselves more than God or we have destroyed even the unit of love of ourselves, which is from charity. God comes first; but immediately after God, ourselves. Because of this love of ourselves through God -- as belonging to God and as His friend -- it is possible to give all our neighbors the same supernatural love.

Evils about us: sinners, enemies

It is a Manichean, not a Catholic, tenet that the body is to be hated. The scourgings of the saints were gone about with the same regret a parent has in spanking a beloved but unruly child. We must, from charity, love our bodies; not for the part, they play in sin, but as things of God, made by God, as being a part of us who belong to God, and as sharers in the winning of heaven and the enjoyment of its triumph. So also, we must love sinners, not for their sins but for their nature, which belongs to God, and for the possibilities they have of sharing in divine friendship. We must love sinners, even though sinners most effectively hate themselves.

There is tragedy in that last phrase, a tragedy that is best expressed in a paradox: the sinner abandons God for love of himself, and reaches the goal of hatred of self; the just man abandons himself for love of God and reaches the goal of most perfect love of himself. Swinburne could write, naively, of "*the raptures and roses of vice*", only because he had got lost in a fog. We do not get raptures and roses from enemies and the sinner is a bitter enemy of himself.

As a concrete test of the love and hatred of men for themselves, let us apply the signs of friendship. A friend does not wish to absorb his friend; he wishes to preserve that loved personality in all its integrity. He wishes good to his friend; moreover, he wishes it effectively, he does something about it, actually tries to get that good done. He delights in the presence of his friend and with him is at peace, for they seek the same goal. The test works out perfectly when applied to the just man relative to himself. He does not wish to destroy his own excellence, rather he desires to preserve that rational part in all its integrity; he wishes good to his soul, to his supreme part, a real, lasting, a spiritual good. In addition, he does something about this wish by his acts of virtue. He delights to enter into the house of his soul, because there he will find peace.

This does not mean that the just man sits down and hugs himself by the hour; but his very fight against sin has the universal appeal of a man's fight for his friends, with its connotations of mysterious communion, long calm evenings, pervading peace. Now let us look at the sinner. He does not wish to preserve the integrity, the interior life that should be his; his sin is a direct attack on it. He does not desire the spiritual goods that are alone goods of the rational part of man; quite the contrary, for he does all he can to destroy those goods. He gets no pleasure out of entering into himself; his life is an attempt to escape from himself. His moments of terror are the moments when he is forced within himself, for there he knows well he will find nothing but war. The unspeakable things that are championed today in the name of love are, actually, not the inspirations of love but of hate.

If the modern world thinks of it at all, it probably decides that Christ was not thinking of Chamberlain and Hitler when he commanded men to love their enemies; imagine demanding a flush of pleasure on Hitler's cheek, a joyful racing of his heart at the mere mention of the name of Chamberlain! Now, no one has made any such demand. Christ did not ask us to feel love, but to have love. Moreover, he did not ask us to love these people as enemies. In fact, as enemies, they are sinners, they have acted unjustly towards us; if they have not and we still think they are enemies, we are being stupid about it. Really, they are friends, doing us good though the momentary bitterness of the good has spoiled our appreciation of it.

We are asked to love them, first of all as men, and secondly as at least potentially participants in the friendship of God; in other words, as belonging to God and as His potential friends. We do not have to kiss them; but we do have to wish them the good of charity, their eternal salvation. The signs of friendship we show them are the signs proportionate to the inner love we are obliged to have for them. We must at least show them the general signs of good will that we show to all men; "*darling*," as a term of address, is certainly not obligatory; "*skunk*" is just as certainly forbidden. Under the stress of some particular necessity, we may be obliged to show the signs of friendship normally reserved to our particular friends -- an invitation to dinner when our enemy is starving or at least a sandwich at the back door; or a friendly approach when we know our stiffness is furnishing him with further occasion for hating us.

Good and evil above us angels, saints, devils

We may be a little exuberant in our estimation of their earthly counterparts, but we do love angels, not only as creatures of God but as active participants in the friendship of God. We can love devils in somewhat the same way we love a friend's horse; their nature belongs to God, they are the creatures of our divine Friend. Yet, they can never be our friends, no matter how chummy we get with them. From our point of view, devils are not an unmixed evil; they are remarkably assiduous exercise-boys who keep countless men spiritually fit, offering them constant opportunities for the practice of virtue in resisting temptation.

We could sum up all of this doctrine on the object of charity by saying, briefly, that by charity we must love God, the Cause of this divine friendship. Then we must love those who directly participate in that friendship: first of all ourselves; then our neighbor, who is associated with us in that friendship, at least potentially; finally, our bodies, which have a share in that supreme happiness of union with God in heaven through a redundance of the glory of the soul. All else is loved solely as belonging to our divine Friend.

Friendship's preferences: The place of God

This is all clear as long as we stick to general statements; but when we come down to particulars, it is another story. There is for example the perplexity of the man faced with choosing between the rescue of his wife and his mother in a shipwreck; or between the starvation of his wife and of his children. Who comes first? What to do? The quest.ion is not settled by the rescuer drowning himself, nor the husband allowing the whole family to starve.

Much of this difficulty is cleared up by a simple distinction. Perhaps the choice will not be made any easier, but it will certainly be made clearer if we remember that there are two kinds of love. The first is *appreciative love*, which corresponds to the objective goodness or lovableness. This is the love, which falls under precept; it is an objective thing, for its object is not something subject to our will, but existing in the ontological order. We are commanded in the appreciative line, the line of evaluation, because it follows the objective goodness; this is nothing more than truth in love. The second might be called *intensive* or subjective love. You find it in full force in the heart of a mother of a worthless son; for it depends not on the objective, value of the thing loved so much as its closeness to us. This love does not fall under precept.

As an illustration of the contusion of this distinction, I was once told by a young nun that she had not written home for nine months, because, as she explained, she had left all things for God. This was a concrete expression of her love of God above all things, even above her parents. In fact, by religious profession God is loved above all else, *appreciatively*; it is perfectly normal to have a much more *intensive* love for parents than for God.

The place of ourselves

In fact we can push this further and say that it is the ordinary thing to have a more intensive love for grandchildren, or even for a chance acquaintance; but if it comes to an exclusive choice between anyone or anything and God, the choice must be in

God's favor. He is the reason for loving all else. In Himself He is the most desirable, the most lovable Being. In this objective or appreciative order, we love God first, then ourselves, then our neighbor; in the concrete, this will at least mean that we can never put ourselves above God, and never commit the smallest sin (do ourselves the slightest spiritual damage) to further the good of our neighbor, even to save him from eternal damnation.

The place of neighbor: Inequality

In our love of neighbor there is, of course, variety; it would be a dull world indeed in which there were none of the ups and downs of love. We have, in fact, a double ground for our preferences, namely, our neighbor's closeness to God and his closeness to ourselves. Their proximity to God determines their objective lovability, as a basis of appreciative love; their proximity to us explains, in a dark manner, the mysterious variety of human tastes in love, as it furnishes the basis for intensive love.

Double foundation: goodness and bonds of union

A man's proximity to God is determined by his participation in divine perfections. Additionally, of all the bonds, which tie one man to another, St. Thomas selects, as the closest, the bond of blood. That is still a little too general to be genuinely informative. Determining it further, Thomas says that we should love parents more than sons, father more than mother, and parents more than a wife or a husband. Understand all this is on the appreciative or objective side. Thomas is arguing from the one consideration of parents as parents. We love them as the principle or source of our being; as such, their claim to love is most like God's own. Parents are the principles of our life, our sons are not; so we love our parents more objectively, but usually we love our sons more intensely, for sons are really a part of us. A father, as the active principle, is more the principle of generation than a mother; on this ground alone, he is to be loved more, though on countless other grounds the claim of the mother may be superior. On this same consideration -- of principle, or source of being -- parents are loved more objectively, a wife more intensely. This same line of argument is extended beyond the bonds of blood and justifiably so. Thus, for instance, we love a benefactor as a principle of a good that has come to us, but a beneficiary as a part of ourselves; consequently the benefactor is loved more objectively, a beneficiary more intensively. All this is not merely academic; it gives the solid basis of rational preference in those crucial moments when tragic preference must be made. Although, it is true, not many men are ever faced with the dilemma of deciding whether father, mother, wife, child or friend shall have the last crust that stands between them all and starvation.

Conclusion: The norm of friendship -- generosity

We can, I believe, sum up this chapter briefly in terms of friendship. Friendship is a mutual benevolent love on a common ground, and has as its normal rule, unselfishness; or, in more simple terms, generosity. Our friendship is as deep as the identification of our will with the will of another; insofar as we see someone else as another self; insofar as we find our happiness in giving good to another, whatever the cost.

Friendship and the nature of man

From the beginning, it has not been good for man to be alone. Man has recognized himself as incomplete; he has sought other selves, and carried that search even to the heights, in seeking a divine Friend. We must share our lives with others because our hearts are so big; we must have the companionship of others because our hearts are so small and weak. Betrayal of a friend is a kind of suicide, with all of suicide's cowardice and despair. It is difficult for a man to live a whole human life without friends, because it is exceedingly difficult to any man to be sufficient unto himself.

The limits of friendship

Yet this yearning of man for friendship, for the completion offered by love, is certain to disappoint when it is restricted to the purely human sphere. There is, after all, a limit to the generosity of men and women, a limit to what they can give, a limit to what, of themselves, they are able to share. There is a much greater limit to their capacity to do the good they wish for their friends, and perhaps an even greater limit to their capacity for instilling generosity in others. Even were we to overlook all these limitations, there is the terrific limitation of time on human love. For, left to itself, the love of men for men must end at death.

Friends of God: Living the life of God
Embrace as wide as the arms of God

It was divinely fitting that this yearning of the human heart should be fulfilled by the only friendship capable of satisfying it. In that divine friendship, all the limitations of human friendship are done away with. There can be no question of the infinite generosity of God nor of His capacity for doing effectively the good, He wills us. His is a creative love. There can be no question of His ability to share His inner self with us. We find the friends of God living the life of God, so much so that this divine life is the very basis of the friendship, the common ground upon which they walk arm and arm with God. We find them loving with the love of God, knowing God as He knows Himself. These friends of God have an embrace as wide as the arms of God, so wide indeed as to include everything: neighbors, friends, enemies, sinners, even irrational creation.

Loving with the love of God

If the patois of friendship be sacrifice, these friends of God have a marvelous fluency. If sacrifice is the rule of thumb by which we judge the depth and value of friendship, its willingness to surrender, it is not surprising to come upon eager, joyful, unquestioning self-denial in the lives of the saints. There is no mystery in the complete surrender of men and women to the love of God; there is no mystery in the young hope, the unfailing joy, tile intense living of the friends of God, whatever be the discouraging circumstances of poverty, suffering and death.

Charity and the modern world:

Doctrines of hate

Doctrines of selfishness

In the modern world, the friends of God are persons apart. They are in the world, but not of it; in fact, quite opposed to what it advocates. There is no echo in their hearts to the ringing appeals for hatred of men for men, class for class, race for race, and nation for nation. They know better than to believe when they are told that it is by hate that happiness is to be brought to the poor that men are to be given opportunities to live full human lives that the evils of the world are to he overcome. For behind all these doctrines of hate are the unholy hosts of selfishness. The man himself, or the class itself, or the nation itself has been made the supreme thing; and that means the death of sacrifice. It means the death of love, for it means that we are no longer able to see beyond ourselves, or beyond that limited sphere, we have identified with ourselves -- beyond the class, the race, the nation. We have closed our hearts to everything else; moreover, we have closed our minds to everything else and so, forever, sealed our hearts in a tomb.

The narrow love of men

Even those who recoil in horror from the doctrine of hate and selfishness to champion a doctrine of humanism -- of love for men, development of the human race and the possibilities of human endeavor -- even these have done little to satisfy the heart of man. They have restricted the human heart to the narrow limits of human love, with all its limitations, above all with its pitiful gesture of despairing farewell at the door of death.

The death of love

These are not the things that satisfy the human heart. It was made for something much greater than all this. Consequently, the human heart cannot stand by unmoved and watch love put to death, whether by hate, by selfishness, or by narrowness. Today the human heart is not standing by, in spite of the tremendous propaganda that attempts to lull it to stagnant inactivity and dull resignation. The human heart today is seeking, as it never sought before, that satisfaction, that fullness, that completion, which can come only with a friendship that is divine. In other words, the world of today is hungry for charity.

CHAPTER IV

SHARING THE DIVINE LIFE
(Q. 27-36)

1. The hearth and the heart:
   (a) A full heart, a heart at home.
   (b) The pilgrim and his homeland (*via et patria*).

2. The expansiveness of love:
   (a) Surrender, not conquest.
   (b) Surrender to God:
      (1) Immediate contact of love.
      (2) The measure of love for God.
   (c) Surrender to friends and enemies.

3. The withering effect of hate:
   (a) Hatred of God.
   (b) Hatred of neighbor.
   (c) The climax of evil.

4. Love in the heart of man:
   (a) Joy:
      (1) An unappreciated possession.
      (2) The sorrow of charity.
      (3) Enemies of joy:
         a. Spiritual sloth.
         b. Envy:
            1. Foundations of envy.
            2. Roll-call of the envious.

(b) Peace:
    (1) The peace of Christ and of the world.
    (2) Peace and action.
    (3) The common goal of men.
(c) Mercy.
    (1) The nature of mercy.
    (2) Roll call of the merciful.
    (3) The excellence of mercy.

5. Love in the world: mercy at work:
    (a) Among the needy -- almsgiving:
        (1) The works of mercy.
        (2) The effects of almsgiving.
        (3) Its circumstances.
    (b) Among the erring -- fraternal correction.

Conclusion:

1. Divine wisdom and Nazareth:
    (a) While God is, the home endures.
    (b) While home endures, God cannot be forgotten.
    (c) With God and the home, the world of strangers is secure.

2. The modern crisis:
    (a) Shall the heart of man be full or empty love or hate?
    (b) Centers of modern attack: God and the home.
    (c) Some results of modern doctrines:
        (1) Shriveled hearts -- hate.
        (2) Enveloping sorrow -- envy and sloth.
        (3) Closed fist of selfishness.
        (4) Crushing hammer of cruelty.
        (5) Seduction rather than correction.

3. The paradox of the human heart.

CHAPTER IV
THE FULLNESS OF LOVE
(Q. 27-36)

It might be a good thing if every small child would, at least once during its too brief term as a child, stray from home and get lost. At least the child would enjoy the strange experience of being coaxed, amused, entertained and caressed in a police station; certainly, the child would learn, as it could in no other way, how big a place home holds in its heart. Everyone takes such a child to his heart because, in some dim way, almost everyone knows what it means to lose home. The mysterious hold home has on the heart of man is so penetrating that if that hold is ever lost, something has been lost of the very nature of man; something of bitterness has entered in.

The hearth and the heart: A full heart, a heart at home

Yet that appeal of home is an intangible thing. Looking back, we can see that home does not necessarily call up vistas of plenty, comfort, wealth or culture. Home reaches more deeply into the soul than any of these things. It is the fulfillment of a hope; we might say that it is an ideal, which is at the same time a memory, a goal and a promise. It keeps before our eyes the wondrous vision of a human heart fulfilled. We look back to it with complete satisfaction; we ourselves naturally strive to establish a home in the world; we hope to see the promise perfectly fulfilled some time, even if that time is not until eternity.

The pilgrim and his homeland (*via et patria*)

Two pictures of home stand out in every Catholic's memory: the home of the Holy Family at Nazareth, devoid of material comfort; and the individual's own childhood home. Both fit perfectly our picture of home. Analyzing both, we come close to the roots of that tug of home on the heart. Call it peace, happiness, or an understanding mercy that made our little sorrows the sorrows of the family; or an open-handed hospitality that made home a source from which kindness went out. So that it seemed quite natural for us to bring our little friends home when they were tired, hungry or hurt. No doubt, in some way, all men have known, vaguely, that all these characteristics of home were the creations of the unceasing activity of unselfish love. What is in danger of being forgotten today is the exact nature of an act of love.

In our judgment of others, we make no mistake about this. We do not think the nasty, thoughtless boy who takes advantage of his mother at every turn, yet runs home sure of being petted and fawned upon, is the least bit better for the love he is receiving. Nor do we think the gangster-son of worthy parents is any less despicable for the trust and love given him by his parents; rather he is a great deal worse. We are quite sure that the mother who insists upon absorbing the whole life of her child, in the name of maternal love, is no mother at all.

The expansiveness of love: Surrender, not conquest

In all these judgments, we are insisting that the act of love is much more a matter of loving shall of being loved. Love does not so much make us a blotter, to sop up infinite caresses, as it does make a dynamo of us to produce untiring action. It is not a matter of getting, but of giving. It does not sit back, with a resigned sigh and suffer love; rather it steps out actively to prove love. For love is an operative habit, being a virtue, it exists to do, to work. Love is not so much a conquest as it is surrender, a surrender that sets us free from the debasing slavery of selfishness. If we look in puzzlement at a woman drudging away at housework in a hovel, and wonder what she gets out of life, we are being hopelessly superficial. For we overlook the fact that she gets the principal thing love has to give the opportunity to serve, to surrender, to prove love by sacrifice.

To fly from love, unless it is showering favors upon us, is to desert love and embrace selfishness. We preen ourselves before an audience, graciously allowing others to recognize our superior goodness; but we demand that they applaud by loving us. This is not love that we are seeking, but flattering that echo our own stupid overestimation of ourselves. There is nothing of love's astonished humility in this. The so-called love that consists in a constant demand for attention is accurately classified if we remember that, to a dishonest mind, the fact of being loved is a source of unalloyed exultation, for, to such a mind, it is proof that success has been achieved in fooling someone, badly.

Surrender to God: Immediate contact of love

Not infrequently, a chance breeze blows back the curtains from the windows of our soul, a passerby is given an unexpected glimpse of the depths of that soul, and friendship begins. Perhaps the immediate occasion is no more than a smile, a kind word, an understanding glance. In somewhat the same way, the favors of God or the high hopes He offers us, push back for an instant the veils that hide His face; we get an unexpected view of the depths of the richness of God. Nevertheless, the benevolence of a man, a woman, or even of God, is not friendship. Friendship is a mutual thing, there can be none between us and God until we have surrendered to Him made ourselves one with our divine Friend. With that beginning of divine friendship, wonders pour into our lives, and among the very first is an immediate contact with God; love lengthens our arms to reach to God Himself.

This immediate contact with the beloved is not peculiar to divine friendship. It is true of all love, for it is always true that the will begins where knowledge ends. Knowledge is the guide, going ahead to hack out the footholds upon which love can climb higher and higher. Now, knowledge is a self-contained thing; it brings things into ourselves, stripping them of their material garments at the door of our soul. Then love goes plunging out to the thing loved, as it is in itself -- whether it wear soiled overalls or royal robes. So charity, love of God, plunges out, not to God as He is known from the things of this world, not even as He might be ideally pictured by the greatest of human minds, but to God as He is in Himself.

The measure of love for God

On its human level, love finds, later of course and ruefully, that not infrequently it has plunged too enthusiastically. For if the measure of lovableness is the goodness of the beloved, obviously we can love beyond measure. Human beings do have their limits of goodness. nut there is no such risk in divine friendship. There is no danger of going too far, if only because it is impossible for us to go far enough. There is no excess in this friendship, for our Friend is the rule and measure of all things, He is the reason for the desirability, the lovableness of every other thing. In fact, the more we love God, the better we love Him. Our external manifestations of our love for God may have to take dictation from prudence; but the love in our heart not only does not need, it cannot stand, careful, cautious calculation.

Surrender to friends and enemies

St. John was not putting it too strongly when he insisted that the man who said he loved God, yet did not love his neighbor, was a liar. For this surrender to God simply has not been made if we have not also surrendered to our neighbor, both to our friends and to our enemies. To the pagan world, love of enemies has always seemed a strange, even a weak thing. perhaps because the pagan did not understand well that the greatest conquest man has to make is not of his enemies, but of himself. Love of enemies is not a weak, but a strong thing; indeed, from the human point of view it is a hard thing. Yet based on divine friendship, it is an inevitable corollary of the solid basis of love of neighbor. If God is our Friend, then in the name of that friendship, we love all that belongs to God; in other words, everything that is.

An opposite extreme view of this love of enemies made men a little suspicious of love of friends; it was so easy, so natural that one reaching for the divine heights might be expected to sniff in disdain at something that was really much too easy. Actually, it is more meritorious to love a friend than it is to love an enemy, all else being equal; for an enemy, if he is truly such, is a sinner. On the contrary, the true friend is virtuous; he is then, by his virtue, closer to God, and by his love for us our friend is closer to us. In other words, our friends have two solid claims to our love; our enemies' case rests only on the fact that they are potential friends of God.

Yet love of enemies is a splendid, Christian thing. Its particular excellence comes from the fact that it is a striking sign of our love for God. Here there can be no doubt that we are loving men because of God; certainly their weakness, injustice, viciousness does not furnish the attraction. Here is one love for men that is above all suspicion; it is a test of the vitality of our love for God, proving to us and to Him that we are ready to do even difficult things in the name of that love. Still, the fact that these things are difficult does not make them better, for it is not difficulty but goodness that determines the worth of a thing.

In its smallest degree, this divine friendship is strong and generous; it pushes the heavy door of our heart open as wide as the heart of God. This wide open door is not natural to us; it is ever ready to swing shut. Perhaps it is closed softly, imperceptibly by indifference; or it may be slammed hard and bolted by hate. In either case, we are imprisoned within the confines of our own heart.

The withering effect of hate: Hatred of God

It seems a tragic, and at the same time, a petty action for a man to lock himself up in his own heart, much more tragic and petty than a man's locking himself in his own house and pouting against the rest of the world. It seems almost impossible that a man should slam the door of his heart against the most desirable, lovable Being there is. Indeed, this would be impossible if we could see God face to face; then we could not hate Him. However, in this life we see Him only darkly through faith, or dimly in his effects in the world.

At the same time, we look about us and see clearly the sorrow that enters into our life, the labor that must go into our understanding, the punishment that must follow on our sins. Additionally, so we can hate God, much as a woman learns to hate her husband, not because of any evil in the man himself, but because of the disorderly way he throws his clothes about the room. We can hate God for sprinkling our lives with the seasoning of sorrow, for giving us the kind of mind that can uncover so few nuggets of truth and with such terrific difficulty, for judging our sins and punishing them. In these cases, we hate God for His effects in our lives, not for Himself; yet we should know, knowing God as we do, that even these bitter tasting effects are solid proof of His profoundly thoughtful love for us.

Hatred of neighbor

If we do succeed in hating God, our neighbor has little chance for our love. That the heavy odor of hate should pervade every corner of a godless world should be no surprise, for in such a world the one foundation that will most surely include all men in love has been denied. The hater of God has made his own life a godless world and so thrown open the sluice gates of hate.

Understand, now, that we are not expected to love a man for his stupidity, his theft of our car, his insults to our family or his contempt for our personal appearance. St. Augustine put the demands of love beautifully when he said: "*If you hate well, then you love; whereas if you love badly, you hate.*" We should hate in our neighbor the things that are not God's, but rather against God; then we are really loving him, wishing the destruction of evil afflicting him and the approach to the Supreme Good. If we love him for the sins he makes possible to us, or for his own sins, then we are not loving him but hating him. In either case, we are committing the gravest sin possible against our neighbor. Now, hate is a helpless thing. We could do much more damage to our neighbor by breaking his nose or ruining his business; our hate hurts no one but the person in whose defense it arises -- ourselves.

The climax of evil

Hatred of God is the climax of evil. All other mortal sins have some little saving element of humanity about them; a thief, for instance, turns away from God because of the particularly attractive loot, as a boy condemns himself to a spanking because he wants to play baseball beyond the dinner hour. Yet, hate is diabolical. In common with all mortal sins, it turns away from God; but not for any other reason, not betrayed by some less worthy love. It directly spurns the divine goodness itself.

The humiliating thing about hate, whether of God or men, is that it always arises from self-pity. Its immediate source is sorrow for oneself, for it arises from envy. Maybe it is the good of our neighbor, or again it may be the good of God Himself, that weighs us down with sorrow. In both cases, the hate that bubbles up is the helpless gesture of protest of a small ineffective, miserly soul; so great is the terror of losing its own closely guarded goods that the very appearance of good in others is taken as a personal loss. The hater has so slight a hold on his own excellence that he cannot risk the presence of the slightest rival; he is, in fact, a man who has been busy lying to himself. By his very envy and hate, he admits that he has realized his own nothingness and is terrified that the rest of the world will discover his own empty secret.

Love in the heart of man. Joy: An unappreciated possession

The circulation of pictures of dyspeptic looking saints was one of the masterstrokes of satanic propaganda. Certainly, this contributed no little to the modern notion that saints are a sour, grumpy lot. Nothing could be further from the truth. The saints are always great lovers; and love floods our hearts with the sunshine of joy, particularly when that love is for a divine friend. Look at it objectively for a moment. This unselfish love has identified our will with the will of our Friend; His happiness is ours -- even as it is between human friends. From the first moment of this divine friendship, our Friend is always and intimately with us: as Lord and Creator to His creatures as the object of our knowledge and love, and by that extremely intimate presence by grace, which enables us to live his very life. Then there is that triumphant joy in our Friends possession of the great good we wish Him, though He does not so much possess it, as He is it. Nothing can threaten His happiness; nothing can dim the joy of our friendship.

This is the pervading influence behind all Christian life: where there is charity, there is joy. In addition, where there is joy, life can be lived intensely, merrily whether the instruments of its living be scrubbing brushes, palaces, failures or triumphs. Charity, you will remember, is the common heritage of every Christian in the state of grace, of everyone who is a friend of God. It is not only the saints who live merrily, but the humblest of men with the least degree of charity. We do not wait for the joy of this divine friendship to hit us with the same unmistakable emphasis as an attack of cramps; nor must that joy be put off until we have reached the heights of sanctity. It is not a matter of feeling, nor is it a matter of mystic heights; our joy is really full with the gift of divine grace.

If we put our minds to it, we can be gloomy even though we are in the state of grace. After all, a man might starve to death because he forgot the ten-dollar bill he put in his watch-pocket months ago; we can frown on the world and ourselves, if we forget the joy that is ours. We can, if we like, allow the joy of charity to be overshadowed by disgust, sorrow at our spiritual negligence, or the misfortunes that enter our life. Nevertheless, if we do, if we forget our joy or allow it to be overshadowed, we are cheating ourselves; the joy is within us if we care to make the most of it. If we insist upon remaining unconscious of the goodness of God within us, of course we deprive ourselves of the radical joy that gives all Christian life its flavor. Consciousness is the minimum requirement for the enjoyment of any good; we can play dead if we like, but then we must not complain that we cannot enjoy the lilies heaped about the coffin.

The sorrow of charity

This does not mean that Christian life has the utterly carefree hilarity of an American Legion convention. This joy is deep bubbling up through every strata of life, but still it leaves room enough on the surface of life for a tart layer of sorrow. We can, for example, have real sorrow for the sins of others, or indeed for anything which works against the presence of God in ourselves or in others. Herein is found one side of the zeal and compassion of the saints for sinners; the other side being the realization of the tremendous boon the sinner deprives himself of by his sin. We can have deep sorrow for our own past sins, but chiefly as they represent a hindrance to our union with God here and now. We can be decidedly sorry at having taken the wrong train, catching pneumonia or scratching the fender of our new car. Now, none of these things should ever plug up the wellsprings of joy that are in the depths of our souls.

This joy, coming from the bottom of our hearts, is full and deep; but in this life, it can always be fuller, for we can always come closer to God. In heaven, that joy is so full that, rather than being enclosed in our hearts, it wraps us about as a bright garment. It is odd that in spite of this solid truth, we have so seldom pictured God as infinitely joyous; that we should even have taken seriously the Puritan's gloomy, grumbling tyrant. The heavenly fountains of joy overflow our being, for they are commensurate to the infinite goodness of God, only God can drain the deep, cool cup of joy.

The world has always laughed indulgently at lovers' quarrels, realizing that the fuel of their fire is usually trifles that will soon burn themselves out. Nevertheless, unfortunately, such quarrels are not always patched up; it is not always necessary to plant a bomb in order to break up a home. A snore is only a trifling thing, but to the victim of insomnia the rhythmic ebb and flow of conjugal snores may completely drown love. In fact, we could make this more general and say that, frequently, human love is broken up precisely because of trifles. When that love concentrates on irritations, defect, sorrow in the life of love, then love is not only cheating itself of the joy that belongs to it, it is preparing the way for the destruction of that love.

The same is true of divine Friendship. When we concentrate on the sorrows, misery and misfortunes of life, we are doing much more than cheating ourselves of love's joy; we are preparing for a flight from that divine friendship, for a horror of divine things, for the time when the flesh shall completely prevail over the spirit. Then in place of friendship's eager joy and its rush to the loved one, there will come that sorrowful boredom and irritation that prepare the way for hate.

Enemies of joy: Spiritual sloth

The human heart simply must have joy. If the joy is not forthcoming from our divine friendship, we shall cast about for companionship that is more agreeable and that means in a realm other than that of the spirit. Our unconsciousness of the good that is ours in this divine friendship practically assures us of a decreasing knowledge of the divine good. The overshadowing of this joy of divine friendship then begins to make possible a positive contempt for the goods of God by a concentration on the evils that affect us. More briefly, we are learning more and more about the attractions of the flesh, and less and less about the joys of the spirit.

The condition towards which we are thus drifting is called spiritual sloth. This capital sin of sloth is not mere laziness. It is not the irritation felt at getting up for Mass on a bitterly cold morning; it is not the reluctance to fasting in Lent, or the embarrassment involved in confessing our sins; nor yet is it the vague sigh that heaves its way to the surface at the mention of the general difficulties of Christian life. It is much more fundamental than that.

It might be called a kind of bored tediousness, a torpor of the mind that moves us to neglect the things of the spirit and to wallow in the warm ooze of the flesh. St. Thomas described it as, "*a sorrow which weighs down the spirit of a man, impeding him from operation.*" It is a strange, perverted sorrow, dank with evil, for it finds the very goodness of God a sorrowful, evil thing and it holds man back from the one thing important in his life -- that action which will lead him to life's goal. Even when this sloth is occasioned by a real evil, a sorrow springing from one's own sin but going to the exaggerated lengths of paralyzing a man, its effects are just as disastrous as the sorrow and tediousness in the face of divine good.

In itself, sloth may be either venial or mortal, according to the degree of distaste within us for spiritual goods. However, in its possibilities it is utterly tragic. It is a capital sin, with the capital sins usual family of unlovely daughters. Sloth is at the same time an escape and a pursuit, an escape from God and a pursuit of the world. On the side of its flight from God, Thomas lists its daughters as, "*desperation, pusillanimity, a stupor of the mind in the face of the precepts of God, and, finally, an indignation against and a detestation of spiritual things*". This last is easily recognized as a gesture of face-saving closely akin to a tramp's attitude towards work. On the side of sloth's pursuit of sensual pleasures, St. Thomas, under the general title of, "a wandering mind", groups such daughters of sloth as importunity of mind -- the faculty of thinking of the wrong thing at any time --, curiosity, verbosity, a restlessness of body indicative of the restlessness of mind, and finally instability. The insight of a saint recognized feverish restlessness as a symptom of laziness.

In other words, we are not seeing spiritual laziness at all if we see it in terms of a rheumatic old negro letting the southern sun seep slowly into his bones. It is an escape, a desperate, panicky flight. There is in it the senseless taste of a man flying from what he knows cannot be escaped; and, at the same time, the weakling's attempt to drown his fright in gulps of sensual pleasure. In a word, sloth is the abandonment of the joy of God for the joy of the world.

Envy: Foundations of envy

There is another capital sin opposed to the joy of charity, namely, envy; and this too drives a man in panic to the embrace of unworthy goods. It too is a flight from sorrow, a perverted sorrow that has for its object, not the good of God, but the good of neighbor. The sorrow we may feel on learning that an enemy has been made chief of police, at our lack of virtue, or at the good fortune of an unworthy man all have some basis in reason. Envy is none of these, for it is totally unreasonable. It is the vice of the man who is broken hearted because some one exceeds him in good; this neighbor's excellence strikes his soul with the shattering force of a deep personal injury.

Roll call of the envious

It is difficult to face envy honestly, for it is the sin of the defeated. It enters intimately into the mock horror at the doings of the "youth of our time", the hard luck story and the whinings of those who are never promoted because some one has a "grudge" against them. In other words, it is a sin common among the old, the plodders and the unfortunate; among those, that is, who have been conquered by age, misfortune or lack of talent. Successful rivalry emphasizes their defeat, renews its bitterness; and they are unforgiving. Petty-minded men are easily envious, for to them all things look big; no matter what excellence a neighbor may have, in the eyes of the petty, he surpasses them by tremendous lengths. The ambitious, athirst for honor, look on the excellence of another as a direct attack on the praise they could normally expect; they too are easily envious.

An interesting angle of this sin of envy, of interest especially in view of the modern discussions of democracy, is given in Thomas' laconic statement: "No one but a fool is envious of someone or something that surpasses him infinitely." Only those just above us, within reach of our clawing hands, excite our envy. In a social organization, then, which puts all men on the same level, there must inevitably be rich material for envy; on the other hand, this gives a psychological explanation of the stability -- desirable or otherwise -- of civilizations, which definitely excluded ambition from the greater part of society.

The unlovely daughters of envy are among the most thoroughly despised sins that gnaw at the foundations of human life. They work up to the crescendo of evil, which is the destruction of the mansion of a man's life: from the sly start of a furtive whisper, through detraction, then to joy in the misfortune of another and sorrow at his good fortune, and finally to the climax of evil which is hate.

The envious man finds life intolerable. We were not made to live with sorrow; and envy is sorrow. We were made to live with joy. Christ accurately stated the whole purpose of His life when He said that He had come, "that our joy might be filled." His directions for fulfilling that joy, even though they insisted on the carrying of a cross, involved no contradiction; men and women are constantly discovering, as He meant them to, that under the cross there is some little taste of the beatific joy that was deep beneath Calvary's sufferings. The combination of the divine and human filled the world with paradoxes; Our Lord seemed to prefer to emphasize, rather than explain them. Being puzzled, men might seek to discover their meaning by living them. Christ, seeing the bewilderment in the Apostles, must have had something of the same divine playfulness in His eyes when he sent them into a hostile Roman world, all the odds against them, with the parting words: "*My peace I give you.*"

Peace: The peace of Christ and of the world

Certainly, the peace Christ gave the Apostles was not the peace sought by a weakling, a peace at any price. With this peace went persecution, mockery and ultimately death. These men were not to be coddled by a surface peace, as they were not to be sustained by a surface joy. In no sense did this peace make pacificists of them; they knew well there were many things worth the price of a fight, even of a fight to the death. Now, no fight could destroy the peace that had been given them. The peace of Christ is as deep as the soul of a man. On that point alone, it is startlingly different from the peace of the world, for only God can reach into the soul of a man and bury peace there so deeply that it will be inviolable to any other force but the will of man himself.

Peace and action

The life of a man who is peaceful with the peace of Christ, does not present the appearance of a stagnant pond's slimy calm; it is much more apt to be a riotous, storm-tossed ocean, with calm, inscrutable depths. By the very nature of peace, such a life will be intensely active; for peace means the completely unified effort of appetites towards a common goal. It is energy streamlined to the utmost. From it follows peace, or rather concord, with other men and with God, again by a union of appetites towards the common end of all. We love our neighbors, not as rivals, but as we love ourselves; and we love both ourselves and neighbors because of God. We do not resent the attempt of other men to reach the same divine end; it can be shared without loss to ourselves. Yet, we do hurl all the crushing power of unified effort against those who would hinder either our neighbors or ourselves from obtaining that goal. This very opposition is directed, not against our enemies, but against their hatred for themselves.

In other words, Christ furnished us with the one solid bond of union in giving us charity; His peace follows upon the identification of a man with his neighbors and with his God. The world has no such basis for peace. Its offer must always be a surface thing; it can only encourage a man to snatch at things and to try, desperately, to protect what other men most surely will attempt to take from him. To put it quite baldly: the peace of the world is really a peace that amounts to oblivion; it consists in attempting to forget what we do not have, and to be satisfied with that which can never satisfy the human heart.

Perhaps a moron enjoys having his teeth knocked out; but surely, it is not a pleasure to which one can become addicted. Yet Chesterton once wrote of the Irish that, "all their wars are merry"; and the name "*fighting Irish*" is never used as a term of abuse. These things may be taken literally in the sense that there is something to fight for; something that is so well worth while that it can be fought for merrily, with a keen realization that nothing that may be lost in the fight can be compared with the thing that might be gained. Still, undoubtedly the person whose mouth waters over the prospect of a fight, just for the sake of the fight, is mentally deficient. In fact, no one loves a fight for its own sake. Even the bully is fighting for peace. For the purpose of every battle is to obtain something that, at the moment, is lacking, something that is considered necessary for the satisfaction of appetite, for perfection. The victim of an inferiority complex lording it over his fellows, the naturally quarrelsome man, the nation with a chip on its shoulder, are all confessing their own deficiencies. By the very fact of the quarrel, they admit a serious defect, that something is yet necessary for their full well-being.

The common goal of men

On the contrary, the man of peace, far from being a frightened weakling, is a possessor of perfection. He has what he needs for his happiness; he is at peace because nothing, no one, can take that happiness from him. It is in this full sense of the word that Christ is the King of Peace. Additionally, this was no less true of Christ nailed to a cross, than it was true of Him in the sanctuary of Nazareth. It is true of his followers whether they stand before applauding crowds and grateful kings or whether they stand alone in an arena. They are possessed of the peace of Christ, a peace that will reach its full perfection, its full activity, its widest scope only when they are with Christ in heaven.

The man whom Christ has taught that love is giving, not getting; who has identified his will with the will of His friend, has deep joy, deep peace. He is one with God and one with men.

Mercy. The nature of mercy

The smile he gives the world is not the ghastly, soulless facial gesture of an indifferent stranger, signaling the mere absence of hostility. It is easy for him to rejoice with men; it is easy for him to be at peace with men; it is easy for him to suffer with men and, if possible, to do something about their suffering. For he is one with men. The efficacy of this union is nowhere more clearly than in the virtue of mercy. It is only by seeing the misfortune of another as somehow our own, that we can be compassionate, can be driven to do something about this misfortune. In other words, for mercy as for charity, there must be some common ground upon which our neighbors and we meet.

Roll call of the merciful

A brother can, without difficulty, be compassionate to a sister; they are one in blood. An American in China finds it easy to have mercy on the misfortune of a fellow American. The old and the wise find mercy easy, for these misfortunes, either have already come upon them or, in their wisdom; they see how quickly the same misfortune might visit them. The weak and the sick normally are quickly sympathetic because of their fellowship of misery. The same truth stands out more clearly when viewed from a negative point of view. The choleric, quarrelsome man is readily merciless. So, too, are those who are sure of their immunity from misfortune: those sure of power, of health, of happiness, the very proud. Indeed, even the man who is sure nothing worse can happen to him and the man stripped of all love are quite apt to be contemptuous of the misery of others. For all these people think only of themselves, breaking off the bond that would unite them to other men.

God is merciful to us, not because He is a fellow compatriot, a blood relative, nor because He trembles at the threat of similar evils, but because He is our friend. In strict truth, our evils, our misfortunes are God's; we are one with Him, not by a physical bond, but by the bond of love.

The excellence of mercy

Mercy is an immediate effect of charity. Now, it must not be understood to flow from charity in the same way as joy and peace. These are acts; mercy is a virtue in its own right. It has its own work to get done; and that work is the moderation of the passion of mercy according to the rule of reason. Understanding this well, we have no difficulty in distinguishing mercy from sentimentality. It is possible to be angry at a judge because the murderer he has condemned has such gentle eyes. Our sympathy for the "poor, misunderstood boy" who has turned a machine-gun on the police may fill our eyes with tears. Nevertheless, not all this is the work of the virtue of mercy. Mercy, in this sense of passion, can be found in cats; as a virtue, mercy must proceed along rational lines to the goal of reason.

We might expect mercy to wear a doleful face because it is based on our ability to suffer with another. Actually, it is a joyous, satisfying virtue. Even its counterfeits are likeable things. The criminal who murders people at night and operates soup kitchens for the poor during the day, is actually enjoying the role of daytime dispenser of mercy. He is, in a sense, playing god. For it is only insofar as we are superior to others that we can be of help to them, supplying for their defects. Mercy is a God-like virtue; indeed, it is a virtue proper to God, one of the chief means of manifesting the divine omnipotence. However, in men, much as they may like to play the part of omnipotence, mercy is not the greatest of virtues; after all, men are not God.

A man does not reach his perfection in supplying the needs of others, but in subjecting himself to God. Only the Being Who has no superior manifests His perfection by supplying the needs of others. Yet among the moral virtues dealing with neighbor, mercy holds top rank, precisely because its act is the act of a superior. Justice must stand at attention when mercy passes by; after all, justice only gives another what is his due. Fortitude and temperance are orderlies of mercy; their work is to control a man's own passions, not to supply for the defects of others. It is true that God will have mercy and not sacrifice; but not in the sense that sacrifice is unnecessary, nor because God and men must take second place to mercy. Now, rather in the sense that after justice has been satisfied, then mercy puts forth its superior, God-like act. In itself, mercy is not at all the greatest of the moral virtues.

When St. Gregory said, "love is not idle", he was saying that a peaceful home life cannot but make itself felt in the community, that a full heart cannot but overflow into the lives and hearts of others. Consequently, when the love of divine friendship fills a man's heart, he cannot sit basking in the sun of his own satisfaction, his hands idle, his mind wandering aimlessly up and down the formal garden of his own delights. If he does, then he is enthralled not by love, but by hypocrisy. This thing is not filling his heart; it is emptying it.

Stingy selfishness is an admission of an empty heart. Beneficence, generous love, is a statement of a heart full to overflowing. It was divine genius that so planned the lives of men as to make of human life a wharf humming with the activity of constant imports and exports; a noisy exchange which all men must frequent. There is no man, however great, who is not in some way inferior to other men; and there is no man so lowly that he cannot help another, and so be superior to another. The spiritual isolationist makes a tragic mistake. For God has drawn us close to all other men by making us dependent on all others; i.e., by making us, in some sense, inferior to every other man and, at the same time, making us superior, in some sense, to every other man.

Love in the world: mercy at work

Understand, the beauty of this truth is not the theoretical beauty of an impractical plan seen in the engineer's office. If we step out of the office into the confusing roar of the construction job where men are building their lives, we see mercy at work -- the divine plan being slowly transformed into the tangible, enduring beauty of heavenly mansions. If we take the "works of mercy" of our catechism days as denoting whole classes of acts, rather than particular deeds, we are given a sharp, quick insight into the deficiencies every man may suffer.

Among the needy -- alms-giving

On the physical side, there are, for example, such things as deficiencies in food, drink, clothing, housing; there will be more particular difficulties, of course, such as come from an intrinsic cause like sickness, or an extrinsic cause like captivity. Even after the living of life is over and done with, there is the neglect and dishonor of an unburied corpse. On the spiritual side, a man may be a spiritual beggar, desperately in need of the divine help we can get for him through prayer. He may be a spiritual infant whose defects of intellect we can supply by doctrine or counsel. He may be suffering from spiritual malnutrition with defects of appetite we can readily supply: such, for example, as sorrow awaiting our consolation. Perhaps he has lost his direction by sin and we can give him correction, or pardon when the sin was against us, or even toleration and patience. No man escapes all these defects; no man is incapable of supplying even one of these defects in his neighbor.

The works of mercy

Objectively and absolutely speaking, a spiritual work of mercy is far superior to a corporal one. Nevertheless, to a wretch shivering in Chicago's merciless winter wind, a treatise on the Trinity is a much lesser gift than the price of a drink, let us suppose, of coffee. Whatever the drink we supply, it will be a decidedly material thing; yet because it springs from charity, it has spiritual effects that wear well through all eternity -- grace, glory, perhaps even the prayer of the needy one for his benefactor.

The effects of alms giving

It is true, of course, that alms giving -- spiritual or corporal -- can proceed from the virtue of penance, or merely from a deep, human fellowship with the unfortunate. Yet, it is equally true that charity cannot exist without alms giving. At least there are times when these works of mercy are solemn precepts, when to ignore them would be to lose charity by violating the commands of God. Surely when we have more than enough for our state of life we cannot be satisfied with talking about love of neighbor while a man in desperate straits starves to death.

Its circumstances

Beyond such a situation, the giving of alms is a matter of counsel: something praiseworthy, pertaining to the perfection of charity. Obviously, a man with just enough food to keep him from starvation is not obliged to give that food to another, even though the two are running a close race to starvation. Nor, normally speaking, are we to be surprised that a millionaire owns two suits of clothes. A man is not obliged to sacrifice what is necessary for his state in life to supply the ordinary needs of others. A case of extreme necessity is of course different; the sanctity of private property does not include the starvation of men nor the wreck of a commonwealth.

As a matter of fact, some states in life forbid alms giving. We are unreasonable if we demand alms giving from a thief; his obligation is not one of generosity but of restitution. A servant may be smilingly open-handed with the goods of his master in the name of mercy: but not with any justification. Our alms giving must proceed from our own abundance, not from the abundance of others. It is well to remember that in our generous sharing of that abundance, the abundance is to be reckoned from our side; in other words, the purpose of alms giving is not to establish a beggar in luxury, but to sustain the life or supply the needs of another. It is much better to give our alms to many poor than to establish one poor man in luxury: indeed, rather than doing him a favor, we may be corrupting our neighbor by the very luxury we so suddenly bestow on him.

Among the erring -- fraternal correction

An equally obvious gesture of a full heart is the correction of those who are making mistakes, though its distastefulness to our twentieth century palates makes its welcome into our own diet dubious and reluctant. In our materialistic reversal of the scale of values, we are profoundly impressed by physical misery, eager to help; but spiritual necessity leaves us cold. Of course, we have excuses. We explain, what hardly needs explanation, that we are not saints; we have troubles enough with our own soul; moreover, the personal life of another is none of our business. Behind all this, too, there is a healthy contempt for the busybody who is forever reforming others.

Now, the life of another is very much our business. By charity all men are one with us; their misfortunes are ours, their mistakes our own. Sanctity is not a prerequisite for correction of others; all that is necessary is sane judgment, for sin is, after all, a mistake in judgment. Indeed, of all the people in the world who lack charity few have a clearer title to that defect than the busybody. The whole purpose of fraternal correction is not to aggravate, humiliate or impress a neighbor, but to help him. If what we have to say will not be helpful, then we cannot excuse our words on the grounds of fraternal correction. A superior, by reason of his office, may be obliged to make a correction and insist on it even when it represents real difficulties for the one corrected; but that is not true of those who have no such office.

The extent of our rationalization in this matter becomes apparent if we probe a little into the reasons for our hesitation. Is it love of this neighbor that pulls the reins so sharply on our galloping tongue? Is it because we know our words will do no good, will perhaps do damage, while kindly tolerance will be more effective than actual correction? Or are we holding back from fear: fear of the reception that will be given our correction, fear of what people will think, fear of appearing holier than another? If fear dictates our silence, we have only the slim comfort of the coward to support us in our silence. It is true that a bank robber is not in an ideal position to chide a pickpocket on his evil ways; but even here, it may happen that the correction offered by a sinner will carry greater weight. He speaks from the experience of misery brought into his life by that particular sin.

Conclusion: Divine wisdom and Nazareth:

While God is, the home endures;
While home endures, God cannot be forgotten
With God and the home, the world of strangers is
secure

It was a stroke of divine wisdom that established that family circle at Nazareth, with Himself as the center, and insisted on the long quiet life of the Son of God in the midst of that family circle. That one picture of Nazareth brought sharply to men's eyes the promise that as long as God is, as long as the inner life of divinity continues, men will not be deprived of that image of eternal divine life, which is the home of man. For God will see to it that men's hearts are filled with the only thing that can fill them -- unselfish love. On the other hand, that act of divine wisdom is a promise that as long as the home life of men endures, as long as men are given some taste of love, peace, joy, mercy and generous beneficence, they will continue to thirst for that which awaits them at the end of life; that as long as men have some taste of that joy which God has prepared for them, God Himself cannot be forgotten. It is a guarantee that with God and the home thoroughly established in the lives of men, the world of strangers is secure. For love is not idle, love cannot stay at home; the full heart of man cannot contain itself, but must overflow into the lives of others.

The modern crisis: Shall the heart of man be full or
empty: love or hate?
Centers of modern attack: God and the home

That one act of divine wisdom in Bethlehem, with its sequel in Nazareth, brings us to the core of modern difficulties. The question before men today is really: will the heart of man be full or empty? Will it harbor love or hate? It is not surprising that modern heresies attack God and the homes of men; these are the guarantees of the fullness of man's heart. Even where God is apparently left intact, the home is the object of serious, bitter and often subtle attack. Still, if love, joy, peace, mercy, and beneficence are not to be found within the home life of man, if there is not to be about his home something of the permanency of heaven, then we can expect the hearts of men to be empty.

Some results of modern doctrines

In the concrete, this means that instead of expanding, overflowing hearts, we shall have shriveled hearts, hearts engaged only on the dreary errands of selfishness and hate. Instead of the rich joy of life, we shall have the sorrow of envy and sloth. In place of the open hand of beneficent love, there will be the closed fist of selfishness, instead of love's eager mercy, the crushing hammer of cruelty. For spiritual correction of others will be substituted their spiritual seduction for selfish ends. Perhaps we could put all this in just one sentence by saying: instead of union, we shall have division, separation; instead of men being at one with one another and with God, each man will be for himself. Unfortunately, no man is sufficient for himself; and he who thinks he is, has no one helping him, not even himself.

The paradox of the human heart

These are not theoretical conclusions, nor are they prophecies. Rather they are the facts of today, facts that are inevitable consequences of a doctrine of hate supplanting a doctrine of love. Our world should have known better than to adopt this doctrine of hate. Centuries of experience should have taught us that the human heart cannot be filled by grabbing at particular things and stuffing them into that heart. Rather experience should have taught us that the only way a human heart can possibly be filled is by emptying itself. Sacrifice is the only language love can speak, and love is the only means of filling the human heart.

It is all of a pattern, that the God Who came to bring us the fullest joy should have died on a cross and warned us to follow in His footsteps; that the God Who came to bring us peace -- Who was Himself the Prince of Peace -- should put us into a world of constant warfare; that the God Who has come to fill the human heart should demand, as the first condition of that fullness, that the human heart be constantly emptying itself.

CHAPTER VII

THE EMPTINESS OF STRIFE
(Q. 37-46)

1. Desolation to the human heart:
   (a) Not mere emptiness.
   (b) But an invasion of reason's domain.

2. Disorder and desolation:
   (a) God and His image: champions of order.
   (b) Disorder a characteristic of hell.
   (c) Disorder and peace.

3. Emptiness of heart and its origin.

4. Desolation by words.

5. Temporal desolation by works:
   (a) Against the universal Church -- schism.
   (b) Against nations -- war:
      (1) Just and unjust wars.
      (2) Clerics and war.
      (3) Moral limits of intelligence corps.
   (c) Against the commonwealth -- sedition:
      (1) Defense of the common good.
      (2) Justified rebellion.
   (d) Against the individual:
      (1) Duels.
      (2) Quarrels.

6. Eternal desolation -- scandal:
   (a) Its varieties.
   (b) Its malice.
   (c) The just man and scandal.

7. First principles of order:
   (a) The double commandment of Christ:
       (1) The end of all other commands.
       (2) The words of the commandment.
   (b) Wisdom:
       (1) Its nature and extent.
       (2) Its beatitude -- "Blessed are the
peacemakers."
       (3) The enemy of wisdom.

Conclusion:

1. Order and the modern world:
   (a) An ordered emptiness.
   (b) An idealization of emptiness.

2. A desolate world:
   (a) Desolate hearts.
   (b) Temporal desolation.
   (c) Eternal desolation.

3. Wisdom of the Word.

▣CHAPTER V▣
THE EMPTINESS OF STRIFE
(Q 37~46)

Desolation to the human heart

A SPRING sky, empty of every cloud, can be a joyful sight. A city street late at night, undisturbed by the click of a single heel, can be as peaceful as a lullaby; yet the same street, totally empty at noontime, speaks sinister threats of war or pestilence. There is a vast difference between mere emptiness and desolation, a difference that we sense immediately when we remember that there are some things that cannot be empty without being desolate. A village, for example, or a human heart, is never empty, though it may be deserted.

Not mere emptiness; but an invasion of reason's domain

In desolation, something is missing; there is more than negation, there is privation. Kilmer's "House with nobody in it" has the sharp, pinched misery of desolation about it; the dilapidated shacks of miners in a mountain country are another tabloid definition of desolation. A house was not built to have nobody in it; nor is the house of the barely existing miner the sort of place a man inhabits if he has any choice in the matter. What is missing, in all these pictures of desolation, is *order*. In them, something of reason has been destroyed; and with its destruction, something in man has been destroyed, for order is the fruit of his reason.

He has stamped his personality on the outer world by his imposition of order upon it; when that order has been destroyed, something of humanity is taken out of the world. Yet desolation is never wholly outside a man; it is also within him. Therefore, the human heart, made to contain so many things, cannot be empty without having something missing that should be there. It cannot be empty without being desolate, because it was not made to be empty.

Disorder and desolation: God and His image: champions of order

That single human fact, so easily verified by looking into ourselves or about ourselves, is a microscope focused on a tremendous truth. Man has been designed after an infinite model. In the infinitely full life of God, there is no room for desolation; and that means there is no room for disorder. By His very nature, all the acts of God will have a perfection of order about them; indeed, such a perfection of order that it is often too great, too far-reaching for our comprehension. To question that order is to question the very nature of God. Man, the image of God will be a champion of order in his own imperfect way. A tornado, a hurtling automobile, a relentless enemy, or the upheaval of sin will all make a wreckage of his life because they desolate that order that is so much a part of him. This is so true that it seems obvious to us that order should be the first law of the eternal home to which we are going. In addition, it seems just as obvious that chaotic disorder should be one of the most horrible things in hell.

Disorder a characteristic of hell

This does not mean that a badly cluttered desk, or a pile of unwashed dishes in the sink, is evidence of a satanic visitation. A sepulchral office, with every document neatly entombed in some drawer, might well seem a fitting likeness of hell to many a man. God can look after the towering essentials and at the same time see to the infinitesimal dust of the non-essentials; but man often has his hands full keeping the essentials straight. It is pleasant, of course, to have a secretary who knows essentials from details, and keeps a measure of order even in the details. Now, it is in an essential order and disorder that a man finds the difference between the chaos of madness and the happiness of sanity; there too will we find the difference between heaven and hell.

Disorder and peace

St. Augustine said all this when he defined peace as "the tranquility of order." You will remember, from the last chapter, that peace is a kind of streamlined activity effected by complete order in the motive powers of a man. By this means might we see that man is neither at war with his fellow men nor with himself; that he is not trying to run in two directions at the same time. In the natural order, the disturbance of peace is visible in war, split personalities, nervous breakdowns, and in the divided heart that keeps the sinner always in misery yet never quite turning to God. In the supernatural order, the remorse from the horror of sin is a testimony of the human heart's yearning for God and, at the same time, of its devastating appetite for the opposite of God as embodied in mortal sin. This is the radical explanation of why a man must either attempt to forget heaven or fight valiantly against sin.

Emptiness of heart and its origin

Just as fullness of heart comes about through the union of wills by the friendship of charity, so emptiness of heart is the result of division, of the crashing hostility of appetites. As by charity, we are one with God and men, by discord we are cut off from the divine will and from the wills of other men. It is a process of isolation. By discord, we bar the entrance to our soul; those bars not only prohibit God and men from entering our soul, they prevent all exits from that soul. They imprison us within ourselves; and the human heart was not made for solitary confinement. In such a cell, the human heart is desolate.

It is conceivable that bitter political enemies may be fundamentally at peace; it is even possible that opposing generals in a war have this fundamental concord one with another. In fact, men can disagree on all but the essentials of human life and still be one with God and with other men. The possessors of peace do not form an association of "*yes men*," never disagreeing with one another. Peace is much more a matter of union of wills than of harmony of opinion. Of course, if the difference of opinion has its roots in an error for which we are at fault, or in our stubbornness, then there is real discord present; because of envy, or because of our rapt admiration for our own excellence, we are giving way to that same desire to cut ourselves off from others, from God and men.

To be at peace with some men and at war with God is no virtue. It is something like forming a union for murderers. There is no absolutely universal bond cementing men together except that of charity. On the contrary, to be at war with men and at peace with God may, quite possibly, be virtuous; it means that we are not so much acting against others, as attacking their hatred for themselves. It is evident then, that if peace at any price means coming to terms with sin, it is utterly vicious.

Desolation by words

It is rare that man is content to keep his emptiness of heart a secret. When that inner discord breaks forth in words, we have the sin of contention. Obviously, this does not constitute a prohibition law against discussion. Not every dispute is a sin, even though someone must be at least partly wrong, even though some disputes are never settled. A very great many arguments are positively virtuous, such, for example, as those against attacks on God or men. The difference between contention and defense of the truth is the difference between a man who will not lose an argument because his envy or pride cannot admit defeat, and the man who cannot lose an argument because he has hold of truth.

Still, even in perfectly legitimate disputes, there are limits. Somehow, we do not expect a nun to descend to altercation over a taxi-fare, though we would not be so much surprised if an excited cab driver expressed himself forcibly. We are quite right, for discussion should be suited not only to the subject matter, but also to the person engaged in the discussion. A bishop, for example, has not the same possibilities in rough and tumble argument as has, say, a top sergeant; in fact, the bishop has no business getting into that kind of argument. In other words, this act of virtue, like any other, must be placed in fitting circumstances; the very circumstances must be in accord with reason. When discussion, however worthy its end, does not keep within fitting limits, then, as St. Paul insisted, it "not only does no good; it does serious damage to those who are listening."

Temporal desolation by works

The inner discord that isolates the heart of a man is like a disease eating its way from organ to organ, gradually disintegrating the whole body. For this discord can never stay within the heart of a man, it eats its way out, disintegrating the unity of man and attacking the institutions which bind men together. We might, quite aptly, compare a discordant will to an engine on an airplane as it breaks loose and smashes back into the cabin. Before, when it was one with the rest of the plane, it served the mighty purpose of rushing the plane and its passengers to their destination with swift, easy movement, now that it has broken loose from the unity of that plane, it becomes an instrument of destruction. Therefore, the will of man, broken loose from the order of God, becomes a smashing destroyer of the unity of men. It stops at nothing; nothing is too great, nothing too sacred for its devastating attack.

Against the universal Church ·· schism

When this attack centers on the unity of the Church, schism is born into the world. Schism is a quarrelsome sin; its enemy, then, is peace. It does not attack the faith, as does heresy and infidelity; rather it concentrates on the unity achieved by charity; it cuts its victims off from the members of the Church and from the head of the Church. It is true that it is against a changeable, temporal thing like ecclesiastical unity, rather than against the unchangeable First Truth; yet, because it reaches out to injure the spiritual good of the whole multitude of the faithful, it well merits a place near the top in the sins committed against our neighbor.

Against nations ·· war

If our modern world had to choose between war and schism, it would emphatically vote for schism as the lesser evil. Even though its object is less sweeping and the damage it does is much less serious, the sin of discord breaking out in unjust war impresses us much more vividly than the sin of schism. Spiritual damage, after all, does not splatter the street with blood. We have reason enough, God knows, for being impressed with the evils of war, but no reason at all for reversing the order of spiritual and material values.

Just and unjust wars

It must be noticed, however, that the clash of armed forces, which constitutes war, is not in itself sinful. Sin enters when the war is unjust. There are today two odd extremes of opinion. The first7 glorifies war and admits no legal limitations to military activity. The other completely condemns war, refusing to admit any justification whatsoever for armed hostilities between nations.

Actually, these conflicting opinions are twin sons of the same horrible mother; they have a common source in atheistic materialism. The fundamental principle of the glorifiers of war is: "*might is right.*" Law, then, is the dictate of the bully. This amounts to a deification of brute strength, an inculcation of the philosophy of the bully; it leaves men much worse off than the animals, for it leaves men shorn of every principle of order and condemns them to the chaos of shifting power, with its inevitable results of constant desolation. The opposite extreme opinion has about it the softness of corruption and disintegration. Behind it is the conviction that the things destroyed by war are supreme in the scale of human values: property, health, luxury, money, even life itself.

Both opinions are evil from their very root; of the two, perhaps the absolute pacifist extreme is the most destructive of things distinctively human, for normally there is apt to be a healthy reaction on the part of the recipient of a bloody nose. As a matter of fact, acts of nations are as subject to moral law as are the acts of individuals; which is to say no more than that the acts of nations are just as human as acts of individuals. They are pointed to or away from a goal that does not vary; they are, then, right or wrong, leading to the goal or away from it. The power that may allow them to escape immediate punishment cannot make good out of evil. On the other hand, there are things worth fighting for, worth the loss of all the material world can offer, worth the loss of life itself. We cannot refuse to fight under any circumstances without admitting that there is nothing worthy of the efforts of a man above what he can reach in the world, what he can touch with his hands.

These modern opinions are not glittering novelties. Man has unconditionally condemned war before. The Manicheans were sure war was always a sin; Luther was convinced that to fight against the Turks would be to resist the will of God, impeding His punishments, while Erasmus, conceding that war might have been justified in the Old Law, maintained that in the New Law of love, it certainly is not. That war, under some circumstances, is justified is not a mere philosophical opinion; a Catholic is not free to embrace or reject it. It is a solemn doctrine of the Church; in fact, time and again through the ages, the Church, through Her councils and Supreme Pontiffs, has urged men to wage war.

Perhaps we could compress the basis for a just war into one word -- defense. The just cause for war is to repulse an attempted injury or to obtain satisfaction for an injury already done. In the first case, we have what is called a defensive war; in the second case, what is called an offensive war. In both cases, we may have a just war, for in both cases action is taken in defense of rights.

Such defense is, of course, desperate, last-ditch defense. If we keep this in mind, it will be clear that no private person has a right to declare war. A private person always has a higher court of appeal; he does not have to settle the matter with his own hands, he can go to the judges of the community and demand satisfaction. However, where the rights of states have been violated, there is no higher political court of appeal; and because there is no temporal power above the state, a recourse to arms is necessary.

To put it another way, a conscientious citizen may decide to devote some of his leisure moments to helping out the state; casting about for a helpful role, he decides to hang a few public enemies on his private gibbet. As a result, there is much indignation among the public enemies. For once, they are right. A man has no vindictive power within the nation itself; it is the work of the community to punish the enemies of the community. The same is true outside the limits of the nation; the private person has no more vindictive power against external enemies than he has against criminals within the nation. He is not the one delegated to care for and act for the community; he has no authority to convoke the whole community, as would be necessary in the case of war. All this belongs to authority, to him who has charge of the community.

Nevertheless, even here, in the case of the governor of a nation declaring war, it is not a matter of any particular person taking up the sword. The sword of defense is given to the soldier by the authorities; and it is given to the authorities themselves by their very office as community guardians. In each case, the sword is not taken up; rather it is thrust upon them. Even though the cause be just, the war is rendered unjust when the competent authority declaring it vitiates its justice by such evil intentions as cupidity, cruelty and the like. Nor is this surprising with a sufficiently evil intention a man can make the love he has for his mother or the support he gives his wife a vicious thing.

The brief, classic statement on the morality of war demands three conditions for war's justification. it must be declared by competent authority, it must be for a just cause, and it must be waged for a right intention. These three must be had simultaneously. War is not just merely because competent authority declares it; it is not just merely because it has a just cause; nor is war just merely because one's intention is very pure. When these conditions are present simultaneously, war is not sinful; it is an act of virtue, a defense of the common good.

Such wars were the crusades. Such a war might have been the war waged by Spain against the Moors. Now, it is not always easy to determine the justice or injustice of a particular war, not because the principles are not clear, but because the evidence is often so difficult to get at. In this case, as in every other case of judgment of a moral act, it is essential that we have the whole story, honestly told; but to break through the protective barrier of propaganda thrown around the evidence of modern wars is almost too much even for the tank-like minds with which nature has gifted historians.

Clerics and war

In a really just war, we are faced with a paradox of an act of virtue being positively forbidden to one class of men, i.e., to clerics. It is not nearly so hard to understand the paradox as it is to understand the leaders of a nation disregarding such a prohibition. After all, these men, by their very office, stand between men and God, bringing God to men and men to God. Contemplation, praise of God and prayers for men are integral details of their work of feeding men with divine food. The government that would force these men into battle must either consider such work relatively unimportant or it must look upon the roar of guns and the desperate clash of bayonets as offering no hindrance to contemplation. In either case, one might justifiably doubt its capacity for guiding the lives of men.

The reasons against clerics' participation in war go much deeper than all this. All the clerical orders within the Church are ordered to the supreme grade of the priesthood, whose work is to offer the sacrifice of Christ on the altar. It is not fitting that such a minister should shed the blood of other men; rather he should be prepared to shed his own blood for Christ, imitating the work that he performs each morning at the altar. He is another peacemaker. His life is dedicated to the salvation of souls, not to the destruction of bodies. So supreme is his office among all the offices offered to men, that not even such a just cause as the defense of the common good justifies his casting aside of the dignity, fittingness and stability of his office of continuing the work of the Prince of Peace.

This does not mean that, at the outbreak of war, all clerics are to be put in glass cases and hidden in bombproof cellars, along with the windows of the cathedral. The purpose of this prohibition on their active participation in war is not to protect clerics from hardships, privations and dangers. By the command of Christ, these things are their normal diet. They are expected to go into the hardships, privations and dangers of war much more gaily than other men, indeed without any of the implements of self-protection that bolster the courage of their fellows. The point is, their work must not be interrupted. They are to work for the salvation of souls, not for the destruction of life, so clerics should be found wherever men are found -- in front-line trenches, in the precarious privacy of no man's land, on sinking ships, in shattered cities. For men, wherever they are, must be given the same spiritual help, the same supernatural nourishment. Clerics not only may take part in war in this fashion; they are obliged to.

Moral limits of intelligence corps

Although we have talked incessantly about war for years, there is one final point about that ghastly business which has been consistently overlooked, that is, the moral regulation of the secret service or intelligence corps. Remembering that war is a moral act, waged by a moral agent, and therefore strictly limited by the precepts of moral law, it becomes evident that an act evil in itself is never permitted in the name of war. There is no cause that can justify a morally wrong act, for an end never justifies the means. A woman prostituting herself to obtain enemy secrets or an expert propagandist concocting an enormous lie to hide the secrets of his own country have merited the bitter names given to perpetrators of the same acts for any other purpose. Not that the moral code is a naive young lady whose notion of honesty is to tell all she knows; it is quite legitimate to allow an enemy to draw wrong inferences, to refuse to tell plans for defense or offense, or any part of those plans, to tell as much as we want to be known. Now, sin, be it very small or very big, remains what it is -- an ugly, inhuman blot -- whatever the purpose for which it is committed.

Behind the deceit and corruption that have so often, marked modern diplomacy lies the foul political philosophy of Machiavelli, with its implication of the absolute supremacy of the state. Today that supremacy is no longer merely implied. The good of the state, as the first and only unchangeable moral principle, has been flatly stated. It has been officially declared, for instance, by the Soviet Party, that the ethical code is entirely subordinated to the service of the proletariat and its class war. In simpler language, in the service of the state or the party, anything goes.

Sane men must recoil in horror from such a conception of the state because it means that the state has taken the place of God. Men who are not particularly interested in God may stupidly think they could put up with such a substitution; but a moment's thought shows the implications for humanity itself. This state supremacy means that human life is stripped of all hope, man is chained down in despair; he is made a puppet of a state, without personal rights or personal goals, with nothing but impersonal service to support him in this life and oblivion promised as the reward of his labors.

Against the commonwealth -- sedition: defense of the common good

Not that full place must be denied to the rights of the state. Those rights are objective and must be respected. Rebels against a just government are criminals, guilty of mortal sin -- a sin directly against the common good of the community, committed from the very beginnings of their preparation for rebellion. This sin of sedition is not an aristocratic sin, which demands capacities for leadership in its victim; it is a common thing, shared alike by ringleaders and camp followers of rebellion. However vigorously they may protest their love of men, actually they rob men of a chance to make a success of human living.

Justified rebellion

There is no stauncher defender of the authority of the state than the Church. Even so, the Church does not mistake the members of a Cabinet for the Seraphim who stand before the face of God. A government can be wrong; it can be tyrannous; it can be greedy and inimical to the common good. When it has become so corrupt, the men who rise up against it are not rebels; they are heroic defenders of the common good. These men are not waging war on authority; the betrayal of their office by those in authority has already stripped them of whatever claim they had to rule others. Unless a rebellion would do more harm to the common good than this present tyranny, it is not only justified, it may even be obligatory.

For now, the state is leaderless except for those whom nature, education and responsibility have equipped to take the place of the traitors to the common good. Nature does not so much take the crown from the former heads of the state, rather she snatches these heads from under their crown; nor does she leave the crown of authority suspended in mid-air. Those equipped by nature cease to be private persons; they are pushed forward by the solemn responsibility incurred by nature itself, to fill the gap created by men who, contrary to their office, preferred their own good to the good of the community.

Against the individual

Even in this case, it is still true that private persons cannot wage war. That principle is universal. Indeed, a private person cannot even wage a little personal war such as is involved in a quarrel or a duel.

Duels

A duel is really an elaborately planned murder. It is an attempt to give dignity and order to an act that is essentially chaotic. There is a solemn, "gentlemanly" agreement as to time, place, weapons; when always, the affair is haunted by the shadow of murder, the persistent danger of death to one or to both parties. It is not surprising that the condemnations of the Council of Trent against dueling are as bitter as deep-seated disgust can make them. Under these condemnations are included, not only the participants, but those who allow it to take place within their territory, the seconds, the spectators, indeed, anyone who has anything to do with the official murder. Rulers who allow the duel are stripped of their jurisdiction, as well as excommunicated, all their goods proscribed; they incur perpetual infamy and are to be treated as murderers. The participant who dies as a result of the duel is forever deprived or ecclesiastical burial. Counselors, advisers, spectators are excommunicated and are under perpetual infamy, and this notwithstanding any privilege or custom, even immemorial custom, to the contrary.

The Council has made it fairly clear that it considers the life of a man sacred. The transformation of a sow's ear into a silk purse is child's play compared to the task of pinching murder's ugly, deformed hulk into the delicate finery of dignity, honor, virtue. There are no grounds to justify the murder of a man.

Quarrels

Dueling and quarreling, for all their show of fire and flashing eyes, plod through the life of a man with all the dull stupidity of Markham's debased "Man With a Hoe." Both are products of anger; and there is no passion that more completely robs a man of his reason. The quarrelsome man may have some little excuse, on the grounds of passion, for his desire to hurt another and have him know he is hurt; yet the act is an unjust invasion of the rights of another; it is contrary to all reason, a stupid thing.

A duel proceeds from a much colder, more deliberate anger; so rarely is there any excuse about it at all. When we go a step further, to calm, deliberate, unjust injury of another, we have come to a savage thing, a product of hate. Its purpose is not so much to obtain satisfaction, as to inflict injury. A knife in the back or a burst of machine-gun fire from a dark alley is not so much the blind, smashing animality of anger, as the cold, diabolical finality of hate. The proverb that it takes two to make a quarrel can hardly be classified as profound; a man must be desperately lonely to quarrel with himself. Still, the implication that both parties to a quarrel are necessarily wrong is quite false. Certainly to defend oneself against unjust attack, such as is involved in quarreling, does not involve moral wrong; indeed, such defense may be positively obligatory in some cases.

This dreadful desolation we have been describing is easily appreciated. We know something of the loneliness of a Catholic heart, which has wandered outside the unity of the Church. We have a vivid realization of the ghastliness of a street spattered with bodies, a heap of brick and mortar that had once been a home, a man gasping out his life from the pistol shot of an enemy, or lying, a sodden, insensible, beaten thing, the victim of brutality. All these strike deeply into our hearts; they are human tragedies and we are very human. Then, too, there has been no lack of emphasis, in this last century, upon the value of the things destroyed by such desolation.

Eternal desolation -- scandal

Yet to eyes accustomed, as ours are, to the horizons of eternity, all this is not the most dreadful desolation that eats its way through the lives of men. There is yet another, which undoes the work of Christ, besmirches the supreme beauty in man and brings on eternal death. It was vivid to the eyes of Christ when He warned us that the man by whom scandal came to little ones would be better off if he had a millstone hung about his neck and were thrown into the sea. We can see how this is so. At least the little ones should be safe; at least they should be spared an introduction to the filthy paths of sin.

Unfortunately, we make the mistake of limiting the words "little ones" to children, whereas, really, we are all children of God. The introduction of any of the children of God to the ways of sin, the accomplishment of the spiritual ruin of any friend of God, merits the terrible condemnation of Christ and will undoubtedly receive the punishments it deserves.

Its varieties

Our generation has been made shockingly familiar with the ruin of little ones. It is true that the despicable drug salesman who introduces marihuana to high school students is primarily interested, not in spiritual ruin, but in money. It is also true that the seducer for purposes of his own pleasure is primarily interested in himself, in the satisfaction of his own appetites. Nevertheless, both have effectively brought about the spiritual ruin of a child of God. They have, as a matter of fact, done much more damage than the moron who attacks a child of three or four.

Both of these men have been guilty of a serious mortal sin against charity; but as yet, this is not that diabolical scandal whose chief aim is the spiritual ruin of another. The Communist, who throws adolescents together in the hope of destroying their moral life, the more easily to destroy their religious life, is in a class by himself. Trudging to the same school is the propagandist who attempts to root out all love and knowledge of God from the hearts of men. These are the works of the devil.

Done by men, they are diabolical scandal. This is the supreme gesture of hate of fellow men.

Its malice

From this, it is evident that, in the theological sense of the term, scandal is not a gossipy passing on of the latest bit of unsavory news. It involves spiritual ruin and it can be effectively committed even when the act, by which it is brought about, is not in itself sinful. The saintly man, who interrupts his lecture on mortification to take a drink of water, has acted in complete innocence; the damage is done because he fails to notice that some wag had put the water in a gin bottle. The scandalizing act need not even be aimed at anyone at all. The gaily drunk young parents, staggering home after a party, are in no condition to aim at anything; yet their synthetic gaiety may well do spiritual injury to their children. In fact, an act of positive virtue may bring about spiritual ruin to others; imagine the effect produced by a Greek priest touring Ireland in the company of his wife!

At this rate, it would seem that scandal is unavoidable. In a sense that is true, for there is no action, which cannot be given an evil meaning by twisted minds. Now, that kind of scandal is Pharisaical; we do not even try to avoid it, rather we give it the healthy contempt it deserves. The scandal that must be avoided (over and above the scandal flowing from sins) is that which comes from the appearance of evil about good or indifferent acts. This is the scandal of "the little ones", the innocent; and the little ones must be spared, even at the cost of serious inconvenience. Surely, the soul of our neighbor is more important than any act we may place here and now, than any temporal thing we may possess. In fact, the very omission of a good work for love of our neighbor is itself a greater work than we could accomplish by going ahead with our original plan.

The just man and scandal

As a matter of fact, a just man ordinarily is not scandalized, because he will not wreck his divine friendship for any human consideration. Of course, he does not scandalize others; not even by that scandal that comes from slight venial sins or carelessly done good acts. This man is not in the habit of doing things carelessly for God; he is in love with God, so he has an eye to all the things that belong to God, a very keen eye for the welfare of the friends of God, who are his neighbors.

First principles of order:

With essential order established in human life, there come fullness and peace. With essential disorder, human life is an empty, desolate, chaotic wreck.

The double commandment of Christ

It is above all necessary, then, that order come into our lives. Christ was not one to overlook the necessary things, particularly since He had so little time to teach us the truth. Therefore, when He was asked to select, out of all the commandments, the principal ones, His divinely wise answer was that there were just two. The first was: "*You shall love the Lord your God with your whole heart, with your whole mind, with your whole soul, and with all your strength*"; and the second, "*You shall love your neighbor as yourself.*"

The end of all other commands

In these words, Christ gave us the objective principle of order, the principle that places man in the proper relation to his goal; for the end of life is the object of charity -- union with God -- and if we are properly ordered to that goal, everything else falls into its proper place. In fact, His one command is, in itself, really enough; it contains all the others. Yet, that there be no mistakes, Christ added: "*You shall love your neighbor as yourself.*"

The words of the commandment

The first commandment states the measure of love for God. We are to love God in the only way God can be loved, without measure. Christ advocates a complete surrender; but a surrender that is not defeat but victory. We are to give ourselves utterly to God: to strain towards Him with all of our will; to have our intellect subject to Him; to have our appetite operating according to Him; to have our external acts obey God. In other words, all principles of activity within us are to be focused, not scattered, to operate in unity, harmoniously and with an effectiveness that can be measured only by God Himself.

As a result of our surrender to God, we have a holy, just and true love For our neighbor. It is holy, for it is for God's sake; it is just, For it wishes him only good, refusing to condescend either to his evil will or to our own evil desires; it is true love, for it is not a matter of getting but of giving. These fundamental commands of Christ are not impossible ideals held out to superior beings; they are commands of which the minimum requirements are met in the observance of the Ten Commandments.

Wisdom: Its nature and extent

These are the objective principles of order. Within us, the principle of order is charity, perfected by the gift of the Holy Spirit, which is wisdom. The scientist can be very learned, but at the same time very stupid; his science does not give him wisdom, for it is not interested in the last things of life. On the contrary, the philosopher must be wise or cease to be a philosopher; he must know the goal, though it be only the unsatisfactory natural goal, or admit he knows no philosophy, since philosophy's one interest is in last causes. In other words, it is only by seeing the goal that we can know where our steps are leading us; it is only by seeing the last thing, that we can understand the first. A wise man is one who has the serene judgment given by a knowledge of the meaning of life.

In the supernatural order, the last things are divine things. To contemplate divine things, and by them read the meaning of the divine and the human order, is the work of the gift of wisdom. This is the third of that trio of intellectual gifts, which fit our mind to wander in the halls of the house of God. As we have already seen, the gift of understanding allows us to penetrate the divine truth; then the gift of knowledge enables us to see the world of creatures in the light of the world of God. The gift of wisdom allows us to contemplate this new world, and see both it and the old world through the serene eyes of God.

The enemy of wisdom

Its roots are deep in charity. By it the end is con natural to us, we judge it as a chaste man judges of chastity, or an honest man of honesty; that is, not clumsily, not laboriously working out an answer, but by a sharp, instantaneous insight into truth. Obviously, the work of wisdom is not something to be explained on natural grounds; it must come from that push of the Holy Spirit to a mind well prepared by the gift of wisdom to receive the movement of God. Yet this wisdom is not a rare, exotic flower. It is one of those extraordinary things that have, by the grace of God, become more ordinary than the common things of life. Everyone in the state of grace has it; and retains it for as long as that state of grace endures. Alternatively, to put it another way, to every friend of God, identified by friendship with the divine Friend, the supreme end (God Himself) is con natural. Mortal sin, then, excluding this divine friendship, knocks out the basis of the con-naturality with the end, which is at the bottom of wisdom. That is to say, mortal sin is an evidence of stupidity, an egregious error about the goal of men.

Wisdom is not limited to that minimum degree which assures us of avoidance of the essential stupidity forbidden by the Ten Commandments. Wisdom can abound, must abound with the increase of charity. It may exist to the degree that enables us to manifest these divine things to others; or even further, to the degree necessary to order and direct others by these divine truths. As that wisdom increases, the cup of life has an altogether different taste; labor gives way to rest, bitterness to sweetness for now we are not turned away from God but one with Him. As a matter of fact, we must have some kind of wisdom if we are to act at all, because we must have some kind of end. In the light of that end, all things will be seen. It may be an earthly wisdom, coming from an earthly end, which gives a man the viewpoint of a mole, burrowing in the things of earth. Or a man may place his end in the goods of the body, gain an animal wisdom and so see the world through the eyes of a pig. Or, finally, he may place his end in his own excellence; the result is a diabolical wisdom, which instead of giving man an outlook, confines all his sight to an insight, the same colossal vanity that blinded Lucifer, the greatest of the angels.

All of these false wisdoms are really stupidity. They are a thick-headedness that misses the whole meaning of life, the whole possibility of man, a stupidity that comes from immersing the senses of man in the earthly things that completely absorb his soul. Naturally, its chief source is to be found in sins of the flesh; sins of luxury are a jealous mistress who demands every instant of a man's time, every moment of his thought, every beat of his heart.

Its beatitude -- "Blessed are the peacemakers"

The inevitable result of stupidity is disorder, chaos. Alternatively, more concretely, it must bring forth a distaste for things of the soul, a hatred of God and, ultimately, desperation. The contrary climax of wisdom is stated in the beatitude corresponding to that gift: "Blessed are the peace-makers, for they shall be called the sons of God." Charity gives us peace; but it is by wisdom that we are able to make peace. Augustine, you will remember, defined peace as the tranquility of order; wisdom alone has the wide outlook of God that makes plain to the eyes of man the meaning of all that life includes, the relation of one part to another and of all parts to the whole. Here we come closer to the imitation of Christ; and our reward is named with becoming beauty when it is said that the peacemakers shall be called the sons of God. That Incarnate Wisdom, the Son of God, first brought peace to men of good will.

Order and the modern world

The world, to which that Incarnate Wisdom brought the principles of order, and so of peace, was a world where order was rampant and yet there was no order. The disciplined order of the Roman legions has become legendary. The administration of Roman justice, the means of communication, the unity of language, in fact everything about the Roman Empire marked the high point of the human effort to be self-sufficient. Additionally, as Chesterton has said, "that effort was a failure and men realized it was a failure."

The entire world was at peace; yet in that world, no man had peace. Men's hearts were desolate. The world was empty. Philosophy had tried to fill that emptiness; so had military power, sensual indulgence and a frigid asceticism. However, all had succeeded only in giving order to emptiness. What was missing was the reason for everything else that is, and without it, nothing had reason. It was time for God to come.

An ordered emptiness

Our world today is a world ordered to its last detail; it is another high point in the human endeavor to be self-sufficient, and we are achieving the same results. We are busily ordering emptiness. We insist on the most perfect order in non-essentials. Everything can be weighed and measured, must be weighed and measured: our food, our clothes, our sleep, our pleasure, our personal habits, our education, our emotional and intellectual and physical life, our houses, our cities, our children, our navies and armies. There is no scale that escapes our passion for order.

An idealization of emptiness

We have gone the Roman world one better. We have not only ordered emptiness, we have idealized it; we have insisted that there be no goal, and so that there be no order. We have deified essential disorder, essential desolation. It is not love of God that we advocate, but indifference or contempt for Him. It is not love, but hatred of neighbor that is our watchword. We will not have wisdom but only learning.

A desolate world

We are just beginning to feel the cold chill of desolation, the chill of empty, haunted hearts, isolated, locked within themselves. We are puckering our mouths against the bitterness of enmity, of schism, of war, of quarreling, even of dueling, though we have thrown away the rapiers. Scandal has become a part of our educational scheme, though we are still shocked at the ruin it causes.

Wisdom of the Word

It is time for God to come among men, for men to open the door to God, even though there be but little room in the human inn. For only God can bring us fullness and peace. It is time for men to listen to the echo of the words of divine wisdom in their hearts, and to know that these two words of the Word of God are inseparable: "You shall love the Lord your God with your whole heart, with your whole mind, with your whole soul and with all your strength, and your neighbor as yourself." "My peace I give unto you." It is the kingdom of God that must be sought first.

CHAPTER VI

THE FULLNESS OF ACTION
(Q. 47-56)

1. Fullness of action and maturity:
   (a) The activity of men.
   (b) Stages of human activity.

2. Marks of maturity in action:
   (a) Current expressions of maturity.
   (b) Men's evaluation of maturity in action.

3. Cause of mature action -- prudence:
   (a) Reason and appetite in prudence.
   (b) Work of prudence as a good habit:
      (1) The work of a virtue.
      (2) Its relations to other virtues.
   (c) The acts of prudence:
      (1) Principal and secondary acts: command. counsel, judgment.
      (2) Conditions of perfect prudence:
         the integral parts of prudence.
   (d) Prudence in the individual:
      (1) In sinners.
      (2) In just men.

4. Origin and decay of prudence.
5. Species of maturity:
   (a) In the state.
   (b) In military organization.
   (c) In the home.

6. Complete maturity: the gift of counsel.

7. Types of immaturity:

(a) Imprudence (precipitation, thoughtlessness, inconstancy).

(b) Negligence.

(c) Carnal prudence (craftiness. guile, fraud).

(d) Worry.

Conclusion:

1. The condition for fullness of action -- maturity.

2. Second childhood of a world:

(a) Modern attempts to attain maturity of action:

(1) Mass education.

(2) Psychological theories.

(3) Democracy.

(4) Totalitarian political practice.

(b) Modern philosophical and political attacks on maturity.

3. The desperately young who will not grow up.

4. The eternally young who are always mature.

CHAPTER VII
THE FULLNESS OF ACTION
(Q 47-56)

Fullness of action and maturity

Human activity is a mirror, which gives back accurate images of men. Among the pictures presented to us by it are two unappealing extremes. One is the image of the dreamer, which, somehow, suggests nurseries, perambulators and guardians; for such a one is never found alone, someone must take care of him. The other is the image of the "go-getter", who impresses us often as a victim of glands, sometimes as a champion of trifles, and always as a nuisance.

The activity of men

Somewhere between these, two is an image that is close to our hearts. It is linked somehow with freedom; it seems to be the fruit of freedom of mind and freedom of heart. Yet freedom of action is not the whole story, or even the most important part of the story, of that ideal which is so close to our hearts. Certainly, the wealthy libertine, to whom riches and complete lack of moral restraint give utter license of action, arouses no writhings of the green-eyed monster within us. We do not particularly want license of action. No one feels hurt at being forbidden to shout or sing in a Pullman car at midnight. If law prohibits a nudist promenade on Broadway we do not consider that the fullness of our action has been impeded, at least not that fullness of action which is the goal of humanity.

Stages of human activity

In addition, really, this fullness is a goal. It is a goal to which we approach, step by step, through all of a lifetime. Today we feel no regret that we cannot lie abed all day, like an infant, ceaselessly gurgling. We admire the ceaseless activity of a child; but we have little desire to throw dignity to the winds and rush about expending the same amount of energy on just such childish ends. We can smile understandingly at the great dreams of youth, and at its self-conscious, clumsy gestures towards the realization of those dreams. Now, that is not what we want. We may sigh a little over lost youth, but not too seriously; we have no more real desire to slip back to our sophomore days than we have to crawl back into our mother's womb. These steps are only stages in our growth to fullness of action. Man's discontent and sense of guilt at not having lived up to his possibilities, at not having continued to grow, give us a negative picture of what this fullness of action should be.

Marks of maturity in action: Current expressions of maturity

If we were to try to put this fullness of action in one word, we would have to say "*human action*", or "*mature action.*" It is an action that should have about it something of the maturity of God. The action we demand of a man should not be the unconscious activity of a tree in a high wind, the narrow efficiency of the brute, nor the childish indirection of the infant. It should be responsible, effective, goal gaining. In a word, we demand an action proper to the image of God: an action proceeding from intellect and will, as God's actions proceed, deliberately, and to ends worthy of such an agent as a man.

This distinctive flavor of human action is to he tasted in such words as independence, sovereignty, full control; yes, even in the word "*humanity.*" It finds practical expression and validation in such things as freedom, responsibility, self-respect, self-control, power, shame and remorse, orderly action in the economic, military and political spheres; perhaps above all in sacrifice. This fullness is truly wisdom in action; certainly, it is truth in action. It is, at the same time, a confession and a boast: a confession of our need of order in life, and a boast of our power to introduce that order into our actions.

If, in our actions, we are to have this note of maturity, which is order, we must have something of the long vision of God. We must have vision, if not of the eternal hills, at least of the footprints of the past, the bustle of the present and the dim outlines of the future. For a definite mark of that, order in action is a provision for the future.

Men's evaluation of maturity in action

That we need, vision for orderly action is a significant truth. It means we must soar past the blind efficiency of irrational creation, past the fixed gaze of sense knowledge, which never goes beyond the present. We must exceed the limits of time and space. Actually, this vision sets man apart from the rest of the universe and brings him very close to God. Man can, somehow, set himself aside from the bustle of life and be a spectator of the whole game of life, even of his own life. He is a provider for himself and for others; in some sense he is a master of his own thinking, of his own action, somehow he directs himself. All this is contained in man's possession of vision: more concretely, it means that for this fullness of maturity in action, we must have a perfection of intellect; for it is only through intellect that we can see beyond the limits of the present. This perfection of intellect is called the virtue of prudence.

Cause of mature action -- prudence

Not any intellectual perfection will do. Many an actress, putting on her make-up, has plotted out the glowing path of her rising star; many a Sunday quarterback has won a game without getting out of bed. Unfortunately, none of this ever got out of the pretty head of the actress, or the sleepy head of the alumnus. Both of these were purely speculative. Here it is not a question of speculating but of acting, of getting things done.

Human action, in this light, is busy with the means to an end, with the attaining of a goal. It is not enough merely to know; we must apply what we know; consequently, we must know that to which we are applying the truths, as well as the truths we are to apply. In other words, we must know not only the universal, but also the particular, the contingent.

When we overlook this truth, we bring about the fatal divorce of speculative from practical intellect. Alone, the speculative intellect precludes all action but the noiseless grinding of the dreamer's dreams; alone, the practical intellect gives us action, but the disorderly, feverish action of the "go-getter." We may take a little of the strain off our spine by holding our chin in our hands as we ponder universal truths; but we will not get much done. It is not enough to sit and think; nor is it enough to rush out doing anything and everything that occurs to us.

Reason and appetite in prudence

Universal truths are extremely practical, for they are the soul of action. All the same, to have them replace action in our lives is like assigning ghosts to stoke the furnace. The external activities of men are the body of action, to entertain that body without its soul is as ghoulish and inane as grouping corpses at a wedding feast. Here it is a question of human action: and such action is truth at work in the singular. It demands a combination of the speculative and the practical; more than that, it means a combination of the intellect and the will, for it is an effective application of truth, and all effectiveness, all movement, must ultimately be traced back to the will.

Work of prudence as a good habit: The work of a virtue

For the moment, it is sufficient that we notice that this perfection of intellect, by the good habit of prudence, has about it none of the danger of lopsidedness inherent in mere intellectual development. This latter may make a man a good mathematician, philosopher, carpenter and so on, yet leave him a vicious man. Prudence perfects the whole man, not just a part of him. In other words, while the other intellectual virtues demand the moral virtues for their fulfillment, prudence is, in a very real sense, itself a moral virtue.

Its relations to other virtues

In technical language, prudence is formally or essentially an intellectual virtue, because it perfects our faculty of intellect; but materially, or simply, it is a moral virtue, because the material with which it deals -- our human acts -- is moral material. Nevertheless, all technical language is a snob, speaking only to technicians; to put the same truth in more democratic terms, the work of prudence is to direct the actions of man to an end; that is, to a proper end, with the obvious implication of a right end to which those actions can be directed, that is, with the obvious implication of moral perfection.

Perhaps this unique position of prudence can be made clearer by a momentary comparison with the other virtues. Prudence does not try to crash the board meeting of wisdom, knowledge and understanding, the speculative virtues, which deal with high, necessary, universal truths; it stays in the outer office, chatting with the stenographer about humble, contingent human acts. Art, the other practical virtue, is busy with houses, boats, medicine, and masterpieces, with things to be made, while prudence is occupied with loving and suffering and hoping and trying, with things to be done. Prudence is distinct from the moral virtues as the intellect is distinct from appetite. It is set off sharply from the theological virtues as God is set off from the feeble deeds of man, for, while the object of the theological virtues is God Himself, the object of prudence is human action.

Yet, while standing out so distinctly from all the other virtues, paradoxically prudence runs through them all, particularly through all the moral virtues. In somewhat the same way the soul of man is sharply distinct from all his members, yet it is in every part of a man or that part is dead. Therefore, too, charity stands out from all other virtues in the supernatural order; yet it is the life and the soul, the living principle of them all.

In the moral field, prudence builds up from nature as a thinker builds up from the naturally known first principles of thought. The starting point and foundation of everything must come from nature. A philosopher, who decides to toss away the natural first principles of thought and construct his own set of first principles, commits intellectual suicide. He is in the absurd position of a man who decided to start life over again without the original dependence on his mother. Both are whimsical declarations of independence; fortunately, for both men, the task they set themselves cannot be accomplished; nature is not to be denied. It remains the starting point and foundation in the world of thought, of action and of being; however we may feel about it.

The starting point in the moral or practical order is the ends of the moral virtues. In the preceding volume of this work, we showed that in human action the end is always the beginning. We must start off with a goal in mind or we wander aimlessly. Additionally, the field of human action is the field of moral action. Understand prudence does not create this moral starting point. Just as the intellectual virtue of knowledge applies, the first principles of speculative thought to arrive at conclusions, so prudence applies the first principles, or ends, of the practical order to arrive at action.

To be more explicit, the ends of the moral virtues are the happy medium of reason. That is neither a pledge of mediocrity nor an excuse for cowardice; rather it is the trademark of humanity. Reason is the rule to which human action must measure up; the happy medium is had when there is neither excess nor defect from that rule. Nature gives its none too gentle push toward that medium of reason by the natural inclinations of the appetite, which are the seeds of the moral virtues. How and through what means man can, in the concrete, attain that medium in action pertains to prudence. That is, prudence in the concrete finds the medium, for it is only by a right disposition of the means to the end that the medium in action is to be found. That is precisely the work of prudence: rightly to order the means to the end.

Perhaps we can put this more graphically by saying that no matter how strong the drive of a particular appetite, or a habit of that appetite, without prudence that drive is as disastrous as the speed of a running man who is totally blind. No matter how great the knowledge of the end or goal may be, if the drive of appetite is not there, if it has been destroyed by bad habits, education, and so on, prudence is as helplessly grounded as an aviator without a plane. No matter how healthy and well balanced our natural appetites may be, they do not suffice in us as they do in the beasts. Prudence, the work of reason, is essential because of the infinite variety of means uncovered by human knowledge and the independence of human freedom.

Prudence is the ideal housewife of a man's inner mansion; it is the virtue that gets things done the way they should be done. It is a virtue, which gives us fullness of action In common with all the virtues all the habits. it is a principle of action; specifically it is the channel down, which flow the powers of the practical intellect into the sea of action.

The acts of prudence:
Principal and secondary acts: command. counsel, judgment

If we remember this effective character of prudence, the discovery of its principal act is absurdly simple. The acts of prudence will be the acts of the practical reason doing things, so of course the principal act of prudence will be the act by which we actually get results. Let us suppose that the thing we are about to do is to go to a theater. That involves, first of all, a scanning of the lists of plays actually in town; we are taking counsel. Then a selection of the best show would be necessary; we have made up our minds. passed a judgment. Finally would come the act of command, or precept, by which we get the tickets and go to the theater. If we stop at the act of counsel, we have obtained some information but no entertainment; if our mental stamina carries us only as far as the act of judgment, we have material for argument but still no entertainment. It is only by the last act, the act of command, that we actually obtain rest for our soul in the make-believe world of the theater.

This act of command or precept, then, is an application of the fruits of counsel and of judgment. It is the act closest to the end of practical reason, that is, closest to action. It is the principal act of prudence. That this is so will be evident if we look at the question from another angle. Let us say that an artist, with his tongue in his cheek (he must be successful to be so free with his tongue), decides to paint the moon as a square. He is poking fun at the art critics. Although we may win a prize, but he has committed much less of an artistic sin than the student artist who. trying desperately to paint the moon as it is actually produces a square moon. We may smile with the first artist, sure he can do much better; we must agonize with the second's pitiful efforts. Now, the man who deliberately swallows poison, knowing full well it will kill him, is guilty of a sin against prudence, whereas the man who swallows poison unwittingly is guilty of no sin at all. The perfection of prudence, in other words, unlike the perfection of art, does not consist in excellence of judgment but in excellence of command. It is not a matter of knowing the rules, but of getting things done.

It may be well here to summarize the detailed analysis of the act of command, which was given in the preceding volume. Taking it apart, we find it has three elements: an element of ordering, of announcement or intimation, and of motion; the first two belong to the intellect, the last to the will. It can be briefly described as effective direction. St. Thomas, placing this act as the principal act of prudence, shows us that Providence, law, government are all acts of prudence, for they are all acts of command: that is, they are all essentially acts of reason, not of will. From this one article of St. Thomas, locating command as an act of prudence, the exact nature of Providence, law and government can be deduced; from the profound analysis of this act of command, the purpose, limitation, extension and obligation of Providence, law and government, can all be clearly and profoundly discovered. This is a significant truth, as we say in some detail in Volume II, for it removes government and law from the field of mere caprice, distinguishes them clearly from mere power or mere will of the ruler, and places them squarely where they belong -- under the protecting wings of reason.

Through all these three acts of prudence, there runs a double note of quick ingenuity and healthy doubt. The more prudent man is not the cautious man who spends three months considering every angle of a problem, in the hope of getting a guarantee of absolute certitude for his solution. Rather the man who considers the pertinent possibilities, makes a decisive choice and swings into action is much more prudent, though he is not denying the elements of incertitude in his choice. We simply cannot have the certitude of metaphysics or mathematics in things human. We cannot know that a banker is trustworthy or a salesman is truthful in the same absolute way that we know two and two are four. That very incertitude gives us an alertness that quickens our faculties, enabling us to peer quickly into all the possibilities, and at the same time to keep ourselves on the watch against mistakes. Certainly prudence must have that note of eager alertness about it; it is not the virtue of a dull, plodding, ineffective man. It belongs to the man who is getting things done, who applies the results of counsel and judgment quickly. For the whole purpose of counsel and judgment is precisely to prepare the way for the supreme act of command, with its effective results.

For the most part, our superfluous anxiety is caused by a search for the impossible, a demand for absolute certitude in human affairs. It simply cannot be had. Aristotle gave expression to the resentment of men and women, tortured by anxiety, against the serene confidence of the really prudent man, when he said that a magnanimous man is lazy and idle. Of course, he is not lazy and idle at all; he merely appears so to us, who are so busy worrying about the things that should be worried about, distrusting those who should not be distrusted. The magnanimous man escapes the excessive fear and distrust of others that drives lesser men into a panic of conferences, advice taking, fence straddling and nervous breakdowns.

When the edict went out from Caesar that the entire world was to be enrolled, Joseph and Mary were presented with a problem for prudence. They had something to get done; they had to make that long, four-day trip from Nazareth to Bethlehem to be enrolled. Therefore, they set about making their plans. What went into those historic plans, which culminated in the birth of God?

First of all, they must have gone over their memories of the annual trips to Jerusalem for the Passover; that would refresh their knowledge of the route and its difficulties, and of the means necessary to make the journey safely. They would have called on their knowledge of the political conditions of the time, the caravan departures, Mary's own physical condition, and so on. Even without being asked, the town veterans of the road would volunteer advice, plenty of it; Mary and Joseph were, after all, very young. With true wisdom, they showed themselves neither proud nor contemptuous, but humbly docile in the face of this advice of their elders. They themselves would have to take care of the inevitable emergencies, which no one could foresee. Mary, of course, would bring along swaddling clothes, because she knew her time was near; but it would be necessary for Joseph to fall back upon his native ingenuity to make the swift decision that would consecrate forever the manger of a stable as the birthplace of God. They were ready then to put all these things together and reason out their procedure. That their reasoning was well done is evidenced by the safe arrival of Mary in Bethlehem, in spite of the rigor of the season, of the delicacy of her condition, of the poverty, which forced them to travel in such humble state.

They were ready to reason out their procedure; that is, they were ready to make their plans, actually to order the means to the goal of Bethlehem; and that reasoning took foresight. They would need circumspection that they might overlook no circumstance of the journey: the cold of the mountains, the possibility of exposure during the brisk nights, excessive fatigue and so on. As far as possible, they would provide for the avoiding of obstacles; for example, they would take care not to attempt a journey through that dangerous country alone, rather waiting, cautiously, to travel along with the group going south for a similar purpose.

Conditions of perfect prudence: the integral parts of prudence

All of these acts go into every work of prudence, however quickly it may seem to spring into being, for these are the necessary conditions for perfection of prudence. Let us run over them again briefly: there is memory of the past and understanding of the present, which covers knowledge already had; then there is the acquisition of new knowledge, either by the experience and teaching of others accepted through docility, or, when time does not permit recourse to others, by our own ingenuity, our own alert shrewdness. Indeed this last is necessary too when we encounter a circumstance so singular as to have escaped the experience of all others. Finally, all these elements are put together as the material for reasoning out a plan of procedure. At that stage, we are ready for the perceptive part of prudence: for foresight, circumspection and caution, i.e., for actual ordering to the end, for attention to circumstances and for the avoidance of obstacles as far as is possible.

St. Thomas puts this in another way when he points out that the highest thing in man is his reason, and the lowest thing in man is the exercise of action by means of the body. In the work of prudence, then, we descend a precipitous hill. We can come crashing down from top to bottom recklessly, without a stop; at the very least, we shall not escape splinters. Or we can pick our way down, carefully, in an orderly, intelligent fashion. If we make the descent humanly, that is, intelligently, the steps we shall take will be: memory for the past, understanding for the present, an alert eagerness or shrewdness for the future; then reasoning or comparing of these elements of past, present and future. Finally, there will be docility in learning from others, for of course, no man is sufficiently clever to know all things himself, nor does his experience cover every possible circumstance. We are then on level ground, ready to order things effectively to the end, attending to all circumstances and possible impediments.

This question in the *Summa* on the conditions for the perfection of prudence is worthy of long study. Invaluable passages are strewn all through it, as though his very generosity had tired a rich man's arm and in a final gesture of beneficent impatience, he had turned the purse upside down. There is, for example, a course in memory training worthy of a modern psychologist packed into the cramped confines of an answer to an objection. Among others, we might mention Thomas' indication of the happy medium between contempt for the wisdom and experience of others, a result of pride in our own abilities, and the fawning dependence on others that leaves us helpless before emergencies -- the sort of thing that leaves a man calling for his mother at the age of eighty. Again, there is his pertinent insistence that the certitude of reason comes from the intellect, while the necessity of reasoning comes from the defect of intellect in man, a remark that might have saved Bergson, and the world, many a headache. Naturally, a man as bold and decisive as Thomas would point out the limits of caution, and do it well. All of these things would repay a much lengthier study.

Prudence in the individual: In sinners

Prudence must be in every man if he is to act maturely. Yet,, such is our jealousy of human characteristics, that even in our immature acts we must cling to some shadow of prudence, some semblance of maturity, though it make our acts as comically incongruous as a bearded infant. The prudent burglar goes through the motions of prudence, but he points those motions to a wrong end, like a star football player making a brilliant run to the wrong goal. That is not prudence, for it is not getting something done; rather it is undoing something.

Again, the irreligious businessman, who spends every hour of the day making his business a success, is using a kind of prudence; he is going to a true goal, but not to a very important goal. He has no justification for indignant recriminations at the desertion of his wife; he has left her long ago for his business. Nor has he any right to cry out injustice when he is told: "*You fool, this night do they require your soul of thee; whose shall those things be which you have provided?*" Of course, the man who merely makes up his mind but never gets anything done has no business rushing to the front when a call is sent out for prudent men.

In fact, the false prudence of the burglar and the imperfect prudence of the irreligious businessman can be present only in the wicked; both neglect the real business of life. The imperfect prudence of the dreamer can be in either good or bad men; but the perfect prudence, which enables a man to get the necessary things of life done, can be had only by those in the state of grace. It is a virtue, which perfects the whole man. We are speaking here, of course, of the infused or supernatural virtue of prudence, which, as a concomitant of sanctifying grace, is to be found even in children who are not yet able to use it.

In just men

This alone indicates the gap between natural or acquired and supernatural or infused prudence. Natural prudence is a human structure, built up slowly through the years by our acts; it must be torn down, brick by brick, with the same tools. Normally we expect to find it in the old: but we are not too optimistic in our search for it in the young. For the young are much more apt to have their reason impeded by the heedless elbowing of passion; moreover they have none of that long experience, age's compensation for the ashes of youth's fire, to fall back on.

Origin and decay of prudence

From this, it is clear that no man can lay the blame of his imprudence on nature; no man passes all of a lifetime searching as helplessly for prudence as an American in Paris searches for the right railroad station. Nature gives us a definite push towards prudence, not only in the natural inclination to the good of reason, but also by the naturally known first principles from which prudence must proceed. It may be that a hotheaded or full-blooded man finds it much easier to be rash than to be prudent; he can blame some of the difficulty of prudence on nature, but if he has coddled his rashness, he must blame himself for the brat's impudence.

In other words, our temperament has not the finality of a death sentence about it; rather it is the challenging note of a bugle call to battle. Nature gives the push, puts no insurmountable barrier in the way, but the perfection of this or any other virtue is ours to attain by the simple expedient of exercise.

The destruction of prudence is no less in our power than is its perfection. We can go about its destruction subtly, by poisoning it with acts of its opposite, imprudence. Alternatively, if we prefer violent means, we can shoot its prospective parents at the altar. You will remember the double element of reason and will inherent in prudence: the element of reason can be effectively excluded either indirectly by impeding reason's control through passion or directly through forgetfulness or ignorance; in either case we leave the will blinded, even if we do not steadily sap its strength or give it the perverted outlook of malice.

Species of maturity

It is a mistake to picture prudence as utterly personal, like the part in a man's hair. Prudence orders the means to the end of man; and that end includes the good of the family and the good of the community, as well as the good of the individual. For each of these goals of man there is a corresponding type of prudence: personal or monastic, economic or domestic, and political or ruling prudence. However, in a larger sense these three cannot be separated. After all, the individual good includes, and in a certain sense is included by, the common good. As a subject, man is a part of society to whom the common good is preferable to personal good; but man, as an individual, possessed of an immortal soul, has a good so far superior to the common good that this latter is itself the means to that supremely personal end.

It is not mere pique at the impossibility of sleep that makes the neighbors call the police when a man is beating his wife. An attack on the family is an attack both on the individual and on the state, for the individual is naturally a part of the family and the family is naturally a part of the state, while every individual, as a subject, is directly a part of the state. Consequently, in his practice of self-control, a man is exercising a part of the rule of the state; more than that, he is engaged in constant practice for that regulation and direction of others, which is necessarily involved in the office of those who have care of the state.

A man who works for the common good is not tossing a coin to a strange beggar from sheer generosity. Without this common good, a man cannot have his own proper good. This truth is fairly evident from the fact that man has a natural inclination to live in society; for nature does not pay much attention to frills, it concentrates on the essentials without which man cannot live. This is a fundamental explanation of the withering effect selfishness has on the very roots of human life. It is a violation of the fundamentals, both natural and supernatural, for both of these rules of human life -- reason and love, prudence and charity -- are given to man in view of his own fullest development.

At any rate, where there is a special object of direction or government, there is a special type of prudence. It may be the prudence, which rules the life of the individual within himself, the prudence which rules the family, the prudence which assures the internal peace of the state or, finally, the prudence which offers protection against external enemies. This last, military prudence, contrary to the absolute pacifist's notion, is not an unnatural, inhuman thing; rather it is a careful copy by human reason of nature's design. Even animals that cannot smile were given teeth; and the teeth serve as well for munching on enemies as for munching on the tastiest food the pet shop can offer.

Nature has given not only an appetite for good, but also an appetite against difficulty, an emergency appetite that finds its object precisely in those things that threaten to destroy or corrupt the good that is the individual's perfection.

Complete maturity: the gift of counsel

It takes a man a long time to grow up. In fact, he does not really reach full maturity until he reaches God. His mind and heart do not reach out with the strong, full gesture of maturity until they reach out for God; nor are his actions fully worthy of his manhood until they exceed it, moving toward the supernatural goal under the direction of the supreme Governor with something of the swift ease of angelic efficiency. We have called these dispositions, which makes a man readily moved by God, the gifts of the Holy Spirit. It is eminently fitting that there be one such perfection of movement for the virtue, which moves man to his action, the virtue of prudence. It is, in other words, essential that the smooth, easy movement of divinity should flow into those stumbling efforts by which alone we can come to God -- our own human acts.

The gift that perfects the virtue of prudence, bringing man to his fullest maturity, is called the gift of counsel. All the same, do not be misled by the name; it is not to be thought of in terms of a board meeting and endless argument. Like all the gifts, counsel proceeds in a manner that can be described by only one word -- angelic. It is not a step-by-step consideration, a weighing of possibilities, but an instantaneous, breath-taking application of supernatural knowledge to individual supernatural work. It is much more practical than a pair of overalls, yet it has the delicate strong beauty of flashing steel.

At the peak of the acts of counsel will of course be acts dealing with the direction of the things most useful to the goal of lite, for, like prudence, counsel is essentially practical. It is highly significant then, that the beatitude corresponding to the gift of counsel should be: "Blessed are the merciful, for they shall obtain mercy." In other words, the acts most useful to the successful living, which is the goal of prudence, are merciful acts; when we can suffer with others, we have begun to live.

We might expect, since counsel is in the practical intellect and is busy getting things done, that there would be no place for this gift in heaven; surely there, with the main task of life done, there will be nothing left for counsel to attend to. Nevertheless, counsel does remain in heaven, at least in a special double sense. That is, we do not forget what we have learned in this life about getting things done, and there are many things to be attended to even in heaven. In fact, here and now we spend a great part of our life sending the angels and saints scurrying about heaven running our errands -- finding health, jobs, happiness and forgiveness for us. It is true, of course, that counsel is not busy about the last goal; nor is there any of that uncertainty and healthy doubt about heavenly prudence and counsel. Rather there is an instantaneous transition to the knowledge of what is to be done and how it is to be done.

All through this second, part of the *Summa* St. Thomas proceeds on a homely principle as refreshing and uncompromising as the earthy common sense of a farmer. He argues that a man who knows a road well has no difficulty knowing when he has left that road. The thing is so utterly obvious that it smothers all disagreement instantly. In addition yet, we too often proceed on the assumption that a knowledge of the road is not so very important if we can only know a great deal about the blind alleys and crooked, wandering paths that get us nowhere. Thomas would argue that a man who knows the width and depth and beauty of purity needs no illustrated booklet of the complexities of impurity to keep himself clean. On the other hand, on a wider scale, a good knowledge of a virtue is the best knowledge of the sins against that virtue, for virtue is the highroad to heaven.

Types of immaturity:
Imprudence (precipitation, thoughtlessness, inconstancy)

In this matter of prudence, for example, we find as many sins as there are conditions and species of prudence. Roughly, all of these sins are reducible to: imprudence, negligence, carnal prudence, craftiness and unreasonable worry. The first, imprudence, is obviously directly against prudence, that is, it is an abandonment of the rule of reason; it crashes down from the heights of reason to the depths of action without any of the intervening steps. It will, then, have none of the perfection of prudence about it. Wherever it is found -- in the individual, the home, the state, the army -- it may include precipitation as against counsel; thoughtlessness as against judgment; inconstancy as against precept or command; and negligence as against the prompt execution of that command. As a result of its rashness and precipitation, imprudence will be incautious and will lack circumspection; because of its thoughtlessness, it will be deficient in docility, memory and reason; and because of its inconstancy and negligence, it will have little of foresight or reasoning.

All this sounds as highly complex in the order of imperfection as prudence's own complexity in the order of perfection. Really, it should be so; after all, it is not the beggar but the millionaire who can be robbed of a million dollars. In addition, all of these sins are brought about principally -- but not exclusively -- by sins of luxury. As a matter of fact, anything, which can absorb the soul in sensible things, can give rise to these sins of imprudence.

Negligence

The negligent man wanders through life in a rosy daze of naive trustfulness. His sin is opposed to the note of alertness, of healthy doubt, which we have said, was universal in all acts of prudence. Still other men fall in love with the daughters of the illegitimate branch of the prudence family. They win to an earthly, an animal or a diabolical prudence, according as the goal whose color lights up their lives is the world, their own senses or their own excellence. Now, in all these cases, the goal is so completely the wrong goal that it draws them in the direction opposite to the flow of rational life.

Carnal prudence (craftiness. guile, fraud)

Where the sin falls, not on the end, but on the means, we have the sin of craftiness, with its execution through fraud and deceit. The very names have a slimy sound that awakens a revulsion in a man enjoying no more than the remnants of moral health. The furtiveness of cowardice and the slyness of trickery have not yet won favor in the eyes of men, in spite of much talk about worthy ends, good intentions, relative values. Even in the moral order, perfume is a poor substitute for soap and water.

Worry

Perhaps one of the most human of the sins against prudence is that of excessive worry. Because prudence does deal with human ends, human actions and human circumstances there must always be a note of uncertainty about it; there is always reason for healthy doubt, some reasonable anxiety and a great alertness. We should have some little anxiety for future things, some concern for temporal things; but if we go to the excess of worry, we are not only being unreasonable, we are falling into a trap that Christ went out of His way to protect us against. You will remember that He pointed out the things that divine goodness has given us without any worry on our part, such as our body and soul; He called our attention, too, to the help God gives the animals and plants, the goods proper to their nature. Certainly, He will not treat us less kindly than He does irrational creation. He went deeper and insisted that it was the ignorance of the Gentiles in spiritual matters that was behind their gnawing concern about temporal things and their mocking skepticism of things spiritual. With us, possessed of the knowledge and love of God, the spiritual things must be first.

Conclusion: The condition for fullness of action -- maturity

Perhaps we can sum this chapter up best by saying that the condition for fullness of action is maturity, a maturity that comes only by the virtue of prudence. In the physical order, we would be astonished to see an infant swinging a sledgehammer or directing a bank. We do not expect a child to produce the works of a man, to have the endurance or intelligence of an adult. That last point is all-important: a man works perfectly only when he works intelligently, and he works with full intelligence only when he is working by prudence.

Men have always sought fullness of action, which is no more than saying that men do not relish being morons; men have always wanted to grow up. Like everything else in the world, men have always sought their fullest perfection; and the men of our age are no exception to the men of all other ages. In fact, we have sought maturity of action rather desperately.

Modern attempts to attain maturity of action

We have resorted to mass education as a means of opening more and more goals to human action. We have championed the political theories of democracy in the hope that men might have greater opportunities for action. We have advanced psychological theories as a means of freeing the motive power of man from all checks. Finally, our age has been swept by totalitarian political practices calculated, and rightly so, to remove the check of an absolute standard of action, allowing men a devastating adaptability to times and circumstances.

All the same, really all of these attempts have been somewhat lopsided; they have looked at everything but the central figure -- man and his humanity. No one of them has been aimed at moral fullness that is at human fullness. Two, education and democracy, have been extrinsic; that is, they have added nothing to a man himself, indeed have neglected man himself, in their concentration on the things outside of man. The other two are indeed intrinsic, the psychological and totalitarian attempts, but they have not added anything to man, not developed anything within him, rather they have taken something of his humanity away from him.

Modern philosophical and political attacks on maturity

It would seem as though our desperate striving for fullness of action is, in reality, a desperate struggle to destroy maturity of action. Let us look at it this way: full maturity of action comes from the effective direction of our action to a worthy, personal goal. Today we talk of motion without direction, or direction without motion, direction and motion to wrong ends, direction and motion to good ends by bad means or even of no motion at all. It would seem almost as if we were trying desperately to dodge the right answer to the problem of full action. Look at these attempts, or attacks, on fullness of action in the concrete. Behavioristic and animal psychologists have denied our self-direction; pragmatists and organistic philosophers have made a strange friendship in denying not only direction, but the things to be directed, the very truth of direction. The emotional philosophers, of the aesthetic, romantic and neo-supernaturalistic schools, attack reason itself, the one directive faculty. Then there is naturalism, in all its weird, irrational forms, denying a personal goal, in this respect taking its place staunchly alongside of humanitarianism and totalitarianism -- all of which, in a real sense, destroy the whole reason for direction by destroying the goal of the individual.

The desperately young who will not grow up

Certainly, we are not growing more mature in our action; we are not attaining a greater fullness of action, in spite of the mechanical and scientific helps that have been evolved to lengthen the faculties of man. Perhaps we are forgetting that human fullness of action is moral fullness of action. At any rate, we seem to be trying desperately to stay young; we have adopted the cult of youth, not only in the physical order, but in the intellectual and moral order. It is as though we insisted on clinging to the gurglings of an infant, the constant activity of a child busy with childish ends, or the large dreams of youth, along with youth's clumsy gestures and self-conscious effrontery.

The eternally young who are always mature

There is a human side to all this, for youth has always been a desirable thing. Age creeps upon us with a definite threat of destruction; and that, perhaps, is the whole explanation of our terribly young world, a world that is so young it is in its second childhood. For if, the men of that world cannot see beyond the limits of the material, then, in their eyes age is a thing of horror, a relentless enemy that irrevocably wipes the individual human being from the world of reality. Yet, if our eyes are lifted up beyond the barriers of nature to the limitless stretches of eternity, then maturity is not something to be feared, but to be worked for earnestly. For then it is not a destruction of youth, but a promise of eternal youth; it is not a concomitant of corruption and disintegration, but rather it is a fundamental condition for eternal life.

☖CHAPTER VII☗

THE FULLNESS OF SOCIAL LIFE
(Q. 57-62)

1. Social life's link to humanity:
   (a) A perfection and a necessity of humanity alone.
   (b) The fundamental social question: the question of right.
   (c) Sole social answers: affirmation and denial.

2. The rights of man:
   (a) Triple sense of "right": interrelations of these senses.
   (b) Origin of all rights.
   (c) Division of natural rights.

3. The social virtue ·· justice:
   (a) The sole virtue dealing with right.
   (b) Justice as a habit.
   (c) Justice as a virtue:
       (1) Its nature and subject.
       (2) General or legal justice.
       (3) Particular justice:
           a. Its material.
           b. The medium it seeks.
           c. Its act and eminence.

4. The anti-social vice ·· injustice.

5. The act of justice ·· judgment:
   (a) Its nature.
   (b) Its conditions.

6. Species of particular justice:

(a) Distributive justice.
(b) Commutative justice.

7. The act of commutative justice ·· restitution.

Conclusion:

1. The purpose of social life.

2. Only norm of fullness of social life.

3. Fundamentals of all fullness in social life ··
truth:
    (a) The truth of man.
    (b) The truth of society.
    (c) The truth of fullness.
    (d) The truth of justice.

CHAPTER VII
THE FULLNESS OF SOCIAL LIFE
(Q. 57-62)

These last few centuries have seen a growing emphasis on the "social life" of the animals. We read so much today of mother apes, bees in the skilled worker class, soldiers of the termites and so on that it takes very little imagination to picture a gray haired ape sitting at the front window, knitting in quiet dignity; a bee trying to dodge payment of union dues; or a West Point for termites. There is talk of monogamy among chinchillas, though we have not reached the point of speaking of divorce courts for cats. Really all this is a mixture of poetry and embarrassment. It is a poetic statement of the constant, orderly pursuance of a goal by the animals; and it is an embarrassment that men continue to be so snobbishly different from all other animals. This class-consciousness of men is decidedly disconcerting when the learned world has worked so hard to show him as nothing more than an animal. We would seem to be faced with the necessity either of lifting up the other animals or of dragging down this animal which is man.

Social life's link to humanity: A perfection and a necessity of humanity alone.

Social life, actually, is a brusque, uncompromising statement of the distinct difference between man and the animal world. Irrational animals have no need of judicial machinery, trade unions or columns on etiquette; man does need these things. Human life cannot go on where the social structure has broken down: a flood will not only do away with the traffic officers, it will release gangs of looters; civil war, a police strike, rampant gangsterism all suspend normal life because all attack law and order. Until they are crushed, everything else must be put aside.

It is not merely a matter of animals not needing this social structure, as a man does not need a bib at table. This is not a mark of superiority but of inferiority; the animals cannot have social life, while man can. We could put this in one word by saying the difference lies in this: the animals are distinctly predictable, while men are quite unpredictable. There is only one path, which leads to the goal of the animals; they must trudge along that path necessarily, naturally. The different paths by which man can reach this goal seem to be limited only by his ingenuity; we find, for instance, vastly different social structures built up by men of different ages, or even by men of the same age in different nations. Indeed, within the same social structure, we have a wide variety of paths by which men find their way home.

It is because man can live such a full and varied life that he is so dependent on the help of others. that he can never be completely self-sufficient, because men are not tied down to one necessary path to the goal, it is possible for men to crash into each other like stars gone wild. Men must have some order, other than the merely physical, to govern their mutual relations precisely because of the great potentialities inherent in their nature.

Perhaps we can put this necessity and ability for social life in the one statement, that man is a driver, not one who is driven. Each man can stand off from the world, or step down into the world and use any part of it; yet no man is absolute master. In other words, the roots of social necessity and the perfection of social organization lie in the mastery of man, which is, at the same time, his perfection and his need as distinct from the narrow self-sufficiency of the irrational world.

The fundamental social question: the question of right
Sole social answers: affirmation and denial

The fundamental social question, then, will always turn about this mastery, this dominion, this right of man. In addition, it is a question that cannot be dodged, that admits of no compromising answer: the only answer possible is a flat yes, or a flat no. That is we must either affirm and defend the rights of man on the sole grounds of his humanity; or we must deny and attack the notion of man possessing rights by reason of his humanity. This denial may take the form of anarchy -- a denial of all rights whatsoever -- and thus solves the social question by denying it. It may restrict all rights to members of a party, and give us

Communism's answer to the social question; it may give some rights to man, but solely as the generous gift of a benevolent state, and then we have the totalitarian answer; it may deny rights to all but those who enjoy power, which is the answer of the slave state to the fundamental social question. All four of these answers are denials of the rights of man on the grounds of his humanity. All of them deny the fact that man is a person, that he has liberties, that he can choose the path to his personal goal, that he has dominion over his acts and over things. In a word, they deny that man is a master.

Obviously, an understanding of dominion or right, then, is essential to any treatment of social life. Fortunately, an understanding of the word "*right*" is made easy by our common usage of the word. When a man is paid back the ten dollars he lent a friend, he may be surprised but he has no reason for gratitude. He is not expected to pin a medal on his extraordinary borrower; he has received no more than his right. We speak of a man having a right to a living wage or to an inheritance, even though, in fact, he is not getting a living wage or is being cheated of his inheritance. Again, and this is particularly true of the Latin form of the word (jus), the word "*right*" is used in the sense of law as, for example, in the Codex Juris Canonici -- The Code of Canon Law. We confirm this usage whenever our rights are questioned, by an immediate appeal to some law.

The rights of man: Triple sense of "*right*": interrelations of these senses

These examples are concrete statements of the triple sense of "*right*." First the objective right, which is a thing as tangible as a basket of groceries, the solid walls of a house or the gay sunshine of a spring day. The second is the subjective or moral right, the moral faculty of doing, having or omitting something; it is by this that we lay claim to the objective right. Finally, the third is law, as we understand it today.

Origin of all rights

These three senses of right are not disparate somewhat like different species of flowers or types of birds. They are as intimately dependent as members of the same family tree. Passing from the objective right through the subjective right to law we are on the same trail that leads from a speck of dust to the Creator of the world; we are ascending from effect to cause, to the origin of right. In reverse order, from law through subjective right to objective right, we proceed from cause to effect. Objective right depends on subjective right, and subjective right depends on law. These three, in other words, are always correlative: ten dollars is not due to a man unless he has some moral right to it; and if he has a moral claim to it, that claim must be traced back to some law, natural or positive.

In spite of our familiarity with rights, it may come as a surprise to us to learn that they are children of law. We have the notion that such invaluable friends as rights could be no relation to law, with its constant imposition of obligations upon us. Our modern emphasis has been to insist upon right, to the disregard of law and of obligation; these latter are medieval, irritating, out-of-date and prudish. Now, the emphasis does not change the facts: right and obligation are twin children of law.

Certainly, there can be no right without a corresponding obligation. To say that I have a right to walk down Madison Avenue is meaningless if other men have not the obligation to permit me to make that amusing promenade. It is absurd to say I have a right to the privacy of my own home, and in the same breath to deny that other men have the obligation to respect the privacy I cherish so. The very existence of a moral right in one man is a statement of a mortal obligation in others to respect that right. This is an obvious relationship of right and obligation. There is a more fundamental tie between them that is too often overlooked. Perhaps it could be stated by saying that obligation is the elder twin; at least the very reason for a right is to furnish a man with an opportunity to fulfill an obligation. If there are no obligations, there is no reason for rights. We cannot separate right and obligation any more than we can slice Siamese twins apart; both are fed from the same blood stream of law, for law, after all, is no more than the dictate of right reason guiding a man to the necessary means to be used for successful living. Because those means are necessary, they carry with them an obligation; consequently, man has a right to the use of those means.

Perhaps this will be clearer if we notice that, when we speak of objective right, we speak of a thing belonging to or being due to a man. That means that this thing has been selected, set apart from the universe, and stamped with the stamp of dominion, of ownership, of right. There are only two dies that can produce that distinctive mark: nature and some will. So reverence is the right of parents by the very nature of their office; reverence may be thrown out the window, stolen, lost but the mark on it is not to be done away with by tearing out the flyleaf. It is the ineradicable stamp of nature. On the other hand, a lesser, but no less authentic, stamp can be made by the determination of a public or a private will; it may, in other words, be produced by way of positive law -- human or divine -- or by way of private law, i.e., by contract. Understand now, that when we speak of determination by will we are speaking of deliberate will in the sense in which it is law; that is, in the sense of a dictate of right reason.

It would be accurate to picture the lesser die, which is positive law and contract, as a smaller, sharper, finer tool used only to bring out in detail the rough outlines of nature's stamp. From our treatment of positive law in the preceding volume, it is clear that positive law is merely a determination of the indeterminate principles of natural law. Consequently, no right can be conferred by positive laws that are contrary to natural law; just as a human mind cannot create the note of necessity that is at the root of obligation, neither can it destroy that necessity. Mercy killing is not less horrible for being permitted by civil authorities or juries; nor is prayer less lovely for being prohibited by a dictator's decrees.

Division of natural rights

Rights may, then, be either hardy plants with roots sunk deep in the inexhaustible earth of nature, or they may be frail, delicate flowers depending for life on the handful of soil in a window box. For the two great divisions of rights follow upon the two great divisions of law, rights may be the immutable, utterly inviolable fruit of the unchangeable natural law, or they may be positive rights conferred by positive law and suffering the same variety, from age to age and people to people, as their generator. In between these two there are a few rights conferred by the *"law of nations"* (jus gentium). We went into this thoroughly enough in the preceding volume to allow us to pass over it now rather hurriedly, merely noting that it is a bridge between the natural and the positive law: distinct from the natural law as depending, not only on nature itself, but also upon some universal contingent fact; distinct from positive law as being framed directly and immediately by reason itself, without any intervening institution. These rights, as determinations of natural law rather than natural law itself, are not strictly natural rights, though they have the force of nature about them.

There is an interesting point, in this discussion of natural rights that is too often misunderstood or totally overlooked. Thomas insists that in the domestic group there can be no such thing as strict rights. He is not, by any means, championing wife-beating, poor cooking or malnutrition of children. His point is that compared to the solicitude essential in this domestic group, justice is a shabby thing. It is true that in this group, human beings have intimate relations one to another: husband to wife, parents to children, master to servant. However, strictly speaking, the relationship is not to another, but to oneself: there is no clear cleavage between these different members of the domestic group we cannot speak here of something being due to "*another*", for they are all, in a sense, one.

As individuals, of course, all of these people have their strict rights; but as members of the domestic group, they are part one of another, with common rather than individual rights. Herein lies the striking difference between the subordination of unity of order in the domestic group from the Catholic point of view, and the individualism and chaos of the modern position. The subordination insisted on in the family is not one of injustice, tyranny or inferiority; in fact mistreatment of a member of this domestic group is as unnatural and disgusting as self-mutilation. The superior or head of the family, in his care for the family, is not a judge doing out justice. In other words, we cannot speak of a man being just to his family any more shall we can talk of his being just to his hands or his feet. In fact, this unity of the family is the natural approach to that identification on common ground of the supernatural virtue of charity.

The social virtue -- justice

The domestic relations of a man pertain much more to his personal life than to his social life. The latter is a matter of things, of actions outside the man himself, of communication with those distinct from himself. In addition to live, this social life man needs special perfection. We have seen more thoroughly in the preceding volume that the tremendous powerhouse of the intellect is put to work by feeder-lines of intellectual habit. The powerful resources of sense appetite are put to work by the moral habits, which regulate the passions. So also, the one faculty by which man can reach out into the lives of others -- his will -- is perfected for social life by a habit; and that habit is the habit of justice.

The sole virtue dealing with right

The mind of man is regulated by the intellectual habits, the passions of man by the moral habits. Still, both of these are matters of the internal life of a man; with no more than this, he would be isolated, turned in upon himself. The habit of justice regulates the external acts and things by which a man comes into contact with others. It is, then, the only *social* virtue. Justice not only wears a blindfold, her face is entirely covered with a grim mask when we picture her as a ruthless avenger. The picture is distorted, for justice is not only the social virtue, it is a sociable virtue; to be seen rightly, it must be seen as smiling, habitually good tempered, considerate of others, not mingling with the world in a sour, dutiful fashion, but positively enjoying contact with men and women. That is why we define justice as a habit by which a man, with constant and perpetual will, gives everyone what is his due.

Justice as a habit

The definition contains three characteristics of justice that allow us to see justice as she is, exposing the grotesque propaganda that insisted she was a harridan nagging at the joys of men. As a habit, justice has about it the smoothness, ease, perfect action and stability of nature itself; and it is this stability of habit, which is the immediate basis of the stability of social life. As a constant and perpetual will, justice escapes the charge of unpredictable moodiness. Here, in constancy, we have the peculiar difficulty of virtue. It is not difficult to be just occasionally, to pay back a loan now and then, return one or two of the books we have borrowed, give an employee a just wage at Christmas time. The difficulty comes in perpetually aiming at that goal of justice; but society is not preserved by an occasional just action, for men do not live together only at Christmas. Looking to another, justice releases a man from the isolation of the concentration camp of self.

Justice as a virtue: Its nature and subject

This last point is extremely important. Justice is a neighborly virtue, inseparable from our neighbor. It is unemployed on a desert island, rushed to death in the market place. When we speak of a person doing justice to his head, his heart, or his hands, we are speaking in metaphors; for the moment we are considering a man's head, heart and hands as existing apart from himself, forming a neighborly group, buying and selling, entertaining and marrying. Actually to postulate justice without reference to another would be like speaking words that had been carefully stripped of meaning. If justice gives another his due, it implies equality; it means giving a man exactly what is his, in strict equality. Equality is a statement of a comparison between two subjects, not of one subject to itself; this latter is identity, not equality.

Justice is inseparable from our neighbor; and it is the only one of the virtues in the natural order that is so linked to others. Just as right is the fundamental social question, so justice is the fundamental natural cement binding men together in society. It is the sole natural means by which right can be guaranteed, the sole means by which men can live together in one unit of society. This truth has been much misunderstood by modern thinkers. The modern mind may be inclined to be irritated at the precepts and prohibitions of the moral order; yet those precepts and prohibitions are, for the most part, the commands of justice. They are not arbitrary infringements of human liberty and dignity, comparable to the harsh orders of a peevish parent. They are the fundamental requirements for human social life. To attack justice is to attack the very foundation of society; it is to build a barrier between man and man, isolating individuals within the impenetrable walls of their own souls.

Justice is no more than a practical recognition of other men as persons, as possessors of rights. As a good habit, and so a virtue, we say rightly that justice makes both men and the actions of men good; that is, it makes both men and actions conform to the rule of reason. Now, the practice of justice, in its baldest statement, means that we refrain from doing damage to another. There is something a little ridiculous in a man's puffing out his chest, elated at himself for having let others alone; and there is something very horrible about the infrequency with which that boast can be made. The outbreak of racketeering is not something totally inexplicable today; it is essentially a denial of the fact that we do not deserve payment for merely letting others alone, for merely refraining from damaging them. The racketeer insists on payment for leaving men in possession of their rights. Our age's skepticism of the absolute foundations of justice is itself a distinct veering toward the viewpoint of the racketeer, a questioning of the sacred personality of our neighbor.

A dishonest lawyer usually knows very well what is the just thing, at least the successfully dishonest lawyer does. That knowledge enables him to thwart justice; it does not make him an honest man. That easily verified fact brings out the profound importance of accurately locating justice. It is not in the intellect of man, as our tricky lawyer proves by his action. It is not a matter of speculation but of action; it must be located, then, in the root-source of all action, namely in the appetite. Moreover, it is to be found only in the rational appetite or the will of man, because it looks to another, a thing impossible to sense appetite with its complete concentration on the immediate, particular, personal good. This is important. To make emotion, a rigidly personal utility, or the blind development of a universal organism the basis of human action is to destroy the basis of justice and so of social life. The anti-intellectualistic and anti-metaphysical philosophies can escape anti-social conclusions only by scuttling logic; in themselves, they are philosophies of selfishness, for they render a man incapable of reaching out to a consideration of another.

To be just, a man must look beyond himself; yet looking beyond himself, he may be amazed, for every man he sees will be a twin: an individual and a part of a community. Some men have been so irritated at what they considered the bleared vision of justice, with its effect of double-exposure that they decided to deny the evidence and maintain either that men were no more than individuals, or that they were no more than part of a community. However, the facts are not destroyed by shaking one's head; our contact with men as individuals must be ruled by one kind of justice -- particular justice; with men as parts of a community, we are ruled by another, general justice.

General or legal justice

It is to be understood, of course, that this general justice is not general in the sense of a general statement or a general panic, as something running all through and found in all the virtues. Its generality comes from the generality of its object, which is the common good. Its work, a decidedly extensive work, is to give the community what is due to it. So, just as charity can and does order all acts of all virtues to the supernatural end of man, so legal or general justice orders all the acts of all the virtues of man to his social end, the common good.

From this point of view, it is evident that general justice has more to do than patrol a beat. It reaches up to the intellectual virtues in such laws as those fixing the minimum intellectual requirements for citizenship. Indeed it may extend even to the exterior effects and acts of the theological virtues when, as in some of the Swiss Cantons, a religious procession is also a civic function regulated by general justice.

Normally it will not be necessary for a citizen to set aside one day of the week for concentrated fretting about legal justice. The state puts its demands clearly and forcefully; and the fair-minded citizen normally agrees to these fair demands of the state. The not-so-fair-minded citizen's disagreement is promptly taken care of by the state itself. However, not all times measure up to the rule of normalcy and when the state demands more than is just, there is no question of legal justice involved. Rather the question is one of tyranny and tyranny's resistance; for the mere fact that it is the state, which makes the demand, is not necessarily a guarantee of the justice of that demand.

Particular justice: Its material

Over and above legal justice, there is a justice that enters intimately into the numberless contacts of our everyday life. If the skeptic doubts the possibility of justice squeezing its way into a crowded subway train, he has only to try jerking someone from a seat onto the floor in order to obtain a seat for himself. Just as fortitude and temperance order a man to his own proper good, and legal justice orders man to the common good, so particular justice orders a man to the individual good of his neighbor. As a social, or neighborly, virtue, its material is precisely the means we have of communicating with others, external things and actions as they coordinate the life of one man with that of another. It deals, in other words, in those things by which men's lives are pulled together or driven apart.

The significance of this determination of the material of particular justice can hardly be over-estimated. On the social side, it makes evident the profound truth that, however dutiful we may be to the state, we cannot ignore man, the individual, if social life is to continue. A community in which all citizens paid their taxes promptly and spent their spare time at each other's throat could hardly lay claim to the unity, peace and harmony that are essential to social life. Individual injustice has furnished the ideal condition for the spread of communism; it is the force behind looting and gangsterism; it was the permanent condition of our early frontier days Obviously if this injustice becomes universal, men cannot live together, although their houses touch one another. In other words, particular justice is absolutely necessary for social life, however much we disregard it theoretically today. A strong police force or a well-trained army is no adequate substitute for it; a society lacking this essential ingredient has within itself the elements of disintegration.

On the personal side the absence of particular justice cuts a man off from the lives of his fellows, puts barriers around his own life that are much more effective than the walls of any prison. A pickpocket may enjoy dense crowds, but not for the fellowship, they give him; and a habitual liar leads as lonely a life as a habitual thief. Indeed, this particular injustice is corrosive of the character of its owner. It means that something is rotten in the will of this man; and, since the will is the source of all he does that corruption necessarily creeps into all his acts, making them crippled, ugly, deformed. When an employer is anguished each week at the sight of the pay-roll scattering into the pockets of his employees, he may be doing no injustice to his employees, but he is not a just man; he does not enjoy his justice. It is true that justice deals with externals, operations or things, and is not primarily concerned with joy and sorrow. Nevertheless, particular justice is not a cold, poker-faced, inhuman virtue. No human virtue can possibly be that. St. Thomas rightly insists that, "*The man who does not joy in his justice is not really a just man*;" for every virtue, like every habit, carries with it its own joy, at least the joy of smooth, easy, natural action.

However, it is well to insist upon justice's exclusive concern with externals, for then we see clearly the impossibility of effective reform from the outside. Justice may prevent or punish the murder caused by hate; but it cannot touch the hate. It may prevent or punish the theft that springs from greed; but it cannot take a step after the greed itself. When there is a constant stream of such unjust actions, proceeding from inner corruption, it becomes less and less possible for justice to be enforced. In other words, the abandonment of a stable, absolute morality, is in itself a guarantee of injustice and, eventually, of social disintegration. This is one of the discouraging differences between the modern pagan and the pagan of antiquity; it is only in our time that it became the fashion to deny a goal, and so an absolute rule, to life and consequently to destroy the foundations of that inner morality without which justice is a practical impossibility.

The medium it seeks

A man might drink a pint of wine before breakfast and be thumpingly intemperate, whereas he could drink the same pint of wine with his dinner and be a temperate man. Nevertheless, if his thirst is for other people's jewelry, it makes no difference whether he quenches it before breakfast or after dinner. For while justice, in common with all the moral virtues, seeks a medium between excess and defect of the rule of reason, unlike all the other moral virtues, the coincides with the medium of objective reality. In justice, that is, the question is always one of equality, or measuring up to something outside.

No man can frown the smile from the face of a summer day. These outside things are not changed by any subjective dispositions of ours. No matter how much of a nervous release it may be for a man to commit murder, no matter how innocently he deprives a laborer of his wages, no matter what pleasure it may give him or how much good it may do the state to choke a crooner -- these things remain unjust. It is always a question, in this matter, of what is due to another; only on that consideration may we judge the justice of a thing.

Its act and eminence

An act of justice seems a simple, unsophisticated thing when we describe it as simply letting others alone. Even when we dismember it, the table is not cluttered up with its parts: it is merely an act placed in the proper material of justice -- external things and operations -- and in the proper mode of justice, i.e. rightly or equally. Yet the just man receives a solemn tribute of respect, as though in his justice we had recognized an outstanding merit, much as a soldier might respect a Legion of Honor ribbon or a Congressional Medal. This respect is more than a sigh of relief because the justice of another is a bulwark to our own rights: justice deserves that respect for it is the outstanding moral virtue. Considered subjectively, this superiority is clear, for justice does not perfect the sense appetite of man which is tied down to the world of sense; this is the work of fortitude and temperance. Justice concentrates on the rational appetite of man, which can go out to others, even to God. From the side of its object, justice does not do the limitedly personal work of controlling man's passion, but rather it escapes the personal in its concern for the good of another or for the good of the community.

Perhaps the more profound reason behind our respect for the just man is to be found in the stamp of humanity justice puts on the activity of man. A man's life is successful only in so far as his life and actions measure up to the rule of reason. Fortitude and temperance do no more than conserve the good of reason, preventing the passions from exceeding it; justice injects rationality into the external acts and things of a man's life. In paying tribute to the just man, we recognize an individual whose humanity stands out in all of his actions, all his dealings with his fellow men. For much the same reason the hypocrisy of the backbiter fills us with disgust; here is a man who has taken reason out of his life with his fellows, here is an unjust man.

The anti-social vice -- injustice

In a word, the unjust man, in his external actions, ceases to be a man; and so ceases to be a social being. He has embraced the anti-social vice of injustice; he has no valid complaint against the ostracism with which society punishes him. In his heart, he carries a contempt for the common good and a contempt for the good of his fellow men; perhaps it would be more accurate to say that he is the victim of his ostracism of society. Another way of saying the same thing would be to say that the unjust man thinks only of himself; even though he be a contemptible sneak thief, he fancies himself a conqueror who recognizes no rights in other men, for he scorns all obligations to respect those rights.

In reality, he is no conqueror but a stupid suicide. In denying his obligations to respect the rights of others, he cancels out, as far as is possible for him, his own claim to rights; for it is a man's obligations, which are the basic claims to rights. This unjust man is an enemy of himself, an enemy of others, and an enemy of society, an enemy more deadly than a plague or a hostile army, for he is boring secretly from within, gnawing at the pillars of the social structure and breeding others of his kind by his every act of injustice.

Injustice is stupid, it is dangerous from a social point of view, in grave matter, it is deadly to the unjust man, for it is a mortal sin. Of course a blow struck in quick, unreasoning anger or short-change given by a flustered clerk will hardly topple the towers of society and will certainly not put a man in the state of mortal sin. An unjust act that, as a result of passion or accident, pops Up its head to startle everyone concerned is not the offspring of injustice; the coolly deliberate depriving of another of his due which is both the fruit of injustice and its seed, is not surprising to the man who has produced it. Indeed, as a rule, he has worked hard at it and may even take a perverse pride in it.

A man cannot enter this vicious anti-social state by falling through a trap door or listening to the glib story of a stranger. He must be willing, while, if he wants to make a good job of it, his victim must be decidedly unwilling. A wealthy man who owns so many automobiles that he does not mind losing one or two, has made it impossible for the automobile thief to do him an injustice.

Perhaps one of the deadliest things that can happen to society is to have confusion arise about the distinction between just and unjust things. The good intentions of champions of suicide, euthanasia, industrial laissez-faire and birth control may be an inspiring thing; but the damage they do to society is not lessened by their sweet simplicity. It is essential for the individual and society that man's acts be just; consequently it is most important that a man recognize a just from an unjust thing when he sees the two side by side. In this human field, as in the other moral fields, virtue gives a man a taste of the swift security of angelic knowledge. The chaste man intuitively recognizes the slightest taint of impurity; the coward cannot hide his cowardice from the piercing mind of the brave man. In the same way, the just man, quickly, surely, instinctively unveils all trace of injustice. In other words, the moral virtues make a man so familiar with the end of these virtues that he can make no mistake about the friendship or enmity a particular means bears to that end. This is the constant help given to knowledge by virtue, the negative help, which removes impediments to intellectual operation, and the positive help, which comes from familiarity with the material of the particular virtue in question.

The act of justice -- judgment

Yet, moral virtue is not the whole story. Rather it is the obscure, profound, indirect part of the story that seldom finds its way into print. In this matter of justice, the virtue of justice disposes a man to judge justly; but it does not don the judicial robes, sit on the bench and pronounce the judgment. Judgment is an act of intellect, while justice is a matter of the will; the actual judging must be done by an intellectual virtue, namely the virtue of prudence.

No one has the right to wander through the hours of the day scattering judgments with the same abandon with which he makes comments on the weather. Licit judgment must be both just and prudent. That is, judgment is not the angry weapon of pique, the sly weapon of envy, the merciless bludgeon of malice nor the panicky blow of self-defense; it must proceed from the inclination of justice, of giving every man his due. Moreover, it is not to be made of the airy stuff of guesswork, nor the eerie stuff of telepathic reading of motives that can be known only to God; solid evidence must go into its make-up, for it must proceed prudently. When it is a matter of public judgment, over and above justice and prudence, authority is necessary, for public judgment has coercive power.

This does not mean that the warning, "judge not", is to be taken with absolute universality. Judgment is not only licit at times; it may even be necessary and strictly obligatory. The prohibition is against imprudence and injustice in judgment; that is, the warning is leveled against the perverse judgment of the unjust man, the temerarious judgment of the fool and the insolent judgment of the usurper of public power.

As a matter of fact, we make judgments of the actions of others, and of our own, every day of our lives. When the judgments are unjust or perverse, we have no difficulty recognizing the fact. We hate ourselves for thinking our friend, the undertaker, is looking for business when he visits us in a hospital. A judgment of this sort is a blow at our own self-respect; we have done something unworthy of our humanity, stripping an action of ours of its reasonable character. Oddly enough, because we have done something unworthy of our humanity, we become more and angrier at the person we have judged, more and more stubborn in the judgment itself.

A much more subtly dangerous type of judgment is that from mere suspicion. It starts off as a vague, even silly idea; but it haunts our mind, repeating its unsavory melody repeatedly, like a tune that hums itself in spite of our irritated rejection of it. The temptation is to look at this judgment a little longer each time it recurs; each time it becomes stronger, until finally it seems to rest on solid evidence. Perhaps it is helped on by the very human desire to be first with a bit of information, the ambition of the keyholer, the eavesdropper and the pseudo-prophet.

Because there is so much adolescent vanity in it, a consideration of the sources of judgment from suspicion is no mean help to avoiding it. There are three unflattering sources of this judgment; by making it, a man has given good grounds for his own conviction on one of these three counts. A gangster is much more suspicious than a saint, for the evil man finds it easy to believe evil of others. We can run off suspicious judgments effortlessly and by the score when the object of those judgments is a person for whom we have contempt or hatred, or of whom we are envious. Finally, we find it much easier to make these judgments, as we grow old. In fact such judgments are themselves signs of old age; they are the distinctive badge of one made cynical by experience, of one who has been disappointed so often in his hopes and expectations of men that now he is rather prepared for disappointment than eager to recognize truth. That he is evil, petty, or sourly growing old -- not even the sprightly newspaper columnist whose suspicious judgments are a part of the breakfast menu can buckle up his vanity with such sagging stays as this.

Whatever the soil that nourishes it, judgment from mere suspicion is always a sin, for it is always an injustice. It may be slight in its beginnings when we begin to doubt the goodness of another; usually this is not fully deliberate. It becomes a mortal sin in its very nature if, without sufficient evidence, we take the evil of another for certain, or flatly against justice when, from mere suspicion and by a solemn judgment, we proceed to the actual condemnation of that person. Of course, to be serious, the matter of judgment must be serious: suspecting the high school girl of using her mother's lipstick need not disturb our sleep; but judging that it was the mayor who committed the murder in the City Hall is quite another matter. For, concretely, that alone is grave matter, which, considering the person judged and the evil of which we convict him, does serious injury to his honor, good name or the opinion others have of him.

We have a real obligation in justice to give others the benefit of the doubt. When you hear your neighbor coming in at five o'clock in the morning it would be much more prudent and just on, your part to decide that he was working a night shift, than to accuse him of sowing wild oats. In other words, when the thing in question is doubtful, to proceed to judgment without manifest indication of evil is imprudent; moreover it is unjust for it is contemptuous of the man we are judging.

It may be objected that we will make many more mistakes in our judgment of men by following this line than we would if, cynically, we refused to give anyone the benefit of the doubt. Perhaps that is true, although it can be seriously questioned. However, even if it were true, it is much better to make many mistakes giving others the benefit of the doubt, than to make a few mistakes suspecting everyone. In the first case, in spite of mistakes, no harm is done either to the one we have judged kindly or to ourselves. We must get over the idea that we can judge men as we judge horses. A horse-trader is rightly suspicious of the qualities of every horse he sees, for his prime consideration is one of intellectual accuracy. Not even the feelings of the horse will be hurt by the cynical dealer. In judging men, it is not so highly important that every detail of our factual knowledge he accurate; gossip is entertaining, but it does not contribute to the intellectual perfection of a human being. It is highly important that we do no man a serious injury; yet if we judge a man to be evil when he is not, we have done him a serious injury, we have violated his right to our good opinion, we have, in a real sense, robbed him. On the other hand, if, mistakenly, we judge him to be good, no injury is done either to the one judged or to ourselves.

Species of particular justice: Distributive justice; Commutative justice

It should be clear, in our day of tardy social legislation, that the individual's rights can be respected or violated, not only by his fellow citizens, but also by the state; that the state as well as the fellow citizen can owe debts to the individual. This obvious fact is a concrete statement of the classic division of particular justice into distributive and commutative justice. We can put all three types of justice -- legal, distributive and commutative -- in order by simply remembering that justice is a social virtue and society is a whole of which the parts are the individual citizens. The relation of the parts to the whole is regulated by legal justice; the relation of the whole to its parts is the care of distributive justice, while commutative justice controls the relations of part-to-part, of man-to-man.

Both commutative and distributive justice are varieties of particular justice; but they are varieties, not alternates, and their differences are decidedly important. No one seriously expects a poor man to carry the same burden of taxes as the rich man; yet we know well that the borrowed fifty dollars cannot be shaved down to twenty-five just because our creditor happens to be rich. Perhaps the average person has never put the thing in such frigid words, but he knows that the equality demanded by commutative justice is absolute or arithmetical, while the equality demanded by distributive justice is proportional or geometrical. The basis of this proportion is the share the individual has in the whole of which he is a part; so, for instance, in an aristocracy, it will be a matter of power or perfection, in an oligarchy the basis will be wealth, in a democracy it will be freedom.

Distributive and commutative justice plays in the same park and on the same-team; their remote material is the common material of all justice, i.e. things, persons, actions. Now, they cannot trade positions with any but disastrous results. For proximately, distributive justice is directive of the distribution of honors, burdens and so on of society; it is the habit behind the distribution of medals and income tax blanks. While commutative justice directs all the exchanges possible between individual men.

The last sentence can be read quickly; but do not be deceived by its brevity. The actual field of commutative justice makes the fencing of it a long, hard task. In later chapters we shall attempt an organized expedition into that vast territory; now, as a slight indication of what will be found there, we may note that commutative justice covers all the involuntary exchanges brought about either secretly by fraud or openly by violence, such as theft, murder and so on; within its territory also are all the voluntary exchanges such as gifts, sales, purchases, rentals, and so on. Even so, perhaps the most important thing to notice at the moment is the strict equality demanded by commutative justice. At least such a consideration focuses attention on the futility of injustice by pointing to that outstanding act of commutative justice, which is called restitution.

The act of commutative justice -- restitution

The fact that a car has wandered into our garage overnight does not make that car ours. A gas attendant who has innocently given gas and change for a twenty dollar bill the kidnappers offer from the ransom money has no right to pass it on to some one else or to deduct his own losses from it. We may have no more than the satisfaction of our spite to show for having burned down a neighbor's house, but we are obliged to compensate him for his loss. To put the matter more plainly, criminal appropriation and unjust damage oblige to restitution in the strict sense of the word; that is even though here and now we have nothing of our neighbor's goods, even though a fellow craftsman has turned the trick on us and picked our loot from an inside pocket, we must still make good the loss. All the same, even where no crime is involved, the mere possession of goods of another immediately involves the necessity of returning those goods to their owner; in this last case, of course, the obligation holds only so long as the things are in our possession.

In other words, we must give every man what is his, strictly, equally. A thing cries out for its owner as a dog cries out for its master. Title to ownership is not lost, like small change, by doing somersaults; it must be renounced or it continues to endure. As long as it endures, no rival title can be established.

Conclusion: The purpose of social life

As we saw in the preceding volume, the norm of the plenitude or fullness of social life is the fullness of individual life within a society. For the purpose of society is to fulfill the natural needs of man; it exists that man's individual life might be fuller, that it might offer greater opportunities for living the life of virtue, for the attainment of individual perfection. Indeed, the ultimate end of the state -- peace and the life of virtue -- is itself a means to the further end of the individual, the perfection of his immortal soul. Society, then, is to be measured and evaluated by the opportunities it gives a man for living his individual life more fully, by the help it offers him to perfect himself.

Obviously, the fullness of social life has a double aspect. One is negative, insofar as society at least takes nothing away from the individual; this means no more than that society observes the natural justice demanded by natural law itself. It respects the natural rights of man. The other, positive, aspect is summed up in the rights society confers upon a man by its positive law, i.e., the further guarantee of help it offers a man for the fulfillment of his natural potentialities.

It is no more possible to deny the preponderance of the individual for the sake of society than it is to shoot off a man's face to make more room for his nose. A denial of the supremacy of the individual is, basically, a denial of social life. A humanitarianism, which insists upon the race rather than the individual, a communistic insistence on a party, a Nazi insistence on the nation, the abolition of the rights of the individual by organismic and mechanistic philosophies -- all of these are logically unjust and inevitably anti-social. They attack the individual in the name of society, and in so doing they attack society itself, and destroy it.

Only norm of fullness of social life

Fullness of social life is possible only when the rights of man are granted on the grounds of his humanity. However generously they are granted on other grounds -- as a gift of the state, as a concession to power, as a temporary expedient -- the fullness of social life is not only limited, it is destroyed. There is only one answer to the social question, a positive answer -- the defense of the rights of man on the grounds of his humanity. All other answers are negative; they are answers that dissolve society but leave the social question unsolved.

Fundamentals of all fullness in social life – truth; of man, of society, of fullness, of justice

We might sum this up in one word by saying that the fundamentals of all fullness of social life are comprehended in one word: truth. For a full social life, the truth of man's humanity must be admitted; i.e. the inalienable, natural rights flowing from the mastery of man, his liberty and eternal destiny must be the foundation upon which society exists and for which it exists. The truth of society itself must be recognized: it must be seen, not as a goal, not as a god, not as an end of all things, but rather as an instrument designed for the fullness of man's life. The truth of fullness itself must be seen: that is, we must know that man's fullness is not an economic fullness, not a sensual fullness, not an intellectual fullness alone, but a human fullness, a full development of man as man.

All of this is no more than a recognition of the truth of justice. For full social life, we must give every man what is his due, we must tell the truth in our actions. We must give man what is his, we must give society what is its own, we must give fullness the recognition of its true nature. On the other hand, in just one sentence, fullness of social life is accomplished by truthfulness: emptiness of social life or even the destruction of society is accomplished by living a lie, by denying the nature of man and the nature of society. These two, man and society, are inseparable. The one springs from the other; but unless we recognize man as the source of society, rather than society as the source of man, we are working for the destruction of both man and the society he establishes.

CHAPTER VIII

THE ESSENCE OF ANARCHY I
(Q. 63-71)

1. Violence in society:
   (a) The violence of defense -- a gesture for peace.
   (b) The violence of attack -- the brutality of madness.

2. Social insanity:
   (a) Its origins.
   (b) A denial of the fundamental character of society.

3. Personal victims of social madness:
   (a) By murder:
       (1) Killing in general.
       (2) Public and private execution of criminals.
       (3) Suicide.
       (4) Killing of the innocent.
       (5) Killing of aggressors.
   (b) By mutilation,
   (c) By beating.
   (d) By imprisonment.

4. Social insanity's attack on property:
   (a) Licentiate and necessity of private property.
   (b) Secret attack on property -- theft.
   (c) Open attack on property -- rapine.

5. Social insanity's attack on the instruments of justice:
   (a) Favoritism.
   (b) Injustice in the courts:
       (1) Injustice of a judge.

(2) Unjust accusation.
(3) Injustice in the accused.
(4) Injustice in witnesses.
(5) Injustice in lawyers.

Conclusion:

1. Social sanity and human life.

2. Social sanity and human dignity.

3. Social sanity and private property.

4. Social sanity and human freedom.
5. Social sanity and the instruments of social life.

Pictures, like persons, remain strangers if we see them in the sad, false light of solitude. Compared with the full, human richness it displays when flanked, say, by the mystery of a da Vinci and the delicate beauty of a Fra Angelico, a Titian in solitary grandeur is reserved, even sullen and pouting. We cannot always gather such a company on the same wall; but we have a mental gallery that can be arranged and rearranged at our pleasure. It would be impossible, for instance, to hang side by side, in the same exhibit, the astounding picture of an angry Christ violently driving the moneychangers from the temple and the pitiful picture of a modern racketeer mercilessly heating a small storekeeper for not paying "for protection." Now, arranged in such significant contrast in our mental gallery, they tell a story that could be told as graphically by no other means.

Violence in society: The violence of defense -- a gesture for peace

The story they tell is the story of the distinction between sanity and madness in the relations of man-to-man. The one is a violence of defense in an attempt to safeguard the right. The other is a violence of attack whose theme is one of disregard of man's needs and man's rights. The one does the work of society, respecting and guarding man's rights, attempting to fulfill his needs; it is an insistence on man's mastery, on man's dominion, on the end of society. The other is the attack of a mad animal. The violence it portrays is the violence of a lunatic, without reason, destroying both the wielder of violence and his victim. Indeed its very attack on the rights of others is an attack based on the attacker's own rights, for it is a denial of his obligations. He is petitioning for isolation, snarling a scornful denial of the human character of his own nature. 7

The violence of attack -- the brutality of madness

These may sound like angry, exaggerated words in which to describe justice. They are not angry words. Anger's mightiest bellows die away to an inaudible whisper before the mutinous protests of wrists and back evoked by a typewriter's tyrannous commandeering of the hours of the clay. Nor are they exaggerated words. Let us look at the facts a moment, at the roots of injustice. There is a common note in the gangster's brutality, the bully's gloating superiority, the hard ruthlessness of a man in power. That note is a note of contempt for the victims of injustice. Additionally, the basis of that contempt? Certainly, it cannot be on the grounds of humanity; even these men recognize that their victims are just as human as they are themselves. That contempt is always based on some extrinsic, accidental consideration as silly as the superiority a man feels looking down at the world from the back of a horse. The gangster is flooded with synthetic courage when he has a gun in his hand or dope in his arm; the bully's stout heart is fed on the fear of his victim; the powerful man can look with scorn on the rest of men because he has wealth to abuse, claims membership in a special nation, a particular party, or because he has a representative position in a state -- all of which give him an opportunity to oppress others.

A denial of the fundamental character of society

Could anything be madder than this? To deny one's own mastery, to cast off one's own sole claim to self-respect, and with this denial to destroy the basis upon which society tests, then, lest there be any doubt of the matter, to confirm these denials by the destruction of others -- reason can find no ground for this sort of thing. Its correlative is no less mad, i.e., the construction of our house of pride on the frail foundations of power or the means to oppress others; the foundations of man's life are not to be destroyed by a half-hour of seasickness or an attack of indigestion. What this really amounts to is a self-condemnation to a life of narrow, withered, inhuman horizons. It is a man's denial of humanity to man.

Social insanity

It is not exaggeration, but charitable understatement, to describe injustice as social insanity. In fact it is a little too kind, for we feel pity for lunatics. Sometimes this social insanity takes a homicidal form; there pity must surely stop, for then it has the ruthless violence and sly cunning peculiar to the insane with all the cool deliberation of a man in full command of his faculties. Still, pity has not stopped. Rather it has gone the lengths of discarding with contempt the sacredness of human life and of seeing in murder the innocence of a guileless child, the courage of a martyr, the sweet smile of a compassionate friend. In such terms do we think of abortion, suicide, euthanasia, and so on. Yet, we shall come back to these things later. For the moment, let us set the record straight by examining the nature of killing in itself.

Killing in general

It must be understood that it is not life, but *human life* that is sacred. This is important if we are to escape the menace of the double mistake induced by current philosophies of materialism. It may not be so strange that materialism should mistake the bottom rung of the ladder for the top; but it is pitiful that the illusion should be so complete as to enable it to break its neck by falling off the bottom rung. This double mistake comes from a denial of any specific difference between man and the animals. Obviously, if no animal life is sacred, then there is nothing sacred about the life of a man; or, proceeding in the other direction, if man's life is sacred, then all life is sacred. These are the two extremes of brutal contempt for, and sentimental mooning over, all living things.

The latter mistake is now very, very old. It was not young when it furnished the material for some of the earliest of heresies; and that was long ago. It was refuted back in the very beginnings of the Church by the simple truth of the profession of the Apostles; they were anglers and it was as true then as it is now, that a man cannot fish for years without killing a fish, or at least hoping to kill a fish. If we are to insist that a fish has a right to its life, then we must insist that a fish has the same mastery of his life as has a man; it is only on the grounds of mastery, of dominion, that we can possibly conceive of right. It is his liberty, responsibility, his ability to use things that lies at the root of man's possession of rights.

Just as indubitably, as man has rights, irrational creation has no rights. It is no sin to use a creature for the end intended by nature. Throughout all of nature the inferior creature exists For the superior; the grass is not violated by the cow, rather it fulfills the end for which it was made.

This is not by any means a license for brutality; a man cannot use animals in any way that pleases him. Accidentally the killing, or even the abuse, of an animal can be sinful. Accidentally! That is, by such actions, a man violates the rule of reason; he is doing a senseless, disgusting thing. He is not using animals for the ends of nature, i.e., for the good of man, he is wantonly, viciously abusing a creature of God. The thing is, in itself, a convincing sign of viciousness. As a violation of reason, it is a positive contribution to an increase in disorderly appetite. There is no reasonable basis for cruelty to animals, not because the animals have rights, but because there can never be a justifiable basis for a violation of reason, for a senseless action. The question of the justice or injustice of killing enters in only where there is a question of a right to life, that is, in the human field where alone it is possible for right to exist. Within that field, the obvious place where human right to life can be questioned is in the case of the criminal, the sinner; for, as Thomas says, "The sinner is much worse than a wild animal. and does much more damage." By his sin, he discards his human dignity as an unpleasant garment, makes himself a slave to sin, and puts himself in the class of irrational creation.

Public and private execution of criminals

Now, it is not on these grounds that St. Thomas will allow the execution of criminals. Rather it is on social grounds. The criminal is a corrupt member of the social body, to be cut off for the health of the whole as a gangrenous foot of a diabetic is amputated to save his whole body. Nor does this make the criminal a kind of martyr for the common good; he is an enemy of society whose attack is repulsed even at the cost of his life.

It would be a strange society, indeed, in which a man, sure of his own justice, could stroll out after dinner and shoot down a few sinners. The nicest thing about such a society would be that it would soon simmer down to just one man -- the best shot. As a matter of fact, there is no open season on criminals. A Klu Klux Klan or a Vigilantes committee, executing justice independent of authority, has no justification; no individual, or group of individuals, has a right to execute a criminal, even though he is beyond all doubt guilty. Execution is a social remedy for a social disease; it is an act in defense of society and so proper to him who acts for the whole of society. Moreover, this very defense of society works an injury to the integrity of society in causing the death of one of society's members. On both counts, of authority and injury to society, it exceeds the powers of any private person. By this right of self-defense, public power is not at all put in the position of fanatical reformers who maintain that right is tight, and must be done regardless of consequences. As a matter of fact, consequences may make right very wrong indeed. Public power is not a bloodhound, existing to track down all sinners; its execution of the criminal is for the common good, for the safeguarding of the health of the whole. The ideal to which public authority looks is the patient wisdom of the divine regime, which often lets the cockle grow, lest tearing it up the wheat also be uprooted.

Suicide

Unfortunately, patience seldom wrings cheers from the crowd. It is not too easy for men to see the stout heart that beats in the man who endures; in fact, paganism went so far in the other direction as to see the supreme example of a stout heart in the man who quits the suicide. The alleged heroism of the suicide has become a kind of dogma that only the irreverent challenge. Of course the spy kills himself to protect the secrets of his country; the military traitor is presented with a pistol, locked in a room, to do "the honorable thing"; the drunken husband is expected to take himself off in favor of the worthy, patient lover of his wife. Apparently it has not occurred to us that the spy might simply keep his mouth shut, the traitor repent the betrayal of his country and take his punishment, and the drunkard give up drinking.

The sane clarity of the Christian view refuses to become confused in such a fog of sentiment. We cannot mistake softness and cowardice for the strong virtue of fortitude. Suicide is the act of a man who admits utter defeat, of a man in despair, of a coward, of one who is afraid to face life. In a way, it is a species of sneak-thievery. No man is lord of his life; he merely has the administration of that life. The destruction of that life on his own responsibility is an injustice to the Lord of life, to God; it is an injustice to the community, of which the suicide is a part; and it is gravely against his serious obligation of charity towards himself.

The champions of suicide allege reasons that drip altruism: remorse, failure disgracing his family, fear of sin, or violation of body. This poor man's family needed the help of his insurance; this other recognized himself as a general nuisance and simply rid the community of that nuisance. Of course, none of these is valid; it is never permissible to do murder that good might come; that the particular murder is cowardly neither justifies nor ennobles it.

Direct suicide must always stand condemned as evil, for human life is a sacred thing; but even human life is not so precious that it may not be lost in the fight for more precious things. Even where the immediate goals sought are not so exceedingly precious, compared to life, if they are sufficiently grave and honest, life may be risked for them. A man may sacrifice his life in warding off failure; a woman may resist to the death or attempt to walk along a ledge fifty stories above the street to escape criminal attack. The chances may be a thousand to one in favor of her crashing to death, for not every woman has had circus training; but she is entirely justified. The difference from suicide, in these cases, lies in the fact that here death is a by-product; it is not the goal of the act. Where the end is honest and the reason sufficiently grave, such by-products can be justified.

Throughout all this discussion, the central and fundamental truth has been the sacredness of human life. It is an important truth in an age where the brutality of materialism is throwing off more and more of its disguise every day. So sacred is human life that no public authority, no private person, can for any reason directly kill an innocent man.

Killing of the innocent

There is a profound significance in the fact that this fundamental truth is so seriously challenged today; challenged, you understand, not in a classroom or a letter to the editor, but in the concrete actions of governments and men. Such a challenge is the execution of hostages as a means of holding off an enemy, or the killing of an innocent but influential person whose death has been demanded by the military authority of the enemy: all this in the name of the common good. On the personal side there is the mercy killing calculated to relieve a man of his suffering, the painless killing of the hopelessly wounded, of the old, the misfit, the insane, social nuisances. The argument even includes an unborn child that the mother's life be saved. All this is murder. The smooth, somniferous length of the words we use to describe it -- liquidation, euthanasia, mercy killing, solicitude for suffering mothers -- does not destroy the ugliness of murder.

Murder is its hideous, loathsome self no matter what name we give it. Society can kill in self-defense. Still, surely the man who violates no rights is not attacking society, nor is he an unjust aggressor threatening the life or property of any individual citizen. He is innocent and his life is sacred.

Killing of aggressors

We have seen earlier in this chapter that it would be a strange society where every self-justified man could execute anyone who did not measure up to his idea of goodness, a strange society that could not endure. It would also be a strange society in which all men followed the gentle Christ's example and invitation to turn the other cheek to an aggressor; a strange society, but one that could endure and with such peace, harmony and happiness as to crowd the outer fences of the universe with astonished angels, anxious to see for themselves. However, Christ's invitation was to the very strong; few men are as strong as that, strong enough to be perfect. Nor does Christ demand the heroic from non-heroic men; not all citizens have to turn the other cheek. They may defend their rights, even to the extent of killing the attacker of those rights.

This is another case of death being a by-product of a legitimate act -- the defense of one's rights. If the intention is good, i.e., not the death of the aggressor but the defense of right, and if there is a sufficiently grave reason the killing of an aggressor is justifiable. Among reasons sufficiently grave for such an action, we might mention defense of one's life, of physical integrity against mutilation, of property, and so on.

However, the act must be one of actual defense of protection of rights that are being violated. We have no right to ambush a burglar and shoot him down because we have heard he is going to rob us the day after tomorrow. Nor can we put a bullet in his back a week after he has successfully looted our home. It would be unjust caution that would move a woman to poison a man she suspects of having dishonorable intentions. As a matter of fact, when a blow on the head of the attacker will protect our rights, we have no right to fire a cannon ball at him; for this act must be not only actual defense, but defense only, i.e., no more force must be used than is necessary for our protection.

It is to be insisted on that the question of self-defense hinges upon violated rights, not on the guilt or innocence of the one violating those rights. The term "unjust aggressor" is not a description of the state of a man's soul but a statement of the objective character of what he is doing. He may be a lunatic incapable of sin; but he is still an unjust aggressor for the thing he does is unjust, even though by reason of his incapacity, it is not done unjustly. In other words, as we pointed out in the preceding chapter, the medium of justice is an utterly objective thing.

Of course, this does not justify the strange reasoning that finds the unborn child an unjust aggressor against its mother because it too, like the lunatic, is innocent of all crime. At least that is the only common bond between the two, their innocence; certainly the child is violating no rights. It is fairly obvious that while every one has a right to life, there are superior duties before which this right must give way; the right to life is indeed a sacred thing, but not so supreme a thing as to justify the scuttling of every other consideration, for physical life is by no means the ultimate value in the human or moral order.

Mutilation

With that limitation of force well in mind, we can insist that it is not only man's life that is sacred; his whole being is sacred. The power that can, in self-defense, proceed against so sacred a thing as his life, can also take action on a lesser scale against its attackers. If society can kill a man for a crime -- and it can -- then obviously it can mutilate him for the same cause; it can pluck out his eye, cut off his ear, or even sterilize him. Now, all these must be punishments; that is, they must he inflicted by public authority, for the common good and *only* for a crime. To sterilize the feeble-minded or the poor is an example of that social insanity which is injustice. These men are innocent of all crime. Yet there is a terrifying indication of how close we are to insanity in the fact that a law for the sterilization of the feeble-minded actually exists on the books of the majority of our States.

The thing is a violation of the fundamental rights of man, of the fundamental sacredness of his being, of rights, which the man himself cannot relinquish. Even if the victim be willing, such mutilation cannot be committed; a doctor performing an operation to sterilize an innocent man, whether at the behest of the man himself, other individuals, or a nation, is violating justice; he inflicts an injury on the individual and on society. This right, of a specific nature, cannot be denied, for a man cannot deny his own nature. The amputation of an arm or a leg to save a man's life is, of course, an altogether different thing; it does no hurt to society and actually saves the individual. Nevertheless, it is worth noting that, however poor a thing the leg or arm may be, if the owner of it wants to keep it no one has any right to take it away from him. There is an implicit recognition of this truth in the hospital practice of insisting upon an explicit permission to proceed with an operation, and an implicit denial in the much-publicized cases of a state or city government stepping in to order an operation on a child over the protests of its parents.

Beating

The bodily injury involved in execution and mutilation, implying as it does an injury to society, can be inflicted only by the state, and then by way of punishment. It is not a power that a governor can give away like passes to the theater; it cannot, for example, be extended to fathers in relation to their children, or to masters in relation to their servants. However, the limitations of execution and mutilation do not reach to the corporal punishment involved in such a thing as a spanking; for this latter does not affect the integrity of the body, but only the sense of pain.

There have been many brutal cases recently of moronic, parents beating children to the point of positive mutilation. This is madness; and it rightly arouses intense and immediate indignation. All the same, within proper limits, the pain of such a thing as a spanking can be inflicted on subjects by way of punishment, not only by the state, but also by parents and masters; for children are subject to their parents, servants are subject to their masters. Understand, however, the question here is not one of the advisability of spanking in general, advanced, as a challenge to modern psychology; but rather it is a question of the justice of corporal punishment. St. Paul himself admitted there were spankings and spankings, when he warned parents against punishments that would break the spirit of their children. St. Thomas puts the question of the value of spanking to one side; he had had a strong-minded mother. He limits himself to the question of justice; and it is important to notice that he solves the question on the basis of authority, and on that basis alone. It is only by reason of their authority over their children that parents have a right to punish them. Almost everyone (with the possible exception of the, parents) will agree that the sticky-fingered child who climbs into strangers' laps on a train could well stand a little punishment. According to St. Thomas, the proper procedure in such a case would be to approach the respective parent and present the case in some such words as these: "Madam, will you please give me permission to give Agnes the spanking of her life?" or "Mr. Jones, would you mind if I gave your pretty child a few clouts on the ear?" In other words, the stranger has no jurisdiction over these children, so he cannot punish them.

As a matter of fact, we cannot even lock a child up to give the neighborhood a few hours of peace; for incarceration affects the corporal goods of man as do mutilating and beating. True, it does not, necessarily, injure the integrity of the body, nor inflict pain; but it does limit man's movement and the use of his body. There is, however, an interesting difference between incarceration and the other forms of bodily punishment, a difference that was brought out clearly by the police of Paris a few years ago.

Imprisonment

At that time, Communistic agitation was running high in Paris and May first was rapidly approaching. At the last moment, some high police official hit upon a simple solution: he would prevent trouble on May first by the effective expedient of putting all known Communists in jail on April thirtieth. The plan was carried out with complete success; Paris, on May first was as sleepily peaceful as a summer day in Avignon, for not a single Communist was out of jail in all of Paris. In this case, incarceration was used, not as a punishment for a crime already committed, but as a precaution against possible, even probable future disturbance of the peace to the detriment of the common good. Evidently, the state cannot cut out a man's tongue for fear of what he may say against the government; nor can it kill a man who may some day lead a rebellion. Now, it has, with no violation of justice, imprisoned men for forty-eight hours for fear of their starting a riot. The difference is that this imprisonment was not inflicted by the power of the state to punish a crime, but by the exercise of the state's rights to command the external acts of a citizen, and consequently to prohibit them, at least for a time, in order to the common good.

Social insanity's attack on property

Over and above the personal natural rights a man has to his life and the integrity of his body, he has other rights essential to his individual and social life. One of these is under particularly heavy fire today: the right to private property. The attack is theoretical and complete on one side in its demand for complete state ownership; on the other it is concrete and terribly effective, rendering more and more men propertyless, indeed even going so far as to wipe out the very desire for property, as happens when the direction of taxation is such as to render private property a burden rather than a help.

Now if it is true that man has a natural right to property, such attacks threaten the foundations of society, as do the other attacks on man's natural rights. What is this particular right and where did it come from?

Liceity and necessity of private property

We have it on the authority of faith that man's right to possess things as his own comes from nature itself. Let us look into that more closely from the philosophical side. Perhaps we can understand it better if we keep in mind that there are two branches of the family of natural rights: one in the direct line from natural law, the other in the collateral line. The first is made up of positive demands of nature; the second follows from nature immediately with no other intermediary than reason itself recognizing a universal fact and concluding from the fact and a direct command of natural law. This may sound decidedly complex; but then the process of boiling water, simple as it is, looks frightening in the form of an analysis. What all this complexity means in this particular case is not difficult to grasp. Natural law does not positively command that all things be possessed in common, just as it does not command nudism; nor does it command that all things be privately owned, just as it does not command that all men wear clothes. Yet, reason immediately concludes from the contingent facts of the world and a direct principle of the natural law, that private property is necessary for man, somewhat as it concludes that clothes are necessary for man. In other words, the right to private property is a natural right of this second or collateral class, a right conferred by the jusgentium, the "law of nations."

Considering man strictly as an individual, it is clear that natural law demands directly and positively that he conserve his own life. This command is not only for today but also for tomorrow; it not only touches the present, it reaches out to the future. A man will grow old, get sick, be hurt in accidents, and if he is to conserve his life these things must be provided for; because he has the obligation to conserve his life, he has the right to the means necessary for that conservation. The fact, however, is that for men in general -- not for this or that individual, this or that small community, but for men in general -- private property, even capital or productive property, is an absolute necessity for the fulfillment of this obligation of self-preservation.

It is rare indeed that a man's concern for the present and the future is lessened by marriage. It still remains to be proved that two can live as cheaply as one; when it becomes a question of six, or eight, or ten eking out an existence, the proof becomes correspondingly difficult. As head of a family, a man must provide for his wife and his children in the future as well as in the present. If he can be sure of their food, clothes, shelter, and so on only as long as he is able to swing a pick-ax ten hours a day, obviously he cannot fulfill his obligations as head of the family.

Under the same conditions, he will have little time for Aristotle, the opera, or meditation. He may not want to attack culture as lustily as all this; but he has a direct obligation from natural law to perfect his mind, his will, his body, to perfect himself as a man. For progress in knowledge, virtue, health, the fact is that some private property is necessary, because some independence is necessary. As head of a family, he has the same obligations towards the perfection of his children. With the full force of natural law, then. man has the right to private property.

From the social point of view, this right is no less clear. Man has a direct obligation from natural law to live in society. Along with this direct command of natural law, there is the evident impossibility of life in society without private property; and, as a consequence, the conclusion of reason to the absolute necessity of private property, a command of the jusgentium.

Today the impossibility of social life without private property is not readily admitted, although it is difficult to understand why this should be so. The immediate end of the state is such internal and external peace as will give men the opportunity of working out their individual perfection, a peace that is obtained by the official and orderly guarantee of the necessities of life, by harmonious regulation of the civil life of the citizens and by protection from external enemies. All this is by direct command of the natural law. One who thinks all this can be done by holding all property in common must have spent his life in solitary confinement; certainly, he is possessed of an incredibly naive ignorance of men.

Men, taken not as they should be but as they are, are distinctly disinclined to labor for what does not pertain to them; they show no ability to move as a mob to widely different, constructive ends; and they do quarrel constantly over their *de facto* possessions here and now. Universalize those conditions and you have made social life impossible.

There can be little question, in the face of the facts, of the difference between the efficiency and solicitude a man gives to the care of his own things and the indifference he betrays in his care of what belongs to the community, or to no one at all. The pet cat and his cousin, the alley cat, lead vastly different lives; public parks, at least in America, are untidy hoydens while private gardens haven't a seam crooked or a hair out of place. Private bank accounts received a much greater share of worry from the citizens than the Federal budget. These are facts.

It is asking too much to hope for quiet order in a community if, for instance, everyone has the right to a dentist's office and his dental tools; if a man has no more right to his bank today than to his neighbor's farm tomorrow; or if every man is to supply his needs in any way and in any place that pleases him. Again, peace is impossible where everything belongs to everybody and nothing to an individual. For men, as they are, will not agree with sweet serenity on the use of these common goods at this particular time. If the family clothes are held in common, an interesting situation arises when two sisters begin their long preparations for the same party; fortunately, the affair is private. In the face of facts like these, universal facts, along with the necessity man has of living in society, there is a positive obligation to divide property into personal possessions.

To put all this briefly: the possession of private property is licit (i.e., not forbidden) directly by the natural law itself; but the necessity for private property is directly commanded by the jusgentium, that is, a direct principle of natural law, side by side with universal contingent facts, forces human reason to this intermediate conclusion. Men, as they are, simply cannot live, as individuals or as social beings, without private property.

Secret attack on property -- theft

An attack on this right to private property is an attack on society. The large theoretical attack of philosophers, propagandists and social theorists is, in fact, much more deadly than the concrete attack made by a pickpocket in extracting a man's wallet from his pocket. The first is a general attack aimed at society as such; the second is a particular attack aimed at one citizen, and only through him at the peace of society. Of course, if all men turn to picking pockets for a livelihood, not even shortening of the working day will save society from destruction.

Now that we have been introduced to a pickpocket, it might be well to get better acquainted. He has his points; at least, in some sense, he is a thoughtful, flattering fellow. He leaves his victim in blissful ignorance of his loss, at least for the moment. In addition, he pays his victim the flattering compliment of fear. To appreciate these good points, we must look at a burglar. The pickpocket is a sneak thief; but the burglar uses force to gather in his loot. In; other words, the burglar cares nothing for even the momentary happiness of his victim and has a thorough contempt for the victim's power of resistance; he has arrogated to himself something that belongs only to the state, that is, coercive power. Overall, the burglar is a very unpleasant fellow.

In treating of this matter of theft, we must deal with the puzzling case of the theft, which is really not a theft. All Catholic theologians admit that a man, to maintain his life, can legitimately take the goods that are held by another. Of course, this right is strictly limited. It must be a question of extreme necessity, and a man must take only enough to relieve his extreme necessity, not enough to keep him in luxury the rest of his life. Moreover, he must not reduce the individual from whom he takes these things, to the same extreme necessity from which he extracts himself. This is really not theft at all; this man has not taken what belongs to another, he has merely taken what belongs to him.

The confusion of the case is cleared up if we remember that the root of man's right to things of the world lies in his ability to use things; and that is, at the same time, the limitation of his right. Things have not been delivered over to him absolutely; nature has given them as a means to be used in attaining his goal. God alone has absolute dominion. Man, then, has a natural right to the use of creatures beneath him as a means to his goal; that this or that particular thing belongs to this man for his particular use is dependent on the determination of positive civil law. The extreme necessity of one man brings about a clash, or rather an apparent clash, between a positive right and a natural right; of course, the natural right wins in such a battle, for the positive right simply disappears. No positive law can oppose, destroy or uproot the natural law.

Social insanity's attack on the instruments of justice: Favoritism

When social insanity invades the government itself, the citizen is in a desperate way. He is in the position of a man who set out to buy a police dog to protect his home, and returns leading a wolf on a leash. The government exists to protect the rights of the citizen and to minister to his needs; when, instead, it violates those rights, it leaves its helpless victim naked and wounded by the roadside, the victim of organized injustice.

It may seem touchingly human for a president to name an attorney general because he likes the man's smile or to exempt his political friends from the boredom of paying taxes. Actually, such a thing is decidedly inhuman for it is a violation of distributive justice; it is an obvious attack on the rights of citizens, an attack that goes by the name of favoritism. The state, through its officials, is obliged to distribute honors, burdens, rewards and helps on grounds of strict justice.

In such cases, corruption has crept into government; and corruption is rarely a static, localized thing. It spreads quickly, silently, with devastating effect, from executive positions into the legislature. Here it will take such forms as legislation favoring or penalizing one class or one section of a country; in other words, it will be legislation working for particular, selfish ends against the common good. No society can stand up long under such mad attacks. Even so, the most devastating damage is done by the corruption of social insanity when it eats its way into the judiciary and the judicial processes. After all executives are changed from time to time; many laws are written on the books and do no more than gather dust; but the judicial processes are continuous, immediately effective, concrete. These processes are the digestive apparatus of society that process of elimination and assimilation must be completely dependable or society is in a bad way very quickly.

Injustice in the courts: Injustice of a judge

A corrupt judiciary leaves a slimy trail of bitterness, anger and despair; and must eventually result in private execution of justice. A judge does the tremendously important work of putting the law to work. He is a public, not a private person; he exercises coercive power on citizens and, by his decisions, gives what St. Thomas calls "private law", i.e., a concrete judgment with the full force of law. Our interest in a law may easily be detached, unbiased, academic; but a judgment will bring us roaring to our feet, as philosophizing drops like a forgotten book from our lap.

The fact that he is a public person does not mean that the judge has no private life; but it does mean that in his judgments he must not act as a private person. His private knowledge of the sanctity of Miss Jones cannot be used to save her from the electric chair when the evidence shows she poisoned the barber for ruining her hair. His decisions must be based on his public knowledge; that is, on the knowledge he has from the law, from the witnesses, from the instruments of the trial. He may insist on a stricter examination of the evidence, because of his private knowledge of the guilt or innocence of this particular person; but it must be on the evidence that he decides his case. He can, and indeed, he should, feel very sorry for the culprit; and this latter may be positively extravagant in his promises to be good in the future. Now, here an injury has been done to another citizen, and to society; the law that demands punishment is the voice of society, it is not the private product of this particular judge. He is no more than the instrument of justice.

The judge occupies a precarious position, delicately balanced. He is not an accuser, nor is he a defender; he is the impartial figure of strict justice; a position extraordinarily difficult for any man to maintain. It is true that in criminal cases, he should favor the one who is accused; but this is by reason of his very impartiality, for a man remains innocent of crime until he is proved guilty, he has a strict right to his good name, to his liberty, and so on. These rights must not be taken from him until he is proved, with a moral certitude, to have forfeited them by definite crime. In a civil case, the matter is a little different; here he judges according to the greatest probability, but again this is no more than maintaining his attitude of strict justice.

It takes little imagination to see what damage can be done to society by the ignorance, prejudice, cowardice, greed or ambition of a judge. His work is difficult and dangerous. For the victim of unjust judgment there is one instrument of defense in the knowledge that a certainly unjust judgment does not bind him in conscience. However, that weapon is so small, so frail, so pitiably individual, the more so since it is coupled with the knowledge that even such a judgment must be abided by if there is any danger of scandal or disturbance of the public peace. In other words, this man is forced back upon the meager resources of individual action, whereas he should be enjoying the rich benefits of social action; he is obliged by his conscience to think always in reference to the common good, whereas this fanatic who has judged him is limited by no other thought than his own selfish interests.

Of course, the judge does not have to bear the whole brunt of injustice in the judicial process. Our own times have made it fairly clear that others can corrupt justice in spite of an honest judge; in fact, anyone connected with the judicial process -- accuser, witnesses, lawyers -- can be the means of introducing the note of social insanity into this social act that should be so eminently sane. Let us glance at these other members of the troupe, which performs in the courtroom.

Unjust accusation

It is not necessary to call out the national guard every time you see a boy stealing an apple. Most modern laws make provision for formal accusation by public officials whose office was created for this particular purpose. Still, a private person may have a serious obligation of denouncing a crime: of counterfeiting, for example, which threatens the common good; or when it is a matter of averting grave damage to an individual, as when the uproar next door indicates that murder is about to be done. In other words by doing nothing more than putting an extra bolt on the door a private person may be guilty of injustice; he makes a more thorough job of it by accusing another of crime falsely, by covering up crime in collusion with the defendant, by losing evidence, admitting invalid arguments, false testimony of witnesses and so on, or even by getting chicken-hearted at the last moment and withdrawing from a case that should be prosecuted.

Injustice in the accused

The citizen is carrying his civic virtue pretty far when he goes to the length of setting bloodhounds on his own trail; no man is obliged to accuse himself. Indeed, among the peoples of our western civilization it is universally agreed that the accused man does not have to confess his guilt, if he is under no obligation in this regard, of course no force can be used to obtain such a confession. The, reason is fairly evident. Secrets are not the proper matter for public judgment, which deals properly with external acts; and if this man's confession is necessary for conviction, certainly his crime is a secret thing. Then too a man must be considered innocent until he is proved guilty, for he has a right to his good name.

Both of these grounds were defended by St. Thomas, but in his time, there were circumstances, which obliged a man to confess his guilt. If, for instance, he had already lost his good name by some crime, there was no danger of injury to his name. If express indications made his guilt apparent, or if that guilt were already half proved, Thomas held that in all these cases a refusal to confess guilt was a sin. The thing is important for it lies behind the medieval use of torture as an instrument of trial. It was only in these cases, where refusal to confess was sinful, that torture could be used; it was argued, that in these cases there was no violation of man's rights in demanding that he admit his crime.

An accused man has a right to every legitimate means of defense. Courtrooms frown on name-calling as undignified and, as a matter of fact, it is a decidedly ineffective defense. Now, name-calling in the modern way of destroying the character of witnesses by false accusation goes far beyond a violation of etiquette; the thing is vicious, unjust, an absolutely illegitimate means of defense. Once a just judgment has been passed, there is no longer any question of legal defense for the condemned man. He cannot argue that he has slugged the guard or shot the judge in self-defense; such resistance constitutes an attack upon the community. He must undergo his sentence. Even so, that does not mean that he has to inflict the penalty on himself; he does not have to pay his own carfare to prison, he does not have to keep himself in jail. That is the work of society; if the opportunity to escape from jail offers itself, the prisoner is not violating justice in taking his leave without consulting the warden. The unjustly condemned man is in a different situation. If his unjust sentence is the result of defective form in the trial or through lack of evidence, he can defend himself, even with violence, against the officers of the state. He is the victim of unjust attack; he is not obliged to submit to that attack unless, in a particular case, there are extrinsic reasons that make it necessary for him to sacrifice his own private goods, such, for instance, as the danger of serious damage to the common good.

Injustice in witnesses

The comely witness, who lies with the grace and facility of long practice, may not have influenced the jury so much by her testimony. Nevertheless, her glib falsehoods have all been charged with a triple spiritual death for her own soul. The witness chair has no value as an alibi for a lie; and since testimony is now seldom given without an oath, it forms an excellent perch for the vulture of perjury. The lying witness then commits a triple sin: of perjury, of lying and of injustice.

Obviously, this business of acting as witness is serious. In fact, it is a business that most of us would gladly escape. Just when are we obliged, in spite of our distaste, to occupy that uncomfortable chair? Well, the obligation is one of charity when our testimony, as private persons, is necessary to avoid damage to our neighbor or to the common good. It will be one of commutative justice if our office entails such testimony; a burly detective, for instance, cannot become kittenish at the thought of facing all those strange faces. It can be one of legal justice when our testimony is demanded by a legitimate judge.

Even if we are obliged to testify, we need not empty out our minds as we would an old purse, turning it inside out. There are some things about which testimony simply cannot be given. The district attorney who would hammer away at the priest, trying to uncover something that was told in confession, is wasting his time. The priest knows these things, not as a man, but as a minister of God; the knowledge is God's and the priest cannot use it. Ordinarily the things learned by doctors, lawyers and so on in their professional capacities cannot be the matter of testimony; these are natural secrets, and it was with this understanding that they were told to these professional men.

However, these professional secrets have nothing like the inviolability of the seal of confession. Sometimes they may be revealed; and sometimes they must be revealed. A doctor, who knows that a mid-wife is constantly procuring abortion, would be obliged to offer testimony to that effect in order to avoid grave evil to the common good; indeed, even where it is not a question of the common good, but of serious damage to an individual, or to the doctor himself, he is not bound to hide these natural secrets.

Secrets are only a small part of the things that need not be testified to. Much of the confusion in this matter comes from the fact that often only a sickly ray of the sun of common sense can fight its way through the dust of a legal library. While it may pain the attorney, it seems obvious that a witness does not have to do himself grave damage by giving testimony, nor give testimony to the injury of a close relative; a father, for example, can refuse to testify against a son. Obviously, we do not have to testify at the command of a judge who has no jurisdiction, nor reply to a judge or a lawyer asking questions not pertinent to the trial in hand. It also seems nothing more than common sense that the detective who has tapped a private phone line or the bored postmistress who has steamed open letters should not be obliged to testify in these matters, for both have obtained their knowledge by injuring others. The milkman, who, on his early morning rounds, has seen a drunken man kill another, can legitimately avoid giving testimony if there is no danger of damage to a third party; for here too, there is no serious question of protecting the common good or vindicating justice, for the drunken man was obviously irresponsible.

Perhaps it would be well to sum all this up. If a man is not summoned by the judge, he is nevertheless obliged to give testimony to save a man from unjust execution, from serious penalty, from the loss of his good name, or from serious damage; a just proportion always being observed between the damage he is trying to avert and the damage he himself will incur. If this testimony is not demanded by a legitimate superior, then a man is obliged in charity to do what he can to bring out the truth; but if his testimony will contribute to the condemnation and consequent execution of another rather than to saving him, then no one is obliged to offer testimony, though that testimony can be required in justice by a superior.

Injustice in lawyers

St. Thomas knew enough about lawyers to be sure they were as weak as other men. They too might become negligent and handle a case carelessly, might let a professional secret slip, use some unjust means to escape from a dangerous situation, or prolong a case to swell the fee. All these are distinctly possible injustices; but they are also distinctly obvious. Thomas neglects them to concentrate on the fundamental injustices that have a much more direct effect on society.

Thus, he insists that a lawyer may not knowingly defend an unjust civil case; if he does, he is not only carrying the burglar's tools, he is instructing him in the use of them. He may start in innocently enough, thinking the case is just, and later discover that it is, as a matter of fact, unjust; but his original innocence does not give him a license for robbery. True he is not obliged to help the opponent, nor to reveal the secrets manifested to him professionally; but he is obliged to give up his part in the case or to induce his client to withdraw the case. In other words, there is no limitation to the prohibition of partaking in an unjust civil case.

In a just civil case, the lawyer's defense of justice cannot be waged unjustly; he has no permission to lie. Yet, of course, he does not have to tell all he knows; in fact, he would be doing an injustice if he did not prudently withhold the things that would impede his case. In criminal cases, a lawyer may defend the accused man even when that man is certainly guilty; the guilt must still be juridicaly proved. On the other hand, a prosecuting attorney is guilty and bound to restitution when he wins the condemnation of an innocent person culpably; indeed, he is unjust when he pursues a trial after learning of the innocence of the accused, or after gravely doubting his guilt. Nor can he dodge the charge of injustice when he injures society by his lackadaisical exercise of his office.

This has been an unpleasant chapter. We might say it had some of the unpleasantness of hell about it; both hell and this chapter are crowded with sins and for all their gaiety, there is nothing more depressingly unpleasant than an empty-faced crowd of sins. Perhaps that is another clue to the unpleasantness of this chapter -- the fact that the eyes of sin are always so terribly blank, so completely unseeing; the lights have gone out behind these windows of the soul and they tell only the fearful message of darkness.

The same unnamed dread of unreasoning blindness is behind the horror that grips a visitor to an insane asylum. An insane man is one who is terribly blind and does not realize it; he is a man who acts against his very humanity. Sometimes it is the less violent insanity of sin, or again the openly violent insanity of mania. In both cases it is the surrender of control, of the foundation of the humanity of man's actions; the insane man attacks himself. The man, who is socially insane, living in society and depending on that society, as every man must, attacks the foundation, the reason for the existence of that society.

This social insanity goes by the very ordinary name of injustice; and it consists in attacks on the rights of man. For it is precisely because of the mastery of man, because of his possession of rights, that society is possible and is necessary.

Social sanity and human life; and human dignity

Social sanity looks upon the rights of man not as rivals to be destroyed, but as a solid foundation to be carefully preserved. To it, the life of man is sacred, above all human power: a thing to be challenged only in self-defense against the criminal, who has already forfeited his right to life. Nor is social sanity deceived by high-sounding terms or pseudo-scientific theories; euthanasia, mercy killing, justified abortion, sterilization may catch the fancy of the unthinking for a day or an hour. However, not very stable castles can be built on air; and the solid rock of social structures is the sacredness of man's life, the integrity of his body, his inviolable dignity as a sovereign being. Eugenics or social inferiority are not seasons for a violation of these things; they are excuses for the inexcusable.

A society that has begun to lose this reverence for man's personal life is a society that has become feeble-minded. When blood purges, murder, and mutilation become the order of the day, or even a part of legal procedure, society has gone mad; it is attacking itself. It no longer functions as a society.

Social sanity and private property

A disrespect for or lack of interest in man's right to private property is a serious threat, because social life cannot exist without private property. Like other natural rights, this one too is at the basis of society; it is, in fact, the concrete guarantee of another fundamental right, the right of human freedom. When a state has begun to look upon human individuals, not as persons, but as things, as slaves, as instruments of social perfection, then that society has gone mad. Social sanity insists that the state exists that men's lives be fuller, not that the state be gorged with the bodies and souls of men.

Social sanity and human freedom; and the instruments of social life

In all these cases, society is openly acting as the enemy of its members; it is feeding on its own body. Nor is the attack less mad when it adopts the disguise of friendship in government favoritism. Rather it is more dangerous because somewhat more subtle; but it is nonetheless a betrayal of the citizen by his government. The dastardly betrayal is complete when a government becomes corrupt in the very acts, which were meant to protect the rights of man and minister to his needs, the very instruments of government and justice. The citizen is being stabbed in the back by a friend who has gone insane.

Social sanity holds fast to a knowledge of both man and society; it does not surrender the principle of social control, because it does not give up its knowledge of man. Additionally, in the last analysis, it is man who is the measure of society, as well as its foundation and its goal. The defense of social sanity, then, will not be brought about in any other way than a last-ditch, desperate defense of the humanity of man.

CHAPTER IX

THE ESSENCE OF ANARCHY II
(Q. 72-80)

1. Universal contempt for pettiness
    (a) The fact.
    (b) its foundations -- the nature of man.
    (c) Pettiness and society.

2. Pettiness and anarchy.

3. Petty injustice in word:
    (a) Limitations of pettiness.
    (b) Insult.
    (c) Detraction
    (1) Thomistic and modern definitions
    (2) its nature
    (3) its comparative malice.
    (d) Whispering.
    (e) Derision.
    (f) Cursing.

4. Petty injustice in act:
    (a) In buying and selling:
    (1) Unjust price.
    (2) Defective goods.
    (3) Business as such.
    (b) Usury.

5. A contrast -- the wide embrace of justice:
    (a) Nature of the potential parts of justice
    (b) Their number and name: religion, piety,
observance, truth, gratitude,
        vindication, friendship, liberality.

Conclusion:

1. Two mistakes on petty injustice:
   (a) Too small to matter.
   (b) Too big for anything else to matter.

2. The conditions of life with others -- strength and largeness of soul:
   (a) Life of friendship:
   (1) With God.
   (2) With men.
   (b) Domestic life.
   (c) Social life.

3. Full essence of anarchy.

Universal contempt for pettiness

The normal response of the human soul to pettiness is a kind of nausea. Pettiness in human nature is as revolting as squalor in a hospital or laughter at a funeral. These two, humanity and pettiness, do not belong together; when we see them so we are scornful, contemptuous, even angry. We shrug off the victim of self-pity impatiently; the misery of the miser moves us to anger rather than pity. In addition, we can fully understand the indignation of the Scots at Sir Harry Lauder's constant quips about their penurious caution.

If taken at all seriously, such an accusation is far from comic. We do not have to hold our sides to keep from bursting with laughter when we see a husband or wife ready to scurry out of marriage at the first wave of misfortune; the victim of envy or jealousy must make a long, long search for sympathy; and the executive who counts the carbon sheets in the stenographer's desk need have no illusions about the stenographer's opinion of him.

Its foundations -- the nature of man

The fact is that man is too big to enjoy pettiness. Bigness is a part of the very make-up of man. By the design of infinite wisdom, he was made to bring all things into his mind and to carry his heart out to all things not to spend his time grubbing in the little plot of his own being. He was born, not to plunge into the swirling waters of the world and drown himself, but to stand aside from the world, even from himself, as the one spectator of the material universe. He was made for infinite variety. He was given the mastery of the universe, all other things being the tools by which he carves out an eternal destiny. He was made to give himself utterly to another, rather than to attempt to gather all things in the pitiful compass of his own hands.

On the other hand, smallness is a part of the irrational world, for that world is fenced in, determined to one narrow path. No creature in that world has an interest, knowledge, an ability outside of itself; it is a world incapable of using the rest of the world as its instrument, incapable of surrendering itself to anyone or anything. It is a small world in spite of its size, its power, its beauty and its ruthlessness. Man's nature has set him apart from this small world and given him something of the infinity of God. His actions, since he is made in the image of God, should be godlike; one of the divine characteristics that must stand out in the acts of a man, if he is to retain the respect of his fellows, is that of largeness, of wide horizons and far off goals. Indeed this characteristic is a condition for the maintenance of self-respect, for deep in his heart; every man is revolted at pettiness, even though the pettiness is his own.

Pettiness and society

The fundamental notions of society are really an insistence upon this greatness of man; nor is this surprising, since society is such an exclusively human thing, a thing that only men need and only men can have. There is, in the very notion of society, an open admission of our need for help, a big thing to come from a man. For society exists that man might live the full life of which he is capable, living with others, but incapable, living alone. At the same time, society is a statement of a willingness to give help to others, to pool capacities in order that all might live a more perfect human life. From both angles, pettiness is always an injury, and sometimes a serious threat, to the very notion of society. To admit the need of help and, at the same time, he willing to help others is the work of a creature who can get outside himself: he can stand aside from himself and see his own insufficiency: and he can see the world through the eyes of another, focusing his own vision to an impartial, even a sympathetic view.

Petty injustice is a deliberate campaign of injury, not of help. No matter how great an injury it may do, it is still petty in itself; it is an admission of defeat, of pique, of envy or jealousy. Violence, in general, is the work of a small soul unable to compete with the talents of another. The violence of petty injustice is the work of a craven soul, of a soul not only too small to compete with the talents of others, but even too small to risk the slightest injury or misfortune to itself in its very campaign of injustice to others.

We might say that this petty injustice takes two forms, apparently contrary, according to the particular angle at which a man looks at himself. In one case it puts up a pretense of pride, claiming its own self-sufficiency because a man is unable to stand outside himself and see himself truly; it is the result of a vision, so short that it never quite reaches to a man's own limitations. On the other hand, this petty violence may set up a constant wail for help, when a man looks at the world and is shocked, aggrieved that the rest of the world can see anything but him, that other men do not spend their time and energy thinking of him. This small soul is quite blind to the rights (let alone the needs) of others but cannot understand why the world should be so blindly cruel as to neglect him for an instant.

Pettiness and anarchy

It may seem a long jump from pettiness to anarchy. Nor does the gap look smaller when we remember that anarchy, etymologically, means "*without a head*." It calls up the dismal picture of jungle law let loose in a civilized community whose government, or head, has been cut off, the incongruous picture of a man thrashing about like a recently beheaded chicken, or the horrifying picture of a man who has lost control of himself, who has lost his head and has become a beast of prey. No, it still seems a long way from pettiness to anarchy; but brings the thing close to human life and the distance disappears.

We live in an age where the shambles of domestic groups are taken as much for granted as a shell hole in no-man's-land. This destruction is laid to cruelty, desertion, infidelity, the third angle of the triangle and so on. Perhaps, in a majority of cases, these alleged grounds are true. Nevertheless, does anyone seriously believe that the course of home life was running smoothly, peacefully, with love ruling supreme, sacrifice constant and generosity the ordinary thing, when one morning husband and wife awoke to discover that lightning had hit their home and cruelty, desertion and the rest were pouring through the hole in the roof?

It is conceivable that a home be broken up suddenly; but normally these big things that destroy a home can be traced back to the constant annoyance of very small things. A man, wrapped up in his business, forgets that his wife and children are human and need some attention, some thought. A wife, now that the excitement of the hunt is over allows her natural slovenliness to assert itself, as she appears at the breakfast table disheveled, unkempt, in a state that adds nothing to the tastiness of the cold toast. The husband may spend most of his time at home pitying himself: the wife may be addicted to tears; or either side may cultivate its will power by the constant nagging of the born reformer. They are little things but by their constancy, the big things come about. It is well to know the tremendous danger of these small things well too, to realize that they are the fruits of a small soul, the products of thoughtlessness, of selfishness, of discontent and self-pity. Now, they are at the root of domestic anarchy.

Considering the place the family must hold in society, this alone would be enough to establish the connection between pettiness and social anarchy. However, the direct connection is close enough in the purely social sphere. A revolution is not the work of a moment but the result of years. Society prepares for a revolution slowly, as steam is built up in a locomotive but this steam is applied to terribly destructive purposes when its inevitable explosion rips society to shreds.

Limitations of pettiness

It must be noted that the word pettiness, as descriptive of the type of injustice with which we shall deal in this chapter, must not be taken for a moral evaluation of this injustice. It expresses the contempt of men for this injustice; it is not a statement of its insignificance. It can be exceedingly grave; and its very gravity does not diminish but rather increases the well-earned contempt given it by men.

There is, for instance, the whole group of sins we include under the term "*sins of the tongue*;" the sins that we confess as uncharitable in a tone that says we know they were not particularly noble, but they are only offenses against charity; and who could blame us for a lack of love for these people? Out attitude is an implicit ignorance of the fact that we are violating justice by these sins we have not merely spoken "unkindly"; we have spoken unjustly, for we have refused others the rights that are theirs. We miss the obvious fact that Christ, commanding the kind word, or at least the kind silence, merely demanded that we refrain from molesting others, that for love of Him we leave others alone.

Insult

There are times when we can work up a kind of pride in these sins. when we boldly insult or revile a man, tell him to his face that he is a thief; taunt him with his deafness; upbraid him for his stupidity, his poverty, or with reminders of the favors we have done him--we claim a double justification. The things we said were true, and they were not said behind a man's back but to his face. Actually, is there a justification for the wounds left in a human heart, for the shame and embarrassment of another, for the loss of his good name with others, or even for our refusal to give the respect to which this image of God has a just claim? All of these sins are direct attacks on the honor and respect due to our neighbor. If our intention has been to dishonor him or refuse him respect, the sins are no less mortal than are theft and burglary, understanding, of remorse, that they can become venial when the matter of our insults is less grave.

We need not be surprised if, at one time or another, our insults explode in our face. Some people just will not take insults, while others will take just so many as a matter of fact, they do not have to submit to such reviling, any more than a man has to stand by meekly while his watch is stolen or his children kidnapped. He is within his rights in resisting an unjust aggressor and it may be the best thing in the world for a novice at the dangerous game of insulting others to discover that it is not always an easy avocation. If our resistance to insult has that fraternally charitable end of discouraging a too facile tongue, it is not only justified, it is praiseworthy. A man in authority, who must maintain that authority, or a man whose loss of honor would result in grave spiritual loss to others, is not only permitted, he may be obliged to resist insults. In both these cases the motive was not so much defense of one's own rights but the protection of the good of others normally we can be much surer of these stainless motives in protecting the honor of another, than we can in rushing to our own defense.

To see these sins as examples of boldness and courage is to blindfold ourselves as we approach a mirror. We are really afraid to look at them closely; if we do, we must see them as truly petty. They are an adult version of the little-boy trick of calling names: a gesture of helplessness, of impotent anger, of contempt. If we turn these sins to let strong light fall on their faces, we shall immediately recognize them as the offspring of stupidity they are the product of a mind paralyzed by anger, rushing madly to the handiest means of venting its passion upon another. Pride, of course, helpfully prepares us for sins of the tongue by keeping us well supplied with contempt for others in the admiration we have for ourselves. All the same, it is really the stupid blindness of anger that usually turns loose the flood of insults.

Although insulting words cut deep, they are superficial wounds compared to the gashes made by the words of a backbiter. An insult is an attack on the respect or honor due a person, i.e., on the external testimony of a neighbor's character. The backbiter digs deeper to attack the very reason for honor: he attacks the reputation or good name of a neighbor. This is a sly, deadly sin, this backbiting, and always committed secretly. It is a cowardly knife-thrust in the back, giving its victim no chance for self-defense: indeed, it is quite the ordinary thing for a victim of backbiting to be unaware of the attack until his good name is entirely gone.

Detraction Thomistic and modern definitions

Modern theologians distinguish between true and false backbiting, calling the first detraction, and the second, calumny. Still, St. Thomas, seeing both, as frequenters of the dark alleys of secrecy and assassins of reputations, makes no distinction. As the thing actually works out, backbiting is rarely limited to the truth, at least by the time it reaches its most deadly stage. I recall a case of backbiting that is an excellent illustration of this fact. A disgruntled mother was stopped by a cheery neighbor as she came out of Mass, just at the unfortunate moment when her mind was considerably disturbed by thoughts of her own somewhat meanly dispositioned daughter. The neighbor remarked happily on the attractiveness and popularity of one of the parish girls passing by. In a fit of spite, the disappointed mother remarked acidly: "*Well, there are some things much more important than popularity.*" The remark was absolutely true and hopelessly banal: it could be whispered in the most innocent ears or shouted from the highest pulpits. Now, it was the starting point of a chain of remarks that practically made an outcast of the innocent victim for at each repetition, more details were added as to what was more important than popularity and much more embroidery was painstakingly added to the original inference that this girl lacked these very important things.

Falsehood, the fitting accomplice of sly secrecy, permeates backbiting as the odor of decay permeates a swamp. It is true that we can ruin a good name by secretly telling unsavory truths, revealing secrets and so on. However, we can also make a boy's theft of a piece of candy sound like a bank robbery by a careful inattention to detail. We can declare ourselves actual witnesses of a murderous attack with an automobile when all we have seen is a friendly gesture of help to a stalled motorist on a cold morning. This sort of thing may demand some creative imagination and a good deal of craftsmanship: perhaps that is why there is something of an artist's pride in the completed masterpiece. Yet, it takes no genius and very little practice to accomplish backbiting without bringing our neighbor's sins into the matter at all: by brazenly denying his good points, maliciously guarding a silence on those good points or stopping the whole conversation cold by a frigid trickle of praise that drops from our lips with the slow reluctance of a drop of water from an icicle.

Sometimes an injury to another's name is necessary, as in the doctor's warning against an engagement to a person suffering from a contagious disease; in these cases, there is no question of sin. Very frequently, the empty-headedness of the prattler saves him from serious sin, for even sin demands some thought. In fact, there is a saving element in most of these sins of the tongue; they are so often slips, words that escape from our mouths so quickly that we cannot even grab the tail of the disastrous sentence. This is not something of which we can be proud, but at least it often indicates a complete lack of malice

Its comparative malice

Yet once the thing is done, injuries to reputation remain unjust, and seriously so, even though there was no malice on our part. Not so serious, perhaps, as murder destroying the life of a man, or adultery attacking his family and the very beginning of life but among the sins aimed against the external goods of man, detraction holds a top place. It is, for example, much worse than theft, for it robs a man of a much more valuable and personal thing than his wallet; but like theft, insults and backbiting demand restitution. They demand that we return to another the most precious of temporal things, a thing nearly impossible of returning -- a good name.

Whispering

A gossip, to be at her (or his) best, really needs cooperation. There is no more complete example of futile effort than a pair of gossips whose alternating silences are not the relaxed, docile attention of a listener, but the tense, eager, unheeding preparation of one waiting to go on the air. It is at least possible that gossip would decline sharply if the quota of listening could be curtailed. All the same, of course, there will always be some excellent listeners; nor do they have all the excitement of malicious gossip with none of the sin. The listener whose ears actually rise up at the first breath of gossip gives full consent to the talk and joins in the sin; so too does the person who could and should stop such unjust remarks. Now, the timid person, the negligent one, or the man who is ashamed to appear in the role of defender of a reputation is normally guilty only of venial sin.

One of the most serious and certainly one of the most contemptible forms of gossip is what St. Thomas calls "*whispering*," and what may be called, somewhat vaguely, tale bearing. It is a complete campaign whose chief objective is the destruction of friendship. In the eyes of Thomas, this was more serious than insult, detraction or calumny: for it is much more important to us that we be loved than that we be honored, while a friend is much more precious than a reputation. Men can live without honor, without a good name, but not without friends, for no man is sufficient unto himself.

Derision

In sharp contrast to the magnitude of whispering stands the pettiest of the sins of the tongue, the sin of mockery or derision. Do not be deceived by its air of jollity or its disguise of humor; it is a petty, vicious snob that considers the rights of others as so many coins to buy laughs. It is the sarcastic weapon of the negative wit. Insult and backbiting strip a man of the external rewards of virtue, honor and a good name, much as a bandit might strip a man of his clothes. Mockery saunters lightly into the house of the soul to rob a man of his intrinsic goods, his peace and self-respect. Its aim is to shame a man, to shatter him publicly that others might make sport of his shame. Christ was a victim of it when the taunts from Calvary echoed back from the walls of Jerusalem; nor has the satanic art been lost through the ages. Its modern masterpieces are government executed Jew-baitings.

The other sins of the tongue treat man's faults and weaknesses, whether real or fictional, with some degree of seriousness. Mockery makes sport of them, thus adding a stinging note of contempt. If the subject matter of our costly joke is only slight, then the sin may be venial; but if our contempt for our neighbor is so great that his sin and misfortunes strike us as merely material for a joke, then our sin is mortal, greater indeed than its fellow public performer -- insult -- for it contains more of contempt.

Mockery is an agile sin that runs up the ladder of gravity with a light-hearted step; it is rarely content to stop short of the top, for it has a reputation for wit to maintain and the strain of the upkeep is terrific. It becomes steadily graver as its victims have greater claim to reverence. Thus to mock a virtuous man and his virtues is more serious than mockery of a sinner, because virtue is man's fundamental claim to honor and a good name. In a society where this is widespread, a man may be seen at his sins, but he has to be caught at his virtues; he will keep them secret, or abandon them, for human nature has no relish for mockery. Mockery of parents is a step up the ladder; it is so revolting a robbery of the reverence due them that it is always a shock to spectators. Only in a depraved society does a laughing slash across the face of a parent win a laugh. We reach the heights of this sin when its victim is God; surely, when the divine claim to reverence is the butt of jokes, reverence is dead in the world and with it goes all pretense at respect for the dignity of man.

Cursing

This same proportional upswing of gravity is found in the sin of cursing, taking cursing, not in the vague, general sense of nasty or irreverent language, but strictly as the expression of evil to another by way of wish or command. As men have greater claim to our reverence and our love, we do them a greater injustice by cursing them.

As a matter of fact, all men have at least a minimum claim on our love and reverence; so no slightest degree of evil wished to men, precisely under the aspect of evil, is harmless. Obviously, it is against charity; and its execution is patently against justice. Nevertheless, notice that the evil must be willed under the aspect of evil. A judge, damning a man to prison, is not guilty of cursing; nor is the citizen who wishes for the speedy capture and execution of a notorious public enemy, that the peace of society might be preserved. The old Irish mother gives effective expression to her impatience when she exclaims: "*I wish the Lord had his soul*!" However, she is not cursing: rather she is seeing even her tormentors through the eyes of that divinely wise love that has worn smooth the hills of Ireland by its long, steady regard.

Cursing directed against God is blasphemy; against the irrational world, it is a waste of breath, for good or evil have no place, where necessity is king; against the devil, it is an attempt to gild the lily. More often than not, cursing is no more than a safety valve blowing off the steam of impatience and anger that have proved too much for a limited vocabulary.

Petty injustice in act: In buying and selling

Some time ago, *The Saturday Evening Post* came out with a cover that brought a chuckle from the nation. It pictured a tiny, meek, sweet-looking old lady looking across a swinging scale, at a butcher who looked as all good butchers should but rarely do. He was fat, good-natured and ruddy, as though he had frequently sampled his own products, all of them, and found them good. He was weighing a piece of meat, resting his hand, meanwhile, gracefully and unobtrusively on the edge of the scale. Both the butcher and his customer had their eyes fixed on the figures of the scale; the butcher with a look of astonishment and the sweet old lady with a smile of serene peace, for underneath the scale her index finger was more than offsetting the weight of the butcher's hand.

This sort of thing never happened; but we feel, somehow, that if it did happen we could enjoy it thoroughly. Our vicarious and fictional satisfaction focuses attention on petty injustice in one of its commonest forms, cheating, particularly cheating in the contract between buyer and seller. Perhaps it is because the average man is such a constant and gullible victim of the cheat that the "*besting*" of a swindler evokes such enthusiastic approval.

Unblushing fraud in buying and selling is clearly unjust and is properly and immediately condemned. After all this contract is a mutual thing, designed for the good of both parties; men are right in hotly resenting its open violation. Now, there are many less patent injustices that are not so heavily frowned on, that are even approved by constant practice. It is, for instance, petty injustice to charge forty dollars for a ticket to a football game -- yes, even for that game! The value of the ticket is by no means equal to the price demanded; the equality of justice has been disturbed and must be restored by repairing the damage suffered by the buyer.

Unjust price

It is argued, of course, that the ticket is worth that amount to the buyer here and now; he needs the ticket and cannot get it anywhere else. That sounds very plausible; but whose need is it? If it already belongs to the buyer, surely he cannot be charged for it, it cannot be sold to him. The seller cannot sell what is not his own; he can charge for the thing he is delivering to the buyer, but he cannot charge for the need under which the buyer labors. The case is altogether different if a man insists on buying my rubbers in the midst of a rainstorm. I am justified in adding to the price of the rubbers the price of a cold in the head, which I shall suffer, by the sale of the rubbers. I am not charging the buyer for his need, but for the damage that will come to me as a result of the sale. A woman, who sells a pet parrot worth five dollars for the price of ten, may be acting justly, charging the buyer for the damage done to her affections and the consequent loneliness of her life. A baseball magnate who would sell his franchise just before a world series is right in asking a higher price, charging to the buyer the loss of gain, which was involved in the sale. In all these cases, the seller is charging for something that is intimately his, not for the need of the buyer.

Defective goods

When we discover that the goldfish we bought at a fire sale looks something like a smoked herring, we should not feel surprised or indignant. That is why we got it so cheap. Obviously, the intrinsic worth of a thing is lessened by its defects; as the worth goes down, so must the price, for the price is primarily the measure of the intrinsic value of a thing. Even so, there are some defects that rule out the question of any price at all. The confidence man who sells glass for a diamond offers material with a *specific* defect; the grocer who gives short weights puts a defect of *quantity* in the matter of the sale: the horse-trader, who sells a blind horse as sound, sells a horse who suffers from a defect of *quality*. Yet, all three agree in selling something that does not exist; they are all bound to restitution, for they have in their possession something that is not theirs, the money for which they have not given value.

The same holds true of a buyer who, by some strange accident, buys a real diamond at a ten-cent store for the usual dime; or who gets too much change from a cab driver. In these cases, the defect is not in the goods; it is on the other side of the contract, a defect in price. Of course, restitution is strictly obligatory. It may happen that the seller of poor goods does so innocently; the butcher, for example, who sells corrupt meat thinking it is good, has committed no sin, no deliberate injustice. Yet the thing is unjust; he has money that does not belong to him and it must be returned to its rightful owner. The advance of science might easily confuse the issue here. Science has been able to produce a substitute that looks like butter, acts like butter and produces the effects of butter; then too there is the abundance of synthetic fruit flavors dispensed at soda fountains, flavors of such delicacy as to move chemists to choose the poetic name of "*ester*" for them. St. Thomas and the men of his time gave no thought to synthetic butter nor synthetic fruit flavors; but they gave much thought to synthetic gold and silver. St. Thomas' answer on the matter of the alchemist's gold and silver, an answer of common sense, still stands for any synthetic product. If science produces real butter, as it has produced real sugars and real alcohols, the product can be sold as real: the synthetic or natural character of its origin is unimportant; it has no interest in a pedigree or a coat-of-arms. What is important is that it have all the qualities of natural butter: that is, that it really be butter, not a substitute for butter. Let us take the case of a businessman with a stock of defective goods on hand. What will he do with them? In a responsible firm, the ordinary thing would be to sell the goods as defective and at a lower price, not only from considerations of justice, but as a protection for the reputation of the firm. Now, what if this particular businessman has no established name to protect, and the defects in the goods are hidden, i.e., they can be detected only by an expert: strict defects for instance as flaws in a diamond or faults in the barrel of a pistol? It is clear that he cannot demand the price he would for a perfect product. Is it enough for him to cut down the price and to say nothing? Hardly. The drop in price will take care of any damage that might otherwise have come to the buyer in the sale itself; but it will not take care of the gun later exploding in the buyer's face, nor of the explosion of wrath from his fiancée who happens to be a jeweler's daughter.

Lowering the price to a proportionate level is sufficient when the defects are evident, when they should be seen easily and quickly by an ordinary purchaser. Hidden defects, however, must be revealed. In fact there are times when even manifest defects must be explicitly pointed out; but this is quite accidental, a matter of protecting a particularly simple-minded buyer, such as the man who might have drowned on the lot he had just purchased if he had not been warned of the tide.

Business as such

We come now to an article of the *Summa* that is a ringing challenge to the modern world, for it is an article that questions the unquestionable. It demands that business itself give the password that will identify it as belonging to the army of acts properly human, the password of morality. How moral is business? How legitimate is trade for the sake of profit? Business is business, but does it need no other references than it can furnish for itself, can it stand on its own feet? Thomas' questions are a challenge, a challenge that comes as a surprise and brings a surprise with it, for business does not answer these questions too brilliantly.

To get at the heart of the question it is necessary to distinguish between trade for the necessities of life and trade for the sake of gain. Trade of the first type is undeniably praiseworthy in itself as serving the very ends of nature. This trade does not belong in the hands of private individuals but rather to those in charge of the domestic or social groups, to housekeepers and to governments; in other words, it is the proper act of those responsible for the necessities of life.

Trading for gain, which is business strictly so-called, i.e., buying for the sake of selling at a profit has the type of face that is automatically cast in gangster roles. When business comes to the house of human acts, it must have its hat in hand, references ready, and perhaps even the company of a police officer to prove that it is not nearly so tough as it looks; as a matter of fact, it is not evil. Still, it has an air of baseness about it. It is ordered to earthly profit, is often accompanied by sins of speech and injustice, and frequently put to work to serve cupidity. To put the objections in plain language, let it be said that business has for its end the making of money; and this is a mere means, a mere tool for a man. Unless it is ordered further, to some such virtuous and necessary ends as to support a family, to the public good, to help the poor and so on, it has no justification in human affairs. When it is ordered to these further ends, it is no longer an end in itself but rather it is the price a man exacts for his labor.

Usury

Usually these extrinsic ends are the ends of the executive and because of them, the ordinary profit of business can be justified; but there is one profit that defies justification, that is always and everywhere wrong, and that is the profit of the usurer. For quite a while after the break-up of Christian unity, the question of usury was soft-pedaled, receiving nothing like the constant attention it had during the middle and later middle ages. One might have suspected that the unclean thing had disappeared from the face of the earth; but of course, it had not. Today more and more is being written on it, more and more questions being asked about it, serious, dangerous questions; for usury today is being pointed out by men who do not speak lightly as the power that makes modern wars possible, modern depressions universal and calamitous, and as the most serious threat to capitalistic civilization which it attacks in the disguise of credit.

At any rate, wherever usury is found it is wrong; and its evil is manifest. It is absurdly simple to understand that to charge a man twice for the same thing is always unjust; yet that is precisely what usury does, it sells the same thing twice. The trick is possible only when the thing sold or loaned is consumed in its very first use, things like wine or sandwiches, or money. When we demand, over and above the return of the original sum of money loaned, an added amount for the use of the money, our act is the same as selling a man a glass of wine and then charging him for the privilege of drinking it.

If we keep this simple statement of usury in mind, it will not be difficult to understand the absolutely necessary distinction between usury and legitimate interest. The latter is charged, not for the mere use of the money as in usury, but on some extrinsic title; this doctrine of interest is not something new to Catholic theologians, there has been no softening of the condemnations of usury, for there has never been a question of the legitimacy of a charge on grounds extrinsic to the money itself. Among such extrinsic grounds for legitimate interest we might mention: positive damage caused to the creditor by making the loan; a special danger to the capital loaned, which justifies a man demanding payment for his risk; the cessation of profit proximately hoped for: or the legal premium (necessarily small) allowed to facilitate exchange.

These two, usury and legitimate interest must not be confused: nor must usury be allowed to masquerade as legitimate interest. For the one, usury is evil and forbidden; the other is indifferent or even good and certainly permitted. The evil of the one is clear to reason and positively declared by the Church the other is permitted by all the theologians. The difference between the two seems, quite clearly, to be the difference between a loan's intrinsic and extrinsic title to a larger return. Thus, for instance, a loan for productive purposes has a certain claim to a larger return, that is to a share in the profits but by the same token, a consequent loss should also be shared. On the other hand, a loan for unproductive purposes certainly seems to have no such title to a larger return. A demand for a larger return because of delayed payment does not seem unreasonable, for it is in the nature of a fine, where the original contract has not been kept, or because of increased loss as a result of the longer term of the loan. Stockholders who are really partners in a business are not guilty of injustice when they receive a dividend, for they share in the losses as well as in the gains of a business.

A contrast -- the wide embrace of justice: Nature of the potential parts of justice

We are not used to such a concentration on the anti-social vice of injustice: consequently, the result of these last two chapters is a somewhat embarrassed discomfiture not unlike that of a student nurse at her first operation or a young priest's first call to a nasty accident. This is one of the difficulties faced by officials who must deal with injustice constantly. The anti-social character of the thing creates such a stifling, unwholesome artificial atmosphere that these officials face a double danger: they may be increasingly uncomfortable in that atmosphere, irritated with an irritation that gradually rises to a climax of disgust, brutality and ruthless condemnation of the perpetrators of injustice or, acclimating themselves to that atmosphere, they may become as anti-social as those with whom they are dealing.

Perhaps a realization of this is at the bottom of St. Thomas' method of treating the virtues and the vices together, never dallying very long at any one vice; but rather giving us, side by side with that vice, the perfect respite had by examining a virtue. Here, coming to the end of this first treatise on justice itself and its opposite vice, he throws open the door to let in a gust of fresh air and to reveal to us the wide, inspiring country, which comes under the sovereignty of justice.

Their number and name

You will probably have noticed, in our earlier treatment of justice, the three outstanding characteristics of that virtue: its regard for others, its note of equality and its note of debt. All the members of the family of justice bear prominently stamped on their very nature one absolutely universal family trait: all of these lesser virtues that come under justice deal with another. They are in some sense social, rather than personal, virtues. A glance at these virtues introduces us to the sources of the harmony, unity, smoothness and efficiency, the joy that has entered human life through man's existence in society. All these lesser parts of justice will fall short of that absolutely essential social virtue itself. Some will lack the note of equality, others that of debt. However, all have essentially the happy end of bringing man to a fuller life by giving him an integral part in a social body.

We shall see them all in detail, one by one. For the present, we must be satisfied merely to name them. These potential parts of justice are: religion, piety, observance, truth, gratitude, vindication, friendship and liberality.

Two mistakes on petty injustice: Too small to matter

By way of summary of this chapter, we might point out that there are two mistakes to be noticed in this matter of petty injustice: one of under-estimation and the other of over-estimation. To those with a good grasp of the serious and important things of life, with a scale of values accurately balanced, the pettiness of this injustice is quite clear: but its very clarity may move them to dismiss these things as trifling, as they concentrate on the bigger, more important things. In this same vein, a man might shrink in horror from beating his wife, but have no qualms whatever of being niggardly with her; while as far as the stability of marriage and the peace of the home is concerned, this niggardliness may do more damage than an annual beating. These things are small; but precisely because they are so small, they can accumulate almost unnoticed until they are an overwhelming force, until they have undermined the structure of society. Then we are astonished at the catastrophe and, belatedly, search for a cause, a big cause, a cause as momentous as the damage that has been done. It will be a very human thing if we pick the wrong cause, or finding nothing proportionate, if we create a cause to satisfy our minds, while we go on carelessly indulging the petty injustice that is behind it all.

Too big for anything else to matter

The other mistake, not uncommon in our day, is made by those who have lost or inverted their scale of values. There are men and women today to whom lying, cheating, petty thievery, backbiting, mockery and so on are so revolting as to be unthinkable as a personal vice. Yet these same people are not seriously perturbed by such things as abortion, euthanasia, suicide. They strain at the gnat, while the camel slides down as easily as a sip of wine.

The conditions of life with others -- strength and largeness of soul
Life of friendship with God and men

Both these mistakes are socially, as well as individually fatal. The absolute condition for our life with others is one of justice. There is no place in social life for either violence or pettiness. Certainly, life with others seems to demand a strength and largeness of soul. There are no stingy saints; for life with God demands surrender, not concessions. In human friendship, no selfish friends are true friends: selfishness knows only one loyalty. In domestic life, there is no marriage for long on a basis of self-defense, whether that defense be thrown up before a career, a "developing personality", freedom or such trifles as convenience, taste, relaxation or shape. Additionally, in society there is no social life for long without regard for others, without justice. For generosity, for surrender, for unselfishness, for justice it is demanded that we have the strength and largeness of soul to get out of ourselves, to give ourselves, to forget our point of view in seeing the world through the eyes of others, even through the eyes of God. We must not only see with the eyes of others, we must work for their good as well as for our own.

Domestic life

In the last chapter, we saw the basic attack on man's rights in the great injustices, in the social insanity directed at the rights of man's person, his life, his integrity, his dignity, his freedom, against his property. In this chapter we have been examining the small, nagging attacks in the home of society; the kind of attack that completely usurps peace and harmony and eventually destroys society as nagging eventually destroys the home. This petty injustice is the injustice of a shrew of society. While it is effective in exploding peace, harmony and cooperation, it is yet so small as hardly to merit our notice let alone our determined opposition. Its pettiness, in other words, is one of its greatest dangers.

Full essence of anarchy

Consequently, this petty injustice plays almost as important a part as violent injustice in bringing about the destruction of society, in accomplishing anarchy, in depriving man of his social head. These petty injustices are the contributions of the small souls, the sneak thieves of society; violent injustices are the contributions of the pirates of society. Both work for the same end: the destruction of the social structure by denying in act and in word the rights of man, refusing him his fundamental rights on the one solid ground on which he can lay claim to them, on the ground of his humanity. Both work to the same end of self-destruction, destroying their own rights by denying their own obligations, which are at the root of those rights. Both work for an isolation, a solitary confinement of man they commit social suicide, but, unfortunately, social suicide is not a crime that can be committed alone. Those who destroy society pull it down upon their own heads, but it also comes down on the heads of all the thousands of innocent men and women who have been big enough and brave enough to make the adventure of life in society.

⌑ CHAPTER XI ⌑

THE FULLNESS OF RELIGION
(Q. 81-87)

1. Subjection and order.

2. Fullness of subjection
   (a) involuntary subjection ·· slavery.
   (b) Voluntary subjection:
      (1) To an inferior ·· degradation.
      (2) To a superior ·· perfection.

3. The subjection of religion:
   (a) Grounds of resistance to this subjection.
   (b) Justice of this subjection.

4. The virtue of subjection ·· religion:
   (a) Its origins.
   (b) Its nature and aims.
   (c) Internal and external religion.
   (d) Religion and "sanctity."

5. The act of subjection ·· devotion:
   (a) Meaning of devotion.
   (b) Its cause.
   (c) Its effects.

6. The voice of subjection ·· prayer:
   (a) Practicality of prayer.
   (b) Prayers to God and to the saints.
   (c) The perfect prayer.
   (d) Subjects of prayer.
   (e) Mode of prayer.
   (f) Effects of prayer.

7. Gestures of subjection
   (a) Adoration.
   (b) Sacrifice.

8. Offerings of subjection:
   (a) Oblations and first fruits.
   (b) Tithes.

Conclusion:

1. Condition for citizenship in the universe --
subjection:
   (a) Of necessity.
   (b) Of justice.

2. Fullness of cosmic social life.

3. Personal effects of religion.

CHAPTER X
THE FULLNESS OF RELIGION
(Q. 81-87)

In one sense, it might be said that the past few chapters of this book, insisting upon the necessity of justice, have labored the obvious. At least it is entirely obvious that for any common life men need peace; when they cannot find it at home they search for it in the neighborhood tavern or the distractions of a nightclub -- a difference dictated not by taste but by finances; when they cannot find it in society, they flee from that society or destroy it. In addition, a fundamental, although not sufficient, condition for peace is justice. St. Augustine's definition of peace as the "*tranquility of order*" has made it forever clear that for common life men must have order, since they must have peace.

As a matter of fact, order is at the same time the fruit of intelligence and the first law of intelligence. When we have come upon a trace of order we can pocket our magnifying glass and light up our pipe with serene superiority; we have hit upon a clue of the first order, we know by this footprint of order that some intelligence has passed by this way. It is the one absolutely infallible sign of intelligence at work. The anthropologist, grubbing about in the ruins of lost civilizations with his peculiar zeal for the past and disregard of the present, hails as indisputable evidence of the presence of man a stone impressed with the note of order, a stone shaped as a tool. He even becomes excited about his discovery.

On the other hand, wherever we see intelligence working we can be sure that order will be stamped on its work. However inept the workman, precisely because he is a human craftsman his work will have a note of order, for to work at all he must work with some degree of intelligence. Indeed, so true is this that men insist upon some mockery of order in that most disorderly of human acts, a sin.

Subjection and order

Now, order, the first fruit of intelligence and the first law of intelligence, comes high; the inevitable price that must be paid for it is subjection. On no other terms can it be had. No compromise can be made, no haggling will bring down the price, no substitute will do; if there is to be order, then there must be subjection. The order of the universe is the result of the working out of physical laws, itself an evidence of the interlocking subjection of creatures, one serving the other. It would be taking too much for granted, no doubt, to see in earthquakes, tornadoes, floods and blizzards the loud guffaws of physical nature at the naiveté of the young people's neat division of spheres of influence and their solemn-eyed agreement to work out matrimony on a fifty-fifty basis. Even so, at least physical nature has reason to guffaw. In the domestic group, husband and wife are not rival rulers or cautious partners making sure of their share of the spoils; nor are they enemies attacking each other's independence. If they are any of these things, the order of the domestic group has ceased to exist, peace is on its way out and the marriage is destroyed before it has begun. The same is true of society, for if citizens are not subject to the government, i.e., if there is not the essential subjection demanded by order, then the social group has ceased to exist.

It is particularly unfortunate that today we think of subjection with a sigh of commiseration or regret; it is a price to be paid, but regretfully, with no more pretense of gaiety than we show to the installment collector. It seems to denote a loss of something integral to the dignity, the efficiency, the self-respect of man. It is an affront to our ideal of "being our own boss."

Fullness of subjection: involuntary subjection -- slavery.

Perhaps our resentment to the notion of subjection is due to some confusion of ideas. It is true, for instance, that a complete slave -- one who is being used by a master for the master's profit -- pays a high price of subjection for the order of the society in which he lives, too high a price. All the same, that is because in his case the subjection is not a means to order but a violation of it. The slave has as much right to resentment as would a cow, which has been bitten by a blade of grass it stooped to eat. A man's subjection, by his very nature, should be a moral subjection, a bowing to moral force, a subjection that leaves him free to lord it over the physical order; whereas here we have physical force subjecting this lord of the physical universe. It is tyranny and injustice, rather than orderly subjection.

Voluntary subjection: To an inferior -- degradation

It is also true that the libertine or the drunkard pays a high price of subjection. It is true that the city, which is practically ruled by gangsters, has also paid an enormous price of subjection. In both these cases, the price paid has ended all struggle, giving an outward semblance of peace; but there is no inner peace, either in the individual or in the society. Rather this is the degradation of cowardly surrender; it is not order but chaos.

In our thinking, we have too often lumped tyranny, degradation and true subjection together. It is a fatal error that tends to drive a man either to despair or to isolation. It is a mistake that should not have been made; a moment's thought indicates that subjection means to put something beneath another; the crucial thing is not to put the higher beneath the lower.

To a superior -- perfection

In other words, true subjection means that things are put precisely where they belong; by it, creatures respond to the order of the divine plan of creation. When things are in their proper place, we have peace, progress, stability, the order that all nature seeks; in a word, we have perfection. The subject angels stand out as perfect in contrast to the rebellious devils; the just man in contrast to the murderer; the peaceful citizen in contrast to the anarchist. In each of these cases, the more perfect is the more subject. In the physical order, the least cell, properly subject and working in harmony with the rest of the body, is certainly more perfect than the cancerous cell, which has turned dictator and subjected all others to its own growth. In the scholastic order, a science that has run wild and subjected philosophy to itself has gone far to destroy both itself and philosophy.

We can put this in another way by insisting that there is only one utterly independent Being, because there is only one First Cause. Anyone or anything else that attempts to play God makes a laughing-stock of itself, even though the audience be sympathetic. Everything else has a place in the harmony of the universe, a right place; that is, a place with something above it and something below it. Everything in the universe has an order to everything else, and that means subjection to higher things and the domination of lower things.

In the human order, however, we tend to resist this self-evident truth, perhaps because it is also self-evident that man is a master. We are apt to push that latter truth still further and make man the absolute master, a master of masters with no one above him and everything beneath him. This picture of man is as fetching as a flattering smile to an old man; but in reality, it has none of the beauty of truth; it is in itself a lie, with all the ugliness and distortion of a twisted word.

The subjection of religion: Grounds of resistance to this subjection

Now, it is a lie that it is not too hard to understand, knowing human nature. If a man confuses subjection with tyranny and degradation, it is not unreasonable of him to rebel against the thought of resigning himself to a regime of tyranny or degradation. Again, in a world where man is so evidently master it is not too hard for an unthinking man to believe that he needs no help, that he is entirely self-sufficient. Nor is it hard, for a man who has others do his detailed thinking for him, to overlook the importance of subjection in his constant concentration on the importance of his mastery of others. It is, then, entirely understandable -- though dreadfully unfortunate -- that our age should look upon the virtue of religion, which is essentially a virtue of subjection, as a little distasteful, at best unimportant and entirely subjective, at worst a weakling's knuckling under to superior power.

Justice of this subjection

In the course of this chapter we shall see that subjection to God, the work of religion, is not a matter of sacrificing our self-respect, but of establishing it: it does not knock the hat off our heads and whip us to our knees as the tyrant passes, rather it moves us to bow our heads in a gracious recognition that can be given only by a master to the Master of all. It is not a subjective affair, a matter of taste; it is not a favor done to God. It is the recognition, in action, of an evident truth; it is an act of strict justice, giving God what belongs to Him. If the language is not too strong, we might say that religion does the honest thing, refusing to take from God what belongs to Him; it is a refusal to steal even from God. At least it is certainly true that the neglect or violation of religion brings with it all the chaotic effects of the anti-social vice of injustice.

We have a hint here of a truth that is astonishing to modern minds. For some time anthropologists have been examining moral codes in their relation to religion and religious things. At times, they have apparently found moral codes that have no relation to religion and have no religious sanction enforcing them. Often, of course, these apparent discoveries have been corrected, for, as the anthropologist knows well, the primitives are no more eager to talk to strangers about their most sacred things than we are ourselves. Nevertheless, at other times continued investigation has failed to show a connection between morality and religion. The point here is that such a discovery of a morality distinct from religion is quite possible. Religion is neither the product of authority nor the radical explanation of morality, at least not on the natural plane. It flows from man's nature and is itself a command of natural law, not the foundation of natural law. A community with morality, a moral code, but devoid of religion, would be a community where the natural law was operating but not perfectly, where one of the commands of natural law had dropped out of sight.

If we look at religion in this way, unadorned, in the simple garments of fundamental truth, it is not hard to understand the hold its beauty has taken on the heart of man. For this is not the glamour of a moment or the attraction of a pose; but the full, free, graceful beauty of nature at its best.

The virtue of subjection -- religion

Religion sees God as man's first and last principle, as the source of all that man is and the goal to which all his desires and actions go; and religion pays the tribute of respect and subjection to the infinite perfection of the First Cause, to the infinite goodness of the Last End. The human heart revolves around these two great centers as planets around a sun. Man has to have a beginning, he must have a goal: a goal and a beginning far above himself. Religion is a tribute to the truth of things as they are.

The beauty and solemnity of religion are no more than the rich trappings in which men have clothed the honor and respect given to the Beginning and End of all things. To expect words to express these things is to impose a burden too heavy for the strongest and richest of words; it is no wonder men have not been content to stop with words. However, even the best man has to offer, the beauty of words and the grace of action, the most exuberant ritual and pontifical robing are no more than clumsy instruments by which the unutterable things of a man's heart are added to the beauty of divine creation. At the same time, they are instruments by which yet more unutterable things are awakened in the heart of a man. Yet however high the heart soar above its sublimest expression, it still pays inadequate tribute to the excellence of the Godhead.

Its origins

Men, of course, realized this insufficiency from the beginning. They did their best to overcome it by consecrating to religion some acts whose very nature is expressive of the highest reverence because they are so completely acts of subjection: the acts of adoration, of sacrifice and of devotion. Additionally, because they felt so keenly the inadequacy of even these sublime acts, men bent all of their minds, their imaginations, their energy to a yet greater refinement of the splendor of these acts. Man's life is permeated with religion because it is shot through and through with its beginning and its goal; man's life is saturated with religion because it is replete with God.

In a word, religion is a thing of justice, giving God what is His due as first and last cause. The payment is not adequate, for God is always infinite and we are always finite; but we pay that debt as far as we are able. The debt is a joyful one. Its payment does not take something from a man; rather it perfects the debtor in proportion to the payment of the debt. God's claims are not the claims of a usurer, pressing a man down further and further into the slavery of helplessness. His claims are like the claims of love, bringing out the best in a man, lifting him out of himself, putting even superior things in his power.

Its nature and aims

You will notice that the object of religion is not God Himself but the debt owed to God; that is, it is not a theological but a moral virtue. It has to do with another, no less another than God; and it has to do with the payment of a debt, with the actions of man. In other words, it is a part of justice, a virtue perfecting the will of man in order that he might give to God what is His due. It is, indeed, the highest of the moral virtues, because, of them all, it comes closest to what is best in man's life -- his end or goal, God.

The coins of religion, which we jingle in our pocket as we go to pay our debt to God, have two sides; on the one is the protestation of reverence for the excellence of God, on the other the subjection of the creature who is man. We cannot split the coin to hand over the reverence and retain the subjection; if we try it we mutilate the coin, not only making it worthless but subjecting ourselves to punishment, We cannot have one side of a coin without the other; they are two sides of the same thing. More concretely, we cannot worship God without subjecting ourselves.

That means that we cannot worship God without perfecting ourselves, for the subjection of religion is the subjection to a superior. It puts man in his right place in the universe; not too high, not too low, but just where he belongs. It is not the subjection of a slave to tyranny, nor of a weakling to degradation; it is the subjection of perfection, the foundation of order and the source of peace, stability and progress in human life.

The peculiar advantage of good books is not that they challenge our stubbornness, nor that they furnish us with material to lord it over lesser men, although they have served both purposes. Rather they are severe masters in whose company a man can grow, can perfect himself; they are towering mountains into which we can fly from the deadly flat landscape of discussions on the weather or rehashes of newspaper accounts. They are higher places, superior to the level of our minds and consequently a means of perfection. When we have learned the entire book can teach us, we have reached its level and must look to something higher if our perfection is to continue. The rule is universal; it is not by contact with inferiors but by subjection to superiors that men and things reach their perfection. The mongrel pet of the lowliest of men improves from even such a contact with such a reason.

Internal and external religion

It is strictly true then that every act of religion is ordered to the perfection of man as well as to the worship of God, for every act of religion subjects man to the one superior to whom he owes subjection. Obviously, the man suffering from St. Vitus dance is not rebelling against God by his queer antics in Church. The external acts of religion are decidedly secondary, though tremendously important; but it is the internal act that is at the heart of religion, for man is subject to God by his mind and his heart. The intellect and will of man, again as the superiors, take the body by the hand and lead it through its carefully rehearsed curtsy, in harmony with the universal law of divine Providence that the inferior reach its end through the ministrations of the superior. The hypocrite, who runs through the external motions of religion because it is good business or fine exercise, is not performing religious acts at all; these are dead, ghastly things. Their soul, the internal acts of intellect and will, is missing.

In other words, the immediate purpose of external acts of religion is to serve as a sign of the internal acts and as a means to arouse those internal acts of religion. We know what the agony in Christ's mind did to His body in the Garden of Gethsemane; we know what the solemn tones of a funeral march will do to a gay laugh or a happy thought. The body and soul of man are much too closely united to escape a constant reaction of one upon the other. It is inevitable that the internal subjection to God in man express itself in external acts. If the external acts of religion are sincerely performed, they must have an arousing effect on the internal faculties of a man. It is hard to feel self-sufficient kneeling down, but easy to acknowledge dependence; it is not easy to wipe the thought of Christ from our minds as we make the sign of the cross, but very easy to see His suffering face. It makes a tremendous difference within the heart of a man whether he folds his hands in a toy Gothic arch or clenches them into murderous fists.

In fact, the external acts of religion have made so much of an impression on men that some insisted that religion be confined to external acts. This idea is carried to its logical conclusion in "religious revivals" where a process of mechanical hypnotism is used to overwhelm the intellect and will of man by his external acts; the result is to reduce religion to an orgy of animal reaction. Other men, who saw clearly the supremacy of the internal acts of religion, insisted that they were the only religious acts; all externals were to be promptly done away with and we were to serve God in spirit alone. That was the strangely inhuman doctrine of the early reformers, a doctrine condemned from the earliest days of the Church.

Both mistakes were made because men forgot, or were displeased with, the fact that they were men. Perhaps this was only a part of that general discontent that moves a man to envy a boy, a blonde to envy a brunette and vice versa; at least it is a decided contrariness for a man to insist upon mere animality, or pure angelism, and refuse to consider the outstanding reality of his own humanity. We are men, not angels, not animals; we know much more of the chill of a dying fire than of the chill of failing charity; the vividness of the color red makes a much stronger impression upon us than the light of divine truth; but we cannot be satisfied to shiver by a dying fire or stand paralyzed by the attraction of the color red. We are a combination of the material and the spiritual; our progress to God must start from the material, the sensible, but it cannot stop there.

The quick prayer we dash off on a cold night before we leap into bed or the creaking genuflection we execute on a rainy fall morning are not done for God in the sense that breakfast is cooked for the children. God is full of glory; we can give Him nothing. This humanly flavored and shortened honor that we give God is given for our sake that we might find out perfection.

Religion and "*sanctity.*"

There is a general recognition of this great truth in the attitude of men to the things and persons consecrated to religion. Churches, tabernacles, vessels of the divine service, vestments, priests and nuns all, because of their dedication to divine worship, are sacred. In the eyes of men, these things are holy. We insist they are holy places, sacred vessels, consecrated virgins and so on; by dedication to the payment of the race's debt of religion to God, they have taken on a personal perfection.

There is a modern confession of a tragic loss of this great truth in the violation of these sacred things. It is not only the brutality that inevitably accompanies the violation of churches, the degradation of the sacred vessels and the attacks upon priests and nuns that make them such shocking things. They are attacks, not only on God, but on the highest goal of men, the goal of perfection; and they are more easily forgiven by God than they are by men. They are a blaring note of disorder and chaos ringing through the human world, a note of uncompromising hatred that fills the souls of men with terror; but they also awaken a desperate resistance in the name, not only of God, but of our very humanity. Not all religious men are holy, but certainly all holy men are religious. In addition, the unholy religious men are unholy precisely because they are so devastatingly irreligious in their private lives. The application of the mind to God implied in religion has sanctity's air of fresh cleanlirless about it, a cleanliness that comes from avoiding the muck beneath man and scaling the heights above him. It is the cheerful cleanliness of Alpine snow; not the frosting on a cake, but the striking garment that covers but does not conceal the massive strength and stability beneath it. A man cannot fix himself to the immovable Mover, the first and last Principle of life, without himself partaking of that divine solidity.

Both sanctity and religion order men's minds and acts to God; but sanctity is a much more universal thing. Religion is a humble maid, busy with the household duties of a servant in God's house of the universe, giving the Master His rightful service. Sanctity involves a total surrender far surpassing mere service, a surrender which can be dictated only by generous love.

The act of subjection -- devotion: Meaning of devotion

As a virtue, a good habit, religion has its proper acts. Its first and fundamental act, the act of devotion, has been more grossly misunderstood and calumniated in our own times than has religion itself. We often speak of devotion in connection with religion as though it were something slightly sticky, sentimental, embarrassing because slightly overdone like a laugh that is too loud or a tear that is too ready. Actually, we come much closer to the real sense of the word when we use it in connection with activities other than religious: the devotion of a man to his work, of an officer to an army, of a statesman to a state, or, in more intimate surroundings, of a wife to a sick husband.

In all these usages, devotion means the will to do readily what concerns the object of that devotion -- the work, the state, the army or the sick husband. Devotion here has the aura of consecration and the bustle of promptness about it. The same is true of devotion in religion; it is the will to do readily what concerns the service, the worship, of God. If, in our heartless scientific fashion, we try to isolate the wife's devotion to put it under a microscope, we find that we have set ourselves too difficult a task. That devotion is always wrapped up in something else, like taking the husband's temperature, feeding, consoling or cheering him. That is the way of devotion; it always wraps itself around other things. It becomes, in a word, the mode of other acts. So we say a man prays devoutly, hears Mass devoutly, and so on; he does not turn out pages of devotion and clip them together to be sent to a publisher.

In both the secular and the religious order of things, devotion is fundamental and universal. That of the wife springs from her love and at the same time builds up, feeds that love. This may be true also in religion; devotion may flow from the deep spring of charity. Now, even without the forceful backing of charity, devotion is the first, the universal act of religion. Just as intelligence is the mode of all human action, or strength the mode of an elephant's action, or silliness the mode of an idiot's action, so devotion must be the mode of all religious actions. If there is no ready willingness upon which to draw there can be no acts of religion, its very first act has not yet been produced.

Its cause

Devotion, then, is important. If we couple this importance with the fact that the cause of devotion, from our side, is meditation and contemplation, we see something of the wisdom of spiritual writers' insistence on regular, daily meditation. At the same time, we are brought to a shocking realization of the danger involved in our modern neglect of meditation for the layman. It may sound harsh, but it is unequivocally true, that his danger is the danger attached to being too busy to think of God. The thought of God and the love that follows it are precisely what meditation and contemplation mean. That thought of God is the cause of devotion must be obvious when we remember that devotion is an act of the will (proceeding from religion, a virtue of the will) and consequently must be preceded by an act of the intellect. In this matter, too the heart cannot run before the head.

Just what thought causes this devotion? What mysteries pondered over by our minds can give us that ready willingness to do what concerns the worship of God? St. Thomas points out two great classes of truth, which are immediate causes of devotion; one positive, the other negative. On the positive side, there are the beauties of divine goodness in itself and in its benefits to us; on the negative side, our side, there are the defects and insufficiencies that drive home our need of God and uproot the great impediment to devotion, which is presumption. God made it easier for us by sending His Son. To our stumbling minds and fickle hearts, the tangible world has an immediate and powerful appeal; ready to our hand we have the humanity of Christ with its infinite material for our prayerful consideration.

We cannot think very often of Christ without seeing the magnificence of His divinity bursting through into His human acts, filling us with awe, love and loyalty to the Son of Mary. Nor can we follow His tired feet through Palestine without becoming acutely conscious of the insufficiencies, the defects of our nature.

Its effects

The goodness of God and the defects of man are so obvious that we can easily take them for granted. Yet that is a fatal thing to do: for it means that for all practical purposes, we take them as unimportant, as deserving of little attention. More concretely, it means that we deprive ourselves of much joy, cheating ourselves of the primary effect of devotion; the joy awakened by humble visions of God's goodness and our high hopes, of service that answers the heart's deepest wishes to repay something of the magnificent divine benefits and to reach for high perfection. We are not yet in heaven, so with this joy of devotion there is a dash of tears to wash our eyes clear for the long vistas of eternity, tears that this goodness is not yet ours, while these defects are so truly our own. Yet the very tears are themselves a joy for the promises they emphasize.

The voice of subjection ·· prayer

Some of the most beautiful pictures that haunt the hearts of men are pictures of prayer. There is, for instance, the picture of Christ praying in tears at the grave of Lazarus, the man He loved; or Christ lonely in the shadows of Gethsemane, praying the longer for His agony. There is the picture of Mary interrupted at her prayer by the angel announcing to her that she is to be the Mother of God. More personal pictures of prayer are scattered through our lives. Memory shows us prayer brightening the beginnings of life as we stumbled through those first prayers, terribly serious, anxious eyes on the loved face that would mirror the perfection of the lesson and lovingly distort it. We see prayers sweetening the end of life in the old woman's weary fingers thumbing her rosary. Repeatedly all through our lives, prayer is a shrill bugle call marking the crises.

Men of our time have not missed the beauty of the face of prayer, but that beauty has often blinded men to the solid character behind that beautiful face. Prayer has been embraced as emotional, and rejected as too purely emotional; it has been praised as a kind of super-poetry, and rejected as nothing but poetry. It has been called a weakness, a cowardice, something unworthy of God and man; a case of God playing favorites, or of men trying to load the dice with which they play the game of life.

Yet, prayer is none of these things. Surely, its beauty is not a shallow, superficial thing but the profound beauty of justice and truth. In no other religious act, short of devotion, does man more thoroughly subject himself to God; that is, in no other act does man so strictly tell the truth about himself as in prayer. Every prayer (using the term now as Thomas does in its restricted sense of petition, exclusive of meditation and contemplation) is a statement of our needs; and the very multiplication of our requests is an emphasizing of the fact that it is God Who is the source of all good. Every prayer is a step closer to God, for how can we ask if we do not approach Him at least with the steps of our mind? Precisely because it is by raising our minds to God that we pray, in prayer we offer God the supreme service, a service not of external things, not of corporal things, but of the highest good we have-our mind.

Practicality of prayer

It is important that we stress the intellectual essence of prayer. We do not ask things with our appetites; prayer is not primarily emotional because it is primarily a request. Prayer is an act of practical intellect, a step towards getting something done; inevitably, it is practical people, not dreamers, who busy themselves with prayer -- women, children and saints as opposed to university professors and artists. Prayer is practical in the same tangible way as is scattering fertilizer on a field in early spring. This is not evidence of cowardice or weakness in the farmer; rather it is evidence of intelligence, and of some not inconsiderable resources. So prayer is not to be considered in terms of fawning on God, of coaxing Him to play favorites, of wheedling Him into a reluctant change of mind. We are closer to the truth when we see player taking a place beside the lightning stroke, the blow of a strong man, or the sweep of an artist's brush. It, too, is a secondary cause. Just as these others do not change Providence but rather fulfill it, so also does prayer; for Providence not only disposes what effects shall follow in the world, but also from what causes these effects shall follow. Prayer is among those things that have been knighted, admitted to the noble order of causes to share something of the causality of God. Our prayer fulfills the condition laid down by divine wisdom for the production of this particular effect.

All this could be put briefly in the one truth that prayer does not change God but it does change men. It lengthens the arms of a man to enable him to reach out beyond time, space, through the portal of death even into the fields of the future. If we add to all this the tremendous power for the suppliant's own good that is given to his prayer by Christ's blood shed upon Calvary, we see the supreme practicality of prayer.

Prayers to God and to the saints

Since religion is nothing more than man's acknowledgment of his dependence upon God, a substitute god will not do; a man simply cannot make a religion of his business, his family, his race or his nation for none of these things are his first cause or his final goal. If he tries it, he is cutting the heart out of his life and inserting a synthetic substitute, casually expecting life to go on as full-blooded as ever. Naturally then prayer, as an act of religion, is to God; as a petition every prayer is a prayer to God, for after all our prayers must be ordered ultimately to grace and glory, two gifts that can come only from the divine treasury.

Here the reformers stopped, recoiling in horror from prayer to the saints. In fact so do we recoil from praying to the saints as we pray to God. Still, we remember that Peter asked his question at the Last Supper through the beloved disciple who leaned on the breast of the Master; we too ask things of God through our friends who are one with us in charity and one with God in the vision of His divine essence. We do not expect the saints to *do* but to *ask* for us.

Of course, we pray to the saints; they love us for giving them a chance to express their love in being our messengers, and we love them for the patient ears and willing feet they lend us. Imagine Catholic life without the millions of prayers that have been said to Our Lady! One of the nice things about getting to heaven before the end of the world would be the enjoyment of the quiet chuckles of the saints as our childish requests come in. Every day the Christmas lists of the very small children of God are pouring in; it would be a grumpy saint indeed who could keep his face straight as he scanned the items: lots of snow for Thanksgiving, a warm sun next week for grandma's visit (she gets rheumatism so), a little dulling for the edge of my tongue, something to be done about my husband's grouches, and don't let Johnny fail again in his examination.

There must be quite a similarity to the child's Christmas list for we can licitly pray for whatever we can licitly desire; that would include all the good things of the world that do not hold us back from God. In a sense, we are turned loose in a toy land with limitless funds! We can, indeed we should, pray not only for ourselves but for others, for all those, in fact, whom we should love, even for our enemies. Prayer is the perfection of beneficence, not its weakest gesture. We make the mistake of thinking ourselves helpless, sighing that we can only pray; if the case gets really desperate we might enlist the help of the nuns. Actually, prayer is the biggest thing we can do, for prayer is one act of ours that is stripped of limitations. It shares immediately in the omnipotence of God.

During their short life with Christ, the apostles made many foolish requests. They asked if they might sit on His right hand in His kingdom; if they might call down fire upon the city that did not receive them; they asked for information on the limits of forgiveness, whether it was seven times; and when they saw the sick man, they asked to be told the secret cause of his illness who had sinned, he or his parents. Now, all these foolish questions were compensated for by that one childishly simple demand they made of Infinite Wisdom: "*Lord, teach us to pray.*"

The perfect prayer

As a result of that request and the graciousness of the Son of Mary, we have the absolutely perfect prayer. It is a prayer of utter simplicity, familiar to every Catholic child yet inexhaustible to the deepest minds. It is the prayer we know as the "*Our Father.*"

We pray to God, not that we might change His will, bending Him this way or that, but that we might cooperate in His causality and that we might awaken in ourselves a confidence in Him. That confidence is awakened particularly by our consideration of His love for us, so we begin with words most heavily laden with love --"*Our Father.*" Our confidence is strengthened by a consideration of His excellence, so we continue "*Who is in heaven.*" To pray perfectly we must not only ask for things that can rightly be desired, but also in the order in which they should be desired, putting first things first. Our first desire rightly falls on the end; so we say with Christ: "*Hallowed be Your name,*" wishing God glory, and "*Your kingdom come,*" asking that we may share that glory, attain that end.

Next come the means to the end: first the direct means, then those that remove impediments to the end. Looking to the first we say: "*Your will be done,*" for we merit heaven by obedience, "*give us this day our daily bread,*" that is, both the corporal and spiritual help necessary to the work of merit. As for the second, well, there are just three things that might block our road to heaven: sin, temptation to which we succumb, and the penalties brought on human nature by the sin of our first parents. Additionally, so we pray: "*forgive us our trespasses,*" that is, remove the impediment of sin that bars us from heaven; "*lead us not into temptation,*" not that we might escape temptation but that we may not succumb to it; "*deliver us from evil,*" that is, from the sicknesses, misfortunes, fatigue and bitterness that have come into life by original sin.

Subjects of prayer

Even without this perfect prayer dictated by God Himself, the Catholic tot saying her brief evening prayers before tumbling into bed reaches heights to which the rest of the universe can make no pretense. For prayer is an act of reason, it involves knowledge of the relation of means to end, the long vision of Providence outstripping time and space. Only a being possessed of intellect and dependent on a superior can possibly pray. God has, or rather is, intelligence; but there is no one to whom He can pray, indeed, no possible need of His praying. The brutes have a generous mead of dependence, but they have no reason; while the damned have intelligence and a superior but their motive power, the will, is so fixed in evil by their deliberate choice of a wrong final end that they are paralyzed as far as prayer is concerned. Only men, angels, the saints in purgatory and heaven can enjoy the sublime privilege and effective causality of prayer. We shall have time enough later on to investigate the prayers of heaven. On earth, the prayers of men are public or private, with this great difference: public prayer must always be vocal. It is said in the name of the whole people; and since it is by word that men communicate, it is by word that the whole people can know that this communal debt to God is being paid. In private prayer, the vocal element is a help rather than a necessity. It is a means to arouse internal devotion as well as a psychological consequence of intense inner fervor; and it is always a pleasing gesture of the completeness of our subjection to God, the subjection of our body as well as of our soul.

Mode of prayer

Vocal prayer cannot, of course, be merely a lip exercise, an indication of dramatic possibilities, or sheer unintelligent mumbling and still claim title to the name prayer. All the same, how much of our mind must be put into prayer? Alternatively, putting the same question in another form, how much damage is done to prayer by involuntary distractions? Certainly, they do not affect the merit of the prayer; that is taken care of by the first intention with which we started the prayer. Nor do they detract from the effectiveness, the powers of entreaty, of the prayer. The one effect of prayer they do lessen or even destroy is the spiritual refreshment and consolation, which normally come from prayer. In other words, we cheat ourselves when we do nothing about these distractions, cheat ourselves of a consolation and refreshment that might easily be ours. On the other hand, we cheat ourselves yet more if we give up prayer in disgust because of these distractions. The essential fruits of prayer, merit and impetration, are still within our grasp; this consolation, like devotion, comes from meditation, that is from thought and, for that, attention is essential.

It was Christ's command that we pray always; but evidently, a waitress who pours prayers into a patron's ear as she pours coffee into his cup can easily be a nuisance. We simply cannot always be praying; there are other things that have to get done, things that occupy all of our minds. What we can do, and what Christ demanded, is to keep our prayer continual in its cause. At the root of prayer, since prayer must be ordered to grace and glory, there is the warm flame of love seeping into the very bones of every action, the desire of charity; that must never fail.

Thomas agrees that if five minutes of vocal prayer makes us growl at the children and abuse our wife, we should have stopped at four minutes. External prayer is precisely to arouse internal fervor, not to ruin our disposition or wreck our homes. Additionally, what is true of the individual and his external prayers holds also for public prayers and the devotion of the whole community; public prayers are not designed to embitter the community or induce a communal pain in the back, but rather to increase the fervor of the whole people.

Effects of prayer

Our evaluation of our prayers is too often faulty. Because, in spite of our prayers, it did rain on Sunday, we decide the prayers were useless; and that means that we are overlooking one of the most valuable effects of prayer, the effect of merit. No prayer said in the state of grace that is, proceeding from charity is useless. It is an act of virtue, the virtue of religion, proceeding from charity and accompanied by humility and faith, the faith that God can give us this request and the humility implicit in our recognition of the need of His help. Moreover, there is no act of virtue, thanks to the suffering of Christ and the power of charity that does not merit grace and glory. Prayer may give us spiritual refreshment, it can and frequently does give us the particular good for which we pray; but it always gives us the most important thing in life, a title to glory, to the goal of life.

It is strictly true then that no prayer is left unanswered. However, in another sense, prayer is infallible. The prayer of the man in the state of grace always obtains what it seeks if the just man asks piously and perseveringly for the things necessary for his own salvation. That absolute statement admits of no exception; but it does demand explanation.

Obviously if he is to have a claim in justice to the thing he seeks, the man must be just, that is he must have grace, which is the principle of merit in strict justice. He asks for himself because, while he can remove impediments from his own soul, he cannot plunge an arm into his neighbor's soul and pull up impediments by the handful. No matter what his influence in heaven, his prayers will not get him things that are adverse to his own salvation; he may ask for a serpent and, while he may get bread, he most certainly has not a chance of getting the serpent. Indeed even indifferent things, since they can be abused by man and contribute to his perdition, may or may not be obtained; his request must be for necessary things if it is to have the note of infallibility. He cannot shout at God like an officer to his orderly; he must ask piously, that is, from the necessary virtues of charity, religion, humility and faith. Nor can he deliver an ultimatum, giving God a last chance to grant his request; he must ask perseveringly.

Christ Himself guaranteed the efficacy of this prayer when He said: "*Ask and you shall receive.*" Now, notice that Our Lord did not say "*within twenty-four hours*;" a man obtains what he prays for at precisely the time when he should receive it. The effect of this efficacious prayer said here and now may not be felt by us, or given to us, for twenty or thirty years. There is a time, not hidden from the wisdom of God, when it will be best for us to receive that favor; that is the time when the goodness of God will see to its safe delivery.

All this is not a denial of the effects of a just man's prayers for someone else; it is merely a statement of the conditions essential for infallible prayer. A man praying for others can merit even the things necessary for salvation for that person; but his merit is not in strict justice but rather by the benevolent friendship, he enjoys with God.

Perhaps one of the reasons why the confirmed sinner prefers to sit to one side and watch other at prayer is a kind of spiritual anemia. Sin does make us puny; above all, it robs us of much of our power of prayer. A sinner, by his prayers, cannot merit grace or glory for himself or others either on grounds of friendship or of strict justice: He has neither the principle of strict merit (grace) nor of friendship (charity). Beyond all doubt the prayer of the sinner which proceeds from his very crime, like the prayer of the assassin that he find his victim quickly and get home to his family, is not heard by the mercy of God. Now and then the things so desperately sought by the sinner are given him by God by way of punishment; for there is no more serious punishment in this life than to be delivered up to sinful desires. All the same, God does, from His extreme mercy, very often grant the prayer of the sinner, which humbly, piously, perseveringly seeks a good thing.

However the sinner is not bound hand and foot and thrown into exterior darkness; not yet at least. In thinking of the sinner's prayers, we must never forget the causality of prayer in a concentration on its merit. The fact that a sinner cannot merit does not mean that his prayer is useless; his prayer too is a fulfillment of divine Providence, a placing of a disposition necessary for the effects decreed by Providence. Without his prayer these effects will never be produced; so that the prayer of the worst of sinners is never a futile gesture, rather it is always a powerful cause,

Gestures of subjection: Adoration

As we come to the next of religion's acts, the act of adoration, it is necessary to insist again that religion pays its debts to God and to none other than God. For just as Catholic prayer has been badly misunderstood, so also has Catholic adoration. In recent centuries, at least, there has been no more constant calumny against the Church than that it adores Mary and the saints. The indignation aroused in those to whom this appeared true was understandable; but the strange intellectual twilight that gave an appearance of truth to such a charge is hard to understand, even harder to excuse. The accusation has its roots in an ignorance both of Catholicism and of adoration.

The generic sense of the Latin word *adoratio* (adoration) is to give honor because of excellence or perfection; its specific sense varies according to the excellencies it honors: thus, the honor given to divine excellence is *latria,* the honor given the excellence of Mary is *hyperdulia,* the honor given to the excellence of the saints is called *dulia.* Yet, in English only the first specific sense of the word "*adoration*" has been preserved, that is we speak of adoration only in connection with the honor given to divine excellence, with *latria.* The whole miserable accusation, then, has come about through reading the English word into the Latin texts. Certainly, no Catholic sees the infinite excellences of divinity in the Maid of Nazareth; to her and the saints we pay an honor, which in English is called *veneration.* God alone do we adore, principally with an internal adoration of heart and mind, secondarily with an external adoration, which is a means of increasing or a result of that inner adoration.

Obviously, we can give that adoration, internal or external, anywhere. We do not have to go to church to adore God; but for the fittingness of the thing, we have places set aside for external adoration, consecrated places whose very consecration is calculated to arouse in us the inner acts of religion. Then too, this consecration is itself a mark of respect for the holy things that take place within the walls of the consecrated place,

In this chapter, we have seen devotion, prayer and adoration as acts that of their very nature do the work of religion, that is, they protest the excellence of God and the subjection of man. We come now to the last of these properly religious acts, the act of sacrifice.

Sacrifice

The striking universality of sacrifice in the history of men of all races and of all times naturally leads us to seek its source deep in the nature of man. The search is not a long or complicated one. Natural reason will not tell man that he is perfect, entirely self-sufficient, self-explanatory, in need of no help and no direction. That type of myth is received for the perversion affected by effete civilization. Natural reason, with the frankness to be expected from nature, says quite plainly that man has and needs a superior and that, in accord with the rest of nature, he must give that superior a proper subjection and honor; but, like all else in the universe, he must do this in a way proper to his human nature.

That is exactly what man does in sacrifice, for the expression by a sensible sign of the honor and subjection due the Supreme Being is in entire accord with man's natural practice of freighting sensible words with spiritual significance, making of them miniatures of his own happy blend of the spiritual and the material. To put the thing in more exact terminology we may define sacrifice as the offering, by a legitimate minister, of a sensible thing through its change or immolation, to God alone in testimony of His supreme dominion. It is a gesture made only to God for it is an expression of that inner immolation of soul that is man's principal sacrifice and that can be offered only to God. God's supreme dominion is sensibly expressed by the immolation or change of the victim; and the sacrifice is offered by a legitimate minister because it is a public act, therefore an act to be placed by an official representing the community itself.

St. Thomas beautifully describes this legitimate minister of the New Law when he calls him "the mediator between God and the people." The priest brings divine truth, the sacraments, Christ Himself, in other words, the things of God to the people; he brings the things of the people -- prayers, sacrifices, offerings and so on -- to God. His, in a word, is the work of Christ; he is another Christ.

Offerings of subjection: Oblations and first fruits

The offerings or oblations of the people, then, pass through his hands on their way to God, to the Church, to the poor. Perhaps the offerings are to be consumed as in sacrifice, or to endure as in chalices, vestments and so on; they may be for the support of the Church, the priests themselves, or the poor. Now, whatever their form and immediate purpose, they pass through this clearinghouse where things divine and human are exchanged.

In the Old Law, specific offerings were laid out in the law itself; it was not whim, but a precept cognizant of her poverty that moved Mary to offer two turtledoves as the price of redemption for her Redeemer Son. In the New Law, under which we live, the offerings are determined by the need of the Church and the custom of the country. In this country, for instance, the offertory collection taken up each Sunday at Mass is the continuation of the custom in the early Church of offering the precise materials for the Holy Sacrifice. These offerings, while voluntary, are also obligatory; after all the externals of worship are obligatory and they are not furnished by legerdemain or a constant series of miracles.

Sacrifice is one type of offering; Another is that of first fruits. In the Old Law, this was literally the offering of the first fruits of the earth, in recognition of the divine benevolence, which gave those fruits. In the New Law, it is regulated, again, by the custom of the country; and the practice has a deep hold on the hearts of Catholics. So much so that even in an industrial civilization, where the very words "*first fruits*" have a bucolic sound, Catholics will be found making some offering, for instance, from their first week's salary at a new job; it is as although they saw, even in the unappealing atmosphere of a smoky factory, the always startling blossom of a first fruit of divine benevolence.

Tithes

Quite distinct from sacrifice and first fruits is the offering known as tithes. They are not directly given to God but are for the support of the priest. They are of natural obligation, since sacrifice itself is a matter of natural law and a legitimate minister is necessary if there is to be sacrifice offered. The legitimate minister of religion does, in the religious order, what the policeman, the fireman or the government officials do in the civil order. It would be unreasonable of us to expect the fireman, between fires, to procure a tin cup and squat beside the blind man on the corner, begging for enough to keep himself alive. He should not have to hold a cup; his hands should be free to take care of fires and thus protect the community. The priest should have his hands free for spiritual matters, and should have them full tending to those matters; he does not have an interval between fires. He should not be forced to busy himself with temporal things, even such essential things as the very necessities of life; his time is too precious and the matter with which he deals is much too important to men for it to be squandered on anything of lesser worth.

Condition for citizenship in the universe -- subjection of necessity.

The fundamental truth at the basis of this whole chapter has been that the condition for citizenship in the universe is subjection. There is nothing in this world that exists for itself; the one universal characteristic of all created things is their interlocking union with everything else in the universe. No individual exists alone; no species exists alone; no planet exists alone: nothing exists in the world for itself alone. Everything reaches its fullest perfection in its relation to that which is above it, in its external end; a lower species is ordered to a higher species, all species to the universe and the universe to God Himself. In all this maze of variety of life and creatures, we find a persistent note of order; and that order is impossible without subjection.

Subjection of justice

For the rest of the world beneath man, that subjection is a matter of physical law; it admits of no rebellion, leaves room for no merit, allows for no mistake. Even so, that cannot be so for man; it would make him a freak in the universe, the one creature in the world not governed according to its proper nature. For man's nature is a moral nature; his subjection cannot be physical but moral, that is, he must give a subjection of justice for citizenship in the universe. Man is not a freak: he belongs in the universe, fits in there harmoniously. Yet he would be no less a freak if he were in no way subject than he would be if his subjection were to be dictated by physical laws. The complete absence of subjection would make him a lonely, isolated creature, insufficient in himself yet having no superior to whom he could appeal for help; at the same time he would be an insult to the universe, for his place at the peak of that universe would be a statement of its incompleteness, a mockery of the mirrored perfection it shows, a grotesque goal for the striving of the cosmic forces of the universe.

Fullness of cosmic social life

Man is a master: but he is a master living under authority. He can say to some things "*do this*" and they do it; "*go this way*" and they go this way: for he too has things under him. He also has something above him; he himself must obey a superior authority if he is to escape the dreary picture of loneliness at the peak of the barren mountains of the universe. Like all the rest of nature, he is made for perfection; and that perfection is to be attained only through subjection to a superior. It is by that subjection that he becomes a law-abiding member of the universe; and his cosmic life can become full only when, with the rest of nature, he subjects himself to his first and last principle. In his case, since it must be moral to be in harmony with his nature, his subjection is accomplished by a recognition of the rights of God; and thereby he establishes a social life with God.

Personal effects of religion

It is by this social life that man obtains help and support for his deficiencies, that his arms are lengthened to reach out to the ends of the universe and beyond. Alone in the universe, man stands a pitiful, bedraggled figure; but taking his proper place in the social life of that universe, he is indeed an image of God.

He establishes social peace with God by his practice of religion, giving to God the things that belong to Him; and by that fact, he establishes his own claim to rights, recognizing his own obligations. His life has a solidity and security about it, such as comes from all social life, but much more profound. He is released from the despair and anxiety as to the origin and meaning of life, for he looks steadily at the beginning of all life and at its end. The personal effects of religion, effects with which we ourselves are thoroughly familiar, are parallel to the effects of individual life in a political group. However, it is necessary to notice here that all that has been said about religion in this chapter is common to all religion in the merely natural order. The supernatural religion of Christ has added notes over and above those of natural religion; it is, after all, supernatural. However, besides those distinctly supernatural notes -- supernatural helps, supernatural instruments, supernatural goals -- the religion of Christ has brought men an inviolable peace as a support for and understanding of suffering, the wide sweep of charity, the courage of humility and the spirit of poverty or scorn for immersion in the material world.

Now, even in the natural order, religion gives man, personally, a serenity, a strength and a consolation that come from diving a social life instead of an isolated individual life. It gives him help and at the same time the ability to help others. It gives him courage in defeat; it gives wisdom as a result of his long view from beginning to end; it gives him mercy in the knowledge of his own need for mercy; and it gives him a much keener sense of justice in his constant payment of his debt of justice to the source of all right. In a word, religion puts man in his right place in the universe.

THE BARRENNESS OF IRRELIGION
(Q. 88-100)

1. The barren human heart and the full human heart.

2. Minimum fullness of religion -- a subjection of justice.

3. The perfection of fullness and the perfection of subjection:
    (a) Of will -- vows:
        (1) Their nature.
        (2) Their utility.
        (3) Their matter.
    (b) Of word -- oaths:
        (1) Their nature and liceity.
        (2) Their triple condition
        (3) Their obligation.
    (c) Of power -- adjuration.

4. Language of the full heart -- praise and song.

5. Barrenness in human life -- irreligious.

6. The barrenness of superstition:
    (a) In the worship of the true God.
    (b) In the worship of false god -- a subjection of degradation:
        (1) Idolatry.
        (2) Divination.
        (3) Observances.

7. Barrenness of religious doubt and presumption:
tempting God.

8. Barrenness of contempt:
   (a) Perjury.
   (b) Sacrilege.
   (c) Simony.

9. The barrenness of atheism.

Conclusion:

1. Twentieth century barrenness:
   (a) A negative statement -- modern evaluation of
religion.
   (b) A positive statement -- twentieth century
subjection:
       (1) Of intellect to falsehood -- rejection of a
First Cause.
       (2) Of life to modern idols.

2. A test of perfection -- the crises of life (birth,
manhood, marriage, sickness, death).

3. The price of perfection.

CHAPTER XI

THE BARRENNESS OF IRRELIGION
(Q. 88-100)

IN these days of travel by air, it is possible to see miles of farms in one glance. Even though the soil of those farms be exactly the same, it is rare to see any two of absolutely equal perfection; and it is not at all rare to come upon startling contrasts of diligence and negligence side by side. One farm will be neat, rich, well cared for and prosperous; while its neighbor is a wild, unkempt, down at the heel failure. The thing should not be surprising; it is, after all, just one illustration of the constant individual variety among men. If their domains were as naked to the eye, we would see the same differences, the same startling contrasts in the kitchens of housewives, the offices of businessmen, the books of bankers and the purses of women.

The barren human heart and the full human heart

If human hearts could be as easily scanned, the view would be no different. Every human being starts life with the rich soil of the human heart, that is, with no more than tremendous possibilities, like a plot of ground that has no claim to be called a garden other than the possibilities of its soil. It remains for the individual to determine whether that heart shall produce all the beauties of which it is capable, or whether its growth will be no more than scrubby, scattered vegetation. The individual determines whether his heart will be full or barren; whether or not it will attain the perfection for which it exists.

Minimum fullness of religion -- a subjection of justice

In our last chapter, we saw that the price of perfection was subjection to a superior; in the human order, subjection to the divine Superior Who is the first cause and the last end. Religion, the virtue which pays that tribute of honor and subjection, does no more than fulfill the demands of justice; yet in that minimum tribute to God lies man's fundamental order, peace, stability and progress. It did not take extraordinary powers of intellect for men to conclude that, if this minimum subjection did so much for the perfection of man, still further subjection would mean still further perfection. In addition then the tremendous truth, the secret of sanctity, became clear to the mind of man: perfection is in perfect proportion to man's subjection to his first and last cause. Still, to go beyond the demands of justice, beyond the demands of nature and the supernatural lawgiver, man is forced to resort to a promise. Man can order, at least to some little extent, the actions of others in his behalf without a promise: he can command inferiors; he can pray to superiors. All the same, for what he will do for others man must order, must oblige himself; he must impose an obligation on himself and that he can do only by a promise. Such promises, made to God, are called vows.

The perfection of fullness and the perfection of subjection: Of will -- vows

Of course, there are many promises that are not vows. The first fervor of Lent may rush us hastily into promises of abstaining from candy or cigarettes, promises to hear Mass daily and so on. These are certainly not vows; they are good resolutions, proposals of sacrifices we are going to try to make, and none too optimistically at that. A vow is a much more serious matter. It is a promise by which we intend to oblige ourselves, to oblige ourselves under sin.

It was this notion of added obligation that made the vows so distasteful to Luther and the Reformers. To them vows were harmful, pernicious, immoral because, by reason of this added obligation, they injured human liberty; they fenced in the activity of man even more closely than did the law. These early Reformers saw clearly that the vows were chains binding a man; what they did not see was that the vows were golden chains, forged by the deliberate will of man, and worn joyfully as a divine trinket. The paradox of chains worn that man might be more free was utterly beyond them because they had lost sight of the fundamental truth that there can be no greater perfection for man than in binding himself to God; that there is no greater freedom than in being subject to a superior; in other words, that man reaches his greatest stature in bowing down in the name of religion.

Their nature

The vows do bind a man, and they bind him to God. Their violation is a sin of faithlessness against One Who has the greatest claim on our loyalty. The vows bind a man to God because they are promises to Him; and by this very fact, they are acts of religion by which a man subjects himself to God.

The modern world's view of religious vows is comprehensively expressed in a great sigh of pity. They involve so much sacrifice! How much these men and women are giving up by their religious vows! Additionally, if people pity us long enough, there is danger that we shall begin to pity ourselves. This view of the vows has never been the Catholic view. To us the religious has been knighted by God, he has received a divine accolade. If the modern view does begin to color the Catholic view, it is because we have, disastrously, begun to absorb an outlook on life that is totally foreign to the doctrine of Christ. Now, such a view cannot be the Catholic view, not only because of its opposition to Christ, but because of the fact that it is always the result of muddled thinking or of no thinking at all.

Their utility

After all, what we give to God is not like the food we give to the tramp at the back door; it is not something we lose and God gains. It is not useful to God; but rather everything given to God is useful to us. This is the other side of the coin of religion: on one side, we have the honor and reverence to God; on the other, inseparably and inevitably, we have the supreme utility to men. In addition, this again is the vast difference between promises made to men and promises made to God. When one of our fellows approaches us to the tune of, "will you do something for me?", we know we are in for it. When God comes asking our promise we can take our treasures out of the strongbox and repack them more tightly to make room for the added treasure that is coming to us as a result of our promise to God. In more concrete terms, the obvious result, for us, of any vow whatsoever, is to give our will a solidity, a firmness in precisely the things it is best for us to do; the things that contribute most to our perfection.

A vow confers a kind of consecration. It fixes our will firmly to good as the oil on a priest's hands fixes those hands to the body of God. It dedicates, not merely the stroke of a brush, the breath of a prayer, or the strong, firm step of a man, but the very faculties by which these acts are produced. It is not a thing of a moment, an enthusiastic cheer which leaves only an echo; it is an enduring, penetrating consecration far superior to the dedication of a medieval knight to holy warfare. A vow has a magic touch that makes a king out of a beggar; for the vows reach out to the whole field of man's activity, and whatever they touch they drape in the gold cloth of religion.

Their matter

A consecrated act is more praiseworthy than its fellow, which proceeds from the good intention of a moment. For this reason, it is a higher thing to do a good act from a vow, because the vow consecrates to God the act and the faculty from which it came. To God, mind you; for unless it is directed to God it is not an act of religion, and so cannot be a vow. A promise made to commit a murder or a theft obviously cannot be offered to God; indeed, even the good things we promise to the saints and Our Lady, unless we understand them to be further directed to God, are not vows but mere promises. Yet, everything that is good and voluntary can be promised to God, can put on the royal robes of religion furnished by a vow.

A cautious man might decide to keep even his small change, and yet make a pretense of generosity by making tomorrow's sunrise or the beating of his heart the subject matter of his vows. However, God is not to be fooled. We must give Him what is at our disposal; our gift must be voluntary. Additionally, even among those voluntary things, we cannot sacrifice a greater good in order to vow a lesser one; for a vow is really a deeper inclination of the subjection of religion. In other words, a vow is a gracious gesture to God; it must be most pleasing to Him and most freely given by us.

On God's side, there is no end to graciousness. We run to the protections of divinity like chicks to the mysteriously dark safety of the hen's wings. By vows, we bring to God, our stumbling wills to stiffen them up, inviting Him into the intimacy of our souls. By oaths, we ask Him to come into our external life with others, to bolster up our means of communication with men by giving our words a ring of absolute certitude.

Of word – oaths: Their nature and liceity

A philosopher who, in a fit of piety, took an oath to the certitude of first principles would make a fool of himself. An oath calls upon God to witness the truth of what we are saying; it is to be used then only when witness is necessary, when we are dealing with things not necessarily true. Our oath taking is always a matter of contingent affairs. Experience has shown that men do lie; again, experience has shown us the definite limitations of our minds. We cannot know the future, the secrets of human hearts; nor can we even know absent things with absolute certitude. Still we must talk about these things, deal with them, on a secure basis. So we call in the help of One Who cannot deceive, from Whom nothing is hidden, and Who cannot be deceived.

By its very nature, an oath contains a gesture of reverence to God; on that score alone, it pertains to religion. Yet that one tenuous claim gives it a part in the consecration of religion and makes unnecessary oath taking illicit. Reverence is not the fruit of light-headedness or carelessness, nor is the danger of perjury a fit companion for the holy band of religious acts. The fact that we run so quickly and easily to God for the help we need does not mean that we take that help lightly. The awfulness of divine majesty forbids our tumbling into that presence in an angry uproar to have the King of Kings settle all our childish affairs. We go about this particular act of religion with caution born of the reverence due to God; our prayers may be an unceasing cascade falling in ever-changing beauty from our lips, but our oaths must be the last desperate S.O.S.

That is, after all, the precise purpose of an oath, to rescue us from the defects that lead one man to disbelieve another. It is no more desired in itself than the captain's call for help with the ship sinking beneath his feet; it is only the necessity of our defects that make it at all desirable. Children, then, are forbidden to take oaths because, lacking the use of reason, they cannot give due reverence to God; those who have already perjured themselves are barred from further oaths because, again, there is the serious danger of lack of reverence for God. Moreover, says St. Thomas, ecclesiastics ordinarily should not take oaths; not because of the danger of irreverence, but because of the implied distrust. Ordinarily their words will not need confirmation. However, in some necessity, in a question of great utility or for the confirmation of some spiritual good, they too may take oaths. Thomas, with his deep reverence for divinity, frowns on oath taking on great feast-days, especially when these oaths have to do with temporal things; but even here, his common sense would not permit him to put up an insurmountable barrier. If there is some grave necessity, the oath may be taken whatever the day.

Their triple condition

Even where there is no danger of irreverence or in utility, there are three essential conditions to be fulfilled for the liceity of an oath. It must not be taken carelessly, as we might toss off a remark about the weather; it must be taken with judgment. It must be done justly, that is, not in confirmation of some future, evil deed. In addition, it must be taken with truth.

Their obligation

Men have been right in considering oath taking as serious business. It is serious and it carries with it a heavy obligation. That obligation is first of all to truth, falling either on the act of swearing itself (in the matter of past or present things), or on the thing sworn to (in the case of future things). Thus, if a beggar has sworn to produce a million dollars within a week, his oath has lacked judgment; obviously he stands no chance of consummating the future act which he has confirmed by his oath. If a millionaire swears to produce a million dollars in the same length of time and within that week loses all his money, evidently he is not obliged to produce the million dollars, not held to make come true what he has sworn to. If a political candidate has sworn to murder his rival, he is not only not obliged to make that oath come true, he is absolutely forbidden to do so. When we call on God to help us, we cannot treat Him as a scullery maid, a simpleton or a devil; we must always treat Him as God. It is precisely that aura of divinity that has given an oath its sacred character.

Of power -- adjuration

A man who walks with God goes much farther than the man who walks alone. That is true, not only of the man himself, but of all of his actions: of his sacrifice, his love, his bravery, even his power. It is evident that a man can firmly order his own dealings with others by promises; when those promises are linked with divinity, they have the solemn sacredness of oaths and vows. It is equally evident that a man can order his dealings with others -- superiors or subjects -- by prayers and by commands. If either of these are linked to divinity or some holy thing, they too take on an added drive, the drive of adjuration.

With respect to inferiors or subjects, adjuration means an added obligation; to equals, an added inducement; to superiors, an added plea. It is really a stepping-up of the power of man through the subjection of that power to the things of God. By that super-charged power, the acts of man surge out of the limits of the human field into the wide fields of nature and into the halls of hell. By adjuration, i.e., by the power of the divine name, men can compel the devils themselves, resisting their attacks and safeguarding men. It is true that trees or mountains do not jump to attention at the command of a man; they are deaf to his puny voice. Nevertheless, a fish did bring Peter the tax money, a mountain did move for Gregory and the birds came to listen to the sermons of Francis. For the irrational world does respond to this divine power in the hands of men; adjuration's added plea to God can induce the touch of the Master to which these irrational things respond directly, as the arrow responds to the touch of the archer.

Great power is too often unsettling to men; the faintest promise of a power greater than that of other men is too often enough to coax a man into ridiculous and tragic mistakes. Such a mistake has been the appeal to the devil for help and knowledge, a gesture of friendship and dependence that is always both a degradation and a tyranny. The long wisdom of experience gathered by the Church, as well as the divine wisdom granted to her for the guidance of men, point out that the devil is a very good person to avoid. When we send out our invitations, we make very sure there is no chance of them being delivered by mistake to a Satanic address; for this wisdom has seeped deeply into Catholic hearts, making them avoid what even looks like a friendly smile toward the devil. In fact, even when our hostility is evident, when we are advancing to the attack openly by publicly compelling him to obey, we must carefully follow the rigid restrictions laid down by the Church. We cannot play with the devil, he plays too roughly for us; we cannot be broad-minded about him, he is too clever for us; we cannot be friendly toward him for he hates us. What we must do, in all common sense, is keep as far away from him as possible.

Language of the full heart -- praise and song

In the last chapter, and so far in this chapter, we have fixed our gaze steadily on the double work of religion: the work of honoring God and perfecting man. Now it is a fact that we cannot fill the human heart and expect a man to keep still about it. He will whistle, hum, sing, shout, or, at the very least, he will talk. He may talk as unceasingly as a young father, making a lovable nuisance of himself; but he will talk.

Psychologically speaking, then, religion must have a language; it must have an outlet for the fullness of heart it brings to man. It is true that, looking at the First Cause and Last End of all things, seeing the ineffable, totally incomprehensible goodness and beauty of that Supreme Being, man is at a lose for words; and he must always be. Such a spectacle paralyzes speech; it is too much for the human mind. Now, the world about us, or the world within us, gives us that divine beauty diluted to a point where we can drink it in; and then inevitably we must at least talk. We must publish the praises of this supreme goodness and this supreme beauty.

In the world of men, every spoken word is in the nature of a revelation. It puts aside the veil of our hearts and allows men, angels and devils to peer into the sanctuary that only God and ourselves enter freely. Every man in the world has something to tell others, some reason for speech, even though he does not add to the wisdom of the world; for he has something that no one else can know in any other way but by his words. He has a heart of his own. Our speech with God and with men have totally different ends. Our praise of God is not to be likened to the slap on the back and the word of commendation given the office boy by way of spurring him on. Our praise of God is to give expression to the fullness within us; to awaken yet greater inner devotion and to stir the sluggish hearts of others to something of the same intensity. It is distinctly not for the benefit of God.

If song or chant accomplishes these ends, it is most useful in the praise of God; and so men have found it, for almost universally song or chant has been associated with the worship of God. There is the obvious danger of making a theater of the church, using a song, not for worship, but for show, amusement, pleasure. Such songs are distractions; they defeat the ends of religion, not lifting men's hearts to God but rather binding them to earth.

Barrenness in human life -- irreligious

The picture of human life insisted on by religion is one of light, of order, of peace; a full-hearted exultation. Religion insists on man's perfection because it insists that man take his proper place in the universe. The rich soil of the human heart is cultivated to its utmost by religion; it is metamorphosed into a luxuriously beautiful garden. On the contrary, irreligious and superstition work on other principles and to other goals. Fundamentally, they put man in the wrong place in the universe; instantly the harmony of the universe and of man's life is disrupted by a flat, tasteless note -- the note of disorder. By them, the rich possibilities of human life are perverted, stunted or even destroyed. Even the richest soil can stand just so much abuse. Our growing American deserts are vague images of the rank growth of neglect or the weary stretches of sterile landscape that are spreading in the hearts of men and women today, like a fire licking its hungry way across a dry prairie. The human heart cannot be full if it is not subject. It can be wholly empty if it is subject to the wrong thing; and that is precisely the work of superstition and irreligious, to release man from subjection that he might be sold into degradation and tyranny.

The barrenness of superstition: In the worship of the true God

It is a mistake to suppose that superstition deals only with false gods and their mysterious powers. Just as a man can speak words of love with hate in his heart or be overwhelmed with sorrow while he maintains the smile on his face, so he can be superstitiously irreverent in the very gestures of religion made to the true God. I have seen a renegade, who had not been inside a church for twenty years, kneel down outside a church and piously touch his forehead to the sidewalk twenty times. He was, of course, flatly and openly superstitious; his religion was an exclusive concentration on externals, insisting that these are the essentials of divine worship. The results of these superstitions are usually weird, though not often as weird as the antics of the Holy Rollers; they are sometimes comic, as is the lusty bellowing of a burglar at his annual camp meeting: but they are always disastrous, for defect in the worship of God is inseparable from defect in the perfection of man.

In the worship of false god -- a subjection of degradation: Idolatry

Principally, however, superstition is engaged in paying divine honors to false gods. Our history is a torn, tattered book with most of the first pages missing; but the comparatively short span covered by what pages still remain shows us a variety of false gods that is a diabolic burlesque of divine attributes. Every creature is a footprint of God and God is not far from anyone of us, but rather intimately within us; and men have made the grotesque mistake of saluting the footprint as the Person who made that print. They have found gods in the plant world, in the animal world, in the human world, in the diabolic world -- yes even in that fragile artificial world produced by the skillful hands of men.

To look back over the barren wastes of that superstition is even more disheartening, more terrifying than to search the ruins of a city for the victims of war. It helps little to realize that behind this desolation was the hate of the devil, with its cynical eagerness to work wonders through the idols of men; for we know well what a great part man's own ignorance and disordered appetites played in substituting the superficial beauty or power of the creature for the supreme beauty and power of the Creator. The children born of idolatry were worthy of such parents as ignorance and disordered affection murder, mutilation, sex perversions have all been put forth in the name of reverence and honor for divinity. In fact, St. Thomas says, there is no type of sin that idolatry does not induce or give occasion for.

Divination

Men blundering about in this murk of sin, degradation and tyranny were uneasy, terribly uneasy. In lieu of the Catholic's trust in the providence of a heavenly Father, with its assurance of help and infinitely wise guidance, these victims of superstition had only the bitter bread of fear as sustenance for the future. They were tempted to resolve their fears by forging yet heavier chains by calling in the demons through the practice of divination. Sometimes this invocation of evil spirits was explicit, a total surrender to evil; at others, the devils were implicitly invoked in the study of the disposition or movement of other creatures for the prediction of future contingent things, a practice that made the flight of birds or the drift of clouds momentous things in the life of a man. Or again, this implicit invocation was contained in some action seriously put forth as a means of discovering the occult.

In twentieth century America, we have all types of superstition still flourishing. The devil is invoked explicitly in the trance of a medium; implicitly in the astrologer's charts and study of the movements of stars or in the deadly serious practices of drawing lots, casting dice and so on as a means of determining future things. All of these are superstition, for all attribute to creatures what belongs to God alone, namely, a knowledge of future things, which cannot be known in their causes. As in the time of Christ, men today are seeking signs, signs that are certainly not given by God; signs that can have significance only if they are the work of the demon.

If we take into account the limitations of diabolic knowledge, and the goal of diabolic hate, all this is evidently a silly, fruitless business. The mind and will of man is a sanctuary to be entered freely by God and man himself, but inviolable to the devil. Moreover, the devil is ceaselessly active, not because of his love for men but because of his hatred for God and everything that belongs to God, particularly for the friends of God. How naive we are to expect favors from an enemy who cannot possibly forget! That things wonderful to our weak minds are sometimes made known through these means only makes the practice that much more dangerous; for then we are disposed to believe these predictions when they do deal with things that can be known only to God or when our enemy, the devil, deliberately lies. We simply cannot afford to associate with the devil, depending on our own powers; we are out of our class intellectually and we shall always be fooled.

The devil might, were he so disposed, make a better job of forecasting the weather than does the official weather forecaster; with his superior intellect, he should be a keener student of natural causes. Nevertheless, very few of the superstitious besiege satanic headquarters with desperate demands for weather charts. The fundamental fault that runs through all divination is an examination of things, not as causes, but as signs. It is not an attempt to gauge the natural powers of these things and their consequent effects; that is an intelligent procedure and divination is far from intelligent.

Observances

As if divination were not irrational enough, men went a step further in demanding that signs work as causes and produce effects to which they had no relation. Muttered formulas, esoteric scrawls, tokens such as a rabbit's foot or a lion's tooth were expected to produce knowledge or health, or to unveil the future. Much of this superstitious practice -- which Thomas calls "observances", and which also goes by the name of magic -- has come down to our time and is actually taken seriously by men and women of this scientific age. Its very irrationality makes it difficult to understand how it could persist; perhaps because attacking the irrational by reason is so much like spearing a dream with a pitchfork. Evidently, a rabbit's foot does very good work in its own line -- the transportation of a rabbit. Still, if it should win a horse race, it is going entirely outside the sphere outlined by nature for the foot of a rabbit; it is not producing this effect through any natural ability or natural power. Rather this effect must be traced to coincidence or to something far above the power of a rabbit, that is, to the power of the devil himself.

No one who has known the agony of tired ankles expects a rabbit's foot to carry the weight of a stallion very far. Since they do believe in the magic power of this token, the very magic upon which they depend is no less than an agreement or contract entered into with the demon; a dangerous, devastating and futile contract for a man. Such a contract might bring some results; for instance, the devil might do something by way of help through his superior knowledge if he were lovingly seeking the good of man -- which he is not. Now, certainly the devil can no more pour knowledge into a man's mind or unveil the future than can a squalling infant. Only God has entry into the mind of man, and only to God is the future present.

Lest there be any misunderstanding, a clear distinction must be made between the futile dependence on mere signs and the use of medals, relics and so on, by the Church. In the latter case, these signs are used from confidence in God or the saints, not for the signs themselves. When we make novenas, the nine first Fridays, tridua, or say five or fifteen mysteries of the Rosary, we are not playing a numbers game; we do not expect extraordinary results from the number nine, three, five or fifteen. We hope for these results from God and the saints to whom these things are directed; the number itself is a test and proof of our sincerity, our perseverance, or sometimes it is itself a charmingly significant gesture of reverence to a divine mystery.

A journey through the barren country of superstition is disagreeable. It leaves a sense of uncleanness, of foul darkness, of unhealthy mystery like that which comes as one stands by the Dead Sea in the short twilight that is no more than a muttered threat, which precedes the blow of night, and looks at the bare, tortured rocks that surround that lifeless sink. However, at least superstition insists that reverence is due to a superior, even though it makes a bad job of reverence or a poor choice of a superior. Where the reverence given by religion in the name of justice is denied to God we have the sin of irreligious.

Barrenness of religious doubt and presumption: tempting God

The first of these sins was exemplified, time and again, by the atheist Ingersoll when he pulled out his watch and dared God, if He could, to strike him dead within five minutes. In the same unholy spirit the soldiers blindfolded Christ, struck Him and demanded that He prophesy who it was that struck Him. These men were putting God to the test; they were doubting the divine qualities of God, for we do not test that of which we are certain. These were explicit temptations of God, acts of open irreverence; normally, God in His mercy ignores these petty annoyances of men, giving them a little more time to puncture the balloon of their pride.

The devil tried to coax Christ into another sin of irreligious, when he suggested that Christ throw Himself down from the heights of the temple in the assurance that God would protect Him. The evil one was playing on our human tendency to exaggerate our own importance, the smiling face we turn to presumptuous thoughts. All the same,, you will remember, Christ did no plunging; He came down from the temple as men should come down, step by step. Paul did not jump off the wall of Damascus expecting God to lower him slowly, safely, even gracefully to the ground; he was let down in a basket, presumably by a couple of very strong men. There is, then, absolutely no justification for the expectations of the student who prays hard to pass an examination but does not bother to study. We are not being pious, rather we are tempting God, when we expect a few ejaculations to take the place of a regard for traffic lights.

In these cases, men spurn the ordinary, secondary causes by which things are normally accomplished and, without necessity or utility, they throw themselves directly upon divine action. They put God to the test through presumption; the failure in the examination and the broken bones are rightly put down to the individual. It is strictly true that God helps those who help themselves. Our very ability to help ourselves is one of the great human prerogatives, a participation in the causality of God Himself that marks us off from the world of driven things. In these sins, there is contained just as much, or more, contempt for man and man's powers as there is doubt of God.

Barrenness of contempt: Perjury

We go a long step beyond doubt and flagrantly violate God's rights when, instead of the humble gesture of reverence, we give Him the gnarl of contempt implied in every act of perjury. The perjurer takes it for granted that either God does not know the truth or that He is ready to connive with evil and confirm a lie. The perjurer, then, is not only a liar, he is an irreligious liar who tries to involve God in the mesh of his falsehood. He is a social threat; he not only perverts the means by which men communicate with each other, he undermines the solid support men depend on for certitude and security in the crucial moments of society's existence. He makes a desert not only of his own life but, to the best of his ability, of the lives of those with whom he lives: his own life by the contempt he gives to God; the lives of his fellows by corrupting the society in which they live.

Sacrilege

Less directly but no less certainly contemptuous of God is a sin that is becoming a commonplace in the twentieth century -- the sin of sacrilege. It is a cowardly, helpless thing, like beating the maids of a man's household through timid hatred of the master himself. Sacrilege attacks holy things, the things that have taken on a divine character by their dedication to God. The particular sacrilege may be accomplished by injuring, insulting or outraging persons dedicated to God, as has happened so frequently in the history of nuns. It may be a somewhat lesser sacrilege of violating holy places, such as the use of a church for a stable; it may be the desecration of holy things such as vestments, chalices, images of the saints. Now, the peak of sacrilege is reached when a man uses the very implements by which divine life is possible to him, as tools to dig his way into hell; when he violates the Sacraments, particularly the Sacrament of Christ's own body. The sacrileges, which involve physical violence, bear the common mark of contempt and spite; they have all the mean destructiveness of helpless anger. God is not destroyed; his religion goes on; nuns continue to scorn the world; nothing is consumed but the rebel who tried to throw a thunderbolt at God.

Simony

Sacrilege is a brutish, clumsy, violent lout compared to the sleekly urbane deadliness of simony. It goes about its work quietly; it does not bomb a church, it corrodes it with the relentless stealth of rust feasting on steel. Simony not only destroys religion in its victim, it throws the filthy cloak of greed around the virgin beauty of holy things, making them repulsive to men. Its barrenness is eventually a sterility of a whole community.

The value of spiritual things cannot be measured in material terms; for the spiritual is always infinitely above the world of matter. Yet simony puts these things up for sale and haggles over their price with all the callousness of a white slaver. Greed blinds a man to such an extent that he can see nothing, not even the things of God, except in terms of money. In a very true sense the perpetrator of simony is a thief; he sells what he does not own but of which he is merely the minister. He is flatly violating the instruction of His master, "*freely have you received, freely give;*" instead, he jingles the thirty pieces of silver and goes gaily about the business of hanging himself.

The barrenness of atheism

In Thomas' treatment of injustice done to God by sins against religion, he makes no mention of atheism. As often happens in St. Thomas, what he does not say is as important as what he says; in this case the very omission has profound significance. On the face of it, there is a direct opposition between religion and atheism. One gives reverence and subjection to the first and last Cause, while the other denies and ignores a first and last Cause. Yet, look a little deeper and you will see that Thomas' omission of atheism wag due to his hard common sense, the common sense that kept him from chasing figments of the imagination when there were things to get done.

As a matter of fact, there cannot be atheism. Man may vociferously deny that he had any first cause, though his very existence reveals the falseness of his claim; but he cannot even deny that he has a last cause, a final end, without paralyzing action and reducing it to the spasmodic twitchings of madness. Man must go somewhere, for his life is a motion and every act is a step toward a goal. Man's goal is his god - - an odd god, perhaps, represented by the figures on a bank statement, the sweetness of pleasure, the exhilaration of power, the oblivion of a party, a state, a nation, or even man's own puny self -- whatever it is that the modern atheist aims at, to that thing he pays the tribute of religion. That is his false god; more hideous, more ludicrous, more pathetic, more calamitous than the ugly idol of a savage.

Twentieth century barrenness: A negative statement -- modern evaluation of religion

The abstract too often leaves us cold. Even so, there is no need of keeping to the abstract in treating of the barrenness of irreligious. A glance at modern opinions of the nature of religion will give us a quick and accurate view of the barren spaces within the human souls of this twentieth century; a vivid, concrete summary of this chapter. According to some men today, religion was born of ignorance, consists in the worship of the mysterious as superior, and is destined to disappear with the advent of knowledge. That is, religion is unworthy of an intelligent man; or, at best, it is an object of amiable toleration because of the practical good it may accomplish among unlearned and simple souls. To other men, religion is a manifestation of fear, cowardice, a desire for escape. It is a perpetuation of the protections of childhood and flight from the realities of life; it pushes a solution of the questions of life farther and farther away, even into a distant, future life. In a word, religion is unworthy of a brave man. Still others see religion as a sop for failure, an excuse for lack of accomplishment and drive, the opiate of the downtrodden keeping them satisfied with the unsatisfying things of life. A thing, that is, unworthy of a successful man.

Or, again, religion is described as an emotional outburst, satisfying the side of man's nature that escapes knowledge. It is a matter of feeling, of religious sense, of religious experience. Consequently, it is as varied and independent as the emotions of each individual; it is strictly personal. At the other extreme is the school, which today looks upon religion as a substitute for intellect or a rival of it. Religious intuition reaches the truth which reason falsifies. Ultimately this means that man is not a rational but a purely emotional animal; his guide is not his reason hut his feeling, even though that feeling be called religious.

A positive statement ·· twentieth century subjection:
Of intellect to falsehood ·· rejection of a First Cause

All this has been a negative statement of modern barrenness. The positive statement is no more encouraging, a statement that is readily had by examining that to which men subject themselves today. There is an almost universal denial of a first cause among contemporary American philosophers; translated, that means that man has subjected his intellect, not to God, but to the falsehood of a self-explanatory world, to a falsehood that the existence of the smallest of things effectively refutes.

Subjection of life to modern idols

If we look at the whole life of man, rather than at his intellect alone, we see that the men of our century have linked arms with the men of all ages in subjecting themselves to something; and they have embraced almost everything that has been offered by the ages in the way of a false god. We too have our modern idols, modern only in that they wear twentieth-century clothes: wealth, success, political prestige, party or race supremacy, even pure selfishness. There have been some men in every age who subjected themselves to false gods in pursuing false goals; which is to say, that in every age some men have subjected themselves to things beneath them and consequently have condemned themselves to degradation and tyranny. Our age is no exception.

A test of perfection -- the crises of life
(birth, manhood, marriage, sickness, death)

If it is true that barrenness is spreading in the human heart of today, that is, if it is true that man's perfection consists in his subjection to the true God whereas men of today are subjecting themselves to false gods, then this lack of perfection should show up in the lives of modern men. Now, does it? Well the natural place to look for an exhibition of perfection or a manifestation of its defects would be in the crises of human life. How do we meet those crises? Do we meet them strongly, as an evidence of perfection; or do we meet them with weakness, cowardice, surrender?

There is no need to develop this thought. Let us just mention the modern attitude toward such crises of human life as its inception. Are we meeting the crises of birth or exhausting ingenuity in trying to escape it? How about the crisis of manhood, when an individual comes to an age which demands that he face his own responsibilities, where he is his own master with his own rights and his own obligations? Are we admitting those obligations, embracing those responsibilities or are we trying to flee from them even at the cost of denying our humanity? Also the crisis of marriage -- are we meeting it squarely or are we leaving doors open, like cautious burglars, that we may escape from it at any moment? Do we face the crisis of sickness or do we hide it away in institutions, pushing it out of our minds while we rush into a whirl of pleasure to drown its least hint? The crisis of death? What is it to us today except the ultimate in despair, the end of all things; not to be met, but to be avoided as far as possible, as long as possible, at any cost -- indeed to be escaped by denying life itself in asserting that only change exists.

The price of perfection

Paradoxical as it may seem, it remains true that man is perfect in exact proportion to the subjection he gives his superiors, to that subjection given the Supreme Being Who is the first cause and last end of every creature. This truth is buried so deeply in man's heart that, however much he may reject God, he will still insist upon subjecting himself to something, to someone, because of that profound realization that only in subjection can he come to perfection. Religion, we have seen, is a matter of strict justice; it merely gives God His due. In addition, we cannot give God anything without perfecting ourselves. There are two sides to the coin of religion: on one side is the worship of God; on the other, the perfection of man. The two are inseparable. As the worship of God is neglected the perfection of man decays; as man perfects himself, so also must he perfect the worship of God. There is no other recipe for perfection than that of subjection, for it is always true that he that will lose his life will save it, and he that will save his life will lose it. It is only by giving that life utterly to God that it becomes solidly our own.

⚏CHAPTER XII⚏

SOCIETY'S DEBTOR
(Q. 100-110)

1. Social debts as links to a principle.

2. Social debt as obligations to one's self:
   (a) As a member of society.
   (b) As dependent from a principle.

3. Subjection to principles a condition of perfection.

4. Subjection to the first principle ·· religion.

5. Subjection to secondary principles:
   (a) To parents and country ·· piety.
   (b) To superiors ·· observance.
   (c) To superior persons ·· dulia.
   (d) To benefactors ·· gratitude.

6. The virtues of subjection to secondary principles:
   (a) Gratitude.
   (b) Obedience
      (1) Its natural origin.
      (2) Its excellence.
      (3) Its extension:
         a. Obedience to God.
         b. Obedience to man.

7. Society's bad debts; philosophy of punishment:
   (a) Revenge by society.
   (b) Revenge by the individual.

8. The unceasing social debt ·· truth.

Conclusion:

1. The importance of beginnings:
    (a) The grain of truth in process philosophies.
    (b) Double error of modern views:
        (1) Unending process.
        (2) Burdensome past.

2. The penalty of separation from principles --
physical or moral annihilation.

3. The perfect subject.

Within recent years, the unsolved problems of an industrial civilization have focused men's minds on a partial truth. Individuals in our own country, and especially the organized groups in our nation, have become acutely conscious of the truth that society owes them certain debts; along with this has come a deeper and deeper appreciation of the great resources of modern society. This double knowledge has resulted in the correction of some long-standing abuses: but it has also been turned to peculiarly dangerous ends. Individuals and organized groups have become engaged in endless bickering as sordid as a family quarrel over the will of a dying parent. Each tries to get from society what belongs to him; but as time goes on and the quarrel gets more bitter, greed gets in its sly whisper and it becomes much more a matter of getting all that can be had rather than of getting what is justly due. Indeed, it seems to have gone to the utterly selfish depths of attempting to get so much that no one else can get anything. There is a peculiar fittingness in the comparison of this state of things to the ruthless haggling of a family over the will of a dying parent. In such a case, the parent is pretty well forgotten; the only important thing about him is his eagerly anticipated death. When that happy event takes place, the individuals of the family will be enriched. Now, as a matter of fact, when the groups or individuals within a society concentrate on what society owes them and fight to get all that can possibly be had from society that society is in grave danger of death; of death by violence. There is an equal sordidness in the family quarrel and the social quarrel; but the latter is more than sordid, it is terribly dangerous. The society, like the dying parent, lies neglected and forgotten on its deathbed; but the death of society will not enrich the social groups, it will destroy them.

Social debts as links to a principle

Society is, after all, a union of men. It is not stronger than the links that bind its members together; and those binding links are the individual citizen's debts to society. Where those debts are forgotten, neglected or denied, society is dissolving; it has become a tool for the aggrandizement of the individual or the group, rather than an instrument for the common good. An acknowledgment of the individual's debts to society is a statement of his dependence on the group, and therefore of the strong tie that binds men together in that common life. On the contrary, a denial of those debts is a boast of sufficiency, an implicit denial of dependence on society or of any serious need of a common social life. The truth, however, is that no man is sufficient unto himself. He never lives alone; he is linked to other men as to a cause or to an effect, he is linked to the whole society as to his principle of social life, of education, of direction, of government. It is unfortunate that today we use the word debt in the sense of the obligation imposed by a usurer. In its truer sense, a debt is no more than a statement of the rights of others; it is an insistence on the minimum of justice. In case of social debts, the word means more than that man owes something to society; it means that in owing something to society, man owes something to himself. His payment of his debt to society is a payment made to himself; a repudiation of that social debt is a repudiation of a debt to one's self. For a man cannot rob society without at the same time robbing himself, just as a man cannot shoot himself without injury to every part of his body; every cell in that body must contribute to the toll exacted by nature tor the repair of the injury. Additionally, man, you will remember, is a part of society, a member of the social organism.

Social debt as obligations to one's self: As a member of society.

The man who cheats society is in the disastrously absurd position of an Alpine climber who cuts the rope from which he dangles by way of proving his rugged individualism. If we could picture a musical note, in a fit of independence, turning viciously on the throat of the singer and cutting it, we would have a fairly exact insight into the full significance of injustice to society. For a man is always dependent; he is always hanging from something, swinging towards something. His position in society is like the position of the trapeze artist as he swings through space from one support to another. Neither is in a position to indulge in snobbery or assertions of complete self-sufficiency.

A man cannot hang in space any more than a trapeze artist can sit on air and defy the crowd's impatient demand for the completion of his act. Man must have something above him and something below him. He must have a beginning and he must have an end. It is precisely in holding to that position, below his superior and above his inferior, that man takes his rightful place in the universe; the maintenance of that proper place in the universe is the absolute condition for human order, human peace, human stability and human progress.

In the past few chapters, we have looked at man's dependence in relation to his first cause and final goal. We have seen that the virtue regulating that dependence, recognizing it, glorying in it, is religion. In addition, religion, it became apparent, was not a matter of personal taste, of caprice or indignity to man; but a matter of strict justice, of being honest with God. From the human side, we saw this subjection to a first and last principle as a fullness of life for man; its denial or perversion, as barrenness, imperfection, sterility in human life.

In this chapter, we shall examine some of the other principles, some of the other beginnings of man and his relation to them; for man has other beginnings. There are other persons, other things under God from which man depends and to which he must be subject, Nor is this so surprising in view of the power, generosity and thoughtfulness of God. He is not a blustering dictator nor a tyrannously timid superior afraid to share his power, knowing that he cannot stand a rival. Rather because He is such a perfect Beginning, He can and does share His divine prerogatives so prodigally with His creatures, even that prerogative of principality with regard to the master creature, man. The phrase "image of God" is not an empty figure nor a bit of poetic fancy; it is a profound truth. Men are made in the image of God not only in their very essence, but in their actions as well as in their goals. Man does have other beginnings from which he depends as he depends from God, either because of the benefits he has received from them or because of their superiority, their excellence in his regard.

As dependent from a principle

A dependable norm for judgment of the relative dependence of man upon the creatures of God is this: a man is dependent upon these secondary causes in exact proportion to their share in the principality of God. That is, the dependence is to be measured by the degree in which these creatures are the principle, the beginning, of man's life, his nourishment, and of his direction to a goal.

God comes first on all counts. Under God, as so many easily graduated steps by which His children can race up to the heights of the divine, there are, first of all, parents who are immediate principles of life, nourishment and direction. The native country (*patria*), the fatherland is in some sense a beginning of his life, a principle of his direction to the goal, of his education as a social being. Then there are the superiors of that society as principles of direction to a goal through the instrumentality of law; in a lesser way, the way of example, there are those virtuous men and women who also lead a man to his goal. Finally, there are benefactors who, while not principles of the common goods, as are the superiors of society, are undoubtedly principles of particular goods for this particular individual.

It is as though God, in His tolerant understanding of the vagaries of the human mind, saw how easily we could be distracted, even entranced by the baubles of life to the point of overlooking the Supreme Being in whom we live, move, and have our being. In the rush of life, man might easily forget or push to one side the thought of the infinite presence of God and His all-powerful causality; so all along the way our feet must tread, God put this variety of highly colored markers sure to catch the fancy of our childish eyes and bring our minds back, again and again through life, to the first Beginning and the last End.

Subjection to principles a condition of perfection.

We are debtors of God as the supreme principle, first and last, and by paying our debt of religion, we perfect ourselves. After God, we are debtors to our parents and to our country as to the chief sharers in the principality of God. Again, this is a debt of strict justice. Its payment involves no more than honesty; and that debt is paid, to our perfection, by the virtue of piety.

Subjection to the first principle -- religion

These two virtues, religion and piety, are not rival creditors clamoring for their share of the slim assets of a bankrupt man. They are intimately a part, one of another. Just as religion fits under justice, so piety fits under religion; as religion is a part of justice, so piety is a part of religion. All the same, it is much more a part of religion than religion is a part of justice; in fact, religion includes piety as the United States includes Illinois or as the human soul includes within itself the powers of a plant and an animal soul. In the concrete, this means that true religion is not a shrewish, jealous wife frowning down a man's patriotic devotion; it cannot interfere with man's duties to his parents or to his country. On the contrary, it is the surest guarantee of parental reverence and of patriotic sacrifice, for by piety we acknowledge a subjection that is only a feeble sharing of the subjection to God; in religion we admit the far greater debt which is the foundation and source of the claim of parents and country upon our reverence and upon our subjection. Religion is the sun, piety the moon of our life of subjection.

Subjection to secondary principles: To parents and country -- piety

To carry the comparison to its concrete conclusion, we may say that parents hold the same place in relation to their children that God holds to creatures. Parents play the part of God, not only in the minds of their children but in actual reality. Under God, they are principles or beginnings as God is the Principle or Beginning. This truth is not difficult of realization in its actuality, especially for a mother or father. It is impossible to look with love's eyes at an infant and not see its utter helplessness. It depends entirely on the parents' thoughtfulness, generosity, willingness to sacrifice -- a dependence that extends not only to the broad essentials of life, but to the smallest detail of personal action and personal necessity. The infant in his mother's arms presents a picture, perfect in its way, of our relationship to God.

However, of course the relation is two-sided. If the parent plays the part of God as the principle of the child, the parent also bears something of the divine responsibility to that child; not only in the few instants of infancy, of childhood and of adolescence, but for the whole life of the child. They do not cease to be parents because their son has had his first shave. Therefore, it becomes the normal and accepted duty of a father to exchange the long hours of the years, the tissues of his body, the blood of his heart for a heritage to sustain his children throughout all of a lifetime. Not infrequently, the love and labor that were spent so generously prove a greater heirloom than piles of gold.

Normally our patience towards, and understanding of, other people's children is distinctly limited, our irritation a ready and reasonable thing. Still, with regard to our own we have something of divine generosity, divine understanding, divine patience; and like the divine, these things escape reason's weight and measure. We may be puzzled at the mother's ecstasy over this child, so patently inferior to our own; how does she ever put up with the noise, the thoughtlessness, the impudence of that brat? While from the front porch across the way, other people are asking the same questions about us. So also might we easily wonder how God ever puts up with us.

A superficial glance at married life today might lead us to suspect that men and women have missed the sublime truth that a parent plays the part of God in relation to his child. As a matter of fact, they have not missed that truth today; rather they are staring fixedly at that truth, but only at the frightening side of it. It is the obligations of parenthood, rather than its privileges, that have caught the modern eye; we see nothing but the terrifying fact that the child, in all justice, makes somewhat the same demands on its parents that a creature does on its God. It takes courage to face that fact, indeed, it takes something of divine courage. Additionally, our age is not a notably courageous age.

On the other hand, the child's relation to his parents is like the creature's relation to his God. The untrammeled development of a child's personality is not sufficient reason for its impudence and reckless disobedience. The child owes reverence and honor to his parents for somewhat the same reason that a creature owes reverence and honor to his God; both are principles, sources, beginnings of life and of direction to a goal. Nothing in the world will ever change this truth; the parents will always be parents, the children always children. Understand, this is a matter of justice, not of love. Love for one's parents can be pretty well wiped out by parental wickedness; but absolutely nothing in the world can wipe out the fact of parenthood. Their just claims to honor and reverence stand forever.

It would be utterly preposterous for a mother, in the name of the equality of all men, to rebel against the one. sidedness of nursing and to demand that the child take on half the burden; on Monday, Wednesday and Friday let the child do the nursing, Tuesday, Thursday and Saturday would be the mother's shift, while on Sunday both could go hungry. Normally, it is the child who should receive help, care and sustenance. Still, it would be a monstrous caricature of reverence that would make a son rush through his dinner in order piously to assist at his mother's death from starvation. In other words, the parents, though they share in the principality of God, are not God. We never have to help God; but our parents are human, they can need help and that help must be given. It is an extrinsic, accidental obligation of sonship; but none the less a real obligation that extends to all blood relatives in exact proportion to their share in the common bond that unites parent and child.

In its own way, a man's country holds the same place in relation to the individual and his fellow-citizens as God holds in relation to His creatures. This, however, is not to be taken in the exaggerated sense of an unadulterated nationalism such as prompts an American newspaper to carry on its editorial page the motto: "My country, may it always be right; but my country, right or wrong!" After all, a man's country is not his God; it shares in some way in the principality of God, but it is not divine. It is not true, as Communism openly maintains that a crime is justified if it is committed from patriotic motives, for the good of the party. Whether it be done in the name of parents or of country, a crime is always against God; and it is only by reason of their share in things divine that country and parents have a claim on our reverence, on our loyalty, on our subjection.

The very reason for giving reverence to our parents and country is precisely because they share in divine principality; consequently, it is absurd to advance that shared principality as a reason for abandoning the divine principality, for not paying God the debt of religion. If our parents are evil, they still remain our parents with a claim on our reverence and help; but not at the cost of our soul. If they are a serious danger to our souls, we must leave them; and give them help and reverence from a spot that does not endanger the rights of God and our obligations to our own soul.

On the other hand, Christ was justly indignant at the hypocrisy of the Pharisees in making religion an excuse for neglecting the duty to parents. An only daughter is not being at all religious when she blithely leaves poverty-stricken parents to starve that she might enter the convent. The obligations to God and to parents do not clash; they have one and the same source, the one includes the other. If in the name of one we neglect the other, we can be very sure that we have completely failed in both.

To superiors -- observance

The complicated group of superiors to whom a man is subject can be seen in their fundamental unity if we picture them as intimately interdependent units of an electrical system. God is the generating unit, the dynamo of principality; from Him the line passes through one transmitting station after another, each of which cuts down the power to fit the particular purposes for which it exists, each receiving a lighter charge of the power from the transmitting station just above it. The station below that of parents and country is made up of the superiors of the state. The virtue by which we are subject to them is called "*observance*" and it stands in the same relation to piety (the virtue of subjection to parents and country) as piety does to religion. These superiors, in other words, have the same relation to parents that parents have to God; the superiors participate something proper to parents, as parents participate something proper to God.

The President in relation to the citizens of the United States, a general in relation to his soldiers, a mayor in relation to the citizens of his city, are all principles of limited direction, of government, of common goods. The obvious implication of this statement of observance is one of fatherly providence on the part of superiors; their citizens are not tools, cogs in a machine or a mere rabble to be used for the benefit of the superiors, they are children with a just claim to fatherly thoughtfulness, protection and help.

These superiors cannot supplant the parents without committing suicide any more than the parents can destroy God and retain their claims to reverence and honor. The transmitting station cannot cut itself off from the generating station and its dynamo and still expect to supply power. We are much more closely united to our parents, more dependent on them than we can ever be on the state. To them our union is substantial, from them we receive such substantial things as life itself, education, nourishment and so on. Theirs is the principality, which is but shared by the state superiors.

The superiors, then, are not brow-beaters nor slave-masters. They are not to be looked on by citizens as enemies, suppressors of liberty, or poachers on the domain of individuality; rather the citizen must see them somewhat as a child sees its parent or a man sees his God. Now, it must always be remembered that these superiors are not God. Not infrequently, they will not even be good men. We give them reverence and subjection, not as God, not even as men, but as superiors. By reason of their official position, we give them honor: by reason of the coercive power they exercise, we give them fear; by reason of their directive office, we give them obedience; and by reason of the labor they expend for the common good, we pay taxes for their support.

To superior persons -- dulia

The next transmitting station that cuts down the divine power of principality is the virtue of "*dulia*". It regulates the honor given on grounds other than religious, blood relationship or official capacity; for the protestation of excellence, which is, called honor is due to all superiors, whatever their claim to superiority, precisely because they are superiors. The name of this virtue is taken from the honor due to a master from his slave. It is a derivation of profound significance when we understand that in absolutely every man there is something superior; in a sense, then, every man is a slave to all other men.

Understand, we do not have to distort our imagination in this search for superiority nor to be hypocritical about it. It would be absurd to pretend that we are in breathless admiration by the small talk of a barber, We need only stick to the truth. If there is any good in a man (and of course, there always is), there is a basis for honoring him. As that good increases, that is, as the man comes closer to his goal, to his God, the reason for honor increases proportionately; so we pay great honor to the saints and the greatest honor given to creatures is given to the saint of saints, Our Blessed Lady.

Yet we find the saints paying honor to sinners. Catherine of Sienna stepped out of a crowd and marched arm in arm down the street with a man condemned to the gallows, ascended the gallows with him and stayed by his side until his death. The same sort of thing is found repeatedly in the lives of the saints; after all, they were doing no more than following the example of their Master. You remember the grave courtesy Christ gave the woman taken in adultery, the tender persistence by which He won over the Samaritan woman at Jacob's well. It would seem certain that it is not necessary for a man to be better than we are to merit our honor; surely, it is not necessary that he be better in every way, or even in any way. In some way or another, he is better than some men.

This does not amount to a kind of auto-hypnotism by which we peer at the world through the eyes of Pollyanna. It is true that it is far from the vague, distorted view given by eyes which are clouded and heavy with experience of evil; but what it really is, is the clear, true outlook that comes through seeing the world with the eyes of Christ, through the eyes that discovered the fearless teachers of the world among the ignorant fishermen on the shore of the Sea of Galilee.

To benefactors -- gratitude

We pay honor to all men. We give subjection to our superiors as principles of our being and direction, as principles of the common goods that come to us. The principles of particular goods are our benefactors and to them we give gratitude. There is a sharp and highly significant distinction between our debts to superiors in general and our debts to benefactors. The former look us squarely in the eye with justice's impassive, impartial face; the latter give us gratitude's open smile, half dare, half invitation, all graciousness. To spurn the first is an injury to our creditors; to dismiss the second is to hurt ourselves. Debts to superiors are statements of the necessity for the equality of things; debts of gratitude are statements of the necessity for the equality of wills. Our benefactors are a step up the ladder of perfection; by gratitude we measure up to that advances, by ingratitude we step down one grade below our own level.

A benefactor has no claim in strict justice to our thanks. As a matter of fact, beneficence has about it something of the satisfaction of mercy; it too, allows a man to play God, distributing his goods to those who have less or nothing at all, even when the goods he so freely gives are no more tangible than smiles. A benefactor really has a substantial return on his action from the moment he gives his gift, independent of any return of thanks on our part. He has had the joy of acting like God. In fact, the smallest act of gratitude on our part immediately puts our benefactor in debt and starts an endless exchange of gifts. So the Magi came bringing gifts to the newborn Infant; and ever since that time the same divine Infant has been giving Himself wholly to men. Simon the Cyrenian helped carry the cross of Christ; from that day forward every man has been helped in the carrying of his cross by the Savior, Who was not too proud to accept the help of a mere man.

The virtues of subjection to secondary principles: gratitude.

If we give it a moment's thought, we easily understand that the obligation of gratitude must be interminable. It arises from a gift freely given; it can be paid, not by a return equal to the original gift -- that way we balance justice, paying a loan - - but by a gift from us, a gift as freely and as spontaneously given. Gratitude's return, in other words, must exceed all claims to justice, just as did the original gift; automatically, then, it sets up the game debt of gratitude in the benefactor. To put the matter more profoundly, we might say that we are images of God even in our actions; as all of creation, which is an act of God, fights its way back to God, to every effect of ours, every one of our acts, is perfect insofar as it finds its way back to us. Inevitably, those acts do find their way back, either by way of revenge or of gratitude. If they do not, that act has been imperfect, as imperfect as would be a work of God that did not seek God. In other words, it would have all the imperfection to be found only in that one creature in the universe that does not come back to God -- a man who has sinned.

Christ gave gratitude's prescription when He said, "*Freely have you received, freely give.*" He started the endless exchange of gifts in giving Himself to Mary as her first Christmas present; all of her life with Him was a loving rivalry of greater and greater gifts. Indeed the lives of all of her children have been just such an endless Christmas, with none of the fears of the specter of January bills and February housecleaning of the gifts Christmas has brought to us.

For, as a matter of fact, there is no one so poor he cannot pay a debt of gratitude. cannot give a greater gift in exchange for what he has received. There is no man so low he cannot put the mightiest in his debt. Christ was not exaggerating when he pointed out the poor widow dropping her mite in the treasury as the one who had given more than all others; for the norm by which gifts are judged is not the pocketbook but the heart. In gratitude's return, likewise, it is not the gift but the will of the giver that overpays the debt; not the thing said, nor the thing done, but the pulse of the heart of the grateful one writing the check that satisfies this debt. In addition, there is no power on earth that can stamp "*insufficient funds*" across the face of such a check.

Whether or not it is more blessed to give than to receive, it is certainly a great deal easier; for the reception of a favor is itself a confession of need. It is for this reason that the proud, self-sufficient man finds it so difficult to receive favors; and for the same reason, the first and most difficult act of gratitude is a benign acceptance of a favor. This whole matter of beneficence and gratitude is one of the heart and not of the hand. Just as we can judge the heart of the receiver by the graciousness, by which he takes the gift, so the heart of the giver is betrayed in the gestures with which he gives the gift. A blackmailer rightly doubts the freedom and affection behind the check his victim surrenders for there is none of the inevitable joy and prompt eagerness inseparable from affection visible in the presentation of this "*gift*."

There are two significant conclusions forced upon us by this consideration of beneficence and gratitude. The first is that a sinner's debt of gratitude for his penance far outstrips that of the saint for his sanctity. The unquestioning surrender and intense apostolicity of Magdalene and Paul are entirely understandable, for they received a greater gift in a double sense: they had less claim on the gift of grace that was given them, and consequently the gift itself was given ever so much more freely. It is true that the saint receives the greater gift objectively; but subjectively the minimum of grace coming to the sinner is like a dime given to a destitute man as compared with a hundred dollars coming to a millionaire. The second conclusion, a rather startling one to our age, is that a prompt return of a favor is more often a sign of ingratitude than of gratitude. There is little of the easy, graceful stride about our rush to return a favor at the earliest possible moment; we feel ourselves forced. Additionally, that is the wrong point of view. Really, it is an attempt to escape a debt that should be a joyful burden, delightedly borne; it is a debt, not of justice but of love and love should not be hard to put up with.

Even though ingratitude is usually a venial sin unless it oversteps the boundaries of justice, it is a contemptible thing. The absolute contempt, which men have for the sin of ingratitude, has been compressed into one explosive word: traitor! Judas has remained the most unsavory character of history because he is the supreme ingrate, the betrayer of a divine friend. Other sins that awaken the disgust and contempt of men are despised not only in others but also in ourselves; our contempt for perversion, bestiality or murder, in other words, is not merely speculative, it is practical for we bend the utmost of our efforts to excluding these things from our own lives. Yet, for some dark reason, the same is not true of ingratitude; that our disgust for it remains largely speculative is evident from the rarity of gratitude and the frequency of ingratitude.

This may seem a large statement. All the same, run through the scale of ingratitude, making sure each note is true. The least sin of ingratitude consists in not resuming a favor, a grade of ingratitude that reaches its peak when we return evil for the good we have received: when we have gone up a step in ingratitude we pretend that no favor has been done us, a condition that reaches its high point in the scorning of a favor; finally the climax of ingratitude is a non-recognition of a favor done to us and its crescendo crashes about our deaf ears when we consider the favor a positive injury. Run over that scale again, listen carefully and see how many of the notes find an echo in our own hearts in our relations with God. How many of the favors of God do we take for granted; how many do we fail to recognize as favors; how many do we positively resent as injustices, punishments, curses? Yes, ingratitude is far from rare however despicable it may be; and no doubt, it will remain so, for only a humble man can be grateful and for humility, we must have the courage to see ourselves as we really are. However, the very contempt for ingratitude is a splendid thing, a ringing assurance of the sound common sense of human nature in its rejection of the stupidities of pride.

Obedience: Its natural origin

It is only to benefactors that unpaid debts escape the anarchy of injustice. To all other principles, we subject ourselves in justice and one of the universal acts by which we put that subjection into action is by our obedience. Yet the very word revolts our jaded appetites as emphatically as the mention of pork to a seasick man. The objections to the very notion pour from our lips with a violence and rapidity that reveals a deep-seated resentment: one man is as good as another, the ignobility of taking orders, the servility of being at the beck and call of a man, the irresponsibility of having someone else do our thinking, the spinelessness of being unable to make up our own minds. How fine they all sound to an independent spirit; and how utterly absurd they are! We have hardly reached the point where it is necessary, as a proof of strength, independence, equality and all the rest, to invade another man's home and beat his wife; it is not degrading for us to respect these rights of a man, nor is it degrading to respect any of his other rights.

From a purely natural point of view, obedience is an absolute condition for harmony with the rest of the universe. All of nature follows the same rule of divine providence, namely, that inferiors are led to their goals by superiors. Men are not only equals, they are also unequals; so much so, in fact, that even in the untainted air of Eden's peace there would have been political organization if Adam had never sinned. It is men, not God, who insist on doing violence to human nature. Men have superiors and they move to their ends as all nature moves to its end, not in violation of their nature but in harmony with their humanity; that is, not physically but morally, by a precept whose answer is obedience. Obedience, in other words, is nothing more or less than a moral virtue by which we obey the precept of our superiors from the intention of satisfying that precept. It is the virtue by which, in harmony with all nature, we are moved to our goal in a manner fitting the high estate of our humanity.

Its excellence

Granted that obedience is not in the same high class as faith, hope and charity, which have God Himself for their object, or even that it is not the supreme moral virtue, for certainly religion comes much closer to God. Still, among the moral virtues, which involve a rejection of temporal things, in order that a man might bow down to God, obedience stands at the very top. By it, man offers that which is most truly his own, his free will; he does what no other creature in the physical world can do, he makes the surrender, which is in itself a conquest of self and of perfection.

In the cosmic order, then, obedience saves man from becoming the one freak in the universe. In the social order, which is after all the natural order for man, obedience is absolutely indispensable. No matter how natty its uniforms, how modern its equipment, how numerous its members, a police force that meets with the combined opposition of all the citizens will be utterly destroyed. Men cannot be ruled successfully for any length of time by an army, a secret police, or a mob of gangsters; but only by obedience. We can put this in one short sentence by pointing out that obedience is justice, and justice is absolutely essential for the social and cosmic life of man.

The superior's precept and the subject's obedience have about them the quiet beauty of a peaceful countryside under a spring sun, the smooth freedom of the long, sure strides of a man. Now, it is not hard to introduce the brazen clash of disorder or the grotesque antics of anarchy. All the smooth grace and freedom is gone from the motion of a man when the hands decide to do the work of the feet. It is unfortunate that this grotesqueness is seen to its full only by the spectators. An industrial captain who, flushed with success in the manufacture of motor cars, decides to regulate the diet of his employees never quite sees what a fool he makes of himself. Obedience, you see, is a respecter of rights; the limits of the rights of the superior automatically mark off the limits of the demands he may make on his subjects.

Its extension: Obedience to God; Obedience to man

It is beautifully fitting, and absolutely necessary, that man give universal obedience to God as the supreme superior; naturally, all movement is subjected to the divine First Mover. Even so, no man is a universal superior, nor is he a universal mover. The obedience we give to any man is limited to the bounds of the subjection we owe him. The feelings of a prince should not be hurt when his subjects ignore the commands he has given in contradiction to the natural law. A governor decreeing a limitation on the number of children his subjects shall have has stepped outside of his field, he is a drum-major playing Napoleon; for, in the things that pertain to man's very being, all men are equal. Human superiors have, as their proper field, the disposition of human actions and human things but strictly, within the limits of the power they enjoy.

Society's bad debts; philosophy of punishment: Revenge by society

Even when the command is within the limits of the superior's power, it does happen, and always has happened, that there are social cheats. The action taken by society against these men who refuse to honor their social debts is punishment. It is an unpleasant subject; indeed, if it were not we would have gone far along the road of degradation, as far as enjoying the pain and suffering of others. Nevertheless, we must not mistake its unpleasantness for an argument against punishment. The mistake is a common one today when men argue seriously in favor of coddling a prisoner like a sick child or of abolishing punishment altogether because it is such a messy, disagreeable thing.

Such arguments do not proceed from a love of humanity but from a flabbiness that shrinks from facing the facts. They overlook the fact that non-payment of social debts really means serious injury to members of the society. To speak of this punishment as the vengeance of the state runs the risk of emphasizing the element of injury to the criminal to the complete neglect of the element of healing the wounds of society and protecting the rights of others; and it is these latter, which are the primary objects of this vengeance of the state. Unquestionably, revenge or punishment is wrong if it proceeds from hate; for then it intends the evil primarily, and gloats on the injury it does to the criminal. Yet, when its sources are charity and justice, as they normally are, punishment is a virtue. It intends such goods as the correction of the criminal, the restraint of his crimes and consequent peace to others, the preservation of justice or the honor of God.

Punishment is not something that may be excused but always demands apology; it can be positively obligatory; it is the state's gesture of defense against internal enemies, as war is its defense against external enemies. If the punishment of the state sometimes seems harsh, we have only to try our sweetest smile the next time we meet a thug to see how far it gets us. He does not respond to a homily on virtue, a paternal slap on the back as emphasis of honeyed advice; the tools of his craft are a club, a gun, a blackjack. This is the language in which he makes himself understood and the language, which immediately brings a glimmer of intelligence to his predatory eyes. He understands a threat to or loss of things by which he places great store: his life, his health, his integrity, his liberty, his possessions, even though at the lower levels of crime, he may not take exile or defamation too seriously.

Not long ago the newspapers reported the case of a judge who discharged a prisoner from the charge of manslaughter as a result of drunken driving. The judge argued that there could be no punishment where there was no guilt and this man was so blindly drunk he could not see to commit a crime. The judge was, of course, roundly denounced in editorials the country over; but indignation does not answer an argument. There was something in the judge's argument, but not nearly enough, as is the way with half-truths; they are always too meager a fare to keep the intellect from staggering into error from sheer weakness. It is true that vindictive punishment must not be inflicted unless there is guilt; but medicinal punishment can very well be inflicted in the absence of guilt, though never in the absence of a cause. Perhaps five or ten years in prison is strong medicine; but there is no doubt that it would impress the condemned man with some personal evils of drunken driving, it might even open his eyes to the enormity of the risks to which he exposes his fellow-citizens, surely it will be a salutary warning to others who find the exhilaration of speed only half the fun of driving. Certainly, the thing should be punished, for, if it is not, only citizens with the reflexes of jackrabbits will survive. Surely, these are causes sufficient for medicinal punishment.

Perhaps the judge had in mind the divine Governor Who never punishes except in cases of positive guilt. Now, if he did, then he overlooked the fact that this Supreme Governor inflicts spiritual punishments; and since the spiritual goods, which these deprive a man of, cannot be ordered to further ends, obviously, they cannot be used as a medicine to ward off other evils. We do not decapitate a man to cure his toothache; nor does God deprive him of the supreme goods to which he can aspire for any lesser end.

Revenge by the individual

It must always be remembered that this matter of punishment is the affair of public authority. A private citizen may defend himself against an attack, even defend himself with considerable vigor; but once the attack is over and done with, the matter is out of his hands. He cannot stalk his attacker, biding his time and pouncing at an unexpected moment; the most he can do by way of revenge is to cite his attacker to public authorities, i.e., he can start his vindication but he may never finish it. The reason is obvious. All punishment involves coercive power because it involves some injury to society in the injury it inflicts on one of society's members; and coercive power belongs only to God and the human superiors who share the principality of God in relation to the common good. In any case, the individual is rarely obliged to seek revenge; it is not so much justice as decency and charity that will move him to take revenge through the state for an injury done to him.

The unceasing social debt -- truth

Social debts are debts to one's self. Nowhere is this more clear than in the social debt paid by the virtue of veracity. It would be enough to prove the point if we merely noticed the scorn and distrust given the two-faced individual or the liar as contrasted with the honor and trust that decorates the life of the straight-forward, truthful man. However, these are external things. Within his very self the liar find. quickly how badly he has cheated himself by his lies as it becomes more and more difficult for him to be what he is, to face the world as it is, to meet life as it is. A lie, you see, is an easy escape, a pleasant substitute for accomplishment and struggle; once we become familiar with that emergency exit our hand reaches for its knob at every hint of danger or labor. The liar buries himself in a false world as sweetly and gently as a man might smother himself in a feather bed.

Christ gave a succinctly profound account of Himself when He said: "I am the truth." Dominic set high goals for himself and his Order when he adopted that single word for his motto: *Veritas*, the truth. For truth and reality are not really different. Christ, as God, was indeed and is the Supreme Reality and so the Supreme Truth; Dominic seeking truth was seeking the world of reality and the God of reality. A false world is like a false step; rather than advancing a man, it throws him down with a jar that hammers at every bone in his body and utterly ruins his disposition. In the same way -- not doing what it should do -- a false word lets a man down hard; it tangles up the line of communication from man to man which is so essential to human life. Imagine the turmoil in the petty details of society if bus conductors, ticket agents and traffic policemen answered all questions with artistically fluent lies; indignation would be a timid word for the outburst of the explorer in search of Brooklyn who was deposited in the Bronx. Men simply cannot live together if they can never be sure they are in contact with one another; and it is by word that they reach each other's mind.

At times, this obligation to tell the truth is one of strict justice, as, for instance, in answer to a legitimate question by a legitimate superior. Still, over and above that strict right, men have a claim in sheer decency, certainly in charity, to be spared deception. However, being truthful is not a matter of pulling the bung from our minds and letting all of our knowledge run out. When a wife asks her husband "*How do I look?*, she is not seeking a diagnosis; prudence will teach him, eventually at least, to restrict his comments to a few large and fairly obvious objectives. When mere politeness moves you to ask after the health of an acquaintance, you stand aghast as he rattles off a long list of his symptoms; this sort of thing is not necessary for social life. Words should measure up to the concept in our minds as things measure up to the concept in God's mind, then both the things and the words are true. It is not impertinent to notice that not all the concepts of God's mind have been expressed in the world of reality. We must tell the truth, yes, but when, where and how it should be told.

The tremendously impossible stories of Baron Munchausen were certainly not lies. They were so evidently and jokingly false that they could never have been meant to deceive; and formally speaking, a lie is the will to say a false thing. Whether or not others are successfully deceived pertains to the perfection of a lie rather than to its nature as a perversion of the gift of speech. The student who knows his matter backwards and gives it that way to his examiners is not guilty of a lie; the manifest hyperbole of a political orator nominating a "*favorite son*", or the demure secretary's "*Mr. Smith is not in*" obviously fool no one. They were not meant to fool anyone; the words have a generally accepted meaning, they are polite forms that even the "favorite son" or the traveling salesman do not fail to understand.

Where the formal will to tell a false thing is present there is always a sin, the sin of lying, never justifiable, never excusable. We can no more excuse a boy for the lie he tells to escape a spanking than we can a man who lies to ruin the character of a rival. The second lie is more serious because it enters the field of justice and takes on the added gravity of an offense to another's rights; but strictly as lies, both are inexcusable. Lies are not sour when they hurt another and sweet when they "*do no damage*"; they are wrong because they pervert the gift of speech. As a matter of fact, they always do damage, social damage, which can never be properly estimated. The life of the party who wrings a laugh from a sullen crowd by his plausible lies is nonetheless a liar albeit an agreeable one. There are not white lies, not even spotted lies; all lies are black with the blackness of sin.

If a girl looking for work as a stenographer is asked whether she has had experience and answers "*yes,*" mentally concluding the sentence, "*in washing dishes*", she has completely fooled her prospective employer -- for the moment at least. All the same, she might as well have saved herself the effort of mentally re-washing the dishes. She has indulged in a mental restriction, which the theologians call "*pure*", though an odd kind of purity it is, for it leaves the lie intact. There is absolutely no way in which that restriction can be detected by any one else; no way in which the concept in her mind can be seen from her words. It has been just a plain lie. The legitimate mental restriction, a restriction in the wide sense, is found in the poor, worn-out phrase, "*Mr. Smith is not in;*" only a moron could mistake the meaning. In addition, such a restriction may, under some circumstances, be allowed. So also may ambiguity or equivocation, for we are not obliged to tell all that we know all the time; here we are not telling falsehood, but rather we refrain from improperly telling the truth.

Perhaps the best estimate of the value of truth is to be found in the effect truth has upon man. Devotion to falsehood produces the social outcast and the sinner. Devotion to truth in the intellectual world produces a philosopher; in the social world, it produces a gentleman; in the supernatural world, it produces a saint. In language dear to our times, we might say that a lie is a kind of verbal perversion that prevents the conception of knowledge in the minds of our neighbors and thwarts the delivery of our own concepts; it is at the same time a verbal birth control and a verbal abortion.

The importance of beginnings: The grain of truth in process philosophies

A summary of this chapter must begin with the truth that man is never through beginning. That he finishes one-step in life merely means that he is ready to take another. If any stage of his life is not a beginning of something else, the man has failed; he has been misled into a blind alley, not led on to higher things and, ultimately, to the Highest Thing. Even when he reaches the end of his life, man comes to the beginning of an eternal life and an eternal act, a beginning that never ends. A man is never really separated from his beginnings; he is always starting things, and all of the things, all the way back in his life, hang together as intimately as the links of a chain.

Double error of modern views: Unending process

This truth has been grasped by modern process philosophies. This is what gives an air of plausibility to their theorizing, this thin thread by which they dangle precariously from the world of reality. Their mistake is in thinking that there is nothing but a beginning in man's life; that life and the world is nothing but a process that does not really begin and never ends, but just flows on. In their eyes, man's life is a bridge that is never quite crossed, an endless treadmill whose only goal is exhaustion. As a result, these philosophies present man's intellect with a tremendous lie; there must be a goal if there is to be any activity, and so there must be not only a beginning, but also a progress to the end, which is the reason for the beginning.

Burdensome past

The second error in these modern philosophies inevitably links up with the first, namely, that all of the past is to be disowned, tossed aside as a man discards his boyhood and forgets it. Additionally, this is held to be true, not only for an age, for one generation, but also for the individual in all the fields in which he moves: religious, philosophical, economic or social. Each individual, each age, each nation starts afresh. That, thank God, is never true. We do not have to shoot our ancestors to prove that we are alive. The loudness of progress in human life, the uncovering of truth, the approach to God, is not something to be handled in a moment, in a lifetime, a generation or an age. It is a slow, laborious, dangerous climb where every foothold dug by our predecessors is invaluable. The past is not a burdensome load we carry on our shoulders; rather it is the springboard from which we plunge into the future.

The penalty of separation from principles -- physical or moral annihilation

Man cannot separate himself from his beginnings without disastrous results. They are an intimate part of him; action against them is a kind of mutilation. If he attempts a moral separation from his first Principle, God, he embraces an eternal hell; a physical separation from the same Principle, if it were possible, would mean instant annihilation. A proportionate note of disaster rings through the world as the result of the blow that separates us from any of our beginnings, our principles; and the disaster will be in exact proportion to the principality, which the particular beginning enjoys.

The waifs' physical separation from parents awakens an immediate response of pity for their misery; they have lost something out of their lives, a precious, indispensable thing. Behind all our irritation there is pity, too, for impudent, disobedient, irreverent children; they also have lost something and lost it forever. Something has been cut out of their lives because they have cut themselves off From a beginning; they have suffered a kind of annihilation and condemned themselves either to a hell of memory or a duplication of the same scorn, insolence and disobedience from their own children. Their life has been dulled, sickened, dwarfed at its start for they have lost subjection and sacrifice, both indispensable to the living of human life.

A man, who has cut himself off from his country, has lost a part of himself, for he is a part of society; indeed, we might say that, as a social being, he has cut himself off from the greater part of himself. He is now a stranger to whom no place is home; he is a stranger everywhere and so is everywhere alone. A man who cuts himself off from his social superiors denies moral force and issues an invitation to physical force. He is a rebel, not only against society, against his fellows, but also against himself. The cynic who refuses the subjection of honor and reverence to men on the score of their virtue condemns himself to blindness; he deprives himself of constant inspiration and anchors himself forever in the sluggish waters of smug mediocrity. The ingrate, refusing to meet the debt of gratitude, scurries to cover from the constant shower of gifts that gratitude and beneficence set up, that constant increase of love, the fullness of a man's life, which comes from beneficent acts of others and their gracious return,

The perfect subject

Man can be perfect; in fact, he was made to be perfect. All of his nature was designed to that end. Now, his perfection is not to be obtained in any utterly self-sufficient sense; he cannot pull up his roots and still expect to grow. He is not alone in the universe: he came from somewhere; he is going somewhere. He has something above him and something below him; something behind him and something before him. In addition, it is only in maintaining that proper position in the universe that a man can find grounds for order, stability, peace, progress and ultimately, perfection. There is a perfection of man, but a perfection that is in perfect proportion to a man's subjection. The perfect man can best be defined as the perfect subject, a truth that was once, not insignificantly, put in the agonized words of the Savior's prayer of perfection: "*Not my will, but Your be done.*"

ROOTS OF RUDENESS
(Q. 111-122)

1. Unity and social life.

2. Separation from the unity of social life ·· exile:
   (a) Physical exile.
   (b) Moral exile.

3. Social exile by defect of truth:
   (a) Simulation and hypocrisy.
   (b) Ostentation:
      (1) Boasting.
      (2) Disparagement ("irony").

4. Social exile by defect of friendliness (affability):
   (a) The nature of friendliness:
   (b) Social effeminacy ·· flattery.
   (c) Social savagery ·· truculence ("quarreling").
   (d) Common origin of social effeminacy and savagery ·· contempt.

5. Social exile by defect of liberality:
   (a) The nature of liberality.
   (b) Social niggardliness ·· avarice.
   (c) Social extravagance ·· prodigality.

6. Perfection of the social instinct ·· the gift of piety:
   (a) The nature of this gift.
   (b) Its distinction from religion, filial fear and the virtue of piety.
   (c) Its extension to all men.

7. Minimum demands for social unity -- the Ten Commandments:

    (a) General character of the Decalogue -- precepts of justice.

    (b) Particular character of the Decalogue:

        (1) Precepts of religion.

        (2) Precepts of piety.

        (3) Precepts of commutative justice:

            a. Against injury to persons.

            b. Against injury to family.

            c. Against injury by word and thought.

    (c) Equity and the Decalogue.

Conclusion:

1. Virtue and society:

    (a) General necessity of virtue in society.

    (b) Particular necessity:

        (1) For protection of others and perfection of one's self:

        justice, religion, piety, observance, dulia.

        (2) For intimacy of community life: gratitude, truth, friendliness.

        (3) For perfection of community life: gift of piety.

2. The Church versus a godless society:

    (a) The enemy and the friend.

    (b) Solver of difficulties.

    (c) Protector of fundamentals.

    (d) Champion of culture.

CHAPTER XIII

ROOTS OF RUDENESS
(Q . 111-122)

A masterpiece, a cathedral or a cottage has a personality of its own. It is lovely, proud, simple, eagerly alive or coldly reticent. All are, in a sense, living even if the life by which they live is the life of their creator. They are solidly units; and by that very unity, they are the closest imitation of that substantial unity which is so characteristic of life. We marvel at them because we marvel at life, and will never have done marveling at it. In both we are marveling at an effect of intelligence deeper than a distinct order, an effect achieved by that order which intelligence alone can produce -- the effect of unity. The artist steps back from his easel and sees that his work is good; into his dead materials, he has breathed as much life as it is given man to give to things, the breath of order and unity. He is in his own way a creator and we honor him for his high achievement.

Unity and social life

Certainly intimate union is a universal characteristic of life. When that unity begins to break up, we have disease; when that unity is completely dissolved, we have death. Additionally, this will be true, not only of the dissolution of the union of soul and body, but of the dissolution of the union between the body and any of its parts. Social life implies an organic unity that is essential to all life; we describe society as an organism whose members are men and women. Pursuing the figure, we measure the vigor of social life by the unity existing between the parts of that social body. Society is healthy, diseased or dying in proportion to the unity of its members.

When one part of the social body is cut off, though the whole body retains its full vigor of life, we have the parallel of amputation. It is injurious to the whole in proportion to the importance of the part that has been amputated; the impeachment of a president, for instance, will be much more harmful than the execution of a gangster, just as it will make a great difference to a man whether he loses a finger or both legs.

Even so, in all cases the amputation is absolutely fatal to the member that is severed from the body. In this chapter, we shall consider the relation of that separation from the social body, precisely as it affects the individual member who is separated from society.

Separation from the unity of social life -- exile: Physical exile.

A social separation is not called amputation, though it could aptly be so called; it is known as exile. Ordinarily we understand that term in a physical sense as calling up the haunting loneliness of "a man without a country." The difficulties of this physical exile are vividly presented to us whenever we enter a Greek candy store or approach an Italian fruit stand. The exile may be voluntary, but the blue sky of Athens and the warm sun of Naples are not to be lightly brushed from a man's mind; nor are the memories of easy, leisurely comradeship, the wild words of argument so quickly forgotten by everyone in preparation for the next discussion. These men will continue to dream their dreams of home as they stand shivering on a New York corner or caught in the clammy embrace of a London fog.

Perhaps the difficulties are more evident when we consider an American expatriate in France, not, you understand, a tourist jumping from place to place but always on his way home, but a man who takes up permanent residence there. Nicodemus long ago was rightly incredulous at the thought of a man being born again; the thing is impossible physically. Spiritually it can be done through the omnipotence of God; socially it is possible to some degree and always with much labor and tears.

That is really what social exile in a physical sense means, i.e., that a man must be born again as a member of another social body. To some degree, it is always a failure. A man's own country is one of his principles, of his beginnings; it is a part of his very self; to be cut off from that country means that a part of a man's very self has been cut out. Our country and our attitude towards it are bred in our bones and in our blood. Away from it, we must always remain a stranger, both in our own eyes and in the eyes of others. It is not merely the difficulty of language, of a mode of thought, of national customs; it is deeper than all that, for it is the difficulty of being grafted on a new principle very much too late in life.

Moral exile

For all of its difficulty, the physical exile is hardly to be compared to moral exile. The physical involves a separation that can be measured in miles and it allows some sort of rebirth in another social unit, however partial and unsatisfying such a birth may be. Yet, the moral exile involves a distance, not from society, but from men, a distance not to be measured in miles but in loneliness, rebellion and despair. It is always an absolute and universal exile from every society, for men are the integrating units of every society. By it a man is marooned on a desert island; or rather, he carries his own deserted island strapped to his shoulders, that is the only ground he can stand on for any length of time and from it, he perpetually scans utterly empty horizons. He is always alone. Moreover, the pain, fears, and labors that go into this exile are much more severe than their parallels in physical exile; for our desire for union with other men is much deeper than our bones, deeper than our blood, deeper than our love for country. It is as deep as the depth of the nature of man.

This moral exile consists in a separation from men; its cause, then, is anything that cuts us off from men. It is a deep-seated loneliness accomplished on one side by driving men from us by injustice, on the other by withdrawing ourselves from men by sins against truth. In this latter case we hide behind a falsehood which has built a wall between ourselves and other men, forbidding all contact; when the falsehood is discovered, men withdraw from us in repulsion. However, the discovery of the falsehood is not a necessary ingredient of the bitter fraught of moral exile; whether or not men see the wall behind which we have hidden ourselves, we know it is there and we know it cannot be climbed from the outside.

Social exile by defect of truth: Simulation and hypocrisy

In the last chapter, our efforts were concentrated on the verbal lie and its poisonous effects. In this chapter, we are engaged primarily in dealing with the lie in fact, the factual lie which is called "simulation." We see the appearance of it in the smile of a guest at his hostess' flat joke. It exists on a mild scale in the attempted, but rarely achieved, nonchalance of a girl whose suitcase has sprung open in a crowded railroad station; as a matter of fact, most of the bystanders do get some little inkling of her confusion.

Understand, now, this is not a condemnation of that attempted nonchalance. Just as in words, we do not have to tell all we know, so in acts we do not have to manifest all that is within us. It is not necessary that every murderer slink through the world glowering at people; nor is every empty-headed person obliged to cultivate an ever more vacant stare. Now, if the acts we do place signify things that are not within us, we are shams, pretending, lying to the world.

There are acts that are not meant to fool anyone, just as there are words not to be understood in their literal sense. A dash of lipstick, even skillfully applied, does not fool the owner of the lips, and does not fool anyone else; it is merely a bit of decoration and is recognized as such by civilized peoples, though a savage might reasonably be puzzled about it. No one interprets a mechanical smile of greeting as a sign of hilarious joy. In fact, our lives are filled with acts that have the air of pretense but which deceive no one. The bustle of a loafing businessman or the whistle of a frightened boy are expressions of a hope or an ideal, rather than an attempt to lie to the world. Because they are easily seen through, they do not separate us from men; often they draw us closer to others in their manifestation of a bond, which appeals to every human heart, the bond of human weakness. We recognize in these people something of ourselves, for we, too, have felt the confusing sting of that same weakness.

The naively innocent approach of a swindler is obviously in a different class from these things. It is definitely the sin of simulation, a lie told to the world, a lie for which both the swindler and his victim must pay. The pious airs of the hypocrite who has no other end in view than to appear holy is also simulation; he too is a swindler. In both cases, the individuals withdraw from men, so far, in fact, as to take on the external appearance of totally different persons, completely obliterating themselves from social contact.

The hypocrite plagiarizes the personality of the one-person men most respect, that of a just man; and this is one of the fundamental reasons for the distaste and distrust men have for hypocrites. These spiritual swindlers are guilty of cheap cheating; their smooth approach obtains the price of respect that men mean to pay to real justice, to real holiness. Moreover, this cheating is a cowardly attack on the really just man, for it puts him under the burden of proving his justice in order to escape the suspicion of hypocrisy that men cautiously advance before tendering their respect. Sometimes hypocrisy is an escape from reality, from the not inconsiderable difficulties inherent in the attainment and maintenance of justice. The hypocrite lives in a child's world of pretense with none of the child's candor. The child knows and admits that he is only pretending, playing a game; but the hypocrite is so deadly in earnest that sometimes he almost succeeds in fooling himself.

Ostentation: Boasting

This pitiful romancing, which is simulation, does not always proceed along horizontal lines; at least the personal boaster builds his act straight up. He must stand head and shoulders above others even though his pedestal be of the fragile stuff of dreams. Strictly speaking, the man who regales his company with his truly great deeds is a bore, not a boaster; he tells the truth, though with imprudent excess. The real boaster is a liar. He climbs up the ladder of fiction rather than stoop to the menial labor of building a ladder of hard deeds. If his boasts are successful men never know the real man concealed behind the boasts; if they are unsuccessful, men do not want to know the real man. In either case, he has effectively exiled himself from men. Thomas says that often boasting is not indulged in to injure others, for the sake of a job, or for profit, but merely out of vanity; as such, it is reducible to a humorous lie. That is profoundly true; and most often the joke is on the boaster.

It is fairly easy to deal with a known boaster; all we need do is listen, sprinkling our silence with appropriate exclamations - *"Oh"*, *"Ah"*, *"How wonderful"*, and so on. It is a much more serious social problem to deal with the belittler. This is no place for daydreaming; in a moment of distraction we may make the disastrous mistake of agreeing with a dinner companion who says "*I haven't a brain in my head,*" or with the university professor who asks, in a purely rhetorical fashion, "*Wasn't that a silly thing to do?*"

Disparagement ("irony")

The boaster stretches the truth out of all recognition; the belittler shrinks it. If the latter is actually fishing for compliments in running down his own good points, he really has the same goal as a boaster; indeed, he might be called a subtle or indirect boaster. When, however, he minimizes his good points or lays claim to fictional bad points as a means of avoiding offense to others, he bends over backwards in his attempt to be agreeable; he gives men a distorted view of himself comparable to a candid camera's view of a contortionist caught at an unfortunate moment of his rehearsal. In either case, he keeps his real self-secret from his fellows; he cuts himself off from men.

When he is actually telling the truth about his failures, not mentioning his successes, he is not really belittling himself because he is not telling a lie. Thus, for instance, a successful author might tell his audience of beginners the now humorous history of his rejected manuscripts with no mention of his successful ones; and he is doing no more than giving them the courage to face the defeats and disappointments that will undoubtedly come their way before success stands at their door shouting for admittance.

We understand this and admire the man's kindliness and thoughtfulness to those budding authors. What is much more difficult for us to understand is the case of the saints' open estimation of themselves as serious sinners, even as the worst of sinners. It is important to remember that the saints were not lying; they were not, therefore, belittling themselves, they were telling the truth. Our difficulty in understanding this arises from the fact that we do not know sin as the saints know it, nor do we know God as intimately, as experimentally, as appreciatively as do the saints. Knowing God, so well they could understand to the full the seriousness of any offense against that divine goodness. Moreover, they knew themselves as they could not know others. Not even a saint is in a position to give accurate judgment of the actions of others because not even a saint can edge his way past the gates of a man's intellect and will. No matter what this other man has done, a saint cannot know certainly (short of a revelation from God) that this man is more seriously culpable than was the saint in his small sin; for the saint knows himself from the inside out. They were not hypocrites, not liars, the saints; they told the truth, the highly significant truth that the smallest of sins is sufficient reason for a lifetime of regret.

Hypocrisy, boasting and belittling are all distinct sins against the truth; they are all means by which a man exiles himself from the men and women with whom he lives in society. However, their distinction represents no bar to the human ingenuity of the sinner; he can contrive to pack all three sins into one and the same act. Thus a man, who would deliberately parade himself in old clothes to indicate great spiritual perfection and humility, would be guilty of hypocrisy in claiming the perfection he had not yet attained; he would be boasting by the very flapping of his rags; and he would be belittling his social position by the age and raggedness of the clothes he wore. This was the sort of thing that so angered the Lord and won his scathing denunciation of the Pharisees' parade of emaciation and sorrow as heralds of their great fasting.

Social exile by defect of friendliness (affability)

It seems evident, then, that a man cannot live in society without truth. All the same, it is equally true that he cannot live in society without pleasure. His very nature, as a social animal, demands not only that he live with others, but that he live pleasantly with them, that he be united intimately with them in a common life. It is extremely difficult to live a common life where the members of the community are not on speaking terms, or where it is perhaps better that they are not on speaking terms.

This might almost be established as a norm for the judgment of social perfection; at least as the society becomes more perfect, the relations between its members are more and more pleasant. Thus, in a community of nuns, where the bond of union is supernatural and each member is striving for a heroic degree of sanctity, the time of recreation sounds like nothing so much as a children's party at its height: none of that gloomy or sullen emphasis on what has been surrendered, but rather an hilarious gaiety that awakens a smiling envy in anyone privileged to eavesdrop on its echoes.

The nature of friendliness

The virtue, regulating this decent agreeableness in our social relations with other men, is friendliness or affability. As a part of justice, it deals with externals, with the signs of courtesy and amiability. It does not demand internal love for others; that is charity's work. Still, it does demand that we treat others decently, pleasantly, agreeably.

Friendliness does not demand that every man be a jester of society; friendliness, in fact, does not deal in jokes but in serious, everyday relations. After all, we can stand only so many jokes; certainly not a gluttonous diet of them all day, every day. Yet friendliness is not a barrier to a joke; on the contrary, it is a distinct barrier to a perpetual listening to the jokes of others, a mere passivity in social relations that contributes nothing but takes all that others give. Where this virtue of friendliness is weakening, social relations will fade to such desperate measures as a dinning radio, a perpetual movie, enough drink for oblivion and a headache, or even to a game of solitaire. Affability or friendliness can go too far, either to the position of the "yes men" of society who, in their desire for peace at any price in their social relations, refuse to hurt anyone's feelings for any reason; or to the degenerating length of flattery. Both are evidences of softness, of flabbiness; the first affects the "yes man" himself; the second saps vitality from those with whom the flatterer lives.

Social effeminacy -- flattery

Flattery can be extremely serious, as when it is aimed at a libertine's conquest, designed to prepare a man for a swindle as we fatten a pig for the killing, or when it is an occasion for sin. Nevertheless, even at its lightest, its obsequiousness is a disgusting thing. It is a foul, enervating cultivation of human weakness, hurrying on the disintegration of the individuals at whom it is aimed. To a healthy appetite, flattery has the taste of too much whipped cream or too much of the poetry of Keats: too sweet, too sensual.

The real opinions of the flatterer are never known. He has cut the links that might have bound him to men and so to the social unit, the links by which we normally communicate with men. Instead, he has chosen to use men as tools, humoring them, toying with them, playing on their weaknesses, and all the while laughing at them behind their backs.

Social savagery -- truculence ("quarreling")

The flatterer is simply too agreeable for any social good; he sins by exceeding the measure of friendliness. At the other extreme is the man who sins by a serious defect of friendliness, the man who can best be described as a social savage. He is not only indifferent to the hurt feelings of another, he actually seeks new ways to be unpleasant; it might be said that the one achievement that gives his sardonic soul pleasure is another's embarrassment or pain. He relishes his reputation of having a sharp tongue, of being a master of invective, of being able to cast such subtly sarcastic darts that the victim is socially dead before he realizes he has been struck. Sometimes we describe him, helplessly, as a difficult person. Now, he is really a savage. Perhaps he does not physically torture his victim, burn him at the stake, rush off with his victim's scalp or make a stealthy attack upon him at dawn. However, he does do all that is the social equivalent of just these things. Many a victim has felt scalped after the attack of one of these social savages; and many a matron, striding victoriously away from an engagement of this kind, certainly gives the impression of having her victim's scalp dangling from her belt even though, with proper dignity, she suppresses her victorious war-whoop. We may be maligning the savages in making a comparison between their physical attack and the social attack of social savages. Normally the savage has some reason for his attack, frequently it was a revenge for serious injustice; but these savages of civilization need no excuse to let loose the terrors of their attack.

It is not difficult to visualize the damage done by the social savage to his victims, particularly with painful memories rendering such invaluable assistance. Yet the damage he does to himself is even more devastating. He immerses himself in that personal provincialism that we call uncouthness; he builds a wall about himself, driving men savagely away from all contact with him and imposing upon himself an isolation that becomes increasingly bitter with the passing years.

Common origin of social effeminacy and savagery:

" contempt"

Like the flatterer, the social savage nurses a contempt for others; specifically, a contempt for their feelings which are not to be compared with his own satisfaction. Yet, even so, his contempt for men is a lesser thing than that indulged in by the flatterer; at least the social savage pays us the compliment of social violence a much more satisfying thing than the secret snigger of the flatterer at the fool who swallows his flattery.

Social exile by defect of liberality

The truthful man and the friendly man give themselves to the social life. The liberal man gives a much lesser gift -- his goods -- but with a similar result of tying men closer to himself, making himself a more intimate participator of the unity of men in the social organism. Taken strictly, liberality is a regulator of the love, desire and pleasure in money and the things money can buy. More remotely, but much more evidently to others, liberality deals with the possessions of a man; in concrete terms, the liberal man uses riches well. The corollary of that statement of the nature of liberality is that the liberal man uses men well, never placing riches above them; his every act is an implicit compliment to his own humanity and the humanity of others, fully justifying the opinion that he is a man of refreshingly sound common sense whose scale of values leaves no doubt but what it is the man who tosses the coin, not the coin the man. As a result, the liberal man never lacks friends. In addition, they are real friends, friends who in their turn, when their means allow, show an equal or even a superior liberality. Indeed, often the shock of personal contact with liberality will awaken a man to the real value of his own humanity and of the humanity of those around him.

The nature of liberality

Liberality is not the greatest of the virtues. It may be one of the least, for it deals with the least of the goods of man. All the same, it is a rough, homely, common sense virtue of tremendous social importance, an importance that is seen best, perhaps, in the sins against liberality.

Social extravagance -- prodigality

There is, for instance, the sin of extravagance, the sin of the man who carries liberality to an excess. He throws money away and, of course, a host of followers gather around him like buzzards around a dead body; yet, paradoxically, the very number of his followers only emphasizes his exile. Soon the extravagant man is forced to think of everyone in terms of a "loan"; his evaluation of humanity goes down steadily and receives a confirmation in the fact that when his money is gone so also are his friends. Even if his money holds out and his "friends" never leave him out of their sight, he gets no closer to men but rather farther away; for he gets little from his friends but the flatterer's contempt for a fool.

On the other hand, the greedy man is even more emphatically severed from men. At least the extravagant, the prodigal man puts men and women in their right place -- far above money. The greedy man puts money above absolutely everything else; even, sometimes above himself, to the point of starving himself in order to amass money. His contempt for humanity is countered by his fellows through their contempt for his greed;

the miser goes into a voluntary exile as effectively as if he had locked himself up in a cell and dropped the key down a drain pipe.

Social niggardliness -- avarice

Avarice, the sin of the greedy man, may seem only a slight sin in its direct opposition to liberality; liberality is, after all, not one of the greatest of the virtues, so avarice cannot be one of the greatest of the vices. Now, avarice so easily steps over the boundaries of justice that it is no trick at all to catch it poaching on the rights of others. There is great danger in its inherent gravity; but that danger is as nothing compared to the danger involved in avarice precisely as a capital sin. Here it is the father of a family; we must reckon not only with the sin itself but with all its dangerously ugly offspring.

In fact, in another place, St. Thomas has called avarice one of the roots of all sins, giving it a place just below pride. As a capital sin, it proudly presents its children to the world: betrayal of friends, cheating, deceit, perjury, restlessness, violence, hard-heartedness. Understand that these are not the enumerations of an orator trying to frighten his audience away from avarice. These sins arc logically, inevitably connected with the sin of avarice. The greedy man is head over heels in love with money; he will hold desperately to the conquest he has made and be on fire for still more of money's caresses. Of course, he will go too far in holding to what money he has; and he will go too far in trying to get more. He will be restless and worried about his present treasure, prepared to go to any violent lengths to acquire more; ready even to deceive men, cheat them, and confirm his cheating and deception by calling God to witness. In his eyes, all these things are paltry compared to the beauty of money. Since he has placed money so high in his scale of values, he will not hesitate to sacrifice men for its sake, even those who are closest to him; even one who is the Son of God, if there are thirty pieces of silver to be had for the betrayal.

We have now seen all the equipment for and the dangers to social life. It is time to look back over it all for a composite view, lest we overemphasize a detail and mar the whole picture. Perhaps it would be better to look up rather than look back, for the unifying power of the social order is the shadow of God hovering over it all, softening the light and tempering the heat of divine power. You will remember that we said religion looked to God as to the First Beginning and the Last End; that piety looked to parents and to country as participating the principality of God; while observance looked to superiors as participating the principality of parents. In other words, we have seen that the relation of parent to child is as the relation of God to His creatures; the relation of superiors to their citizens as the relation of parents to children.

The benign paternity of God smiles on the whole social structure. Every unit of it is a mirroring of the divine Fatherhood, a ray of that source of light, dimmer as we get farther and farther away, but immediately dependent on that single source of brightness. It is because of the principality of God that parents have a claim to reverence from their children; it is because of the principality of parents and country that superiors have a claim to obedience and reverence from their subjects.

Perfection of the social instinct -- the gift of piety

The perfection of social life is seen in the concept of paternity. The perfection of our payment of social debts, social obligations, is seen in the reverence and honor given to God, our common Father. To look at God as our Father is an appealing thing and yet it is a difficult thing. It is appealing because it touches the deepest chords in our nature. We are His children more truly than we are the children of our own parents; we owe Him a deeper, more perpetual debt; to Him we come with our smallest troubles, our smallest joys, at every critical moment in our life, and, with even more familiarity, in those moments that are not at all critical. Even so, it is a difficult thing because it is not easy to be familiar with God. For that we need help, help, in fact, of a member of the family of God; the help of God Himself, God the Holy Spirit. We need both a divine push and a responsiveness to that push such as is offered by the gifts of the Holy Spirit; and this particular responsiveness for social perfection is given to us as the gift of piety.

The nature of this gift

The gift of piety makes us easily and promptly responsive to the movements of the Holy Spirit. It inspires us to look upon and to reverence God as our Father, as the Father of all men, as the benign Father of all humanity. The operation of this gift is more or less taken for granted by the Catholic; familiarity with God seems natural to him who has been addressing God as Father since he was first able to lisp a prayer. He has been a member of the household of divinity for so long that it almost seems too ordinary a thing to single out for special consideration; but it is no ordinary thing to belong to the family of God. That family relationship which is the bond of our union is more penetrating than the bond of common blood; it is as deep as our dependence on God. The gift of piety in action, then, gives us a model for our reverence to parents and superiors for, in a lesser way than God, they too are our principles, our beginnings.

Its distinction from religion, filial fear and the virtue of piety

It must be clearly understood that the gift of piety is not the virtue of religion; this latter bows to the first principle and the last goal, by its subjection paying a debt of justice. Nor is it the virtue of piety by which we give reverence to our carnal parents; rather the gift of piety looks to the very source of parenthood. It is by no means to be confused with that fear which is a reverent awe of divine majesty. Rather this is a child's response to a loving Father Who is God.

Its extension to all men

The gift of piety represents the climax of social fitness. It is a statement of the sublime heights to which a man can climb in his social life, a height reached not by tearing down but by looking up. It is social manhood, with all the full strength and vigor of adult age. We have come a long way to this full social manhood from its feeble beginnings of social infancy; for there it was a question of just the minimum strength and vigor necessary for life itself. Alternatively, to abandon metaphorical terms, we have come a long way from the minimum demands of justice, which were the absolute essentials of social life, to this peak of social fitness, which is the gift of piety. Nevertheless, it is essential that we have a very clear idea of those bare essentials of social life, those demands of babyhood; for they remain the essentials of any stage of social life.

Minimum demands for social unity -- the Ten Commandments

The minimum demands of social fitness are stated in the Ten Commandments. It is most fitting that those commands should have been underscored by the finger of God; for without them we cannot hope for life either in the kingdom of man or in the kingdom of God. Like all things essential -- like breathing, seeing, digesting -- these precepts of justice have an air of easy naturalness about them. They all deal with justice and justice is the most evident of our obligations. If a man's horizons are limited to his own mirror he might, by a peculiar blindness, see himself as self-sufficient, completely in command, with obligations only to himself. However, as soon as he steps out into the world of men, these illusions are shattered; other men will not let him make the mistake of thinking they do not count, they will insist that he see that he has obligations to others, that he is not the lord of all men but rather the companion of all men. These precepts have their easy air not merely, because they flow immediately from the first principles of natural law, but also because their obligation is so easily seen and so readily agreed to by man.

General character of the Decalogue -- precepts of justice;
Particular character of the Decalogue

All of the Ten Commandments are really commands of justice; they demand only that we respect the rights of others that we refrain from injury to another. Naturally enough, the supreme rights of God are protected first: the first two commandments removing the injuries or impediments of superstition and irreligious; the third, with the impediments removed, gets us down to an actual payment of our debt of religion. In the fourth commandment, the rights of parents, country and superiors are protected; and finally, in the others, the rights of men as men have their sacred character written on them by the hand of God, rights that embrace the personal, the domestic and the proprietary fields. Additionally, the protection given is absolute, against all injury, whether by thought, word or deed,

It is to be understood, of course, that these commandments are not licenses to do anything that they do not mention; adultery is by no means an exhaustive statement of the sins against purity. Rather these commandments are general or root terms, but statements that include all sins against justice. We are not asked to stretch our imaginations to cover all impurity with the blanket prohibition of adultery; that particular sin is mentioned because it is the most obvious violation of justice in the line of impurity. Thus, also, the inclusion of all superiors under the fourth commandment is not a matter of reading things into the orders of God; reverence to parents is simply the most obvious of the obligations of reverence, that which will be most easily seen and readily agreed to by men.

In other words, the Ten Commandments are the least statement of the secondary principles of the natural law in their most obvious application. Their form is merely another example of God stooping graciously to our level, making as easy and obvious as possible the path by which we shall find our way home to Him.

Equity and the Decalogue

There is one particularly noteworthy characteristic of this law, which makes a fitting conclusion to St. Thomas' tract on justice. In human law, our obedience can never be absolute; sometimes it would be evil to follow the letter of the law, against justice and against the common good. After all, human legislators are not omniscient; they do the best they can, striking an average and legislating for what usually happens. In individual cases, which of course they cannot foresee much less legislate for, something special is needed to preserve justice; some special virtue which will really protect the lawgiver's intention of meting out justice. It is not an attack on the majesty of law but a defense of the honesty of both law and legislator to insist on the special virtue of equity to protect justice in the individual case.

Now the peculiar characteristic of this divine law is that no equity is needed. Indeed no equity is possible; this law deals with what happens, not in most cases, but in absolutely all cases. It flows from the roots of nature itself and the greatest injustice that could be done to the individual would be to enable him to pass out of the limits of this law. God did not overlook anything, there was no individual case, which He did not foresee or could not legislate for; for God, you see, is not a human legislator. This law commands the essential; it is not affected by circumstances, by this or that age, this or that economic development. It is the law for all men, in all times, under all circumstances. Perhaps all this is said very simply when we insist that the virtue of equity is the superior rule of human action and there is no higher rule of human action than the law of God; or, still more simply, God is God and man is man even in the business of legislation.

Conclusion: Virtue and society: General necessity of virtue in society

Let us try to sum up, not only what has been done in this chapter, but in the past few chapters on justice. Let us take one last glance at the social life of man. In the preceding volume of this work, we spoke of virtues, identifying them as good, operative habits, as the habits, which were the immediate principles of good actions. Now it is precisely by action that men come into contact one with another; it is by this that men are linked together, and it is by good actions that men are bound together in one social unit. Why? Because it is only for good actions that men need help to struggle on to perfection. No man needs help to fail, to commit sin, to degrade himself; but he does need help for fuller life, for the development possible through social life. The virtuous man, then, is the best citizen; he is linked most closely to other citizens and, at the same time, he offers most to that common life of society.

Particular necessity

This may have the hollow ring of a pompous platitude; but let us look at it more closely in the light of what we have seen in these last few chapters. For a fuller perfection for ourselves and for the guarantee and protection of the rights of others, i.e., for social life, the very least requirements are justice, religion, piety, observance and dulia. To go up a step higher to more perfect social life, we must have gratitude, truth, friendliness, liberality. Finally, for the complete perfection of social life, the gift of the Holy Spirit, which is piety, is necessary. All of these are habits; all are good, operative habits. In other words, all of them are virtues; and in proportion as they are more perfectly possessed, the individual becomes so much more of an asset to society.

According as a society is made up more fully of virtuous men, men possessed not only of the virtues demanded for the minimum of social life, but also those which make for the perfection of social life, that society is more perfect. Virtue is not something that can exist in society without hurting anyone's feelings or impeding the flow of traffic; it is something that must exist if society is to exist. It is by virtue that men are tied one to another; and it is in that linking of man-to-man that society has its essential origin.

The Church versus a godless society:

The enemy and the friend

This will, I think, make clear the real issues involved in the modern battle, which is becoming more and more an open fight, the battle between the Church and godless groups. This consideration of virtuous society certainly seems to show that on the outcome of this battle hangs the fate of society itself. There is considerable confusion in men's minds today as to which is the friend, and which is the enemy of society, the champions of godliness or the champions of sanctity; but the issue is clear and the answer simple when we understand the relation of virtue to society. Any group that abandons virtue, that condemns it, that does its utmost to root it out, is beyond doubt society's bitterest enemy. Any group that cultivates virtue that insists upon its practice as the uppermost concern in the life of a man is by that token alone the most valuable friend that human society can have.

Solver of difficulties

Indeed, we are doing the Church an injustice if we stop at the insistence that she is the friend of society. We are not saying nearly enough when we go further and maintain that, because of her exhaustive knowledge of and championship of virtue, particularly of the virtue of justice, she has the answer to the problems of society. The Church is more than a friend, more than a solver of difficulties; she is the protector of the absolute fundamentals of social life. Not, you understand, of the absolutely essential virtue of justice alone; but of the very integrators of society -- of the family upon which it is modeled and from which it proceeds. There is still one-step to take: the Church is the protector of the very humanity of man, without which anything human, society included, is utterly inconceivable.

Protector of fundamentals

In this chapter we spoke of the social savage and noticed his provincial character of uncouthness; he has cut himself off from men and that separation has made itself evident in his very uncouthness. Culture is one of the products to be expected of social life; as a part of social life, it should be brought about by precisely those things that are most conducive to the perfection of social life. As the social life improves so the deeper and greater should be the culture it produces. Yet, if we ask what are the things that are most conducive to the perfection of society, our only answer can be, the virtues: justice, religion, piety, observance, gratitude, truth, friendliness, liberality and the gift of piety. Culture and the virtues, then, are not to be separated.

Champion of Culture

The significance of this truth can hardly be overestimated. Obviously, it means that culture is not something to be found in the books that have been read, the plays that have been seen, the languages that have been mastered or the tastes that have been acquired. All of these are more or less superficial indications of an intense social life, past or present; but they are superficial and they are merely indications. They can be, and in fact have been, cut off from the deep roots and living sources of social perfection from which, originally, they spring. It is possible to have an entirely artificial culture, an inherited culture, for instance, which has no relation to the age in which a man lives. Still, of course such a culture is decadent.

It is a far cry from that living culture which explains the French peasant's contagious pleasure and proud welcome of a stranger to his evening repast of bread, wine and cheese or the protective strength in which the voyager is enveloped as the Irish peasant, with one and the same gesture, throws open the door of his cottage and the door of his heart. An artificial culture is separated from the life of a society and is as ghastly a thing as theatrical make-up seen in bright sunlight. Just as the perfection of social life is rooted in the perfection of virtue. so also, the truest culture is something that need not be coaxed along in a kind of social hothouse. It is the inescapable product of a man, a virtuous man, living in society.

CHAPTER XIV

THE FULLNESS OF COURAGE
(Q. 123-127)

1. The oldest of the virtues:
    (a) The word "fortitude" in antiquity.
    (b) Double significance of the testimony of antiquity.

2. The great impediment to human living -- cowardice.

3. True and false courage.

4. The object of courage:
    (a) Fear and daring.
    (b) Dangers of death.
    (c) Other dangers.

5. The acts of courage:
    (a) To sustain and attack.
    (b) The joy and sorrow of the act of courage!
    (c) A norm of courage -- emergencies.

6. Instruments of courage:
    (a) Tranquility
    (b) Anger and desire.

7. The place of courage among the virtues.

8. The courage of martyrs:
    (a) The nature of martyrdom.
    (b) The virtues behind martyrdom.
    (c) Perfection of the courage of martyrdom.

(d) Causes of martyrdom.

9. The breakdown of courage:
   (a) Cowardice.
   (b) Fearlessness and its causes.
   (c) Daring.

Conclusion:

1. Progressive need of courage:
   (a) for human life.
   (b) for Catholic life.

2. The tragedy of fearlessness

3. The course of cowardice:
   (a) Factual cowardice.
   (b) Factual and philosophic cowardice.

4. The moderns and the martyrs.

CHAPTER XIV

THE FULLNESS OF COURAGE
(Q. 123-127)

Dreaming has played its constant part in the life of men from the very beginning. For the most part, it has always been considered a luxury to be saved for the odd moments of life. The man who spent most or all of his time in dreams was decidedly an exception; he was a man apart, sometimes looked upon kindly, sometimes not so kindly. In addition, it is a not inconsiderable compliment to the non-dreamers among men that so few of the dreamers have starved to death.

Much of human progress has been due to the long dreams of far-seeing men -- translated into action by the non-dreamers -- but for the most part men have concentrated much more on the present than on the future, there have always been more laborers than seers, more realists than idealists. In a way, this was an inevitable corollary of the recognition of the fact that there is always considerable difficulty in the business of living humanly. At times men have exaggerated that difficulty to such a degree as to drive themselves to despair; but from the beginning, men saw the fundamental necessity of facing life's difficulty. They saw clearly the need of something within a man that would ward off the threat to the humanity of man's life and actions, for they were keenly aware of the positive existence of such threats.

The oldest of the virtues: The word "fortitude" in antiquity

The depth of this universal conviction is seen from the fact that the particular virtue by which man wards off such threats -- the virtue of fortitude or courage -- has given its name to all the virtues. The Latin and Greek words for "virtue" also mean fortitude or strength; in fact, going a little deeper, we find that the word itself is sprung from the same root from which, in both Latin and Greek, we derive the word man. It would seem that there was a kind of identification of manhood with courage. When we push the etymological investigation a little further and discover that from these same roots came the words for robustness, virility and even the name of the god of war, there can be no doubt that the men of antiquity believed that humanity and strength were inescapably linked.

Double significance of the testimony of antiquity

In this sense, the virtue of fortitude or courage is the oldest of the virtues. It was one of the virtues immediately recognized as such by all men; and that recognition hag left its permanent mark both upon the life of man and the human accounts of virtue. Not all this discussion of words and their roots is merely academic; it is a testimony to two fundamental truths of human life, i.e., that courage is necessary for human life, human action and human responsibility, and that cowardice is a denial or an escape from humanity.

The great impediment to human living ·· cowardice

In other words, it has been clearly seen and frankly admitted by all, from the very beginning, that a man must make the conquest of fear before he can begin to live. He must sustain that conquest of fear as long as he hopes to continue to live humanly. For he is surrounded, indeed, penetrated with dangers; if he shrinks from those dangers, he is forever paralyzed. The dangers will not be dissolved by his cowardly attempts to escape them. Even a poet cannot lie long on the bosom of mother nature. The picture of nature as a kindly mother and man as easily masterful are fictions of the French Encyclopedists concocted from the dreams by which they tried to escape the gutters of Paris. Nature is not the type of friend to be chosen for a stroll along a dark, quiet street; at least not until she has been searched for weapons. She is a constant threat to man. In winter, he may freeze to death, in summer he may be felled by sunstroke; in the fall or spring, wet weather may bring on pneumonia. Hail, snow, lightning, floods are not friendly gestures to man or his works; the wild beasts that inhabit the face of the earth are not rollicking pets, growling and grimacing to amuse man. Even in his own nature, man will find what is perhaps the most serious of all threats: the threat of the foulness of degradation, of slavery, of despair if the animal side of his complex nature gets the upper hand.

Human life is no adventure for a coward; either cowardice must go or the humanity of man's life must go. Because men have always rightly prized that by which they are men, their very humanity, courage has always been given recognition and honor from all men of all times. It is of the brave man that it is so constantly said: "There is a man." We find it easy to understand this because it is easy for us to understand the great love we have for our own humanity. We cannot hate people because they too can love, can will, can understand, can fail; these are all distinctly human things that serve as bonds tying us closely to all our fellow men. We may be jealous of a brave man, but we cannot hate his bravery: rather it is as entirely natural for us to give spontaneous expression to our respect for courage, so natural, indeed, that often anything remotely resembling true human courage has received the applause of men.

True and false courage

If we stand breathless and safe on a sidewalk watching a structural steel worker, forty stories up, stroll around on the beams of a skeleton building, or sit in a ringside seat and watch the professional boxer advance undaunted in the face of what, to us, would be serious danger, we are letting our applause trickle over the edge of the full glass to fall wasted. These men are not so much brave as experienced; these things are no longer dangerous for them. Certainly the cashier who laughs in the face of a bandit under the impression that it is all a joke is stupid not brave.

The mere facing of danger does not make a man brave. In a fit of anger, a man may plunge headlong into danger; but he is nor brave, he is inhuman, he has allowed his passion to take control of his action. The attraction of money, the search for pleasure, the horror of pain, of disgrace may all cast a man in an heroic role for a moment. Now, it is only a role and only for a moment. When the footlights are out and the curtain is down, the appearance of courage is wiped off with the make-up; for none of these enable a man to face the task of living humanly. A false mustache does not fool nature. To face nature, the dangers that nature offers to human living, the threats that humanity itself offers to the life of man, it is necessary to have courage that is authentic.

Additionally that authentic courage is the moral virtue, which makes a man prompt to undergo the dangers and support the labors of human life according to the demands of human reason, not according to the demands of ignorance, passion, mistaken enthusiasm or a diabolic slavery. It is important that we insist on that note of reason in fortitude, the note fundamental to all virtue; for insistence on the reasonable control and regulation of courage accurately outlines the part of fortitude in human life.

After all, the perfection of man consists in the good of reason, in following the rule of reason; that is, his perfection consists in living humanly. The essential rectification of reason itself is accomplished by the intellectual virtues, particularly by the intellectual virtue of prudence; the establishment of reason's order in the outside world of human things and human actions is the work of justice. There still remains the establishment of that order of reason in the inside world, the world within a man himself; and that is done by removing the impediments ordered to reason by the passions: first by the impediments offered by way of repulsion which are handled by fortitude; then the impediments offered by way of enticement or allurement, which are the proper material of temperance. The first takes care of the irascible or emergency appetite; the second, of the concupiscible or mild appetite.

The object of courage: Fear and daring

Fortitude, then, is a kind of bodyguard of reason. If its frowns do not scatter the threats to reason, it resorts to blows. Anything that might overthrow the sovereignty of reason by repelling a man from the road down which reason says he must go is a proper target for the thunderbolts of fortitude. That is, fortitude deals with the dangers and labors of human life; or, more strictly, with the passions of fear and daring aroused by these dangers and labors. For, after all, danger and labor do not necessarily drive a man from the road of reason; a man can get to love his labor or to relish danger and so find in the two no particular obstacle to reason's sovereignty. It is when they are feared or when they arouse a reckless daring that there is talk of reason's abdication; and it is then that fortitude must come to grips with reason's enemies to insure the reasonable character of a man's life.

Dangers of death

The work of fortitude or courage, then, is to limit fear and restrain daring. In fact, we can limit the principal object of fortitude by a simple appeal to experience. The man who can lift fifty pounds can lift five, the musician who can play Bach will hardly find great difficulty in the simple finger exercises of a beginner; so a man who can face the supreme dangers of life will hardly shrink from life's petty threats. That is why fortitude's primary object is to prepare man to face the greatest dangers of life; not that it sits back waiting for the supreme danger to show itself, but, equipped for the main force of the enemy, it makes short shift of his advance patrols. In a word, the object of courage is to prepare a man to face death, for death is the most terrible of all corporal evils, destroying as it does all corporal goods.

Other dangers

There is a great significance in the fact that if we are to be brave we must face death itself. For by this it is plain that, since death is the greatest thing we have to fear, our life is by no means a thing of terror; all that we have to fear is corporal perils. Considering the high goal and splendid possibilities of man, it is a petty thing that threatens human life, a mere corporal evil. Yet, because the corporal is an integral part of man's very nature, even this danger is not a petty thing to a man.

However, it is not lack of fortitude that pulls the covers over our head at a loud peal of thunder or the stealthy tread of a burglar at night. It is not cowardice that snaps shut the unfinished detective story and sends a man scuttling off to bed when a window shade all unexpectedly runs up with a bang at midnight. These things can happen to the most idle of men; whereas Christian courage has its work cut out for it precisely in the pursuit of good; it strengthens man to face the dangers and impediments that may hold him back from the attainment of good.

Every virtue, as a good habit, drives on to its own particular good; in fact, every virtue is unsatisfied with any but the highest good in its own line. No virtue staggers through life in a middle-aged weariness whose illusion is disillusionment and to which compromise is a way of life; virtue is not to be satisfied with a partial or half-hearted control of reason in its own line. It insists upon a whole and complete subordination to the commands of reason. Fortitude is no exception; it trains its guns on the higher dangers that are connected with the pursuits of the higher good. In his attempt to express this thought and summarize the principal objects of Christian courage, Thomas hit upon a happy phrase. He says the object of fortitude is to enable a man to face death in a public or private war; that is, in defense of the high human good which is the common good, or in pursuit of the divine good of virtue.

Not that we need a bullet-proof vest for the practice of chastity; virtue does not hold out the same extreme and constant threat of death as is to be found in the attack of an infantry company on a machine-gun nest. Nevertheless, the practice of virtue is really a first-class war, a war that endures the length of a lifetime. Indeed, among a people hostile to Christian ideals, or in a time of positive persecution, the practice of virtue may involve greater and more constant risks than a private faces in a physical war. At any rate, fortitude is always necessary for a man because a man is always at war. There is no Maginot Line in which he can take his secure comfort. He is always engaged in his private, inner war of facing down the threats and labors, which make up so much of his living and which, rightly handled, form the stepping-stones by which he climbs to divine heights. In an almost infinite series just below the threat to the common good and to the divine good of virtue, are ranged the whole gamut of grave evils that make human life such an adventure and that threaten again and again to swamp the heart of a man with a tidal wave of fear. Precisely as difficulties, these evils are handled by the corresponding virtues. Thus abstinence from overindulgence in drink, with all the difficulty it involves, is taken care of by the virtue of temperance. Yet, as sources of fear, these evils are the proper material of fortitude. Because a whiskey bottle does not roar like a lion, let no one think the drunkard is not afraid of drink, terribly afraid; in his fight he needs much more than the help that temperance can give him, he needs the solid strength of courage. In a very real sense, courage plays its part in the practice of every virtue, for every virtue has its difficulty and every difficulty can be a source of fear to man.

The acts of courage: To sustain and attack

Of the two passions, fear and reckless daring, with which courage must deal, by far the most difficult is fear. It is much more fundamental, more vehement, more completely opposed to the whole vital motion of human life. Fortitude and reckless daring have something of the external resemblance of twins; the one is too boisterous, always looking for trouble, a bit of a swaggering tough, but it is a much simpler task to tone down the boisterousness than to stiffen up the collapsing backbone of a man stricken with fear. It is not nearly so laborious to let off steam as it is to build up. Consequently, the principal and most difficult act of courage deals with the passion of fear. That principal and most difficult act is to stand firmly in the face of danger in spite of fear, to sustain the danger and difficulty. An actual attack on difficulties is really a much easier, a secondary act of fortitude.

This is hardly the common estimation of courage. The smashing attack of a cavalry charge has a stronger appeal to our imagination than a man's dogged refusal to quit; yet if we look at the matter closely, we are forced to admit that we have been captivated by the vividness and swift movement of the dramatic rather than by the solid worth of courage. The truth of the matter is that it is much harder to stand up before an enemy who is admittedly stronger, to hold on knowing that defense is the limit of our powers, than it is to lash out in a joyous conviction of strength, ourselves becoming the attackers. The attacker, you see, has his difficulties still before him, they are future rather than imminent; and it is much more difficult to face present difficulties than future ones. It is more difficult, though far less dramatic, to cling to resistance in the face of a beating while the weary hours, days and years stagger on, than in one swift movement to smash against an enemy.

The joy and sorrow of the act of courage!

Perhaps some of the inaccurate estimates of courage are due, in some measure, to the semblance of defeat in merely sustaining danger. Undoubtedly there is an appearance of inferiority, of bruising physical defeat, of hopelessness where all we can do is just hold on; all of these things are, indeed, present in the act of courage which is sustaining, but we are blind indeed if we do not see, shining through these ragged garments, the beauty of the courage that refuses to relinquish the good. As a matter of fact, we do, and not infrequently, see through that fog of defeat to the splendor of the victory being won by courage. We do not think for a moment that the courage of a bully is to be compared to that of his much smaller victim who refuges to be bullied, though he cannot help being beaten; however inferior he may be in skill and strength, we refuse to admit that the prize-fighter who goes down again and again and refuses to stay down, refuses to admit defeat, is in any way inferior to that of his conqueror.

We may admire the fighter's courage but we certainly do not envy his pains and aches when the fight is over and done with. There is always a sad side to the act of courage. There is physical pain involved; a tremendous sweep of the passion of sorrow; there is even spiritual sorrow in the will. In Christ's long agony, His body was racked from head to toe with physical pain; He Himself said that His soul was sorrowful even unto death; and at that last moment, sorrow invaded even His spiritual faculties and brought forth that desolate question: "Why have You abandoned me?" Courage is not all a matter of parades, bright uniforms, applause for the returning heroes and modest disclaimers; it involves sorrow, sorrow in plenty. All the same, it also has its joy.

The sustaining of labors and dangers will never rival a cigarette as an after-breakfast pleasure; it does not bring a physical pleasure that will cancel out its physical pain, nor does it offer a breakwater against the wave of sorrow, which comes from the sense appetite. Nevertheless, it does bring a spiritual joy that more than cancels out the intellectual sorrow, the sorrow of the will. It brings a joy of manhood, even of super manhood; the joy of acting for ends worthy of a man and even above men, i.e., for the ends of fortitude and of charity. Indeed, in the operation of the supernatural or infused virtue of courage, it has happened, not rarely, that this spiritual joy has been so great as to make a man insensible to all else, even to terrible physical pain. Many of the martyrs slipped through the door of death as a child slips through the door of sleep, with the quiet radiance of a smile, while their executioners were gripped by horror. It was Judas who despaired, not Christ; it was the Roman jailors who wept, not Cecilia; it was Thomas More who ascended the scaffold laughing and joking, not his executioner.

Now, this is extraordinary. Most of us must face our danger, our labors in the conviction that there will be pain and sorrow connected with them, pain and sorrow, perhaps that will shake the very foundations of our soul. However, whatever it be, that pain and sorrow is as nothing compared with the joy of following in the footsteps of a Master Who was neither a coward nor a fool; Who was, besides being God, also a man.

In the preceding volume, treating of the passions, we spoke of the man who, in a rush of thoughtless anger, flares up to a fighting fever and is willing to face any enemy; but then, just as quickly, he cools off, is willing, indeed, anxious to quit after the first blow has been struck. He has suddenly discovered that there are other angles to this business of fighting, angles not at all pleasant. Opposed to this type of fighter was the slow starter, the doggedly persevering man whose actions were ruled by reason; he has thought things out carefully before, has foreseen the danger and in spite of it, gone ahead. That is the difference between the passion of daring and the virtue of courage.

A norm of courage ·· emergencies

For fortitude or courage is a virtue, and like all the moral virtues it is ruled by reason. If given a choice it would prefer to have a little time to think and prepare for the dangers it is about to face. Yet an emergency, which gives no time for thought, is one of the best test of courage. Given time enough, even men without the virtue of courage might possibly fortify their souls against danger; but in the split second given for action in an emergency, our nature and that second nature, we have built in through habit come instantly to the surface. A hero is not made on the instant that he leaps to rescue a child from an onrushing truck. He is made in the long, slow years before, while courage was being grafted on his very nature through the formation of habit.

The naturally timid man, who must have a wage increase to support his family, acts with deliberate fortitude when he paces the outer office and calls up all the reasons he has for anger and resentment at his present salary. When there is a little time to prepare, a brave man quite deliberately selects the tools for his action. If attack be called for, he will wield such an elusive instrument as moderate anger, which, of its very nature, rises to attack an enemy. It may be he will have to go deeper and call on the passion of sorrow as a means of arousing anger, or, with true diplomacy, call in the quietly powerful force of desire to emphasize the good, which defeat would have him surrender. He is not being cowardly; he is a strategist coolly making sure of his supplies and ammunition before launching an attack.

Instruments of courage: Tranquility

For anger, sorrow and desire are helps for the lesser act of courage, which is attack. No passion offers any help to the more difficult act of holding on in the face of fear and danger; that is a product of reason alone. To hold to good in spite of danger demands a tranquil soul, a calm willingness to face loss, even to seek loss rather than run; and no passion is a help to tranquility. It is not by passion that a man weighs his chances and his choices; it is not by passion that his choice falls upon the goodness of his reason, his humanity, his God, a choice that turns an undaunted face to whatever loss, whatever pain, whatever sorrow may be necessary to hold on to the one thing that counts. No one has yet been able to give an answer to that one question of Christ: "What shall it profit a man if he gain the whole world and suffer the loss of his own soul, or what return shall a man make for his soul?" There is no answer. There is no choice for a brave man. His courage consists precisely in acknowledging that fact and refusing to tell himself there is a choice in spite of the unceasing flow of sophistries suggested by cowardice.

Difficulties and dangers are the air courage breathes, the food on which it is nourished. If we were to identify difficulty with virtue (a frequent enough mistake), then fortitude would stand at the top and charity at the bottom; for there is nothing more difficult than courage and nothing more joyous than charity. All the same, difficulty is not the norm of excellence in virtue;

rather, that norm is the good at which a particular virtue aims. On this ground, fortitude must take a lower place. Its work is the humble work of a per-cursor, preparing the way of other virtues, leveling the hills and filling the valleys; removing the impediments that hinder the smooth, swift action of other virtues.

The place of courage among the virtues

Of course, fortitude is far beneath the divine virtues of faith, hope and charity whose object is God Himself. Even in the order of the moral virtues, fortitude ranks beneath prudence, which has the order of reason essentially, and justice, which produces that order in the external world. Fortitude has not the order of reason, nor does it produce that order in the world; rather, it protects or conserves it. It is a bodyguard of order. Yet, because it does protect reason against the more serious threats, it ranks above temperance. Temperance, too, guards reason; not against fear and danger, but against the soft blandishments of pleasure.

Still we must not think that, because fortitude sits towards the end of the table, that it is not a member of the family of virtue but merely a faithful old slave, tolerated and loved in an aloofly superior fashion. It, too, is a cardinal virtue, along with prudence, justice and temperance; it, too, is a root virtue dealing with an outstanding material of human life, a virtue that has for its characteristic note an element that is universal in human living. Dangers and difficulties are not affairs that enter into only some few lives; nor is firmness a thing which can be missing from the life of any man. This is the solid foundation of antiquity's judgment on the importance of courage; for courage must run through all of our lives, all of our acts.

The courage of martyrs: The nature of martyrdom

A more graphic appreciation of the importance of fortitude and its great power can be quickly had by a moment's thought on its supreme act. As that highest act of courage is finished, the gates of heaven swing wide and a brave man, who has produced that supreme act, that singular testimony to Christian truth, which we call martyrdom, in one-step passes from earth to heaven. No martyr sneaks into heaven like a thief; there is no martyr who stumbles into heaven as though he had been hurled along by a hurricane of prayer. There is no hesitation or dallying along the way for the martyr that he might shine up just a little more for a fitting entry into the city of God. Rather the martyr sweeps into heaven like a conqueror coming home. That is precisely what he is. He has lost his life in order to find it; he has made the difficult choice of death in preference to desertion of the faith or of virtue. He has conquered death like his Master; and often he has a penitent slipping into heaven in the wake of his royal welcome, for many a martyr has brought his executioner to heaven.

Every martyr goes straight to heaven. That is a tremendous effect to be produced by any virtue, in fact, the supreme effect of all the virtues. How can it be produced by this humble precursor of the virtues? The temperate man does not walk straight from death into life because he has refrained from taking enough drink to keep him from walking straight in any direction. The humble cannot slip by purgatory by waving their humility as a kind of passport. Nor does the penitent's regret necessarily entitle him to an instant embrace by the King of glory. Christ Himself gave the answer to the difficulty when He said: "Greater love than this no man hath, that he give up his life for his friend." That is the real secret. Courage has not worked alone in martyrdom but with the mighty impulse of charity, of friendship. Consequently, it has carried far beyond the ordinary ends of courage to the end of charity, to God Himself.

The virtues behind martyrdom

A devil's advocate has no case against a martyr. Such a man is certainly a man of virtue. He has stood firm in truth and justice, which is the very essence of virtue. He has held to the good of reason in its proper object, which is truth, and in its proper effects in the appetite of man, that is, justice or sanctity. He is a brave man, for he has stood against the great evil of death in a private war for the divine good of virtue. He is a man of faith, for he has witnessed to that faith even at the cost of his life; and he is a man of charity, for the norm of friendship is sacrifice and he has made the supreme sacrifice.

Perfection of the courage of martyrdom

The lukewarm religious who, in an attack of self-pity, sighs resignedly of the "living martyrdom" of religious life is babbling nonsense. Living martyrdom is as hopeless a contradiction as a self-pitying religious. A man must die to be a martyr; death is of the very essence of martyrdom, for martyrdom consists precisely in spurning all corporal goods to testify to the faith. After all, a man might give up his goods, his friends, suffer pain, all as a means to securing his life; or he might sincerely think himself willing to make the supreme sacrifice until he hears the whiz of the headsman's swinging ax. Indeed, a man might actually be willing to make that sacrifice; but the fact is that he has not passed the supreme test until he has actually died. He cannot be a witness because his surrender of all for the truth of the faith is not evident to the world.

The virgin who dies in defense of her purity is a martyr; so also is the priest who loses his life by administering the sacraments during a plague. For while it is true that most of the canonized martyrs have died in persecutions of the faith, and so in defense of the faith strictly so called, many others have died for the faith in the sense of the Christian life. It is not merely the refusal to deny the faith in words, but also the refusal to deny it in acts that is the cause of martyrdom. The work of any virtue can be the cause of martyrdom if, as is always the case of a man in the state of grace, the work of that virtue is referred to God by charity.

Causes of martyrdom

The Catholic in Russia or Germany today who loses his life because he refuses to give up his Catholicity or any act demanded by that Catholicity, is truly a martyr; in fact he would be so even though the political authorities were acting against Christianity for purely political reasons. This man would die precisely because he was a Christian. Such men have voluntarily suffered death in the sense of preferring Catholicity to the preservation of their life.

The fact that a man is running full speed away from the enemies of the faith and is killed by a bullet in the back does not deny him the palm of martyrdom. In spite of his desperate effort to escape, the sacrifice of his life was a voluntary one; in fact, the reason for his very flight was his staunch refusal to give up the faith. However, we cannot make a martyr out of the man who is killed in his sleep or of the drunkard who is garroted as he lies in the gutter. Neither of these men were capable of sacrifice. The Holy Innocents are the solitary exception; they were martyrs although they were incapable of a voluntary acceptance of death by their own wills.

Socrates, dying for truth, or a criminal who could save himself by a lie but refuses to, could not claim a martyr's crown. They might be called martyrs of natural virtue; but certainly, they are not martyrs of Christ, nor have they a claim to martyrdom's reward. The same is true of the Christian who values his faith highly, so highly that he does undergo death rather than apostatize; but not highly enough to surrender the concubine with whom he has lived for years. There is something fine about this unswerving firmness of the human will; but not that supernatural fineness that gives a man in an instant the splendid beauty that could come to him only through a long period of suffering in purgatory. There is something fine about these things because there is something brave about them. These men have been courageous with a natural courage; but natural courage does not win us the supernatural rewards of heaven, precisely because it is only natural.

A soldier who dies in defense of his country, that is, in the practice of the virtue of observance, might well be a martyr; but he is not evidently so, for it is not evident that the practice of this particular virtue was referred to God. The Crusaders against Islam were certainly fighting for the faith, though their efforts were much more concentrated on shedding other men's blood for Christ rather than their own. In view of the dangers and difficulties they deliberately faced, we cannot deny that they were brave men; many thousands of them undoubtedly were martyrs, but it is also quite possible that many, many other thousands were not.

However, martyrs are found not only in arenas, armies, persecutions; they are to be readily found in much less publicized activities. An obvious example of our own day is that of the Christian mother who will not countenance the destruction of her unborn child as a means of preserving her own life. Alternatively, again, there is the Catholic wife who refuses, in defense of justice and purity, to stoop to perversions of nature, even though such things might ward off a serious threat to her life.

An American magazine recently published the results of a scientific canvass of American women as to their attitude towards birth control and their reasons for their attitude. Among reasons offered in defense of the practice were economic considerations, the fear of giving birth to defectives, the desire to give better education to their children, the refusal to have children until they could be better taken care of, and so on. The significant thing about this list of causes is that it contains no mention of personal fear -- the fear of pain, of loss of beauty, of death. The reasons not alleged are even more significant than those that are given.

The breakdown of courage: Cowardice

They give a modern picture of a very old thing. The martyr stood in the arena before thousands and his courage left the bitterest of his enemies in a kind of awe. The coward hides his cowardice and leaves even himself ashamed. The brave man is a conqueror; the coward is conquered by fear. The coward slinks away, without engaging in battle, to a defeat that robs him of a chance to lead a human life; he capitulates before the obstacles that must be removed before the march of life can get under way. Moreover, he knows he has been defeated. He knows that the contempt of men for his cowardice is but a vague hint compared to the roar of disapproval that must come from his inner self. He is in perpetual hiding, even perpetual hiding from himself.

Fearlessness and its causes

It is not, of course, wrong to feel fear. A good ghost story should cause goose flesh and shivers; a mysterious noise at night might well make our knees knock and our teeth chatter. There are things that should be feared, things like snakes, broken legs and tornadoes; but we should fear those things reasonably, not suffering damnation in an attempt to escape snakes. For if, feeling fear as every man does, we allow that fear to take command of our action, then we are cowards.

If we have no fear at all, something is lacking in us. We may be freaks. We may be too thickheaded to appreciate the danger, so stupidly puffed up as to think nothing can hurt us, or so devoid of love that we do not care what is taken from us. In any case we are not more human, but distinctly less so for our fearlessness. We have no cause for pride or boasting; rather, we have something to be ashamed of, something that must, at all costs, be kept from the children.

Daring

Only a superficial examination can mistake rash boldness for bravely. There is as much difference between the recklessly daring and brave men as there is between the brave and the cowardly. Both the coward and the reckless one have allowed reason to crumble before the onslaught of passion; one makes a man run away, while the other makes a man rush to attack. Now, both prevent a man from being human here and now. Both have cut off human living at one of its starting points.

Progressive need of courage:

For human life and for Catholic life

Summing up this chapter, we can say that it takes courage to be human. It takes even more courage to be Catholic. In addition it takes still more courage to reach those sublime heights of Catholicism which are called sanctity. On the other hand, to put it another way, courage is necessary for the practice of virtue. As a man becomes more and more virtuous, he faces more and more difficulties and so needs more and more courage. Man needs courage to face human life, for human life cannot be lived without virtue, without good habits, without reason being in command. By Catholic life a man steps above the limits of mere humanity; he must not only be human now, thoroughly human, he must be divinely human; his ends are no longer the ends of mere man but the ends of God. Courage, in a word, is not a momentary stop at the important way stations of life's beginning and its end; it is a virtue that is progressively more necessary as life advances, as life becomes fuller, more successful.

The tragedy of fearlessness

The tragedy of fearlessness lies in its inability to see the necessity for any courage because of an inability to see any difficulties, any dangers, anything that needs to be feared. The fearless man is really a little worse off than the coward. The coward, at least, realizes the need of courage along with his realization of his own lack of it; the fearless man not only lacks courage, he does not realize his deficiency, and would not trouble his head about it if he did.

The course of cowardice: Factual cowardice

Fortitude, then, is progressively more necessary as we approach the heights of human life. There is progress in cowardice, too, but it is a burrowing into the depths rather than a scaling of heights. Its first stage might be called factual cowardice, the cowardice involved in fear, sin, irresponsibility, but coupled with the admission that all of these things are wrong, irrational. It is the cowardice of the Catholic succumbing to sin, but admitting that he is committing a sin.

Factual and philosophic cowardice

The next step down may take some considerable time for it involves a denial that fear, sin, irresponsibility, are wrong, irrational, cowardly. Sometimes this is merely a case of rationalization, of excusing ourselves even to ourselves; though we never quite succeed in completely convincing even ourselves. In our own day, another step has been taken to a philosophical denial of the principles that make these things wrong, of the principles that make courage itself necessary; and that means, ultimately, a denial of the principles that make human life possible.

It is no longer a shock to hear the spiritual character of man's soul denied; his free will and his consequent possibility of sin are constant subject matter for denials, as also are eternal life, eternal rewards, eternal punishment. Plumbing still deeper into individual life, the significance and responsibility of human action itself is called into question; it is made an animal act or a mechanical reaction, but is not allowed to remain the action of a human being. Finally, the individual human life itself is embroiled in a mass movement of some kind or another that robs it of any importance, of any significance, of any hope.

We can actually trace those steps of cowardice historically. The per-Reformation abuses were evidences of factual cowardice; next came the Reformation denial of theological truths and the modern denial of philosophical truths; the third and final step was taken in the modern mass ideology that has completely swallowed the individual.

The moderns and the martyrs

These steps of cowardice are so many stages in man's flight from his humanity. Actually, the coward can never escape. Both the moderns and the martyrs are in the same arena of human life; and the modern coward has no more chance to escape from human life than the martyr had to escape from the lions. The obvious difference between human life and the lions of the arena is that the lions would devour the martyrs whether they ran or not, whereas human life devours only those who attempt to run from it. There is an odd paradox here: we cannot run away from human life because we are human, and yet, precisely in attempting to run away from human life we cease to be human, we become cowards. The martyrs were much more careful of the supreme act of fortitude. They were the supremely brave men of our race; they continue to be a graphic statement of the human need to face issues, even when those issues are roaring lions.

GREATNESS OF SOUL
(Q. 128-140)

1. General attitude towards the heroic:
   (a) Admiration.
   (b) No serious desire to imitate.
   (c) No dismay at lack of this desire.

2. Defect of this attitude:
   (a) Defective basis of it.
   (b) Catholic's knowledge of this defect:
      (1) Evidence in face of sanctity.
      (2) Element of heroic in all life.
      (3) Element of heroic in all courage
      (Integral parts of fortitude).

5. Heroism in greatness:
   (a) Greatness of soul ·· magnanimity:
      (1) Its nature.
      (2) Its instruments.
      (3) Its opposites:
         a. By excess:
            1. Presumption.
            2. Ambition.
            3. Vainglory:
               a) A capital sin.
               b) Its "daughters."
         b. By defect ·· pusillanimity
   (b) Greatness in work ·· magnificence:
      (1) Its nature and extent.
      (2) Its opposites:
         a. Meanness (parvificentia).
         b. Waste (consumptio).

4. Heroism in labors and dangers:
   (a) Patience.
   (b) Perseverance:
      (1) Its nature and limitations.
      (2) Its opposites:
         a. Softness (effeminacy).
         b. Pertinacity.

5. Heights of heroism -- the gift of fortitude.

Conclusion:

1. Heroism and hero worship:
   (a) Difference between reaching for and looking at the stars.
   (b) Decline of heroism -- stars for a few only:
      (1) Vicarious heroism -- hero worship.
      (2) Abandonment of the heroic.

2. Heroism and human life.

3. Heroism and modern life.

CHAPTER XV

GREATNESS OF SOUL
(Q. 128-140)

General attitude towards the heroic: Admiration

A few years ago, Colonel Lindbergh returned from his triumphant flight over the Atlantic to a spontaneous public reception in New York. It seemed that the whole city turned out, eager to express its admiration for the daring of this lone aviator; the admiration was enthusiastic, even hysterical. Absolutely everyone had a splendid time, except, perhaps, Lindbergh. When the crowds finally scattered to their homes, they had no envy in their hearts, no grumbling dissatisfaction on their lips that it was Lindbergh and not themselves who was the hero. Apparently, everyone was satisfied that Lindbergh should have the glory, the medals, the place in history.

No serious desire to imitate

For the most part, that is the attitude of the average man towards the heroic. He does not envy a hero, has no earnest desire for the heroic himself, except by way of a relaxing dream. The family butcher around the corner may enjoy reading the life of Napoleon or following the progress of a modern war; but he has no serious desire to be a great military leader himself, After all, there is no secret ruthlessness within him, he has no desire to kill people; the monotony, discipline and rigidity of army life do not make his mouth water; he has no desire to wander over the face of the earth. Rather he is quite satisfied with his humble business, with the peace, kindness and quiet of home life.

Additionally, in that he is much like the rest of men. When the hard working lawyer relaxes with a detective story at the end of a grinding day, he does not seriously look forward to the day when he himself will be unearthing clues. He has no taste for manhunts, no affinity for criminals, no relish for the constant threat of a bullet in the back. So it is with all the rest. The daring aviator, the racing automobile driver, the animal trainer and all-around daredevil -- we can enjoy their exploits. We are thrilled by them, admire them, but as for personally imitating them -- ah no.

No dismay at lack of this desire

We have no more desire for that than we have to be suddenly turned into an angel. Moreover, we show no more dismay at our lack of desire than we do at our reluctance to rise promptly on a cold morning, or our cowardice in the face of a cold tub before breakfast. In fact, we can laugh a little about all this. It is a weakness we have in common with practically all men, the ordinary attitude of ordinary men; not something, we have to be ashamed of. Heroism is something for the exceptional, the rare man. Heroes are few and far between; as for the rest of us, well, we simply trudge along our mediocre way.

Yet there is something wrong with this point of view. In our last chapter, we saw that courage was essential for the living of human life; and that courage could not exist without its primary object -- the facing of the danger of death. Everyone, then, not only can but must have the courage to face death itself. In other words, everyone must have something of the heroic in him.

Defect of this attitude: Defective basis of it

This modern attitude towards the heroic is incomplete, half-baked, something like a half-considered opinion. In addition, its incomplete character is due to the modern identification of the heroic with the venturesome. In other words, we have identified the heroic with the lesser, the easier act of courage, namely, the act of attack. Men do not particularly like to attack, either other men or things; the crunching bones in an adversary's face under the blow of a fist is not music to the ears of the man who struck the blow, if he is normal. Attack is an emergency measure with considerable distaste attached to it, even if it is easier; people do not enjoy rushing down a fire escape in their nightclothes, even though they do it readily as the easiest way to meet the emergency of fire. So men show no dismay at their reluctance to engage in this emergency action, which we have called heroic.

Catholic's knowledge of this defect:

Evidence in face of sanctity

Still, there is another act of courage, the act of sustaining dangers and difficulties, of holding on. The Catholic, above all others, is familiar with this other side of courage; he knows well that this other is the principal, the chief act of courage and that it enters into the field of the heroic. He is constantly faced with this type of heroism and he gives it an honor and respect, which he accords to no other courage. He is, in a word, familiar with the saints and their sanctity. In the depths of his heart, he realizes that courage cannot go beyond this; this is heroism that touches the sublime.

Yet a man cannot merely cheer as sanctity goes by and, when the parade is over, go home well satisfied with himself. True, there is not a universal eagerness among Catholics to imitate sanctity; but it is also true that the Catholic cannot be too complacent about his lack of imitation of the saints. He knows that, through the grace of God, this heroism is in his power, that it is his persistent clinging to things that do him no good or to trifles that holds him back from reaching these sublime heights. Sanctity inevitably awakens shame and compunction in the bystander, not merely satisfied admiration. Frequently it begins a movement of personal reform; yet often it stirs up a violent hatred that is directed much more at sanctity's implied rebuke to the sinner than at the saint himself.

Element of heroic in all life

For heroism is not to be identified with venturesome attack but with courage. It is to be found plentifully in daily living. Since courage cannot be separated from living, neither can heroism; indeed, its very height will not be in the secondary but in the primary act of courage, not in the act of attack but in the act of sustaining, of holding on.

Element of heroic in all courage (Integral parts of fortitude)

Strictly speaking, heroism is nothing more than high courage. It is found chiefly in the supreme act of courage, that is, in facing the dangers of death; and those dangers can be met either by sustaining or attacking them. In either case, there are some necessary acts without which the act of high courage itself cannot possibly be produced. For attack, a man must be straining for the stars. That is, in his heart he must have great hopes for great things, hopes so great for things so great that all else sinks into insignificance; so great, indeed, that they give a greatness to his own soul (magnanimity). Moreover, there must be a magnificence to his action corresponding to the soul's greatness; the execution must be as splendid as the inspiration. For the act of sustaining a man must have a wall of patience built around his soul, a wall that tosses back the waves of the tremendous seas of sorrow that rush at his soul to leave it a wretched, broken thing; it is a wall that must not weaken, must not break, must not allow the smallest leak. Then, too, he must have a bulwark of perseverance to withstand the ceaseless continuity of sorrow's pounding on his soul day after day, month after month, year after year.

If these four -- magnanimity, magnificence, patience and perseverance -- are restricted to meeting the dangers of death they are not virtues, but rather integral parts of the virtue of courage. They are acts that must run along side by side with the acts of courage if that act is not to fail.

In lesser dangers and lesser difficulties, each of these four is a separate virtue. Let us look at it this way: if we consider each difficulty, each danger, as a fragment blasted from the rock of the supreme danger and difficulty, which is death, then in handling every one of these fragments we find some of the gold of heroism in the shape of magnanimity, magnificence, patience or perseverance.

On the other hand, looking at it in a different way, we could consider each difficulty, each danger, as a preparation for the supreme danger. Each particular difficulty, each particular danger pours some of the concrete of heroism into the foundations of the soul; it builds in these four habits that eventually make the ultimate heroism a kind of second nature to us. This truth is not hard to check. A girl who has pampered herself for years, naturally finds it practically impossible to make the sacrifices demanded by married life; in a very short time, she seeks escape through the emergency exit of divorce. Or, again, the sham battle of mortification makes the real battle against temptation somewhat of a routine matter for which we are well prepared; on the contrary, the tremendous penances of Martin Luther, taken in long separated gulps, were positive detriments instead of being helps to the real battle. Human nature does not become anything all of a sudden. We were made to live in time; and it is in time that we build up our characters.

Heroism in greatness: Greatness of soul -- magnanimity

The first of these fragments of heroism, magnanimity, implies a great heart, a heart enlarged, reaching out to great things, to things that are difficult, precisely because of their greatness. Just as courage, moderates fear and daring to the end of courageous action, so magnanimity, looking to a great work, moderates the expectations of honor. These expectations must not be too great, lest in a kind of despair we begin to be satisfied with petty things, counting their honor as great; nor yet must they be too small, for then a man will also refuse to undertake great things, considering them petty, not worth while, as does the cynic to whom all honor is more or less of a joke.

Its nature

The magnanimous man is not a publicity hound with his nose turned to the wind to catch any slightest scent of honor. His interest is in great works, works worthy of honor. His virtue of magnanimity moderates the hope of future honors and the joy of present honors by way of guaranteeing the accomplishment of the great works, which are its proper object. Of course, the magnanimous man has a real regard for honor; as a matter of fact, a man with no regard for honor will do the most despicable things with a kind of gusto, with the strange pride of a gangster kicking an insensible victim or a seducer wrecking the home of his friend. However, because he seeks the works and not the honor, the magnanimous man is not upset when due honor is not given him; nor is he impressed by too much honor, for he is far from a fool. He is not crushed by dishonoring attacks. He is above honor and dishonor, though he is dealing constantly with honor; for he knows that the due reward of virtue can come only from God.

Let us put this from the point of view of magnanimity, as a protector of reason's command. The serious threat to the command of reason does not come so much from the intrinsic nature of man's own passions; they were made to be subject to reason. Rather it comes from the extreme desirability of external things, especially from the attractions of money and honor. Of the two, the attraction of honor is by far the greater, since, as a witness to virtue, it is so close to that supreme value in human life. Unquestionably, there is something of the supreme about honor, its blood is royal. It is given to God and to the best of men; to avoid its contrary men have sacrificed all else. It is, then, a thing for which men we going to reach desperately; but a thing about which mistakes are so easily made that a virtue regulative of the appetite for honor is absolutely essential. We need a virtue governing our expectations of this witness of virtue from men.

Even to our loving eyes, the contours of our soul may have a closer resemblance to the flat monotony of the western plains than to the New York skyline. Yet greatness of soul runs through all of life, all of virtue, all of our works. Wherever there is an aspect of greatness, there magnanimity must be at work. Perhaps it is only such a relative greatness as our Lenten fast as compared to the asceticism of a saint; nevertheless, it is true greatness for us who have such a vague, nodding acquaintance with hair shirts. In a word, there is greatness in every human life, even the smallest and meanest of human lives,

This relative and hardly discernible greatness allows us to escape what absolute greatness never avoids -- the sharp, hard thrusts of the gossips' chatter. The magnanimous man is called a "glory-hunter"; he does aim at big things and they do bring glory. "He moves so slowly", and that is true, for he is looking at great things and they are not many; it is only the trafficker in trifles who is a hustler, a "go-getter." "He is lazy, even his voice is slow and heavy"; again there is some truth in this, for the magnanimous man is mixing only in great things, arguing only about great things; and great things are not only rare, they are not the sort that have to be bickered about. These are the things that grab hold of the very heart of a man or they do not touch him at all. "He is unsociable", because there is no need for him to parade his own excellence. "He is impractical", because he is not producing many results but only big results. "He is hard", because he is not a whiner, because he is above external things and not to be overcome by them. Sometimes he is too truthful because he has none of the fear that makes a timid man lie. In other words, he has time to live, to think, to act, because he is not overwhelmed with a mass of trifles; his eyes are on big things and everything else is unimportant to him.

Fortitude and magnanimity go well together; the one is the head of the family of courage, the other a favorite son. As they walk down the street together, heads will be turned to follow their progress: both are strapping fellows, strong, resolute. The one is the grim, tenacious fighter, strong against evil; the other, in its young strength in the pursuit of good, is not so much involved with security against evil as with the robust confidence that is stimulated rather than downcast by the very magnitude of the task it sets itself.

Its instruments

The greatness of its works, taking greatness in its absolute meaning, demands that magnanimity make use of wealth as an indispensable instrument. Great works erected by dreams come tumbling down at the trumpet blast of the alarm clock; wishing produces its wonders only in fairy tales; in the hard world of reality, it takes money to produce great works. In other words, wealth is an instrument of this virtue; but it must be clearly understood that it is only an instrument. It is not an integral part of the virtue, nor is it a necessary condition for the interior, and principal, acts of the virtue, the acts which actually expand a man's own soul.

Its opposites by excess: Presumption

An evidence of this limitation of wealth in magnanimity is seen in the fact that wealth often proves an obstacle to the virtue, sending a man hurtling after petty things under the impression that they are big. It frequently induces a kind of blindness to the really great things that leaves its victim as pitiable a figure as a physically blind man in the midst of Broadway traffic. He may mistake riches themselves for greatness and wave his bankbook as sufficient proof of his right to admittance everywhere and under every condition. In his blindness he may think the top rung of the social ladder is the peak of human achievement; the isolation of snobbery, the sweep of ruthless power, or even the very clothes with which he covers his nakedness, may seem to him goals worthy of a great soul. Yet by all these things, he condemns himself in the eyes of God and men as possessing a small soul. He makes a burlesque even of presumption; and presumption itself is no more than a mockery of magnanimity. He has merited not honor, but contempt, for he has abided by greatness as it is judged by fools.

Hardly less pitiable is the sin of presumption itself. We are saddened rather than angered by the powerful dictator's decision to design a whole city, the great industrialist's attempt to bring peace to the world personally and in short order, or the monk's efforts to improve on the doctrine of Christ. All these men have taken on works that were too big for them; they have been guilty of presumption, not as it is a sin against the Holy Spirit, but as it is opposed to magnanimity. No matter how small the scale on which the presumption exists, it is always a distressing thing to witness. Its victim is out of his depth. He is in a constant state of panic; in a fever of fear, jealousy, overwhelmed in hurried, desperate work. Ultimately, he is a bitterly disappointed, if not a broken man. It is significant that it is impossible for a man to aim too high in the life of supernatural virtue. Here it is not a question of establishing a proportion between our capacities and the work we try to do; from the beginning, there has been no proportion. Yet there is always proportion, a proportion that comes not from us but from the omnipotent, infallible help of Almighty God.

Ambition

Presumption aims too high; ambition does not aim too high, but it does aim at the wrong target. It speaks the language of magnanimity with all the peculiar inversions of a foreigner; it works out the problems of greatness like a dishonest child who gets all the solutions from the back of the book with none of the argumentation by which those solutions were reached. For ambition aims, not at great works, but rather at the honor they bring; it embraces the conclusions of greatness and snubs the labors of the works themselves.

Of course, it makes a man as helplessly vulnerable as a spoiled child. If he is not given his proper place at a banquet, he pouts in sullen silence or roars in anger; yet he is delighted if a headwaiter mistakes him for a visiting dignitary and gives him honors to which he has no claim. He gulps down honors with the uncouthness of a glutton; even the honors of God. To him the works are always unimportant; he lives on an airy diet of honor like the mythical honeymooners who lived on love alone. He must inevitably discover that it would have been much better to stop long enough to take a few bites of the solid sandwich of the works themselves. As a matter of fact, he has less and less interest in, or effort towards, meriting the honors upon which his life so desperately depends. He is like an athlete hoping for great victories, yet doing nothing about getting into condition, even going without food.

The ambitious man does not feel towards his honor as the saint feels towards his sanctity, satisfied to have it unknown to the world. He is no shrinking violet; he is not embarrassed by the plaudits of men, he gloats over them, for he seeks not only honor but honor's effect, which is glory. The more dazzlingly his light shines before men, the more pleased he is; he wants desperately to make a name for himself, though he is not particularly interested in laying the foundations which would justify that name.

Vainglory: A capital sin

It is not wrong, of course to have glory, or even to desire it. All the same, vainglory is something else. The latter has furnished a living for those creative artists who manufacture coats-of-arms for non-existent family trees; but economic reasons will not suffice to excuse the cultivation of vainglory. It hardly needs cultivation at any time; it springs up in the oddest places and settles down comfortably for a long stay, as much at home in the murderer's pride in his crime as in the physician's joy in the great name he has among the patients of his insane asylum. Its future is secure, its home safe, in the heart of the man who makes glory his god.

All this may sound a little extreme. Now, in our daily lives we do seek honor for non-existent works and purely fictional virtues. We accept honors for things as unworthy of honor as brigandage in the business world, lying in the political world, successive polygamy in the domestic world, and godless broad-mindedness in the individual world of our own soul. Indeed, honor will be accepted from people who are utterly incapable of giving it, even from fools.

When we do these things, we make a fatal mistake. Perhaps, in itself, the sin of vainglory does not exceed a venial sin; it may, of course, be mortal if we glory in material that is mortally sinful or make glory our god. Even so, what is more far-reaching in its tragic consequences is that this sin with which we have become enamored, is a capital sin.

Ordinarily we lump this sin with pride in our enumeration of the capital sins; but, theologically, pride is a concentration on one's own excellence, whereas vainglory is a concentration on the manifestation of that excellence. It might be called a sally of pride from behind its fortifications into the world of men. Certainly it is a stiff-necked pride that will not surrender an inch; as it elbows through the world of men it dispenses, with equal prodigality, blows and yawns, for in its negative activity it is a ruthless fighter while in its positive form it is the greatest of bores.

Its "daughters."

To the vainglorious man, disobedience is a factual manifestation of his excellence; discord proves the superiority of his will; quarreling is by way of showing he will have the last word; while stubbornness is his idea of superiority of intellect. With the last opponent shouted down, the way is clear for vainglory's positive action: for boasting, hypocrisy, the eccentricities of singularity by which it hopes to stand out from the crowd. Vainglory, like presumption and ambition, dare not saunter through the town undisguised; men have not yet reached the stage of honoring any of these things unless they parade as magnanimity. They do have an air of greatness about them; though, in them, there is much more of air than of greatness; they are the sins of windbags but they may fool us until they are punctured.

Its opposites by defect -- pusillanimity

No such mistake can be made about pusillanimity. Its victim can never be mistaken for the possessor of a great soul; by the very fact of his sin, he is defeated, for in the face of greatness he collapses. His pettiness of soul may be the result of an under-estimation of his own power or of an over-estimation of the greatness of the work that faces him. Whatever the cause, whether intellectual or emotional, the pusillanimous man is a pitiable figure as he stands paralyzed, mentally wringing his hands. Such a man was the servant of the gospel story who buried his lord's talent in the ground through fear of his master's harshness. In a milder form, it is seen frequently in men possessed of all the gifts -- clever intellect, kind heart, good personality, splendid health -- but who slip through life as unobtrusively ineffective as a figure in a dream. Pusillanimity wraps its feeble fingers around the life of the procrastinator, particularly the procrastinator in a position of authority, the man who can never quite bring himself out of the agony of his indecision.

Watching the small-souled man writhe in the agony of his fear, we pity him. We must, indeed, be extremely careful that contempt does not enter our thoughts; for it is easy to be contemptuous of so unnatural a thing. Man's soul is not small, it is big; made For tremendous things. Everything in nature moves to the act of which it is capable; this man shrinks from the very thing of which he is capable. Man naturally seeks good, he does not run away from it. Pusillanimity has the pallor of an anemic perversion in contrast to the ruddy, open face of nature.

It is interesting to run through the lives of the apostles with an eye to their greatness or smallness of soul. Those of whom details are recorded all had their moments, at least, of greatness. Nathaniel, recognized as the guileless Israelite, immediately made his gesture of subjection and his recognition of the divinity of Christ. The two pairs of brothers, Peter and Andrew, James and John, left their nets, their ships, their fathers without a backward glance, to follow Christ. Matthew, without a word, rose up from his tax-gatherer's booth at the word of the Master. Peter again and again showed promise of greatness, though his weakness prevented the execution of his works from coming up to their inspiration. Perhaps Thomas' contrasting decisiveness was one of the reasons Christ could be so easy on his tardiness and his hard-headedness; you remember, when Christ decided to return to Judea for the sake of his dead friend, Lazarus, even though his life had been threatened there, Thomas, in an almost matter-of-fact heroism said: "Let us go also and die with him."

There is great significance in this. Moments of pettiness come to nearly everyone. Some men can go all through life without a single moment of greatness. Yet, one flash of the splendor of greatness is a promise that justifies an unlimited investment of confidence. The apostles were to be leaders of men, indeed, leaders of the universe back to Christ and to God. Obviously, there is nothing more impossible than to work under a pusillanimous leader, watching helplessly while things go to pieces through his indecision. It was, then, essential that the apostles have greatness of soul or at least a promise of it. If we could speak on the purely human level, we might well wonder how many anxious days and nights Christ spent watching for some little promise of greatness from the soul of Judas, the traitor.

Greatness in work -- magnificence:

Its nature and extent

Greatness of soul is absolutely necessary if we are to get great things done. It is also necessary if we are to get great things made: but in this respect, greatness of soul is a distinct virtue, the virtue of magnificence. It is the virtue of the builder, the virtue that has produced the cathedrals, masterpieces, even celebrations of great pomp. For the most part, it is not a personal affair. As a general rule, there is little call for magnificence about our own person or in the details of our daily lives, diaries are usually a bore and full-length mirrors are mortifications as well as decorations. Now and then, we are magnificent in a personal way -- in things that happen once in a lifetime, like a marriage celebration, or with what we expect to last a lifetime, as in the construction of a home. However, usually magnificence spends itself on the things of the community or the things of God.

To accomplish great things, we must lay out great sums of money. Magnificence, dealing with those expenditures, also deals with love of money, as does liberality; but the latter handles the small change of life, magnificence carries the checkbook. It is, then, obviously, impossible for a fifteen-dollar-a-week stenographer to undertake works that demand huge expenditures; yet she can be magnificent, at least in the sense of the inner, and more important, acts of the virtue of magnificence, just as a man can be stingy with nothing to be stingy about. Nevertheless, even in the sense of external magnificence, this girl putting forth what to her is a tremendous amount of money, has a solid claim to the title of magnificent, even though that magnificence is relative and not absolute. Paradoxically it is much easier for the poor to be magnificent than for the rich, for five dollars can be spent in five minutes whereas it takes time and considerable thought to dispose wisely of a million dollars; and, as a matter of fact, the poor are much more frequently magnificent than the rich.

Its opposites: Meanness (*parvificentia*)

At one extreme from magnificence is the vice the English Dominicans translate as "meanness." It is a particularly venomous kind of stinginess that attempts to make great things without spending the money demanded by their greatness. As the illiberal man pays out money slowly and painfully, so the stingy man, using stinginess in this special sense, parts with his money as though he were saying a final farewell to a friend. He has, indeed, more reason for his reluctance; no matter how he pares down the expenses, the costs will run into huge amounts. It is this vice in action that has brought such bitter complaints from American labor on the score of unjust wages; where it shows up in inferior material or workmanship, it makes huge concrete piers dissolve like sugar to the astonishment of the citizens who were not in on the deal, or a highly modern overpass in a great city collapse under no heavier a weight than the silence of the night.

Waste (*consumptio*)

At the other extreme is a vice that might be called "waste", what St. Thomas calls "consumption." It also disregards the proportion between the dignity of the work and the money paid for it; it is quite willing to pay out money that would build a skyscraper in the actual erection of a birdhouse. In both meanness and waste the norm or medium of reason is violated. By the first, the sinner usually injures others as well as himself, as, for instance, by lowering wages below a living scale, using inferior material, skimping on the actual details of the plans, and so on. By the second, the sinner usually injures only himself, unless, and this is not too rare in American life, it is the community money, which is being spent. In this latter case, we describe this sin in one short word that has an ugly sound: graft.

Magnanimity and magnificence are the dust of the lesser heroism that is scattered through life. Both are kin to that act of courage, which is attack, for they deal with a good, which does not repel but rather attracts men. There is something of a rush about both of these virtues. Now, there is a greater side to heroic courage, the side that consists of enduring in spite of dangers and difficulties. The dust of this heroism is scattered through life much more prodigally and it goes by the names of patience and perseverance.

Heroism in labors and dangers: Patience

These two do not wear the fine raiment of magnanimity and magnificence. They are not nearly so attractive at first sight and they are easily under-estimated; it is not hard to miss the splendid heroism of a man if he is lying in the dust. Yet something of the splendor of this courage was caught in Christ's simple exhortation: "Possess your souls in patience;" its full brilliance bursts upon us when we remember that no one can follow the path of virtue long without patience, and the path of virtue is the path of heroism. Patience, after all, deals with the sorrows of life; it holds the soul upright under the crushing blows of this sorrow. The extent of sorrow in life is an indication of the extent and necessity of patience. Only so can a man possess his soul; for possession implies quiet ownership, calm dominion, and it is patience, which quiets the uproar of the passions and vices. Patience not only forbids unjust revenge, as does justice; it not only bars hate, as does charity; or anger, as does meekness. It even excludes the undue sorrow that is the root of all these sins. Patience is one of the humble, workaday virtues; but it is, in a real sense, the root and guardian of all virtues, not causing them but removing the impediments to their operation. Do away with patience and the gates are open for a flood of discontent and sin, for sorrow will still find its way into human life.

It is not patience that enables a prisoner to endure indignities calmly that he might later on have a better opportunity for revenge against the guard. Patience endures evil, not to commit evil, but rather that evil may not be committed. It finds its place in our daily lives in such crises as the separation from friends, the death of loved ones, sickness, slander and misfortune.

The natural question is, just what can patience do in the face of these things? Well, if we have it on its lowest level, we can at least endure these things without telling the neighbors about it. On a higher level, we bear with these things without telling ourselves about it over and over again in the kind of whining self-pity that sours human life. On its highest level, patience enables us to endure sorrows with positive joy.

That is a hard thing? Yes, it is. In the natural order it is nearly impossible, done only in view of some much greater natural good; although long experience may give us a kind of hopeless resignation from the realization that impatience does not help but rather increases sorrow. In the supernatural order, God's patience with our own weaknesses, forgetfulness and ingratitude, is a constant example before our eyes; we can never draw a curtain over the spectacle of Calvary's divine patience; and the sublime patience of the saints is not something we are ever in a hurry to forget. Then, too, the realization of its power to satisfy for our sins, its significance for heaven, and closer friendship with Christ, through its power of merit, is a constant spur to our patience. In a word, supernatural patience can be a joyous thing; but even supernaturally, it is never an easy thing.

We resent an inhuman harshness and brute stolidity that leave a man insensible to sorrow. Additionally, we are right in our resentment. Man should be touched by sorrow, by his own sorrow and the sorrow of his fellows; the man who is not so touched is vicious with the vice of insensibility. On the contrary, if sorrow affects us so deeply that we withdraw from good in order to escape it, then we, too, are vicious; we are guilty of the sin of impatience. This sin crowds many of our days with its trifling manifestations; we may not be at all embarrassed by it, even a little vain about such evidence of a strong mind and will. The truth of the matter is that impatience has nothing whatever of strength in it, but much, very much, of a terrible weakness; it is a confession of our inability to stand up before the rush of sorrow, even trifling sorrow. It stamps us as the vanquished mourning our defeat.

Perseverance: Its nature and limitations

Patience runs all through life because sorrow runs all through life; and, because our human life is measured in time, the courage of perseverance must color every work, every day, every life. Perhaps it is because we are made for eternity that we find it so hard to face the difficulty of time; whatever the reason, we do find duration itself a great difficulty. We do not hesitate to give our dinner to a hungry man; yet we find it extremely difficult to give up a small part of that meal for the forty days of Lent. We do not mind a day's work; but the same work day after day is an altogether different thing. It is easy to give a moment's kindness, but not a lifetime of kindness. For real lengths of time are a serious obstacle to human living.

Perseverance is a dogged, unswerving, unbeatable courage whose beauty and grace are often hidden in the weary stumbling of its walk and the gray fatigue of its face. No military bands greet perseverance; no trumpets salute it, no parades are staged in its honor, no decorations publicly conferred. There is not even the human help of racing blood that comes in facing open attack. Perseverance knows only the dull, relentless thud of the moments of time and the fighting heart holding fast to the necessity of fighting through to the end.

Still, not even this heroic courage is sufficient to cover the whole span of a lifetime, not even when it is the result of the supernatural virtue of perseverance. We went into this question in more detail in the preceding volume; here it is enough to recall that for this endurance we need a special gift of God, the gift of final perseverance. A gift, that is, which meets not this or that work, not this or that span of time, but the whole long sweep of a man's life from birth until the moment of death.

Its opposites: Softness (effeminacy)

It is the defect of this courage of perseverance that is the distinctive mark of effeminacy. It is not the muscles or the gait of a man that stamps him as effeminate, but his inability to carry through. In fact, a more expressive word for this condition would be a literal translation of the Latin term, i.e., softness; it means yielding easily to the lightest touch. This man is not giving way before terrifying fear, he does not surrender to the strong rush of pleasure, he crumbles before the almost negative touch of sorrow at the lack of pleasure. He is incapable of facing the long span of the difficult and the laborious because he cannot go so long without coddling.

Pertinacity

At the other extreme is the hard, stubborn, pertinacious man. He does not know when to yield; or knowing, refuses to give way. He does stand up before difficulties and we often give him a mistaken admiration for the beating he can take; but the admiration is mistaken. For usually it is pride making him hold on, a pride that springs from a secret fear of being considered an inferior, or perhaps an unreasonable joy at winning through these difficulties. Actually, stubbornness exceeds the limit of perseverance by excess, as effeminacy does by defect; both are unreasonable, inhuman. Life does not consist in taking a beating, looking like a conqueror, or stamping on difficulties; it consists in following reason's rule to reason's goal.

Heights of heroism ·· the gift of fortitude

All the same, even with all this splendid equipment of courage, it is altogether above human nature that a man win through to every end. conquer every danger and be bolstered up by a confidence that excludes even the small tugs of fear at his heart, and this not only in great works but in the small, arduous tasks of everyday life. There is a crown of courage that alone makes such heroism as this possible to man; that is the gift of fortitude, a gift of the Holy Spirit by which a man wins through to the end of ends, the final end which is God Himself.

Undoubtedly, the pagans did have courage. Nor is this surprising in view of the fact that every man must have some courage to avoid collapse in the face of life. However, it is only the infused, supernatural virtues of fortitude, magnanimity, magnificence, patience and perseverance which make heroes out of every man; that demand that every man be courageous in the work of living.

In our day, some strange things have been done to the concept of the heroic, and with some weird results. The cult of success, progress or accomplishment has won a fairly universal favor, with a consequent identification of heroism with the courage of attack. Some of the weird outgrowths of this have been to give us the absolute dictator and the soldier of fortune. The thing was inevitable because the norm of our judgment has been the norm of success. It might easily be that the man we admire is a successful lunatic, but still he is successful and so is a hero to his people. In the name of progress, we must snub everything that is old; there can be nothing solid worth holding on to because everything is changing, going forward in the name of progress. Consequently, patience and perseverance have been classed as the defects of weaklings or failures, of those who are not in the march of time toward success.

Heroism and hero worship: Difference between reaching for and looking at the stars

One serious result of this has been to split men into two uneven groups. One is the very small group that may reach for the stars; the other is the tremendous majority who are forbidden to reach for the stars. In other words, we have left the average man with no stars for which he can reach, we have taken the heroic entirely out of his life, even out of his hope. Because stars are for the extraordinary, the rare heroes, ordinary life has become a dull, drab thing; and human nature is not satisfied with dullness or drabness, not with the glory of eternity haunting its dreams. Therefore, we have resorted to that vicarious heroism which is hero-worshiped. We let someone else take care of our heroism for us; in our admiration and applause for their great acts, we satisfy the yearning of our hearts for the great things for which we were made.

Abandonment of the heroic

Radically that means that the ordinary man of our century has become resigned to the loss of the heroic, or at least, he has been forced to a frank abandonment of the heroic. He does not like it. If work and difficulty, family life and virtue are dull, drab things they will automatically become things to be escaped from, not sources of inspiration; to them man will stoop only under considerable duress, a physical duress that is the instrument of slavery.

Decline of heroism -- stars for a few only: Vicarious heroism -- hero worship

The fact is that human life cannot go along humanly without heroism; nor can the human heart endure without heroism entering intimately into its actions and its goals. It cannot be satisfied with vicarious heroism, mere hero-worship. For courage is as necessary for the living of human life as air, or food, or drink; not only the courage of the venturesome, but also that principal courage that holds on, even when holding on is the best a man can do. Christ did not take the heroic out of the average man's life; He frankly insisted that that life was permeated with the heroic. Works and labors, difficulties and perils are not drab necessities but constant inspirations, constant sources of greatness, constant tests of tremendous courage.

Heroism and human life; heroism and modern life

The men of our day need heroism in their lives not one bit less than did the men of Christ's day. Thus, today we see the instant appeal of such a dogma as that proposed by Communism, which gives the man in the street a part in the things that he considers heroic. It is an attempt to re-establish a star in the firmament of the worker and the attempt has had considerable success, even though this star is utterly worthless to the individual worker himself. At least it is a star and he can reach for it. In the Christian life, there can be no individual the firmament of whose life is not filled with stars. There cannot be a day in that life in which he is not only permitted, he is obliged to reach for the stars. His whole life is an adventure of incredible courage toward incredible goals and fought with weapons of incredible strength.

The Christian can admire heroism. He can pay it the tribute of respect, which comes naturally from the human heart confronted with great courage. Yet, much more than that, he himself can be a hero; indeed, he must be a hero. In addition, so it is that the tribute he pays to heroism is one much more deep, more understanding, more heartfelt. It is the tribute of one hero to another, even though that tribute is the tribute that the Christian sinner gives to the sinless Christ.

THE HUMAN ANIMAL
(Q. 141-145)

1. Prerequisites of mastery:
    (a) Something to be mastered.
    (b) Something that can be mastered.

2. Modern protestations of slavery:
    (a) Puritanism.
    (b) Pagan psychologies.

3. Catholic protestations of mastery:
    (a) Vindications of history.
    (b) Vindications of facts.
    (c) The balance of reason.

4. The virtue of mastery -- temperance:
    (a) Its position as a virtue.
    (b) Its objects.

5. Conditions for the integrity of mastery:
    (a) Love of the beauty of temperance -- "honesty."
    (b) Recoil from the disgrace of baseness --
shamefacedness.

6. Double defect of mastery:
    (a) By deficiency -- insensibility:
        (1) Distinction from self-denial.
        (2) Opposition to nature.
    (b) By excess -- intemperance:
        (1) Its puerility.
        (2) Its gravity compared to cowardice.
        (3) Degree of disgracefulness.

7. Species of mastery:
   (a) In works conserving the individual: abstinence and sobriety.
   (b) In works conserving the species: chastity and purity.

8. Virtues connected with the virtue of mastery:
   (a) Continency.
   (b) Clemency.
   (c) Modesty.

Conclusion:

1. Implications of the denial of mastery:
   (a) For the truth of human nature.
   (b) For the maturity of human nature.
   (c) For the dignity of human nature.
   (d) For the beauty of human nature.

2. The difficult condition of mastery -- battle.

3. The champion of man as man.

CHAPTER XVI

THE HUMAN ANIMAL
(Q. 141-145)

It was not mistaken strategy that moved the devil to offer Eve the prospect of becoming like God. His appeal was to nothing less than complete dominion, perfect mastery; and the appeal of mastery to our nature is constant and profound, precisely because man was made to be a master. The prospect of mastery immediately sets man afire because his nature responds to the goal for which it was created, so powerfully, indeed, that age after age man rises repeatedly to the bait of false mastery.

Prerequisites of mastery: Something to be mastered

The push of nature towards the goal of man is not sufficient to accomplish the fact of mastery. If he is to be master, man must at least know what mastery means. He must realize that perfect physical development, sharp intellectual gifts, a balance of powers are in themselves insufficient to make him a master. Put this splendid creature on a desert island and it is impossible for him to be a master for the simple reason that there is nothing to master. On the other hand, let an absent-minded bank teller, deceived by the familiar bars, wander into a lion's cage and he, too, is faced with an impossibility of mastery, though for a different reason. In the first case, there was nothing to master; in the second, the thing could not be mastered by this man.

Mastery, if it means anything, means to bring something or someone under our command. Unlike God, we do not create our subjects; we must subdue them. That which is to be mastered must be presupposed to our action; granted the subject matter of opposition, there must be a capacity for mastering it if man is to be master.

Something that can be mastered

It may seem that we are laboring an obvious point here; but the point has been and is being missed, as happens so often with the obvious. It is a fact that man can be and must be a master if he is to remain a man. He is possessed of a complex nature whose elements will not live on equal terms; one or the other will take charge. The spirit pulls against the flesh and the flesh against the spirit now as in the days of Paul, indeed, as in all days since the expulsion of man from the garden of Eden. Here in America, we are officially dedicated to the ideal of freedom, which, if it be not meaningless, is a dedication to mastery. We refuse to entertain the idea of man subjecting himself to his equal or to his inferior. It is a political insistence flowing from Christianity's supremely valuable contribution to Western philosophy, the concept of personality, of individual dignity and responsibility. The same concept is at the rock bottom of Christian ethics; without it, these ethics have no meaning.

Modern protestations of slavery: Puritanism.

Yet, in spite of our political insistence on the concept of freedom, we have repeatedly denied freedom, for we have denied mastery. In the early days, we denied freedom by denying the possibility of mastery, refusing to admit that there was something that could be mastered. The Puritans' rigid gloom was well justified, granting-their principles: if man is utterly corrupt and an utterly helpless tool of a viciously unjust divinity, how can he be otherwise than sunk in gloom? The slave does not gloat over the chains that tie him down like a dog. What is there to fight about if there is no chance for mastery; what is the ground for rejoicing when there is no possibility of triumph? It is the hopeless slavery of a man who is beaten before he can strike a blow. The one thing he can do is resign himself to his fate, admitting his slavery, his lack of mastery.

Pagan psychologies

In our modern days, slavery is no less thoroughly championed, though on different grounds. Our modern contention is that a man cannot be a master because there is nothing for him to subdue. The modern slave-dealer insists that man is entirely one-sided, he is merely an animal; the one course open to him, then, is to give that animality its fullest development, its fullest play. If that be true, then we can no more be masters than can a cat or a worm.

The important point of all this is that none of it is true. Man is by his very nature free, he can fight and win. Man has a soul as well as a body; there is something to fight and subdue. This very truth makes the hell of slavery, to which the moderns have delivered men, just so much more bitter. Eventually the victims of this betrayal of humanity will realize that they could have been masters; later on, when the gilt wears off passion and leaves its dull baseness plain, they will see the extent of the swindle that has been perpetrated, a realization that is almost enough to destroy all hope. For then they will see that they have indeed sold their birthright for a mess of pottage, and that the pottage itself has spoiled. It has always been true that the stars are clearly visible from the depths; that it is the saint or the great sinner who has the real view of the splendor of God. So also, it is the man who is sunk into the depths of slavery who can appreciate to the full the possible mastery, which he has forfeited.

Catholic protestations of mastery:

Vindications of history

There is an amusing angle to this constant denial of mastery in American history, an angle that seriously calls into question our boasted sense of humor. To appreciate it, you must remember that during that short span of our history Catholics have held fast to unchanging ethical and dogmatic truths; the Catholic position on purity, justice, lying, the sacredness of contracts is exactly the same today as it was when judges wore wigs. In Colonial days, the Catholics were considered a corrupt people. They were fast, loose, immoral; to them any means were justified by the end, even murder and lying. They were not people with whom one could do business safely, for by their very principles, their contracts with Protestants were not binding. They were the children of the harlot of Babylon, unfit companions for God-fearing men, enemies of the Christian state, to be denied every share in community life. Today Catholics are considered hopelessly rigid, prudish, medieval. They demand altogether too much of human nature, even the impossible. They have never caught the full significance of the sacred catchword "business is business;" they are the enemies of pleasure, of full, free, joyous living. They try to fit every age into an ethical pattern of two thousand years ago instead of keeping up with the times by molding their ethics to the customs of an age.

Vindications of facts

Odd, isn't it? Still more odd, when it is realized that the accusers have always been the one hundred percent Americans of their time. Yet all the Catholic has done is to hold fast to essential, even obvious, truths. He has steadily maintained that man is man, has an intellect, a will, a spiritual soul, and that man alone is possessed of these priceless gifts. In the eyes of the Catholic, it is these things that distinguish a man from all else in the universe; these things can be, must be in the forefront of his life, his action, his thought if he is to be truly human. In a word, the Catholic's crime has been to maintain that a man is a human being; not merely a helpless pawn, not merely an animal but a human animal who is master of his destiny. Man has a body; he may have to apologize for the shape it is in, but not for the fact itself. There is nothing evil about it; it is part and parcel of him. Now, that body destroys itself when it takes charge of man's life. Man has something to subdue -- his lower nature; moreover, he can subdue it. He is free precisely because he is man: and the principal work of his life is the maintenance of that mastery which is essential to the humanity of his life. Man is not evil, he is not utterly corrupt and helpless because of his corruption. Nor have men nothing to subdue; men are not merely animals, as the moderns would have it. There is joy in life, great joy; but it is not merely animal joy. In spite of the uncouth mouthings of the monk who was so terrified at his own weakness, in spite of the intellectual blasphemies of an arrant theologian of gloom, in spite of the unscientific dreams of pseudo-scientific philosophers and pseudo-philosophic scientists, man continues to be man. He can never escape from his humanity.

The city of Washington is honeycombed with slanting streets -- the Avenues. They are a boon to taxi-drivers, shortening distances (there are no meters) and relieving all boredom as they converge en masse in circles. They are also, I am told, evidence of very intelligent planning. For the ordinary driver or the stranger in Washington, they are a source of that amazement that is induced by a sleight- of-hand trick. For instance, you start out for a walk down Pennsylvania Avenue. Of course you take the north side of the street to get a better view of the buildings; and suddenly the Avenue is gone from under your feet and you find yourself in the oddest places, perhaps gaping at the display of a second-hand furniture emporium. I have been witness to the complete befuddlement of a driver who found himself still on the same slanting street but going in a direction opposite to that in which he had started, with no reasonable explanation of the marvel. It has often struck me that these Avenues are graphic representations of the path of reason. It is so very easy to wander off that path and find oneself in the oddest errors. A Washingtonian, as the years bring him wisdom, learns to keep alert on these slanting streets; so also a reasonable man eventually learns that he can never cease his alertness if he is to keep to the path of reason.

The balance of reason

Reason demands a delicate balance between extremes. It is the peacemaker of human nature, so it is always a target for shafts from both sides, both extremes. Father Cormier, a saintly Dominican Master-General, once held a visitation in Rome. A visitation, for those unfamiliar with that democratic procedure, represents the opportunity given to every individual in a convent to express his mind on how things are running, how things should be run and what things should be stopped from running. In the course of this visitation, the Master-General heard that the procurator should be removed because the food was abominable, there was not enough of it and the members of the community were practically starved. He also heard that the procurator should be removed because the table was too rich, they were living like kings, and the spirit of monastic observance was being undermined by his catering to positive gluttony. When the procurator came in, the Master-General outlined the double complaint; in answer to the procurator's puzzled question as to what he should do, Father Cormier said: "Continue, continue. When you are attacked from both ends, you are probably not inclining too much to either one or the other."

It is not only easy to embrace an extreme, there is a guarantee of assurance about it. There will always be applause for the extremist no matter which extreme he embraces; and there will always be a double opposition in store for the man who rejects both extremes. Moreover, the medium of reason seems often an uncolorful, ordinary manner of procedure. Actually to embrace either extreme means a lack of balance. As an indication of how profound an impression is made on our minds by the garish colors of extremes, there is the fact that we introduce something of these extremes even in our thinking about the moderate refusal of extremes. Certainly, there is a lack of balance in our general thinking about temperance. The very word calls to mind the fanatical reformer or tavern brawls. All the same, whether we speak of temperance in the sense of teetotalism or of sottishness, we always think of temperance in terms of drink alone.

The virtue of mastery -- temperance

That is quite unjust to temperance. This virtue of mastery has for a field of battle all of the pleasures whose allure may draw man off the course of reason. It is not to be conceived of in terms of a puritanical enemy of pleasure; nor is it to be greeted by the sigh of a man arising from a Lenten breakfast. It is not the enemy of sense pleasures in their human limitations; it is their enemy only in their bestial excesses. It is a virtue. That is, it is a good habit proclaiming present and past mastery of reason, protecting, as well as predicting, the humanity of future actions.

Temperance does not attack sense pleasures; rather it guarantees them. It imposes the norm of reason on the mild or concupiscible appetite of man; it guarantees that the goal of man, the good of reason, will not suffer interference from sense appetite in its own search for sense good. In a word, it protects that happy medium of reason, which is the absolutely essential condition for peace and progress in human life. Its goal is not repression or inhibition; it does not frown down all that is attractive in life. Rather it insists on the full freedom that can be given only by control, the control of reason.

Temperance does not speak so softly as to be unheard; nor does it shout so loud that it deafens its listeners. By its very nature, it is moderate; perhaps that is why it goes unnoticed in a crowd and can so easily be taken for granted. Its note of moderation runs through all of human action, all of human passion because the note of reason must run through all of these things. In this sense, temperance is not a special virtue, but a condition of all virtue. In the same sense fortitude's firmness, justice's rectitude, and prudence's rationality are notes of all human actions precisely because they are human, reasonable; for these things are the notes of reason.

Its position as a virtue

However,, taken more strictly, temperance is a special virtue: it has its own proper work to do. We can see this quite easily by comparing it with the work of the other virtues. Justice establishes the order of reason in external things; within the world of man, the interior world, the order of reason is not established by the strictly moral virtues, it is conserved. Additionally, it must be conserved not only against all that might drive a man from reason, through fear or recklessness (the work of fortitude), but also against what might coax a man away from reason, i.e., from the pleasures that are moderated by the virtue of temperance. In a word, fortitude and temperance protect the mastery of man's reason against the impediments offered by his double sense appetite. Those, which arise from his irascible or emergency appetite, are taken care of by courage; those from the concupiscible or mild appetite are handled by temperance.

The passions can be compared quite closely to the sled dogs of Arctic travel. These dogs are powerful, indispensable for man's travel, with great staying power and a marvelous capacity for work; but let them get out of control, and they are vicious enemies more seriously threatening the life of man than the freezing cold and heavy snows, which, normally, they enable him to escape. The passions, too, are powerful things, indispensable for man's travel to his goal. They have tremendous staying power and great capacity for work. Even so, let them get out of control, and they are the most vicious enemies a man can have, threatening not only his life, but his very humanity. The difference is that the passions are at home in harness; that is where they belong, they are human passions, designed of their very nature to obey reason.

Temperance works to moderate the passions of the concupiscible appetite; but indirectly it also moderates the emergency appetite, and from this double moderation proceeds the moderation of human acts. In a real sense, then, the conserving action of temperance is a radical thing. You will remember, in the preceding volume, it was pointed out that emergency passion depends on and arises from mild or concupiscible passion; so that a man who had no love whatsoever could not hope, be reckless or angry. In handling the prior passions, temperance makes no little contribution to the regulation of the consequent passions of the emergency appetite.

The point is important, particularly in view of many of our modern reform methods. We are attempting the hopeless when we disregard the prior passions and try to cope with their consequences. There is an inherent contradiction in our policy of championing the necessity of unrestricted natural appetite in academic circles, while we put policemen on corners and laws on the books to thwart the consequences of such "naturalness". To spoil a child, thereby cultivating uncontrolled concupiscible passion in it, and at the same time to be furious, embarrassed or puzzled at the outbreaks of temper, fear or despair, is to wonder why the roof falls down when we tear out the foundations.

Its objects

If we wish to state the objects of temperance concretely, we could say that it deals directly with the passions seeking or enjoying sensible good, i.e., the passions of love, desire and joy; by way of consequence, it deals indirectly with sorrow at the absence of these goods. Its remote material, the forest upon which it draws for the lumber of its house, is the use of things that are necessary for the conservation of nature; the planed lumber which goes into the home of temperance is the love, desire and pleasure which come from the use of those things so necessary to nature; while the completed mansion is moderate love, desire and pleasure in those necessary things.

A precise notion of the object of temperance can be had by a glance over our shoulder at fortitude. Fortitude looks primarily at the supreme danger of death, because every virtue aims at the highest perfection of its faculty; if a man can face the danger of death, of course he can face lesser dangers. In the same way, temperance aims at the moderation of the supreme pleasure; the man who can keep the supreme pleasures in hand can, without difficulty, control the lesser pleasures.

Really, there is no room for argument as to which are the greatest of sense pleasures. Nature has treated us as children, taking no chance on our mistaking the less important for the more important. Just as a child can accurately judge the preference of the parent by the reward or threat attached to this or that particular work, so we can judge the intentions of nature by the reward or threat attached to this or that particular act. Sense pleasures are the rewards of nature attached to the things that nature particularly wants done; as an act is more intimately connected with an end principally intended by nature, its attached pleasure is greater. Consequently, the acts connected with nature's two great ends of conservation of the species and of the individual carry with them the greatest of sense pleasures. Because the species is much more directly intended by nature throughout the physical world, it is precisely in the acts conservative of the species that the supreme sense pleasure is found.

St. Thomas summarizes all this briefly when he says that temperance, principally and properly, moderates the pleasures of the sense of touch; secondarily it moderates all lesser pleasures insofar as they have reference to this fundamental pleasure of touch. Still, notice that he insists it is moderation, not destruction, of pleasure, which is accomplished by temperance. An oversight of this distinction is at the bottom of a very common mistake. Thus, it is insisted, with an ominous seriousness, that none of these things are to be done for the pleasure of doing them, we are not, for example to eat for the pleasure of eating. So with the best of intentions a person starts to eat for the glory of God or for nourishment; he has been very careful, locked all the doors and windows, posted his guards -- but there stands pleasure in the very midst of his good intentions, grinning its carefree grin. Of course, pleasure comes in. There is a sense of pleasure necessarily and naturally connected with the very use of the necessities of life. Temperance does not touch that pleasure; it cannot touch it. Temperance does not blast out any part of our nature; it does not ask that we keep a few drops of castor oil on our tongue all the time to counteract the natural pleasure of eating. It insists on moderation in those things that add to the essential pleasure, that make that natural use a still greater source of pleasure.

As a matter of fact, to place any one of these acts merely for the acts themselves, solely for the pleasure of it, is psychologically an extremely difficult thing for the ordinary individual. It is when we are very hungry that food tastes particularly good; the pleasure is meted out by nature in proportion to the demand of nature for this particular act. It is a long job to accomplish the perversion that would enable us to eat for the joy of eating. It demands that we twist nature badly; the effort and time necessary for that well-accomplished perversion will leave us no doubt of its evil. Now, until we have that assurance of perversion the pleasure of these natural acts does not represent any considerable material for worrying purposes.

If we remember that temperance is not a destroyer of pleasure, we shall soon see that it is not a repellent, worrisome thing. It is by no means a constant source of irritation designed to keep us constantly unhappy. Rather, it has an air of tranquil beauty about it, like the beauty of a calm sea, a Swiss valley farm seen from a mountain top, or a child's face immediately after a bath. Christ's calming of the storm at sea was more than a gesture of protection and comfort for the apostles; it was a miniature of temperance executed by a divine hand.

The material of temperance can most readily and moat thoroughly disturb the tranquility of the soul of a man. These things are so close to the fibers of a man's being that any disorder in them is a fundamental disorder for the whole man. They, above all other things, can besmirch the beauty of a man's soul, for they are the least in man and drag him down to the lowest level, like the basest of metals mingling with the purity of gold. They represent the common link between man and the animal world; they can easily become heavy enough to drag man down to the level of his fellow animals.

Conditions for the integrity of mastery:
Love of the beauty of temperance -- "honesty"

Yet, temperance is a source of beauty in a more positive way. A human nose is a thing of beauty if there is not too much of it; the very essence of beauty is proportion, a rich, brilliant order. Temperance has as its striking note precisely the note of moderation, of order, of proportion. Moreover, it is a brilliant order; it is the order of reason shining through the lowest things in man, giving them a consecration, a halo, a striking elevation like that given a speck of dust caught in a ray of sunlight. It is true that temperance is not the greatest of the virtues; but it is one of the most lovable. It does not reach out directly to the high, divine things, nor to the great goods of the whole community of men. It does not face the tremendous dangers and difficulties as does courage; it is not even the most useful in the lives of other men. The fact is that temperance is an intensely personal virtue, as beauty is an intensely personal thing. It walks through life as humbly busy as a housewife; every minute of every day, it has work to do keeping the house of a man's soul in order.

Yet, it is a constant inspiration to other men, as beauty always is. It is a refreshing touch of the breath of God's order, like the gust of a cool breeze on a summer day. It is a tranquil prophecy of a beauty awaiting us, or a reminder of beauties that have been carelessly mislaid, beauties that can be won, or re-won, by everyone. There is, therefore, no great mystery in Christ's choice of his most beloved disciple; there is no real psychological puzzle in the humble fascination that kept Magdalene so very close to Mary the Virgin. Beauty has always been loved by men who were made for order, even by the greatest of men -- the man Who also was God.

Recoil from the disgrace of baseness – shame facedness

A keen appreciation of this beauty of temperance is quite essential for the perfection of the acts of temperance. To be truly temperate a man must have, first of all, a love of the beauty of temperance, a love that Thomas calls "honesty." In a larger sense honest or honorable does not express an idea different than that of virtue; indeed, it is not different from the humanly beautiful, the humanly useful, or the humanly delightful. However, in this special sense, in which Thomas uses the word, honesty looks directly at the beauty of temperance and falls in love with it. His keen appreciation of that beauty makes a man recoil from the disgrace, the baseness of intemperance; it gives him what Thomas calls "shamefacedness." This is the thing that makes the memories of a sinner so bitter; that, in its preparatory state, makes the steps of the saint so very careful. It is this saving sense of shame that makes the knowledge of our evil by those close to us so very painful; they know us so well, their judgment of us is so accurate that our shame is almost a constant thing.

We are made for beauty, even for divine beauty. We are in love with beauty even when we have destroyed it in ourselves. When that beauty is wiped out of the life of a man, he has lost a priceless treasure; when the sense of loss of the beauty is completely gone from the heart of a man, he has gone far along the road towards surrendering his humanity. He has cut off one last link binding him to the moderation of reason that must be the keynote of human life.

Temperance, however, is not an empty-headed beauty, highly decorative but socially intolerable. As we get to know her better, we find a solid common sense and a profundity that distracts even from her beauty. One of the great slanders against her common sense persistently arises from the practice of mortification. It is no doubt astonishing to an outsider to hear that mortification is not a condemnation of sense pleasure but a recognition of its intrinsic worth and desirability. Our Lenten penances do not come about because we look on these pleasures as somehow suspect or even possibly evil; it is precisely because we insist upon their innate honesty that these penances have such a particular significance.

Double defect of mastery:

By deficiency -- insensibility
Distinction from self-denial

The condemnation of sense pleasure as evil was the slimy error of the Manicheans, which Dominic stamped on as vigorously as a man would stamp on a snake. The Puritans' repulsion to any expression of the mild or concupiscible passions came from the same unclean error. The athlete in training is not inhuman because he limits his social engagements; the invalid recovering from typhoid fever is not condemning food when he abstains from corned-beef and cabbage in spite of his great hunger. Why then should the penitent be suspect of inhumanity when, for greater health of soul, he denies himself something on the physical plane? This is not a kind of angelism that attempts to deny the physical in man; it is a surrender of something good in itself for higher ends. Indeed, it is nothing more than that profound common sense which dictates an entirely different diet for the nun dedicated to contemplation and the brawny bricklayer whose contemplation fights with the fatigue of his body for a place in his life.

Opposition to nature

The condemnation of pleasure as evil belongs to the unwholesome vice that Thomas calls "insensibility." It is the vice of people who shudder at natural pleasures as somehow uncouth and demeaning. The shudder is, of course, directed against nature itself and the ends of nature: but nature refuses to be embarrassed by the snub. As a matter of fact, such an attitude has no claim whatever to the superior airs it flaunts; there is nothing of piety or religion about it, its calm acceptance of men's respect is a sheer swindle. It is rather an object of pity, or even of contempt.

By excess -- intemperance: Its puerility

At the other extreme is the puerile sin of intemperance, a blind plunge into the dark depths of the pleasures of taste and touch. It is puerile. Not that it is common among children -- quite the contrary; but it makes children of men who should long since have ceased to be children. The appetites of the intemperate are themselves spoiled children, paying no attention to the commands of reason; and as a consequence these men miss the sublime order and beauty of temperance. Their appetites are given their own way, become more and more imperious, more and more insistent on their own immediate objects to the disregard and ruin of all else. The corrective measures for these unruly appetites are the same as corrective measures for unruly children, i.e., coercion. For being resisted, the appetite is corrected, brought under the moderation of reason. Where that coercion is not applied, the house of the intemperate man's soul is comparable to a house full of children where the parents have lost absolutely all authority; or, more tragically, it is like a country devastated by civil war.

Its gravity compared to cowardice

Intemperance is an immature sin but it is not an insignificant sin. Objectively it is graver than cowardice, the defect of courage. The coward, after all, has much more excuse than the intemperate man; he is escaping from the serious dangers of death, so at least he is trying to conserve his life -- surely a much more necessary thing than the satisfaction of the desire for pleasure. The prospect of pleasure does not paralyze a man's mind as does great fear. There is, too, an element of regret in cowardice, a regret that increases with the increase of fear; but the intemperate man becomes more breathlessly willing as his passion approaches a white heat. Granted that in the abstract there is much more distaste attached to the objects of intemperance than to those of cowardice; but in the concrete, the opposite is true, for the increase in willingness is automatically a decrease in distaste. In addition, it is worthwhile remembering that human actions are never in the abstract, always in the concrete.

The odds are always in favor of the intemperate man. He can always and easily find a remedy. As a matter of fact, he has constant practice in his battle against these impediments to the control of reason, and he can enter that battle with none of the tremors that danger inspires, for there is no danger involved. On the other hand, the poor coward comes face to face with the danger of death all of a sudden; that is, he has had no practice sessions, and the exercise of courage here and now, in these circumstances, will be decidedly dangerous.

Degree of disgracefulness

However, intemperance is not the greatest of sins. In fact, it is not at all the one distinctive mark that separates the sheep from the goats; while mortally sinful, it is of the lesser type of mortal sin, for in it there is less of that formal aversion to God that is the determinant of gravity and which is so pronounced in the spiritual sins of pride and envy. You might say that the intemperate man approaches even his sins shamefacedly. Additionally, no wonder. These sins do have the greatest infamy and shame attached to them. It is a shame so great as to be, in a sense, contagious; a temperate man, forced to watch a glutton gorge himself, gets up from the table feeling a little sick, a pure man forced into even momentary contact with a libertine feels himself a little besmirched. This, you understand, is no justification for the hypocrite gathering up his skirts as he carefully circles around the penitent sinner. The question here is not of contact with penitents but of contact with sin; and it is one of the marvels of grace and self-denial that shines out so brightly from the lives of the Sisters of the Good Shepherd that they can be so obviously unbesmirched who, for the love of their Master and in spite of their own great love of purity, spend all of a lifetime in contact with the leprosy of uncleanness.

From what we have seen of the beauty of temperance, it is not hard to understand something of the ugliness of the sins of intemperance. These sins befoul a man for they are directly opposed to the proportion, the moderation which allows reason to shine through the things common to man and brutes, glorifying them with the glory of humanity. These sins shut off that transforming light of reason and plunge man into a world of darkness, of monstrous distortion and of unholy delights that ultimately destroy him. Of course, a man can get hardened to such a world for a while. He can get used to such a darkness to the extent of blinding himself to all light; he can so accustom himself to uncleanness as to overlook the slime that clings to him. Nevertheless, all this is only for a time; eventually, perhaps too late, something of his pitiable condition will dawn upon his drugged mind. Then only the all- powerful grace of God will save him from despair. Meanwhile the objective baseness and disgrace is rather increased than decreased by his careless acceptance of them.

All that we have said in this chapter has been an exposition of the virtue of mastery and its opposite, the virtue of temperance and the vice of intemperance. In the next few chapters, we shall go into the different species of the virtue and the connected virtues one by one and in considerable detail. In this chapter, I should like to mention these other virtues, more by way of mapping out the immediately future study than by way of exposition of these virtues. In other words, this brief mention will be an attempt, in a rough, general way, to familiarize us with the country we are about to explore; and, at the same time, it will give us a glimpse of the perfection of the order of St. Thomas' procedure.

Species of mastery: In works conserving the individual: abstinence and sobriety

In works conserving the species: chastity and purity

The different species of temperance cover the pleasures that draw men away from reason, particularly the greatest of these sense pleasures. Thus, the pleasures attached to the natural works by which the individual is conserved are the material of abstinence and sobriety: the one moderating the pleasures of food, the other those of drink. The pleasures attached to works conservative of the species are taken care of by chastity and purity; the one taking care of the substance of these acts, the other of the surrounding circumstances.

Continency, clemency, modesty

The virtues connected with temperance -- as friendship, gratitude, and so on are connected with justice -- moderate the internal and external movements of the soul towards some good. Thus for the movements of the will obsessed by passion there is the virtue of continency; for the movements of the sense appetite against things, there is clemency; towards things modesty. Modesty itself is of several kinds: modesty of soul or humility; modesty of body; and, finally, modesty in externals. In the next few chapters, we shall investigate each of these virtues and in so doing, we shall see more of the deeper beauty of the virtue of temperance.

By way of summary of this chapter, it is well to notice that however mastery is denied to man -- whether by a denial of the possibility or of the material of mastery -- the results are inevitably the results of intemperance. If a man believes it is hopeless to fight, he will surrender; and surrender here means acceptance of slavery to the sense appetite. If he is convinced, there is nothing to fight against, that he should embrace the sense appetite without restraint, then every last barrier to the free play of those passions is removed. In each case, the result is the result of intemperance, with all of its ugliness, all of its degrading implications for human nature.

Implications of the denial of mastery: For the truth of human nature

In addition, these implications are definitely degrading. Actual intemperance itself means that for all practical purposes, a man is only half a man; that half of him which is animal. The reasons alleged as justification of intemperance broadcast the same unflattering lie: in one case insisting that man is totally corrupt; in the other that he is not a man at all. Thus intemperance, both in theory and in practice, is an open confession of the inhumanity of man.

For the maturity of human nature

There is always an implication of immaturity in sins of intemperance; an insistence that a man pay as little attention to reason as an adolescent pays to the wisdom of experience; a contention that man has no more possibility of putting order in his life than has a child as yet incapable of reasoning. Intemperance argues, in other words, that human nature cannot take care of itself, cannot induce order, proportion, moderation in its own house.

For the dignity of human nature
For the beauty of human nature

Additionally, that is no less than a denial to human nature of the one solid ground it has for dignity and self-respect; for it is a denial to man of the command of his own life. The human individual is thus robbed of that personal responsibility, that personal control, that personal reward or punishment that is wrapped up with the inherent dignity of human personality; of course, he is denied the possibilities of human beauty. Obviously it is impossible for such a man to let the light of reason break through his animal nature to give it a consecrated halo, which is its right as a sharer in the domain of reason; and which reason itself has as a reflection of the light of divine reason, divine wisdom.

The difficult condition of mastery -- battle

There are reasons for a man's surrender of his mastery and his return to slavery. Perhaps one of the most outstanding of those reasons is the difficult condition attached to the victory of temperance, that is, the condition of battle. It is a peculiarly difficult battle, for its end is not to destroy an enemy, or break the power of an opponent; rather it is to keep intact all the power and energy of the opposition and put it to work under control. It demands a fight, a severe fight, a constant fight; and, too frequently, it means many and many a failure. A man can escape the fight either by joining the opposition or by abandoning all hope; either way he surrenders the prize that makes the fight worthwhile, the prize of mastery. Perhaps another, somewhat less tangible, reason for man's surrender of his human ideals is the very darkness of the world of intemperance; the lens of our eye will not register this beauty in the darkness and we have no infra-red camera of spiritual discernment to reveal it to us. Indeed, we have become so blind to beauty that even physical beauty must be hacked to pieces by a tape measure before we dare to give it its palm.

The champion of man as man

The Church today, as in the Colonial days, as indeed in all days, is the champion of temperance. In one age, she was mocked as the slatternly mother of looseness, of ungodliness, of frivolity and pleasure; in another age, she is mocked as the narrow, sour-faced advocate of conservatism, rigidity, prudishness, angelism. As a matter of fact, she is none of these things. She is the champion of the humanity of man. She insists now, as she always has, that man is a rational animal, that is, he is a human animal. He has a body as well as a soul; both integral parts of his composite nature. He has a body, but it is a human body; therefore, by its very nature, it is to be subject to the rule of all things human, to reason. Today, as in all days, she insists on the note of beauty in human life and action, which is moderation, because in this age, as in every age, she insists on the characteristic note of reason in the living of human life. She stands by the fundamental truth, that the human animal is a master. She will continue to urge men to fight for that mastery, to refuse to give it up whatever the sacrifice demanded for its maintenance, because she knows that a man cannot cease to be a master without at the same time ceasing to be a man.

THE FREEDOM OF PURITY
(Q. 146-154)

1. Modern concern about chastity:
   (a) Its basis.
   (b) Its motives.
   (c) Its implications.

2. Roots of freedom:
   (a) Proximate and remote sources.
   (b) Its reason,
   (c) Internal and external.

3. The garrison protecting freedom:
   (a) From the abuse of food -- abstinence:
      (1) Its nature.
      (2) Its act -- fasting
        a. Purposes.
        b. Naturalness.
        c. Allotted times.
      (3) Its opposite -- gluttony
        a. Its modes.
        b. Intrinsic gravity.
        c. Its daughters: unseemly joy, scurrility, physical uncleanness,
           loquaciousness, dullness of mind.
   (b) From the abuse of drink -- sobriety:
      (1) Its nature.
      (2) Its opposite -- drunkenness.
   (c) From the abuse of sex -- chastity:
      (1) Prudishness versus modesty in words.
      (2) Considerations for accurate knowledge of Catholic position on sex.
      (3) The consecration of matrimony.

(4) The excellence of virginity.
(5) The excuses for lust.

Conclusion:

1. Impossible dreams of a slave world:
   (a) Moderation without a norm.
   (b) Humanity without purity.

2. Human ends and slave ideology.

3. A generation betrayed:
   (a) The modern pagan and purity.
   (b) The Catholic and purity.

4. Freedom and slavery.

CHAPTER XVII

THE FREEDOM OF PURITY (Q. 146-154)

There have been many good men and women in America who have lived their lives in cheerful innocence of the conditions by which they were surrounded. When they heard booming attacks upon a new paganism or ringing accusations of an abandonment of Christian ethics, they smiled; "excited Jeremiahs," they said, "terrified at the recurrence of very human evils which no age has escaped." They felt satisfied, mellow and very wise; for to the pure all things are pure, especially if the pure are a little on the slow side. All the same, within these past few years, the complacency has been supplanted by a horrified disbelief; these cheerfully innocent people have received a bad shock.

Modern concern about chastity: Its basis.

They are in the position of the Austrian shopkeeper who smiled at the thought of his country ever disappearing from the map of the world; and then, one morning he looked out his window to see company after company of German soldiers trampling on the kindly old heart of his beloved Vienna. Recently these cheerfully innocent people stepped out of their homes one fine morning and were promptly buried under an avalanche of facts. Studies reported the progress of unchastity and the diseases connected with unchastity: odd defenses of chastity appeared written in a tone that indicated chastity was definitely in need of defense. Inquiries had been made on the subject scientifically, very scientifically: college girls and boys had been interviewed, figures were tabulated, the opinion of women of all classes had been obtained on birth control and marriage; statistics had been gathered on the sale of sex-stimulating drugs to children and the manufacture and sale of contraceptives. One great magazine proved that this latest industry is now one of the great American industries and one of the greatest of rackets; it named names and went unchallenged.

After the first terrible shock of facing the facts, the naively innocent person cast about for some encouragement; and promptly found it. In this progressive twentieth century, it was a good thing to shelve Paul's warning that these things should not so much as be mentioned among Christians. After all, an aroused public opinion has tremendous force. With the aid of that public opinion, the church will now get somewhere in its fight for purity. Everything is going to be all right; now it is not so much a question of arousing the public to the need of purity as it is of furnishing that aroused public with leadership to the goals of purity.

Its motives

A little more profound consideration of all this talk about chastity and unchastity would have uncovered two worrisome facts. First of all no one seems to have anything very cheering to say about the present state of affairs. The reports, which have been made, can certainly cause no joy in heaven; and there can be little reason for their causing joy on earth. Of course, there is no one who believes that these reports and statistics tell the whole story; rather they are a delicate insinuation of the corruption, which has taken place in American morals. The story of unchastity is never easily come at, particularly for national publication

The second disillusioning fact is that, in all this uproar about chastity, the concern has been almost exclusively with the threat to the body and material happiness, not with the threat to the soul and eternal happiness. For the most part the considerations have been purely animal, the worry has whirled about a purely physical sun. In other words, there has been no real concern about chastity but simply the same, old, jittery concern about health that always haunts the mind of a man to whom death is oblivion.

Its implications

Because the desire behind all this is not to be pure but rather to be healthy, we find no distinctly human -- that is no distinctly moral -- reason alleged in favor of chastity. The force behind the whole campaign is stark fear. It was not mere coincidence that a national campaign against venereal diseases synchronized with the excited discussion of unchastity. The coward is faced with an unpleasant choice: he must take chastity or physical misfortune. Neither is attractive; he might have to down the first as a preventive dose, but he reaches for it with the resigned lassitude of an invalid taking bitter medicine. Under these circumstances he will, of course, try every escape offered by mechanical and medical ingenuity before he takes the desperate step of embracing chastity. Chastity will be practiced reluctantly and violated cautiously; and this is, I suppose, something of that lukewarmness that nauseated Christ Himself.

The implication is inescapable. We have missed the significance of purity for human life. Perhaps there is no more damning indictment of our age than that tragic oversight. As if in confirmation of the truth of the indictment, many of our intellectual leaders look upon chastity, particularly pre-marital chastity, as a thing against which nature protests vigorously in the form of natural punishments, abnormalities that border upon insanity, and seriously threatens the sanity of man. Purity is an attempt to thwart the natural, to trick it, confine it in an artificial frame. Catholics make a medieval hullabaloo about what is, at its worst, a human peccadillo.

Roots of freedom: Proximate and remote sources

We have missed the intimate interrelation between purity and humanity. In some mysterious way, we have overlooked the obvious fact that since human life is a reasonable life and human activity is a rational activity, of course human passion is passion under reason. The name of this supreme passion under reason is purity. The attack on purity is an attack on the domain of reason; its defense in the name of purely physical considerations is itself an attack on the humanity and freedom of man.

Its reason

The world of reason is a world where freedom holds sway and where physical force is helpless; it is a moral world. Because a man has a spiritual soul and thus an intellect and will stretching out to the infinite reaches of the universal good, there is no particular good that can overwhelm his appetite. He can take a particular good, or he can leave it alone; because he can see its goodness or, on second glance, he can see what of goodness it lacks. On the long shopping tour that makes up his life, he does not have to take what he can get for the pittance sense appetite gives him to spend; his wallet is choking and he has unlimited resources to call on. He is completely master of his shopping for only one-thing exhausts his resources, that is, God Himself.

Internal and external

The key to the whole situation is spirituality. The proximate sources of man's freedom are his soul, his intellect and his will; behind them stands the sole possible Author of spiritual substance, the infinitely powerful God. Because a man is spiritual, he has liberty; because he is spiritual that liberty has eternal significance. That is, the use or the abuse of liberty is for eternity, for the spiritual, as incorruptible, exists for eternal ends.

A man's will or intellect cannot be handcuffed. As long as he remains a spiritual being with reason in control, he can never be enslaved. He possesses an internal liberty much more important than any external, civic freedom; an emperor, after all, can be a slave to himself, while a slave can be completely master of himself, can be most free. External liberty is as perilous a thing as a heart worn on one's sleeve; it can be lost, whereas internal liberty can only be surrendered. No force, intrigue, trickery can take it away from us. In addition, this is precisely the liberty over which purity maintains such a jealous guard. It is unfortunate that men and women today are inclined to look upon the fight for purity as a little abstract and academic. Like so many moral questions, it apparently has no immediate pertinence to individual life. A man instantly and vigorously resists an attack on his property, his children, his wife; but an attack on virtue is different. Here he considers himself off to one side, a spectator not greatly interested in the winner of the argument. The thing is important, for these questions have a profound personal significance for every individual. The drastic consequences of modern attacks on the spiritual soul, the intellect and the will of man, the bitter attacks on God, are much more serious than any physical attack on a man himself, his family or his property. This attack on the realm of the spiritual is not so much a matter of beating a man to the ground as of disemboweling him.

Surely, what threatens the spiritual and rational in a man threatens his freedom, for it is precisely upon that spiritual foundation that he builds his claim to freedom. When the body, the sense appetite, and the world of the present take precedence over the soul, the will and the world of eternity, man is no longer free. He is a slave; that is, he is no longer a man.

In this material of temperance there are three serious threats to the sovereignty of man's reason, The threats are extremely serious because the material is so extremely necessary that nature attaches to it the greatest sense rewards, lest its primary ends be overlooked or neglected. To take care of the possible sorties against his reason from this material, man is equipped with a garrison of virtues specially equipped for this kind of enemy and this type of warfare. There are only three in that garrison -- abstinence, sobriety and chastity -- but their fighting qualities more than make up for their numbers.

Still these three are not enemies of man's nature, not even of his sensitive nature. They can be rightly understood only when they are seen as guardians and protectors of man and his nature. Their presence in a man has exactly the effect of a well-disciplined garrison in a stronghold of restless subjects. They prevent mob-rule within a man and turn the violently restless energies of his passions to the common good of the man himself. Understand, this is not a question of using these subjects as a tyrannous master might use slaves merely for his own end. Reason is not working against the passions; it allows, indeed, insists upon their attainment of their own proper ends. Those proper ends of the passions, with their rich contributions to the welfare of the whole man, are defeated and trampled underfoot by the rioting of the mob of undisciplined passions.

The garrison protecting freedom:

From the abuse of food -- abstinence; Its nature

If it were a virtue merely to abstain from food, then by implication, the taking of food would be sinful. It is this sort of absurdity that is somehow wrapped up in the defense and attack of the modern negative "protectors" of liberty. A man can and does refuse food; perhaps because he has no appetite or is starving himself to death. Neither case involves a question of abstinence; the whole point of the virtue is the note of reason it insists upon in the we of food. The man who gives up coffee as a penance, even though it makes life miserable for his family, is not an abstinent man; neither is the ascetical tyro who stays up night after night praying only to fall asleep over his work during the day. These things are unreasonable so they cannot be virtuous. The virtue of abstinence is in operation only when the bounds of reason are carefully observed; its precise work is to restrain man's use of food to reasonable limits.

Its act -- fasting; Purposes

Abstinence holds a man back from abusing food. Fasting, an act of abstinence, goes a step further and holds a man back from what might very well be eaten without any abuse whatever. Again, we must insist that this is not a condemnation of food. Eating enough certainly cannot be anything but a cause of joy, except perhaps to a grateful beggar to whom the experience is astonishing in its novelty. To refuse to eat what is no more than enough, if it is to be, virtuous must be reasonable; and it can be reasonable only because it is aimed at ends higher than its immediate purposes.

If I have a healthy appetite for a bit of steak, an entirely reasonable amount in entirely reasonable circumstances, yet I refuse to eat it, then I have some explaining to do. If the refusal was for no reason, whatever it would be an act of insanity; if it proceeded from a conviction that food itself is evil and to be avoided, then it would be vicious; but if it is for some higher end, like training the soul or satisfying for sins, it might well be virtuous. We get a realistically concrete view of the higher ends of fasting by looking back to the first week of any Lent. After a few days of highly successful mortification, we have a definite sense of satisfaction, of pride in ourselves, of highly human accomplishment. You see, we have been fully in control. That is the really solid basis of that sense of satisfaction and superiority over our old selves. We are being super eminently human and we know it. We are experiencing something of the joy of being human.

To recognize those high ends in detail no more is necessary than to see them. By fasting, we let our appetites know beyond any doubt that reason is the head of this household; and by that very fact, we give our appetites invaluable practice in subjection. This practice is important, for it is always important for a man to be rational, to have his reason in control. Going up a step higher, fasting is clearly a kind of restitution. Every sin is a stolen pleasure, for every sin is at least an overindulgence of will; fasting sun renders a legitimate pleasure, thus both satisfying for the debt of sin and impressing us with the true nature of sin. We cannot fast very long and not realize that no one ever gets anything out of sin, not even a pickpocket or a bank robber; everything that apparently comes out of it must be given back, even though that restitution take all of an eternity.

Looking at fasting on a still higher plane, it is not hard to see in it a disposition to contemplation. In the old public school schedule, a singing class was held immediately after lunch. The schedule was good, however bad the singing might be; for surely it would not be as bad as the thinking turned out on a full stomach. Whatever the physical background may be, psychologically it is sure that full satisfaction of the appetite for food makes the mind dull; it is apt to act like a puppy, crawl off to some warm corner and go to sleep. Thus, monastic fasts are not idle gestures of melancholy or of distaste for the pleasures of sense. The primary business of monastic life is always contemplation, and fasting is an excellent disposition for it. The evening meal in a Dominican House of Studies is usually light; from September to Easter, it is extraordinarily light. It is not coincidence that the most fruitful periods of study are the morning (after a positively featherweight breakfast) and the evening or, as far as that goes, the rest of the night. There may be elements of discomfort; but, after all, a monastery does not exist for comfort but for contemplation. The very discomfort becomes eminently reasonable as a means to the higher ends of truth.

Naturalness

From all this it might be erroneously gathered that fasting was the product of Christian asceticism. Nothing is further from the truth. The value of fasting as a means of satisfying for sin, controlling and elevating the mind has always been common knowledge among men; so much so that fasting was a common practice even among primitive peoples, so common as to justify Thomas' statement -- long before anthropology elbowed its way into the halls of science -- that fasting is a command of the natural law precisely for these three reasons.

The natural law did not, of course, tell an Iroquois that he must fast on Friday, nor the African pygmy that he must observe the Ember Days; it said nothing to the Eskimo about Lent. The actual times for fasting are positive law's determinations of the indeterminate general precept of natural law.

This explains the universal character of the Church's insistence on fasting. It does, of course, recognize special impediments, such as exist in children, working men and beggars. Now, even here, the dispensation from the fast does not mean an excuse from mortification; otherwise, it would hardly be a privilege, a favor done for an individual, rather it would be a tragic deprivation. St. Basil could not understand why anyone could not fast: the guest-list of the rich was incomplete without fasting, it was an old table-companion of the poor, to women it was as natural as breathing, to children it was like water to a young plant, while as for the old, why the long years had made it second nature to them.

Allotted times

With the purposes of fasting well understood, the fast days appointed by the Church take on new beauty Surely there is no more fitting time to satisfy for our sins and prepare our minds for the consideration of eternal things than in the days that prepare us for Christ's death and resurrection; how can we better appreciate the great saints' entry into heaven, the full meaning of the great feasts, than by preparing our minds to appreciate the splendid goals they hold before our eyes? All the same, it is not enough to lift ourselves to the plane of the angels now and then; that is where we belong all of our lives. To bring this truth home, we are made to fast in each of the four seasons of the year and for three days as a symbol of the three months that make up the divisions of the year: we call those days Ember Days. During those days, priests are ordained and all the major orders given; a fitting time in which to prepare ourselves to celebrate the birthdays of these other Christs.

Its opposite -- gluttony; Its modes

The delicate fineness achieved by fasting is quickly perceived by a contrast with the effects of gluttony. It is much the same contrast as that between the perfectly conditioned dancer and the man who has let himself go to seed. On one side, there are clean, hard muscles, moving rhythmically under perfect control with a grace that is almost fluid, the grace in motion that a woman so often possesses in repose. On the other side, there is the puffy flabbiness, the disintegration, the softness of a man many years older than his age.

It is to be understood that gluttony is not merely a matter of pleasure in food nor of quantity; rather it is a desire for food or an enjoyment of it that surpasses the bounds of reason. If we think of gluttony only in terms of quantity, we might well echo Augustine's delightfully human confession: "Who is it, Lord that does not eat a little more than necessary?" Gluttony must be thought of, not in terms of quantity, but in terms of reason. As a matter of fact, it can be committed -- a sin of desire -- on a desert island with no food to be had, or at a breakfast table buoyant under the airy weight of two pieces of toast. Lt may be accomplished by the man who goes at his food too ardently or by the kitchen nuisance, the nibbler, who simply cannot wait for his food. The varieties of gluttony are really extraordinary: the gourmand, for instance, who gravely superintends every step of his food's preparation; the dainty one to whom an undisguised piece of beef would be obscenity; the man who eats by the dollar sign, subsisting on a diet equivalent roughly to caviar and champagne. The real epicurean, sinning by a wholesale perversion on the side of quantity, is at present somewhat rare; at least there is little trace in modern records of architects designing a vomitorium as the logical companion of a dining room.

Intrinsic gravity

In itself, gluttony is usually a venial sin. It is only when we make food our goal to the extent of turning our backs on God for it that it becomes a mortal sin. Certainly, the man who would deliberately eat himself to death for the pleasure of his food has carried this sin to its extreme. This inherent lightness of the sin of gluttony may be puzzling by reason of its very close parallelism to contraception. Both are against nature in exactly the same way: by perversion of a faculty, using for an end that which is meant by nature as a means, deliberately frustrating (in the case of the epicureans) the end to which those means are ordained. The difference between the two is that gluttony does not impede the primary physical end of nature -- the preservation of the species; nor does it, usually, seriously impede the secondary physical end of nature, the conservation of the individual's own life. The sins against nature are not grievous simply because they are against nature; their gravity is in exact proportion to the impediment they place to the attainment of the ends of nature.

Its daughters: unseemly joy, scurrility, physical uncleanness, loquaciousness, dullness of mind

From this, we might conclude that gluttony is a disgusting rather than a serious sin. It is disgusting; but it is also terribly dangerous. It is a capital sin and a list of its unlovely daughters explains a great deal of our disgust with it and all of its perils. Gluttony brings the animal in man so emphatically to the forefront as to give the impression that the mastery of reason had been done away with. Reason is drugged, heavy-eyed, sluggish, as contrasted with its alert vitality in the mortified man. With reason asleep or so nearly asleep, the rest of man runs wild: there is unseemly and riotous joy in the appetite, a loquaciousness in speech and a scurrility of action -- all more or less out of control. The crowning touch of distastefulness, made proverbial in the spotted vest, is a physical uncleanness that goes unnoticed by the glutton.

From the abuse of drink -- sobriety: Its nature

Overindulgence in food deprives a man of his mastery stealthily, little by little and day by day. However, overindulgence in intoxicating drink has none of this cowardly finesse about it; it hits a man over the head and throws him helpless in a gutter. It represents a very special threat to reason and so must be mastered by a very special virtue, the virtue of sobriety. Sobriety and teetotalism are not synonymous terms; as a matter of fact, sobriety is not interested in total abstinence. Its interest is in the note of reason, the note of freedom and mastery that must shine forth from a man's use of intoxicating liquors.

Its opposite -- drunkenness

Thomas thought that this virtue was particularly necessary in youths, in women, in the old and in those who hold positions of honor. We confirm this contention again and again by our varying attitudes towards drunkards; to us, a drunken high school boy, a drunken mother or a drunken governor are all much more shocking sights than a drunken sailor. Why did Thomas pick out these particular classes and why are we so instinctively in agreement with him? Well, obviously, the old and those in authority should be those in whom reason is particularly flourishing; in youths and women, sobriety is more necessary because if the added inclination to concupiscence -- in youths by reason of their very exuberance, in women (says St. Thomas) because they are so apt to let their heart rule their head.

This does not mean that a husband can get drunk with impunity while his wife commits the same act only under penalty of sin. Deliberate drunkenness is a mortal sin in anyone. It involves the deliberate loss of the use of reason for the sheer love of the drink. That is, drunkenness is a deliberately immoderate use, an unreasonable use, of intoxicating liquor with serious results to the mastery of man.

From the abuse of sex -- chastity: Prudishness versus modesty in words

For the rest of this chapter I shall do what has not been done in any other part of this work and what shall not be done again in the two volumes that will complete it. I shall depart from the order and the actual material of St. Thomas. I believe the reasons I have for this procedure prove clearly that it is the wiser thing to do.

St. Thomas was the angel of the schools, relieved miraculously from all temptations against purity from the days of his young manhood; yet he could and did have a profound knowledge of impurity. In the course of his Summa, he wrote a scientifically exhaustive treatise on purity and impurity designed especially for physicians of souls. Certainly Thomas with his angelic purity, saw the deep wisdom of Paul's admonition against discussing these things, indeed, against even mentioning them; but he understood it with this very reasonable condition: that is, these things are not to be mentioned among Christians unless it is necessary and in precisely the way, that such mention is necessary.

Yet in spite of the fact that Thomas observed the admonition of Paul and at the same time wrote a thoroughly scientific treatise on the subject, I am abandoning the order and the material of that treatise. I am quite sure I am not being prudish about this thing. Prudishness refuses to talk about these things for one of two reasons: either because it can think of nothing that can be said (an implicit condemnation of sex as evil) or because it can think of nothing that dare be said. In the first case, it shrinks from an unutterable evil; in the second it admits the evil but does no shrinking whatever, at least in private. Now Catholic doctrine is not prudish. It has much to say about sex, all of it good, much of it extremely beautiful; but what it has to say is said in the proper place.

Considerations for accurate knowledge of Catholic position on sex

The Church does give a detailed treatment to these subjects, but not from a lecture platform or in a book for general consumption. This is a matter for personal direction, or for a small group whose needs can be accurately and personally gauged. In this chapter, then, I shall not say all the Church has to say about sex; I shall give only the general truths, the foundations of the Catholic attitude toward sex, with no details and no illustrations. The rest of this chapter then, will not be a shock but a revelation of the beauty of the Catholic position; unless my exposition is very bad indeed.

The Catholic position on sex has frequently been misunderstood because men and women have been content to contrast the Church's high esteem of virginity with its unrelenting, unconditional condemnation of lust. Both of these are facts; but the important thing is the reason behind these facts. All slander to the contrary, neither of these facts constitute a condemnation of sex, nor are they the product of an aversion to sex.

The consecration of matrimony

There is much less likelihood of mistaking the Catholic attitude if we consider the Catholic view of matrimony and the purposes of virginity as the means of arriving at the beauty of the Catholic doctrine. These two considerations emphasize the character of the Church as continuing the life of Christ. Its viewpoint is also divinely human; it, too, lifts men up to divine heights yet fights every encroachment on the humanity of man. The Church is a most human mother, not condemning food, drink, or any aspect or manifestation of man's human love.

It is from the nature of love that the human character of sex is alone intelligible. From the work of the preceding volume and of this volume, we should be thoroughly familiar with the notion of love. All benevolent love, all love of friendship, is defined as wishing good to another. In its last analysis it is no less than an attempt to identify the wills of the two friends; as far as is possible, we are one with our friend, his good is our good, his evil, our evil. In the case of high human love, men and women labor all their lives to make that love clear, to show that they have really and completely identified themselves with those they love. It is this desire to express the genuine character of love that is the force behind all sacrifice, all dedication, all surrender in love.

It is not surprising that when the Church, or Christ Himself, was seeking a fitting expression for the highest things a man can reach; both Christ and the Church should come back again and again to the same figure: the nun's vows which dedicate her life to God make her the spouse of Christ; at Holy Communion the Catholic receives the bridegroom of his soul; the saint, scaling the last peak of heroic sanctity, is said to be mystically married to Christ; the Church itself is the spouse of Christ. This seems to be the only figure that even approximates these sublime things. Why? The reason is because matrimony and the acts proper to matrimony are the highest physical expressions of human love. We must always take love on faith. We try to make that love evident by clumsy words, by a kiss, and embrace; but only in heaven can we be sure of the mutual character of that love, for only in heaven shall we be privileged to see the very souls of others in the essence of God. Until such a time, we must build our lives on the signs of love.

Sex in human life has two outstanding purposes. One is the expression of love. It is something uniquely human, for only human passion can carry a message and has a message to carry; only human passion can have a meaning given it by the individual. It is a messenger; if its message is not authentic, it ceases to be human. It exists for a purpose and must never be considered apart from that purpose; with that purpose in mind, it can never be identified with anything else but the high holiness of human love. The second purpose, also uniquely human, gives human beings a share in the greatest work of God, a share in the procreation of the completely spiritual, the immortal soul that comes from God and goes to Him, the soul that was purchased by the blood of God and is destined to eternal citizenship in heaven.

When the Church insists that the marriage contract is a matter of strict justice, she is not replacing love by a heartless commercialism; she is merely insisting on a guarantee of the absolute minimum necessary for love. Surely, the man who refuses the demands of justice to another cannot pretend to be wishing this other good. Marriage, then, is a consecration. Everything about it has the air of the sacred, everything. It is not something to be tolerated, to be smirked at, to be nonchalantly handled. The celebration of a marriage is always a fitting place for the presence of Christ, even when the provisions for that celebration are so inadequate as to demand a miracle to supplement them. It is divinely fitting that marriage should be a sacrament, one of those channels down which gushes the grace that is the life of the soul; for it is beautifully fitting that the highest expression of human love should be a means of that grace, by which it is possible for us to share in divine love.

Naturally, the Catholic is indignant at the psychologists who see no difference between these human physical acts and the physical acts of the animals. Naturally, he is disgusted with the brazen champions of license and selfish perversion; he does not look upon these people as slightly imprudent juveniles who have dragged dusty skeletons out of a dark closet; they arc vandals, desecrators of most sacred things. Of course, sex is a serious threat; but only because it is so necessary to nature that it carries with it the supreme sense pleasure. Its possible threat is not a reason for surrendering to it or for discarding it; but for protecting it with a virtue, the virtue of chastity. With that protection, sex becomes, not a threat to human life, but a means to eternal life.

The excellence of virginity

It is only with all this in mind that we can understand the Church's attitude towards virginity. Virginity, as such, has nothing desirable about it: it might be a vicious fruit of the vice of insensibility; among the Jews, it was a source of shame to a woman, and rightly so in view of each woman's hope of mothering the Messiah. It has its special value in Christian thought, not for what it is but for what it aims at, not as an end but as a means. As has been said so often in this work, man's goods can be summed up under three headings: external goods,

goods of the body and goods of the soul. External goods are ordained to the body; the goods of the body are ordered to the soul; and the goods of the soul are ordered to God. To abstain from external goods for the sake of the body is reasonable; to abstain from corporal things for the good of the soul is eminently reasonable. It is because of this higher spiritual end that virginity has its privileged place in Christian thought.

Virginity has the same relation to purity that magnificence has to liberality; it carries the bankroll, purity handles the small change. For virginity is not the sun render of illegal pleasure for divine good; it is a gay discarding of perfectly legitimate pleasure for a more perfect and more direct surrender to God. Sacred as matrimony is, virginity is its superior. Here we approach the heroic; here the human is put aside for the divine, the body for the soul. Christ, choosing a virgin mother, taking a virgin disciple for His closest friend, or Paul championing virginity was not an enemy of love. Rather they recognized the truth so many ages have missed: the Christian virgin is head over heels in love. So true is this that the sacrifice of human love, this utter dedication to the divine, is demanded as the only adequate expression of the virgin's love. The difference between the love of the virgin and the love of the wife is that the virgin rushes directly and immediately into the arms of God, while the wife goes to. Him through the holy, natural, and beautifully graduated steps of human love.

For all its bright' young beauty, virginity is not the greatest of virtues. It reaches the heights of chastity, but those are not the supreme heights of virtue. Even among the virtues whose work is to sacrifice, virginity must take a low place: the martyr gives up his life, the religious gives up his will, the virgin merely surrenders the legitimate pleasures of the physical side of man.

The excuses for lust

Man heartily dislikes to have his sins wandering about the house of his soul naked, he must clothe them, even though the best he can offer is the shabby garments of sophistry. He is, after all, a rational animal to the very roots of his being; he may give up reason, but he cannot altogether do away with the appearance of reason even in his sins. As a result, every age has alleged its reasons for lust; though of course there are no reasons. In our own day, the variety of excuses is positively bewildering. There is, for instance, the psychological excuse that chastity injures a man, makes him neurotic in its fight against nature. The sophistry proceeds from an identification of human and animal nature. For the control of man's passion is not an unnatural thing, even for those passions; as an integral part of man's nature, they are fulfilled only in their obedience to the rule of man's nature, to reason.

A little more subtle is the personality excuse. It argues that sex experience is necessary for a full development of personality, for an emotional richness that can be had in no other way. Additionally, this in contradiction to history: in spite of the splendor of Dominic's apostolate, the beauty and depth of Thomas' poems, the sweeping accomplishments of the tender maid of Sienna. When, please, should emotional richness be reached for? At ten' or twelve, or sixteen, or thirty, or ninety? Why then? Less convincing (if possible) is the "wild-oats" excuse; early unchastity is necessary for later stability in chastity, though even modern psychologists have a great deal to say in direct contradiction, in their investigations of habit formation. Then there is the supposedly unanswerable excuse of impossibility, the excuse that rests on facts, the sweepingly insulting excuse that judges all men and all women from subjective evidence. It is an insult to human nature when it argues from natural powers; it is an insult to God when it does not admit the effectiveness of His omnipotent help. Perhaps the climax of irrationality is reached in the spineless plea that personal impurity does no damage to anyone else. As a matter of fact its damage is widespread; not only does it damage the individual, but all those with whom he comes into contact by his sin, his future family, his wife, the society in which he lives, the soul of the individual and all the souls he will drag to hell along with himself. There is still one more excuse: the Christian standard of purity, we are told, is out of date, it is a relic of a medieval ethical system. The argument is based on the absurd proposition that human nature comes out in a different model from age to age; that its ends are not the same, that the steps by which it reaches those ends are not the same, and that the powers within a man by which he takes those steps are different from age to age.

A defense of impurity simply will not stand rational criticism from the point of view of experience, of history, of psychology, or of principle. Men and women of today realize this, at least vaguely. For, in spite of all the modern talk in defense of intemperance, in the concrete they are disgusted with those who carried these modern principles to their logical conclusion: the glutton, the drunkard, the libertine. These are the wrecks of humanity. Men and women today may be willing. to smile at the rocks upon which they have been wrecked; but they have little sympathy or understanding, certainly no love, for the hulks of men these principles produce and abandon.

Impossible dreams of a slave world:

Moderation without a norm

It would seem that our modern world is cherishing an impossible dream. There is, regardless of the principles, a demand for moderation because of the disgust and distaste for the ultimate excess dictated by the principles. nut it is a moderation to be dictated by the individual and by social appearances; ultimately such a moderation is reducible either to satiety or to what the community will tolerate. For if there be no standard objective of the individual, the limit can be set only by this individual's appetite or the appetite of his fellows; that is, by a satiety which becomes constantly harder to achieve.

Humanity without purity

These moderns expect to achieve moderation without a norm; they expect a man to be human without being pure, for they shrink in horror from the excesses of impurity, thereby emphasizing their demands for humanity in the actions and life of a man. Yet the control of reason, the control of virtue, by which alone such purity can be achieved, is lightly dismissed or violently ejected.

Allegedly, this modern campaign is based on a protective affection for men, aimed against the absurdity of taking peccadilloes seriously, or the tragedy of thwarting nature by artificial limitations. Actually, it has come about through a depreciation of personal human ends. An individual must have personal ends if he is to live a personal life; and if he has such ends, he will face conflicts in attaining them. Moderation, purity, humanity, all imply severe conflicts; the lack of them means the absence of conflict through abject surrender. The modern conflict is rather a mass conflict; we are seeking mass ends rather than individual ends. This gives us the comforting anonymity of a crowd and the coward's strength in the violence of a mob; but it also condemns us to personal oblivion, to being lost in the crowd. If we renounce the responsibility of personal, individual conflict, we must also renounce personal, individual ends.

Human ends and slave ideology

The underlying tragedy of this situation awakes real pity in any thinking observer. For the men and women of our day who are championing or practicing unchastity have not, for the most part, come to that state by any long process of neglect, corruption and self-indulgence. It is something that has been imposed upon them from above. They have not come to this condition of themselves; they have been led into it. This generation is a generation that has been betrayed, betrayed by its intellectual leaders, its teachers and its writers, those whose solemn responsibility it is to lead men, not into the depths of slavery, but to the heights of human freedom.

The modern pagan and purity

The Catholic and purity

This fact is one that must be seen by the Catholic; and it immediately abolishes any excuse he might have, or think he has, for joining the mass movement away from purity. The Catholic has not been betrayed. His leaders have insisted now, as always, upon the essentials of purity, its absolute necessity for human life. He has not been trapped, or coaxed, or threatened into a sacrifice of his humanity; rather every force has been brought to bear to make him realize more and more keenly the place of purity in human life. The modern pagan may have some excuse for his disregard for purity; in fact, it seems to me quite possible that many of them may escape a great deal of moral responsibility. Yet, for a Catholic, there is no escape from these facts of life and his responsibility toward them.

Freedom and slavery

To the Catholic it has always been apparent that a man, to remain a man, must be free in the all-important sense of internal freedom. He may be beaten to earth by the might of a dictator; he might be sold into bondage by the greed of a usurer; but no force in heaven or on earth can throw his intellect and will into chains. The Catholic has known, and knows today, that there is no more serious threat to that internal freedom, that sovereignty by which the humanity of man is guaranteed, than the threat involved in the appeal of unreasonable pleasures. So the Catholic has known, and knows today, that purity and the demands of purity are not an infringement on his freedom, not a high fence enclosing his actions in a narrow, sterile field; rather they are the solid protectors, the solid guarantees of the freedom man must have, if he is to be a man.

⫷CHAPTER XVIII⫸

THE FULLNESS OF TRUTH
(Q. 155-165)

1. Conquest and peace:
   (a) Incomplete conquest.
   (b) Complete conquest:
      (1) To destruction of subjects.
      (2) To salvation of subjects.

2. The conquest of temperance:
   (a) Incomplete.
   (b) Complete.

3. The second line of defense ·· continence:
   (a) Its nature and work.
   (b) Its opposite ·· incontinence:
      (1) Its subject.
      (2) Its comparative gravity.

4. Completion of the conquest of temperance:
   (a) By restraint of anger and its act:
      (1) Clemency and meekness.
      (2) Their opposites:
         a. Anger:
            1) Licit and illicit anger.
            2) The species of anger.
            3) "Daughters" of anger: indignation, swelling of mind, blasphemy, contumely, quarreling.
         b. Cruelty.
   (b) By moderation of lesser pleasures ·· modesty:
      (1) Its nature.
      (2) Its species.

5. Humility's conquest:
   (a) Its nature as a virtue.
   (b) Its object and effect.
   (c) Its place among the virtues.
   (d) Its opposite ·· pride:
      (1) Nature and subject of pride.
      (2) Its varieties.
      (3) Its gravity and relation to other sins.
      (4) The first sin of pride ·· original sin:
         a. Its nature.
         b. Its penalties.

Conclusion:

1. The abundant life and truth:
   (a) Fruits of living a lie.
   (b) Dangers of living a half-truth.

2. Inhuman world is a world of fiction.

3. The "mild" virtues and human life:
   (a) The world and the "mild" virtues.
   (b) Christ and the "mild" virtues.

CHAPTER XVIII

THE FULLNESS OF TRUTH
(Q. 155-165)

For complete peace, complete conquest is necessary; for if peace is to be had there must be complete mastery. For us of the twentieth century, there is no reason for the question of peace and disorder, conquest and defeat, to remain on the purely speculative level; we live in an age where war is never declared, yet where war never stops. Of all men in history, we have only to look about us to get a complete picture of peace and its opposite; our notion of the nature of conquest does not depend on subjective scrutiny or hypothetical procedure. The thing is presented in such graphic form as to make its impression ineradicable.

Conquest and peace: Incomplete conquest

It is not because of any particularly brilliant analysis on our part that we see clearly that conquest can be incomplete for two reasons. The most casual observer can see that the Japanese conquest of China and, some time ago, the English conquest of Ireland were both frustrated in their completeness by an enduring hostility of the subject people; a condition in startling contrast to the quiet and order of a recently conquered Spain. On the other hand, with little imagination and even less historical knowledge, we easily understand the tragic incompleteness of a conquest that has been limited to the possession of the enemy's strongholds. In either case, the quiet of night and the very innocence of the smallest village are but aids to a stalking terror and a haunting fear. In place of peace, there is the sinister silence of an unsavory district late at night; death is coiled tense in the shadows, ready to strike at any moment.

Complete conquest: To destruction of subjects

Unquestionably, if mastery remains in question, terror rules the land. Yet not every complete conquest gives peace; its gift may be the bitterly final blow of death. With an essentially hostile people facing an invading army, conquest must remain incomplete as long as any of these people remain alive; complete conquest can be had only at the terrible price of a total destruction of a whole people. Certainly, such a thing is not to be described as peace. In other words, peace can be had by complete conquest, only when the attack is not upon a people but upon the enemies of a people; then only does completion of a conquest bring the saving tranquility of peace's order to a whole nation.

Temperance is essentially a conqueror; it aims at the conquest of the disorderly passions within the kingdom of a man's soul. No other conquest of that kingdom can ever be complete, short of destruction of the man, because it is only this conquering army with which man's full nature is in sympathy. To every other he remains stubbornly irreconcilable, for he was made for the orderly proportion of reason. Only the complete conquest of temperance can bring him peace. If some other conqueror, say anger, or lust, or fear, or sorrow, invades the domain of reason, sweeping away all opposition, it has not yet fully conquered; it cannot control this essentially hostile subject. Behind the conqueror's lines, there will be the gnawings of conscience, lonely unhappiness, fear of the quiet moments of solitude, a rending and tearing of the soul of a man that threatens his very sanity.

The conquest of temperance: Incomplete

Quiet can be had by such a conqueror only on condition of the total destruction of reason in man, a conquest that brings not peace but death. Fortunately, this is a conquest that is never quite accomplished; even in hell, man's nature protests against the tyranny of the conqueror, though there be no hope of ever overthrowing him, even with all eternity for the sedition. The conquest of temperance, then, is man's one hope of peace within his own kingdom.

Complete

Still, that conquest must also be complete. Temperance fights the enemies of man; it has the whole of man's nature in sympathy with it. There is no danger of trouble behind its lines;

it has no need to station large garrisons to hold down a rebellious populace. It can concentrate on the armed opposition, massing all its forces at the front with an easy mind. Now, if it operates only against the out. standing citadels of the enemy, leaving marauding bands free to roam the country spreading terror and death, surely it cannot bring peace. Rather, its great conquests are made a mockery by the disorder, confusion and sudden terror that plagues the very subjects it has come to save.

To put all this in plain language, we saw in the last chapter that the principal citadels of intemperance were stormed by the virtues of abstinence, sobriety and chastity. They openly attack the serious threats to the sovereignty of reason, which are inordinate pleasures of food, drink and sex; by the conquest of these things, they break the backbone of the enemy's resistance. All the same, this is not enough.

They are the main body of temperance. They bear the brunt of the attack and they do it well; but if the conquest is to be complete and bring peace, there are still the mopping-up operations to be gone through. The flanks of the main army must be protected; the lines of communication guaranteed against guerrillas; and the people at home must be allowed to live the quiet, industrious, humble life that is essential for the continuance of the fight. All of this is accomplished by the potential parts of temperance.

Before launching on a lengthy investigation of the mopping-up operations of these virtues, we must look at a constant precaution that is absolutely necessary for the protection of the main army; that is, the strong second line of defense against vicious counter attacks of the enemy. Experience is more than a sufficient witness to the possibility of inordinate passion; and that means that experience vouches for the possibility of temperance being overwhelmed by the rush of passion. Indeed, unless temperance is momentarily overcome, there can be no such thing as passionate desire for unlawful pleasure.

The second line of defense -- continence: Its nature and work

The actual presence of such passion does not mean that man has already suffered the defeat of sin. Whatever the character of the passion, it remains merely a movement of sense appetite until it wins deliberate consent; only by deliberate surrender on the part of reason can sin be incurred. The point is extremely important; for ignorance of it has been the swampland from which hordes of worries have descended upon men, pricking and buzzing, inexhaustibly replaceable by still others of the pests. No matter how long a passion may last, how violent it may be, what effects it may produce, how unclean or guilty it may make a man feel, it is not sinful until it is embraced. Or, to go back to the original metaphor, passion is never sinful until the second line of reason's defense has crumbled, until the continence of the will has broken down.

Continence here is taken, not in the sense of virginity or chastity as it is frequently taken in English, but in its own special sense: a firmness of will holding to the stronghold of reason, regardless of the violence of the attack of passion. Its material is the material of temperance, i.e., those passions which entice man from the path of reason, particularly the strongest of those passions -- the passions for food, drink and sex. However,, in another sense, its material is different. It deals only with the passions that have run wild; while temperance deals with these passions in themselves. The work of temperance is to keep passion from running wild, whereas continence faces the fact of a violent uproar and confusion that has already trampled temperance underfoot.

Perhaps a clearer notion of the work of continence can be obtained by looking closely at the act of the will, which is election. That act is like a village belle with two suitors -- the reason and the sense appetite. When the village belle turns up her nose at the threats, bullyings and coaxings of the latter and graciously gives her hand and her heart to the former, we have continence effectively at work. On the contrary, when sense-appetite sweeps her off her feet by its cave-man tactics, incontinence has carried the day.

The continent man is a sick man who has found an excellent doctor to keep him on his feet, while the temperate man is so healthy he has no need of a doctor. His virtuous good health frees him from the crushing setbacks of passion's counter attach on virtue; he simply does not have inordinate passion. However, we must not consider continence a rather unimportant substitute called on now and then to fill up the space normally occupied by temperance's column. If we remember the frequency of passion's attack in some men by the very season of their physical make-up and call to mind the constancy of the stimulus to passion, we get some little idea of the importance of continence. Obviously not everyone can be barricaded behind the protective walls of a monastery; nor can anyone seriously propose blinders and earmuffs as a kind of monastic substitute for laymen. Continence guarantees man humanity in his life and his actions in spite of the physical temperament that is his, in spite of the tremendous temptations that will batter against his senses. Understand, continence does not do away with passion, or with the effects of passion; but it does hold to reason and to virtue.

Its opposite -- incontinence: Its subject

From these same considerations, it is dear that incontinence is a tragic thing. It is a fact of human life that the occasions and temptations to these sins do appear with fair frequency. Moreover, these movements of passion are going to continue, whether we like it or not. To an incontinent man, that means he is going to face the defeat of sin repeatedly. The forces of reason are going to be conquered in him, the note of humanity plucked from his actions. He has no second line of defense, so that the very appearance of disorderly passion is practically a guarantee of sin.

Its comparative gravity

Incontinence, though it is a deliberate choice of the will, has not the malicious gravity of intemperance. The incontinent man is not a keen-eyed searcher for sin. Rather he blunders into it, and then, when passion has subsided, nothing can hold him back from throwing himself at the feet of Christ, overwhelmed with horror and shame at what he has done. On the other hand, the surrender of incontinence is a more craven thing than the capitulation to anger. The things it embraces are much more base than the offerings of anger. The passions to which the incontinent man succumbs do not operate violently and openly, clubbing a man down; rather they slink to the attack with a certain secrecy and subtlety, on tiptoe as much for flight as for attack. Nevertheless, in their actual operation there is little of regret and much of pleasure; whereas anger is always in mourning. It is true that incontinence does not represent as much difficulty in its reformation as does intemperance, for intemperance is a matter of habit, while incontinence is a matter of passion. The latter is a momentary lapse rather than a solid fortification built up against reason itself. Yet, it is a difficult and discouraging sin with which to deal. When its victim comes shamefaced and penitent, asking another chance, it is not enough to point out the evil of his act; he has a bitter and complete knowledge of that already. He needs the internal strength of grace against this passion; and he needs the external help of correction and advice to learn where and how he can begin to resist passion. For each setback given to passion weakens it, impressing upon the sense appetite a note of difficulty, even of impossibility, that decreases the hope of gratification which is its constant spur.

It is extremely important that the incontinent man submit his difficulties to someone for correction and advice. There is, after all, a right and a wrong way to fight passion; a rightness and wrongness that must frequently be judged in the individual case. It may, and frequently does, happen that the individual actually increases, fortifies and deepens passion by the very method he has chosen to fight it. A direct, frontal attack on passion is an almost natural response to its impertinence; yet a direct attack is frequently a disastrous mistake. It serves too often to concentrate our attention more profoundly on the objects of passion, feeding it, puffing it up by giving it a totally undeserved importance and emphasis. Moreover, it saps our powers of resistance by the constant haunting worry or panicky fear, which it almost necessarily engenders. The incontinent man needs both internal and external help. It is tragic, then, for him to limit his call for assistance to purely internal help until his enemies have attained such proportions as to necessitate a long, discouraging, drawn-out battle.

Completion of the conquest of temperance:

By restraint of anger and its act

Now, let us get back to the mopping-up operations. Here we are promptly brought into contact with two virtues that were close to the heart of Christ, and very far from the heart of a pagan world. You remember the bitter eagerness of the apostles to call down fire from heaven on the cities that did not receive them; and the clemency of the answer of Christ: "In addition turning, He rebuked them, saying: You know not of what Spirit you are: the Son of Man came not to destroy souls but to save." You will remember, too, the brutality of the Pharisees in their desire to punish the woman taken in adultery. Christ's verdict in that case -- "Neither do I condemn thee. Go in peace and sin no more" -- has echoed in the hearts of sinners ever since.

Again, Christ never tired of asserting His meekness. He was proud of the fact that He was "meek and humble of heart." To a pagan world, as to our world, this was a confession of weakness. No one takes the meek man seriously, least of all the modern world. Actually, Christ's description of Himself as a meek man was a simple statement of great strength. The meek man, seen rightly, is a fearless rider of a wild steed, which he has so subdued that it swerves to his lightest touch. For the work of meekness is to restrain anger within the bounds of reason; in that note of restraint, meekness finds its common bond with temperance.

Clemency and meekness

The meek man is truly a conqueror; he has subdued the wildest of the passions of man, the passion that strikes most suddenly and most devastatingly. This is not a task for a timid rabbit of a man, but for a man who could withstand the power of the Roman world and the prestige of the princes of his people. The pagan world had no use for meekness, just as our world today has little use for it. Imagine, if you can, a Hitler smiling in gratified vanity at the aide who has just called him meek! You see, the pagan world is so very unsure of itself it simply must make blatant gestures of power, supremacy and fearlessness;

otherwise, someone might suspect the truth of its fundamental powerlessness. Christ could be meek because He was so thoroughly a master.

The companion virtue of meekness -- clemency -- moderating the punishment inflicted by anger, is even more thoroughly misunderstood by the modern world. It has been scornfully confused with sentimentality or sympathetically opposed to severity. Now certainly clemency is not sentimentality. Christ was clement; but He was not shaken with great, gushing sobs over the poor, misunderstood hypocrites. He condemned them. In other word,, Christ did not allow his feelings to take command over reason. Additionally, clemency, like all the moral virtues, imposes the order of reason, it does not oppose it. Consequently, it is not opposed to severity, for both severity and clemency are according to reason. The severe man is not unreasonable; he is inflexible in the infliction of the punishment that reason declares should be inflicted. Clemency diminishes the punishment when reason declares that such punishment should be diminished. In other words, it is not the reasonable element in punishment that clemency opposes; rather that reasonable element finds unflinching support in clemency as well as in severity.

Clemency is the fruit of a certain refinement of soul in the literal sense of the word; that is, in the sense of a steady elimination of impurities, often enough by the extreme method of fire, until eventually the crystalline purity of the best in man stands out in undisputed supremacy. It implies a wholesomeness of affection that abhors wanton injury to another. Therefore, it is quick to detect when a man has satisfied reason's demand for punishment, rushing to release the sinner; for all along it has loved the man, even while consenting to his punishment. Of course, it is not to be understood by the provincial uncouthness of soul that has no particular interest in others, much less sympathy for their suffering. Perhaps as great, a note of triumphant reason as the mildness of clemency is the justice of it, the justice that insists on proper punishment, in spite of its deep feeling for others. It must always be a stranger to a pagan world, which has enthroned selfishness.

Their opposites ·· Anger: Licit and illicit anger

Both clemency and meekness have to do with anger; the latter restraining the passion of anger itself, while the former moderates anger's act of punishment or revenge. Still, it must be remembered that anger, like all the passions, is not evil in itself. Some men can be splendidly angry, as Christ was at the pettiness that quibbled at healing a man's infirmity on the Sabbath day; there are times when our failure to be angry is a weakly vicious thing, when we hold back the punishment because our love is not strong enough to be just, a sickly, diluted love unworthy of a man. Considered objectively, anger's act of punishment can be seen as a gesture of self-defense, or of defense of a loved one with whom we are one. It is only when it gets out of control, when it is not defense but attack, or when its defect leaves a man supinely defenseless that anger becomes a traitor to man and delivers him up to the mob rule of sense.

Normally we are a little too mild in our judgment of anger. Perhaps it is not so much our fault. It is a human mistake to overestimate the beauty of a plain girl when she has been so lucky as to discover an incredibly ugly companion; naturally, when we see anger in contrast to the hideousness of the other sins that injure our neighbors, we too are fooled.

It is certainly true that anger has none of the vicious desire to hurt that is proper to hate. It is not as childishly petty as is envy with its willingness to sacrifice another to satisfy its desires for glory. As a rule, anger has an air of respectability as astounding as the clean-shaven face of a tramp. At least it always proceeds from an unjust injury and acts in the name of justice, seeking a balance of the justice that has been disturbed. However, for the violence, the speed of its attack, anger gives way to no other sin.

The species of anger

To get some idea of its unfortunate personal and social effects, we have only to look around us. There are such victims of anger, for instance, as the sharp, quick-tempered people, violently angry at trifling pretexts, people who give themselves no peace and have the rest of the family on tiptoe with their fingers crossed hoping to avoid a storm. Then there is the bitter man, who hugs to his breast the injury, which is behind anger; he croons to it, rocking it back and forth in his mind day after day; a gloomy person with a ready reason for sorrow and self-pity. He exudes ill humor and becomes a nuisance to himself. Finally there are those stern, unforgiving people who hold a grudge forever -- proudly. Their thoughts are focused, not so much on the injury they have suffered, as on the revenge they mean to enjoy; they will not rest until they have "got back" at their enemies. It is the kind of anger, which splits families as an aerial bomb splits a house. Sometimes it produces the somewhat comic result of people living in the same house, sitting at the same table, like so many plants that have reached a certain resemblance to humanity but not to the extent of sharing in the gift of speech; so they go on vegetating, but saying not a word to each other.

Over and above this personal and social disagreeableness of anger, there is its extreme danger. It is a capital sin. When it moves in, we can expect the rest of the family anytime. It may not look so bad itself when it signs the lease; but wait until the daughters arriver One glance at them shows us sufficient grounds for constant civil war in the house of any man.

"Daughters" of anger: indignation, swelling of mind, blasphemy, contumely, quarreling

The eldest daughter, born before anger had reached full maturity, is a burning indignation. By it, we put people, especially those who have injured us, in their proper place, as an irritated parent sets an obstreperous child in its high chair -- joltingly. The place we choose is, you may be sure, a very lowly place; and it gets lower at every opportunity. A very satisfying sort of anger that yet is never satisfied. The second daughter is a crowd in herself; at least when she enters a man's mind there is room for little else, her baggage is so huge and so stuffed with schemes for revenge. The angry man uses every idle instant to concoct these terrible things for an enemy; indeed, the unholy ambitions invade his very sleep. St. Thomas describes this state accurately as a swelling of the mind; it is just that. Eventually it bursts into wild, disordered confusion of speech -- the product of a man who is positively stuttering with anger. It goes farther and breaks out into injurious speech, either against God in the form of blasphemy, or against men in the form of contumely. It reaches its peak when it expresses itself in actions, not mere words; the thing that Thomas packs into the one word "quarreling," but which reaches out to all the injuries, which it is possible for us to inflict upon one with whom we are angry.

Cruelty

Inordinate anger is opposed to meekness as weakness is opposed to strength. When the act of anger, punishment, escapes the control of reason, it is the opposite of clemency; and the opposition here is that of justice to injustice. The contrast of cruelty and clemency is a contrast of a rough, primitive rawness and finished smoothness of careful craftsmanship. Where the one is eager to mitigate punishment reasonably, the other is unreasonably eager to sharpen the punishment.

Even cruelty clings to a shred of rationality; that is, it does not punish without some vague reason. When this last bit of reason's bright garment is torn off, it gives up all claim to decency and stands forth naked as savagery. Then it no longer looks for guilt as the basis of punishment; rather it looks to the perverted pleasure to be got from the torture of other men. It is a bestial thing, this savagery, revolting to the soul of man, as is all bestiality masquerading in human form. Perhaps one of the most terrible of anger's natural punishments is inflicted upon a man when after anger has died down, he is brought face to face with the damage he has done in his passion.

By moderation of lesser pleasures -- modesty: Its nature.

In completing the conquest of temperance, clemency and meekness have the difficult assignment of moderating the wildest of the passions. Modesty has no such difficult work; but that does not mean it is unimportant. In fact, one of the reasons for our underestimation of modesty is precisely because it has an air of mediocrity about it. It really deals in the small change of moderation; its very material is mediocre, for its work is to keep in check the lesser pleasures that enter into a man's life.

These latter are not in a position to overwhelm reason; rather they are constant and vicious irritations, like ragged bands of guerrillas that are not at all particular as to which side they prey on. They can, given latitude enough, lay a man's life in waste; always, they can prepare for the collapse of the defense against the immediately serious threats inherent in the greater pleasures.

Its species

In our last chapter, we noticed the different species of modesty: modesty of soul, of mind, of body, and modesty in externals. In this chapter we shall begin our detailed examination of these different kinds of modesty, but shall limit ourselves to the very first -- that modesty of soul which is called humility.

Humility's conquest: Its nature as a virtue

It is another much misunderstood and unappreciated virtue. We sometimes confuse it with a laughing protestation in denial of excellence, a denial that must itself be protested according to the rules of the game. I remember the bitter taste this odd humility left in the mouth of a New York taxi-driver on one of the rare occasions when he ventured out of the safe haven of the city. After working a half-hour under a hot sun on a dusty road, changing a tire for an immaculate, but helpless, young lady, he straightened up in triumph and was effusively thanked. He shrugged, smiling, and said: "It was nothing at all. Glad to do it." Perhaps figuring he was an expert in such matters, the girl took him at his own evaluation and offered him a dime. One wonders why more heroic rescuer. are not manhandled by the people they both save and insult, shrugging off the rescue as "nothing at all; think nothing of it." There is no difficulty in seeing that this sort of thing is not humility; for obviously it is not the truth.

Neither is humility a kind of hypocrisy that beats its breast and blunders into things because of its shyly downcast eyes. Yet we find it hard to be sure of this false humility because the really clever hypocrite is not easily discovered; at least, it show. up one of the causes for the disrespect, men have for humility, for men rightly condemn hypocrisy as a cowardly device. Then, too, humility has an abject look in modern eyes, for it does imply a recognition of one's limitations; and the pagan world does not dare admit limitations in its attempt to be wholly self-sufficient.

Its object and effect

Humility, in actual fact, is not a self-condemnation to obscure stagnation unworthy of a man. It is not an enemy of magnanimity's straining for the stars; rather it is a necessary companion to greatness of soul. Let us look at it this way. In every great work, there are two elements: one of great goodness, which is mightily attractive; the other of great difficulty, which is mightily repulsive. That part of courage, which is magnanimity, holds the soul of a man firm that it might not recoil before the great difficulty and give up the work. Humility holds the soul back, lest, captivated by the goodness of the work, a man be fooled into attempting the impossible. Both keep man's efforts within the field of reason; both insist on man's measuring up to his capacities. The one insists that he must not fall short of those capacities; the other keeps him from overshooting the mark. Certainly, there is nothing of defeatism here.

Its place among the virtues

Humility, then, moderates our appetite for excellence, it does not destroy that appetite; its work is to keep our hope reasonable. It has been said repeatedly for ages, that humility is truth. Additionally, that is true; but not so true that it can be left just like that and not be misunderstood. The crime reporter who thinks he is another Shakespeare may not be insane, but he is certainly not humble. There is an element of truth necessary for humility; at least a man must recognize his limitations if he is to keep his hope from aiming too high. Nevertheless, humility is not an intellectual virtue; its place is in the appetite of man, a faculty that searches for the good rather than the true. Truth is rather the rule of humility than humility itself; the two are so intimately connected that there is no danger whatever of humility blushing furiously at the detection of its lies. It does not tell lies but lives the truth.

This explains much of the puzzling self-contempt in the lives of the saints. Humility is characteristically marked by subjection. Because a man recognizes his own limitations and deficiencies, he is able to see the perfections of other men and of God. You might say that humility recognizes the truth of man's humanity and so sees the perfection of God's divinity. Every man is a mixture of the divine and the human in the sense that in every man, there are the things that are God's, namely, perfections; and in every man, there are things that are his very own, i.e., defects and deficiencies. Humility has an eagle eye for both divinity and humanity; it is not to be confused and blinded by any blending of the two. So that if we consider what has come from ourselves, each of us not only can but should be subject to what there is of God in every other man; in that sense, and in that sense alone, humility makes a man subject to every other man, even a saint to a sinner.

To reverse the process, and subject what is of God in us to what is of man in another, would be irreverent, perhaps blasphemous. On the other hand, even to place side by side the purely human things in ourselves and others, or the purely divine things, and still insist upon a universal subjection would be stupidity, not humility. The fact is that some have greater gifts from God than others, that some have less defects than others. Humility does not counsel stupidity, much less does it allow the living of a lie.

One of the early calumnies against the Christian religion, that it was a religion of slaves and weaklings, was due as much to this emphasis on humility as it was to the historical character of the early converts. Yet Christ did not come to make men slaves, to send them groveling in the dust; His own summation of His mission was that men "might have life and have it more abundantly", that their "joy might be full." Nor did the early Christians misunderstand His aims when they insisted on humility, for one of the explicit lessons He gave was "learn of me, for I am meek and humble of heart." The question is not so much a matter of attempting reconciliation between irreconcilables -- the subjection of humility and the full, joyous abundance of life; it is rather a matter of understanding that one cannot be had without the other. Humility, as a matter of fact, places the very first condition of progress towards a full life, the condition of subjection. Showing a man his limitations, keeping his hope" within the bounds of his abilities, humility keeps a man in his proper place; and this not in a particular respect, but universally. Consequently, it cuts out at the roots the great obstacles to happiness, the obstacles that consist in putting ourselves above all others, in seeking our own excellence, caught up as a sleepwalker by his dream to wander blindly out of our proper world. That obstacle goes by the name of pride.

Just as in society it is the law-abiding citizen, that is, the citizen subject to authority, who is in a position to make the most of and to contribute most heavily to the common life, so also in the world of reason it is the man who is subject who gets most out of and puts most into the life of reason. Indeed, humility gives us that invaluable subjection, not only socially but universally. The virtue is absolutely fundamental, for it removes a fundamental obstacle. Granted that it is not a virtue by which we run to God, still without it the other virtues would have to be expert hurdlers to get anywhere. From another point of view, humility is a guarantee of a right sense of values. It is a calm, clear-sighted virtue, not to be seduced by the tempting prospect of earthly greatness at the cost of spiritual greatness; there is about it a great deal of that hard-headed common sense that comes from living close to the soil, close to the world of things as they are. In addition, humility does give us this spiritual common sense, enabling us to see and to act towards things as they are.

Its opposite -- pride: Nature and subject of pride

The humble man has his feet solidly on the ground. He lives in a world of reality, while the proud man lives in a world of fantastic fiction. Yet in our time it is the proud who are called realists, the humble who are called dreamers. On the very face of it, our evaluation is wrong; pride seeks impossible things -- hardly the objective of a realist. Situated in the first principle of motion in man, in his will, pride drives him to impossible goals that utterly surpass his powers. Whatever the proud man handles must be draped in the flimsy glory of fiction; even though he has nothing at all, he must boast of things as though they were really his. What he has, he ascribes to his own excellence and his own activity -- the perfect author of the success story; or if, grudgingly, he admits God as the author of these perfections, it

435

is to be understood that God could not very well do anything else but give these gifts to him, considering his outstanding character.

The proud man must be outstanding; he is a hopeless victim of a spiritual claustrophobia. He must be conspicuously singular in his excellence; so he must despise the accomplishments of others, so petty in comparison with his own. He is a swaggering little boy playing out his dream, swelling with the importance of his deeds of conquest and, eventually, so lost in his dream world that he cannot bear a return to the world of reality. He cannot be himself, for that self is so very small in so big a world.

Its varieties

As humility makes a man universally subject, so pride makes a man universally rebellious. A superior with a proud subject on his hands can resign himself to sleepless nights; there is no point in thinking up arguments, such a subject does not proceed on reasons; cajoling, threatening, bribing are all useless. For the thing resented is the very relation of subject and superior; the only place the proud man occupies with some peace is the superior's chair, and that at the cost of peace to the rest of the community. You see, his rebellion is a sweeping thing that makes no exception; indeed, at its worst, it makes no exception even for the sovereignty of God.

Its gravity and relation to other sins

In itself, it is a mortal sin; in fact, one of the gravest of sins, for it excels in that aversion from God that is the formal malice of sin. It is, of its very nature, a rebellion and it is rebellion that makes the gravity of sin. In a very real sense, it is the first of all sins, the queen and mother of all moral ugliness. Not for nothing does it wear a veil over its face even in the privacy of a man's own soul. We do it an injustice when we call it a capital sin; it is at the root of absolutely every sin, for pride is the undiluted essence of rebellion, shared in some measure by every sin.

The first sin of pride -- original sin: Its nature

Even in the point of time, pride is first. It was the sin that destroyed the original perfection of man. It has not changed a bit since; then, as now, it was that same insistence on supremacy, on outreaching one's self, on complete self-sufficiency. Of course, Adam did not expect to set himself up as a divine equal of God; he was wiser than his sons who made that absurd mistake. Even so, he did mean to be self- sufficient, to be under no one; in a word, to be more than a man. It was a fantastic fiction; but it is still a best seller in every corner of the world.

Its penalties

Looking at the person of Adam and his excellence as head of the race, we might say his sin of pride was more serious than that of Eve; but then there is a great deal to be said for Adam. After all, he did not succumb to the smooth lies of the serpent, but to the sweet cajolings of his wife. He did not coax anyone else into sin (there was no one else, as a matter of fact); perhaps his love for Eve had something to do with his sin, a muddled notion that it would be better to sin with her than to remain virtuous without her -- a dilemma that no one had proposed to him. At any rate, he reaped the prompt fruits of his rebellion against God in the rebellion of his own flesh against his spirit; and this was the start of that long war between the flesh and the spirit, which will continue until the death of the last man. Along with that rebellion of sin came death, liability to injury, cold, hunger, sickness and all the rest of the ills of man; and gone was that magnificent sovereignty over the physical world that had made the first man so truly the lord of the world.

We may sum up this chapter by insisting that man wins peace only by being true to himself: that is, by holding to the regime of reason in all of life, and so also in the field of pleasure and of sorrow. It is not sufficient to hold to the necessary moderation in the greatest of joys; the least must also be kept in check. To maintain that the conquest is over when the greater aims of temperance are roughly attained, though the lesser aims ate neglected, is a lie that is peculiarly dangerous because it appears so innocuous. As a matter of fact, it is a half-truth that distorts the life of a man, swelling some very human inclinations to inhumanly dominant proportions, shriveling others no less human to a pitiable, even contemptible condition.

The abundant life and truth:

Fruits of living a lie; dangers of living a half-truth

There is no abundance to a lie, whether that lie is told in words or in actions. It has sprung up without roots in reality and it lives on stolen air and stolen light: it must be poisonous if it is to assure itself of continued life, for all truth is its enemy. Obviously, we can expect no rational fruits from so irrational a thing as a lie. That our expectations have not been too pessimistic can be seen, even though we have no taste for history, no love for labor, no time for reading beyond the morning newspapers. Where else does the contempt for meekness, for clemency, for modesty and humility come but from this half-truth? We have almost forgotten that these are human things, necessary things, even indispensable things. They call up pictures of timidity, sentimentality or prudishness; while anger, cruelty and pride, though perhaps reprehensible, are certainly manly. The half-truth has made us miss the whole truth, that is, all of the truth: for it is the first group -- meekness, clemency and all the rest -- that are truly manly; it is the second group -- anger, cruelty and pride -- that are unworthy of a man.

Inhuman world is a world of fiction

These virtues are not popular in a pagan world both because the pagan world is so terribly unsure of itself that it must always broadcast its assurance, and because the pagan is always so unutterably alone. Being alone, the pagan must stand on top or be trampled. He must live in a world of fiction because the truth of his own limitations makes his world too hopeless for the continuance of human life. His world must be an immodest world for it must be a liar's world; it cannot see the truth, or seeing it, cannot bear its too bright face. For the proportion and moderation of reason always carry with them the inevitable connotation of subjection; they present man with that profound paradox: conquest can come only by subjection.

The world and the "mild" virtues;

Christ and the "mild" virtues

It would be true to say that our world has a contempt for these milder virtues because our world has come far from Christ; but it would also be true to say that our world has developed a contempt for these mild virtues because our world has come so far from human life. Human life is a life of reason. If that life and action is to be human, reason must be the master in command; and reason cannot be in command as long as these marauding bands of guerrillas are left free to prey upon the peace and security of the kingdom of man. Reason's conquest must be complete or a man will be haunted by stalking terror and imminent death; and it is precisely these milder virtues -- clemency, meekness, modesty and humility -- that make possible the completion of the conquest of temperance. Christ insisted, in word and action, on these milder virtues because He came to bring us peace, a fuller, a more abundant life. He was not condoning, much less urging, softness or sentimentality and timidity, the evasion of all conflict. He knew what temperance demanded for complete conquest, what courage, honesty and sincerity must go into it; for He knew well what was in man. It is perhaps because this perfect Man, Who was also God, knew man so well, that He could insist that man never has reason for pride in that which escapes the control of his reason.

✠CHAPTER XIX✠

MODESTY AND MIRACLES
(Q. 166-178)

1. The Miracle of modesty:
    (a) Modesty and sophistication:
        (1) The innocence of modesty.
        (2) The wisdom of modesty.
    (b) Personal graciousness by modesty.

2. The material of modesty.

3. Modesty of mind -- studiousness:
    (a) Its nature.
    (b) Its opposites -- curiosity and negligence:
        (1) Knowledge and sin.
        (2) Knowledge and the occasion of sin.

4. Modesty of body:
    (a) Of bodily movement:
        (1) In serious action.
        (2) In recreation -- eutrapelia:
            a. The purpose of play.
            b. Sin in play:
                1) By excess.
                2) By defect.
    (b) Of dress:
        (1) Virtue in dress.
        (2) Sin in dress:
            a. By offense against custom.
            b. By excess and defect in affection for dress.
        (3) The apparel of women.

5. Apostolic graces -- the boundlessness of work:
    (a) Apostolic grace of mind alone -- prophecy.
    (b) Apostolic grace of mind and emotion -- rapture.
    (c) Apostolic grace of speech -- the gift of tongues and speech.
    (d) Apostolic grace of operation -- the gift of miracles.

Conclusion:

1. Modern immodesty.
    (a) Extreme of immaturity.
    (b) Extreme of senescence.

2. The fruits of immodesty.

3. Modesty, miracles and achievement.

CHAPTER XIX

MODESTY AND MIRACLES
(Q. 166-178)

The modern contrast of modesty to sophistication is the contrast of a blushing, clumsy, country boy to the worldly-wise debutante incapable of embarrassment. Sympathy may be all with the country boy; but envy and admiration are for the debutante. When the two, sophistication and modesty, meet there is a tolerantly amused smile for modesty, as though it were a passing phase in life with its attractive sides, like missing front teeth or marble playing; sweet, innocent ignorance that will not, alas, endure for long!

The Miracle of modesty: Modesty and sophistication:

Actually, there is much more than amusement and tolerance in that smile of the sophisticate. Modesty is a kind of miracle to the sophisticate; it does to the heart what a miracle does to the eyes and to the mind. It focuses the heart, startlingly, on things long dreamed of, a focus that makes the rest of the world disappear for just an instant. The smile for modesty has a touch of remembrance in it, of regret, of envy, and even a little of inspiration. In the face of modesty, the human heart goes a little home sick. Sophistication's greeting to modesty is a tribute; for modesty is a realization and a statement of what men would like to be, because that is what men were meant to be.

The innocence of modesty

In a sense, modesty is innocent. Its goals are the clean, windswept goals of virtue, goals whose reflection gives a calm, clear quiet to a face. It is innocent in the sense that it does not seek dark corners, secret rendezvous, it does not start with guilt at discovery or blush with shame in remembrance. Now, it is not ignorant. Rather, it is very wise, very learned in human things. It is saturated with rationality: contact with it is as refreshing as the deep, eager breaths of sea-air by a man coming from the heat of an inland city. It gives us a sense of freshness, of cleanness, as though we had just been scrubbed inside and out.

The wisdom of modesty

Its real characteristic, however, is rational balance. It is not lop-sided as is the sophisticate, the playboy, the libertine, and, sometimes, the scholar.

All modesty has the quietly satisfying qualities that we associate with the atmosphere of home. Its joys do not intrude themselves violently on our attention; they penetrate us comfortingly as the warmth of a fire on a raw evening. Modesty works unobtrusively for a happiness that is almost unnoticed until it is gone; like lost innocence, or the unheard noises of summer whose absence make a winter day so deathly still.

Personal graciousness by modesty

It is extremely difficult to describe the part of modesty in human life; that part is so elusive, intangible, yet so solidly real. Perhaps we could call it "personal graciousness." The air of it has been caught in Chesterton's melodious phrase: "as on a stairway go in grace." It has the serene beauty of unhurried movement, the mysterious penetration of a deep chord of an organ. It becomes almost tangible in the face of a saintly old priest, or the eager unselfishness of a very young nun. Perhaps all this may seem much too figurative to be of great help; but, as a matter of fact, we realize the difficulty in everyday life and, in trying to describe the possessor of modesty, we fall back on such utterly simple statements as "wholesome", or, with very special emphasis, we say "he is good."

The material of modesty

Perhaps the root of the difficulty is that the pleasures with which modesty deals are really an undercurrent in our lives. The pleasure of reasonable hope, of knowledge, of sincerity, of affability, of play and of dress are all a background without which life would be an empty, barren thing. Yet, they are only a background; they are not the principal figures in the finished tapestry of life.

Modesty of mind -- studiousness: Its nature

Obviously, some regulation is necessary for our appetite for knowledge, for here, there are two natural inclinations, either of which may well pull a man off the road of reason. Long before he can rattle the change in his pockets, a man starts to ask "why"; he has a natural inclination to truth. All the same, just as truly he has an inclination to avoid the labor inevitably bound up with that vehement inclination of mind which is the one road to knowledge; study is hard, hard work. As a very humble testimony to the truth of these statements, we have such institutions as truant officers and report cards.

Still there are some things, which a man must know; at least in their regard, his distaste for labor must be moderated. There are other things that man should not try to know by his own powers, so the inclination to knowledge must also be reasonably directed. Both of these ends are achieved by the quiet operation of the virtue of studiousness, steering a man safely past the stagnation of stupid negligence and the restless uneasiness of curiosity.

A doctor is seriously obliged to know something of surgery before he throws open his beautifully equipped operating rooms to defenseless patients; a priest must know moral theology before he opens the confessional slide; and a wife should know something of the fundamentals of cookery before she serves up the products of her art. In other words, if his distaste for the labors of study escapes the control of reason, with the result that man is ignorant of what his state in life obliges him to know, he may be guilty of sin. Indeed, the sin may easily become mortal if the missing knowledge is of serious obligation. Normally, the civil authorities insist upon adequate knowledge where ignorance will have serious social effects; except perhaps in the matter of cooking. However, curiosity is not taken very seriously. It is true that, in itself, there can be nothing wrong with knowledge. It is one of the highest works of man; evil in connection with it is quite accidental, as in the man who sins by pride in his knowledge or uses it as a means to further his sinning. Now, the appetite or desire for knowledge can be, and frequently is, evil. That is, it can become curiosity.

Its opposites -- curiosity and negligence

The man, whose zeal for knowledge is merely a tool of pride, can lay no claim to the rewards of virtue. On a less spectacular, and certainly more futile, scale, curiosity shows itself in the mother of ten children who spends hours learning the intricacies of bridge, leaving the children with the impression that they are orphans. This sort of thing particularly disgusted St. Jerome; he voiced his disgust in no uncertain terms in his complaint against priests who were putting aside the gospels and the prophets to read plays and to sing songs.

Knowledge and sin

In both these cases, the necessary studies have been neglected for the study of that which certainly is less useful, often only possibly useful. The thing is unreasonable; but still it is not quite so unreasonable as the attempt to know a truth above our powers. Thus, a philosopher might madly attempt to comprehend infinity by natural reason; or a man with no mathematical ability might give himself a headache studying Einstein's theory of relativity. Men do not particularly care for headaches as intellectual rewards, even when they are overreaching themselves in the field of knowledge. To contrive the one and avoid the other they have sometimes allowed curiosity to take another and more dangerous form; namely, that of superstition by which, under the guise of knowledge, they sit at the feet of diabolic masters. This is the curiosity of the Ouija board and the séance room that gives man a preview of hell and starts God on His way out of a man's life.

Curiosity did not really kill the cat. It died from some other cause, for curiosity is a human ailment, the exclusive property of the being who can abuse his faculties. It is a distinctly human affair and it can exist in almost any walk of human life. The ubiquitous little sister, the pest of the household, who does not miss a thing about the house, not for any particular reason, but just because she has to know, is not so far removed from the scholar whose knowledge is rigidly divorced from God and is an end in itself. Both are curious; and the scholar is very much more dangerously curious than the child.

Knowledge and the occasion of sin

Neither the corner loafer, who subjects every passing woman to his critical scrutiny, nor the old lady in her rocking chair on the front porch tabulating every activity of the people across the street, do themselves any good. Rather they are setting the stage for the prompt appearance of sin; they also are curious, and dangerously curious. In fact, we can see too much for our own good, particularly when we meander about the universe like a woman who saunters through a department store "just looking."

It was with this in mind that Chrysostom, and Thomas much later, warned against the danger of indiscriminate theater going. Their argument was that we shall have trouble enough avoiding temptation under any circumstances; at the very least, idle curiosity will furnish us with just so much more material for trouble. In going to the wrong kind of play, or going to all plays indiscriminately and with unreasonable frequency, we indulge an idle curiosity in finding out things that would never have entered the course of our ordinary life. We are feeding ourselves with materials for trouble.

Modesty of body

Of bodily movement in serious action

Of course, the family across the street and the woman who has just passed the corner do not imagine that they move in a world of the blind. They know their external movements are not somehow mysteriously invisible; nor do they take offense at others for looking at them. They realize, at least dimly, that their external movement serves the double purpose of mirroring their inner life and of putting them in social contact with others. These aspects of external movement are taken for granted. Still, it follows from this that these externals, too, must have their share in the beauty of moderation that reason's rule gives to the things of a man. From the social angle, this beauty of moderation is effected by affability or friendliness; from the personal angle, by veracity or sincerity, always with an eye to the particular person and the particular circumstances. The effusively silly greeting of a none too bright high school girl would be a little astonishing coming from a bishop; yet we do not expect the bishop to wear his pontifical robes in swimming. We demand that a man be reasonable in his external actions; but he need not carry dignity to the point of absurdity.

However, we do make a constant mistake in this matter on the basis of veracity or sincerity. We feel rather proud of ourselves for following the deceptive maxim "be yourself", more classically stated as "to yourself be true." All the same, the maxim is a little too easy; it tucks the excuse of temperament into our vest pocket to be readily presented as sufficient explanation of almost any eccentricity. It is good to be true to one's self; but that should not mean that there is nothing to be done about the peculiar individual one happens to be at this particular stage in life. We are not always as God made us; "sometimes we are a great deal worse." Thomas insists that there should be an element of the studied in our voice, our laugh, our walk, our conversation. The nuns presiding over a girls' school, insisting that there is a correct way to sit, to walk, a cultured modulation of voice, and so on, are not necessarily snobbishly rigid formalists. Rather they maintain that even in these things we have a right to expect the beauty of moderation that is our privilege as reasonable beings. It does not follow that a man's actions should have that theatrical deliberation that shrieks for a spotlight; but it does follow that into those actions should go an earnest weeding out of defects, a campaign of elimination which makes for personal graciousness and which is nothing more than an insistence on the beauty of reason's order breaking through all of a man's life, even through the externals of that life.

In recreation -- eutrapelia

Perhaps nowhere in all his works does the humanity of St. Thomas appear more clearly than in his defense of the universal sway of reason, a sovereignty that he argues must extend itself even to the play of men. Here in this tract on modesty St. Thomas gives his philosophy of fun. He has compressed it into three articles; an extremely brief treatment that is yet a noble human document, worthy of the tribute of familiarity from any age.

The purpose of play

It seemed obvious to the greatest scholar of the most scholarly century that fun is necessary to human life. When a man has pushed a wheelbarrow all day, his body is tired. If he is to do the same thing the next day, he must do something about the bodily fatigue; he must give his body some rest. Exactly the same thing is true of the soul. Even though there are no such things as spiritual wheelbarrows, there is a weariness of soul that is exactly proportionate to the intensity of a man's mental efforts. It is true that speculative work causes a greater soul-weariness than does practical thinking; but the latter, precisely as thinking, has the same, though a lesser, wearying effect. In other words, man's mental powers, like his physical powers, are definitely limited. When a man reaches, or goes beyond, those limits, he becomes tired -- tired both mentally and physically, for in the labors of the soul the body must also work. If he expects to continue that mental work, he must give his soul a rest: and the rest of the soul is called play or fun, that is, words or action in which we seek nothing but physical or animal pleasures.

It is a very human thing, when we are loaded down with work and we see another stepping out liltingly for a good time, to feel very virtuous in our condemnation of such frivolous waste of time. There are so many serious things in life, so much to be done that it is childish and silly to fritter away precious time in amusement. To combat that notion St. Thomas records the story of St. John the Evangelist. Just such a serious-minded person caught St. John one day playing a game with his disciples. The saint was roundly rebuked for activities so unworthy of an apostle. Instead of arguing the point (people as serious as this will argue forever), St. John picked up a bow, handed it to his reformer and asked him to shoot an arrow at a target. The man did. St. John asked him to shoot repeatedly. Finally he asked what would happen if arrows were shot indefinitely from that bow. His critic, in some irritation at so obvious a question, answered that of course it would break. St. John said that exactly the same thing would happen to a man; unless he gives his soul a rest, he too will break.

The whole idea of amusement is really an application of the orator's technique to individual human life. Cicero gave the counsel, entirely approved by Thomas later, that when an orator talks over-long, when he notices his audience getting restive, he should say something novel or, in keeping with the circumstances, something ridiculous. In other words, the orator must give his audience a let-down, a rest, a break from the mental effort of following his argument. Amusement gives a man a let-down, an interruption of the mental effort of thinking.

The very purpose of fun, then, indicates its need for regulation. Fun should clearly interrupt the labors of the soul, but not upset rational balance, not induce hysteria or stupor; it is meant for a rest. It cannot turn about obscenity or crime without defeating its own ends; these things do not give quiet but torment to the soul. The general term human activity is a description of man's play as well as his work; even in his play, there must be the human note of fittingness to persons, places and time. We are right in our judgment of the man who relaxes by shouting operatic scales at three o'clock in the morning. He is not only lacking in a sense of humor, he is beyond question lacking in the virtue, which regulates fun, the virtue of eutrapelia; for surely such relaxation is not rational.

Sin in play: By excess

It is to be well noticed that the whole purpose of play is to rest the soul. It presupposes work and looks forward to more work. In the absence of that mental activity which makes play necessary, amusement becomes a terrible bore, as distasteful as a steady diet of spinach or six months in bed. Even too much of it in one dose destroys the sparkling relish of it. Of course, the retired businessman promptly lies down and dies; he has nothing to do but rest. While rest is fine as a recuperation from work or a preparation for work, rest for the sake of rest is really a killing thing.

The wit whose humor is discourteous, scandalous or obscene is clearly not practicing virtue, any more than the man whose relaxation consists in murder or theft. Obviously, amusement is not always virtuous. These things cannot be excused on any grounds, let alone on the flimsy grounds of fatigue. In fact, the possibilities of sin in play are considerably varied. Thus, for instance, fun can become such a fever in a man as to destroy all else, inducing a man to sacrifice his family, his work, even his God for such trifles as a horse race, a golf or a poker game. Then it is a vicious thing with none of reason's beauty about it.

In a less ugly, but more undignified manner, we can sin in play by a disregard of reason in the circumstances of our amusement. The things that are done may be just clean fun, and highly amusing; but somehow we do not expect a President to sneak into a dark alley at night to shoot dice, or a portly matron to skip rope by the hour in front of the parochial school.

For most of us, the work of the virtue of eutrapelia is to restrain fun from getting out of bounds rather than to coax us into taking some relaxation. In other words, a man is much more liable to sin by excessive play than by lack of all recreation. After all, a little fun goes a long way. Recreation is a seasoning of human life; a little touch of it is sometimes exactly, what is needed to give a tang to a flat day. Yet, we cannot live on recreation any more than we can on seasoning: and too much fun can spoil a human life as completely as too much seasoning spoils a meal.

By defect

Yet fun is so necessary to human life that the total lack of it is unreasonable and vicious. The wet blanket at a party is a burden to himself and to others; he takes no pleasure himself and cramps the pleasure of others. In fact (and the phrase is that of Thomas), the man, who never says anything ridiculous and is a nuisance to those who are joking, is vicious. He is not to be complimented for his serious frame of mind but to be condemned for his lack of reason.

Modesty of dress: Virtue in dress

A recent biography of Phillip II of Spain gives a little incident indicative of the wide, sympathetic understanding of the Spanish people. Towards the end of his reign, the king decided to determine by law the amusements of his people, their titles of address, even their very clothes. Instead of rising up in anger against the tyranny, the people smiled at one another and said: "His majesty is growing old." While there was solid reason for resentment, there was also solid reason for sympathetic love; he had long been a just, thoughtful, hard-working monarch. While it is true that civil legislation must remain general, since no government can descend to the intimate details of personal life without becoming ridiculous, the same is not at all true of the legislation of reason, of the moral law. We cannot smile tolerantly and say that reason is growing old because our conscience descends to the smallest details of life. Reason must descend to such details, for even the details must be reasonable, that is, they must be human. Even here, in these small details, we shall find virtue and vice, reason or unreasonableness.

Naturally, reason takes in such a detail as dress. Additionally, that very statement is a declaration that virtue plays a part in dress. Indeed, this is clear from the innate dignity of man, as well as from the natural inclination of his sense appetites to disregard reason. If that were not enough to convince a man, there is concrete confirmation in the prompt action of the police against the man who goes to certain excesses in dress. This moderation in dress is the task of that virtue of honesty of which we spoke in an earlier chapter. Then we noticed its necessity for an appreciation of the beauty of temperance. It seems particularly fitting that the virtue, which is appreciative of beauty, should have the details of human dress under its wings. In other words, the regulation of dress is not in the name of shame alone; but also in the name of dignity and of beauty. Here our modern judgment is correct.

Sin in dress: By offense against custom

The appearance of a man in full dress on a South Sea island might be just as shocking as the appearance of a South Sea islander on Fifth Avenue in a costume of leaves, a very few leaves. In either case, the costume would be as out of place as a sour note in a symphony orchestra. Such a man simply would not harmonize with the whole of which he is a part; and we can sin in dress by open violation of custom. This, you understand, is not a condemnation of variety in dress; for the very variety may be a part of custom and custom is something to be respected.

The business of legislating details of dress is extremely tricky; St. Thomas, with the profound wisdom that was his peculiar excellence, was much too wise to attempt it. He gives no measurements, names no high or low limit, hands down no pattern. What he does do is to give us general principles, which form the basis of the reasonable in dress.

By excess and defect in affection for dress

The woman with a gown long out of style is not a willing sinner against custom, whatever her nonchalance; and no secret police are necessary to insure the prompt discarding of straw hats on the day appointed by custom. For most of us, there is little temptation to sin in dress by opposing custom. We are much more likely to offend by vainglory, a silly sort of offense that proceeds on the presumption that our very clothes give us a title to esteem. A man can, of course, sin by the inordinate sensual pleasure he gets from clothes; by his over zeal for personal comfort in dress; or finally by sheer foppishness. These are, respectively, violations of the virtues of humility, of contentment (that is, satisfaction with the suitable) and of simplicity. At the other extreme, is the sin in dress by sloppiness or raggedness; a condition that is a product either of effeminate neglect or of a thirst for attention as strong as that evidenced by the fop.

The apparel of women

All of this general doctrine on clothes will also hold for women's apparel; but over and above these principles, some special consideration is necessary for women's clothes because, says St. Thomas, they may serve as a means to arouse the lust of men. Actually, St. Thomas' article on women's clothes is a defense of reasonable fashion, in contrast to the devastating condemnations of the Fathers. The Fathers were often orators, thundering against the abuses of their time; St. Thomas was a theologian, considering things in a calm, clear, objective light. He spoke quietly and with the strict accuracy of a theologian.

It might well be wondered what a friar of the thirteenth century could have to say about women's clothes that would be of any interest to the twentieth century. Well, no one can say that St.

Thomas, did not have his eyes open; there was little of Europe and life in the thirteenth century that he missed on his slow journeys by foot up and down the land; he moved freely in the greatest courts of his day, What his own eyes did not show him of woman's dress he could well learn from the thundering of the Fathers against the corruptions of a decadent Roman Empire. Not even the twentieth century sophisticate could tell the ladies of that era very much.

St. Thomas saw it as reasonable for a woman to adorn herself with an eye to men if she had a husband, if she wished to have a husband, or if she merely had an open mind on the subject. However, a woman who had no husband, did not want a husband and did not mean to have one, or whose state in life forbade marriage, had no business aiming her dress at men. Now, of course the thing happened. If it was to arouse the interests of men, then her sin was mortal or venial according as she seriously intended to arouse lust, or merely acted from frivolity, vanity or ostentation. In other words, St. Thomas understands the Fathers as forbidding, not moderate, reasonable adornment, but the excesses of sinful, immodest and unreasonable ornamentation.

Some of the Fathers inveighed against the defacing of God's work by yellow paint, black powder, rouge and dye. There must have been some ghastly make-ups in those days. St. Augustine considered the accomplishment of a paler or rosier complexion by means of paint as a lying counterfeit.

Thomas approached such a touchy subject cautiously and humanly. He admits that St. Augustine has something in his contention of counterfeit, presupposing of course the optimistic intention to deceive by an extraordinary painting job. Even so, painting one's face is not a mortal sin, unless it is done for seriously evil ends. Nevertheless, getting back to the counterfeit idea, St. Thomas notices that it is one thing to counterfeit beauty and quite another -- and a lawful -- thing to hide a disfigurement. It is a very neat distinction, which suggests that accuracy would demand a change in the name of those shops that in our age are called "beauty parlors."

This completes the tract on the virtues. It finishes the long statement of the principles of the fullness of human life; not only of human life, but of that divinely human life in its incredible abundance, reaching out to divinity and eternity, the abundant life that Christ came to bring us. The virtues, natural and supernatural, are the instruments of personal perfection; they make life personally successful. In a word, they make a man good.

Apostolic graces -- the boundlessness of work

Horizons such as these would seem wide enough; but they are not wide enough for God. From time to time He gives men more startling glimpses of His divine power and generosity through the graces that are ordered, not principally to personal sanctity, but to the sanctity of others; the apostolic graces. They do not make the individual good, but they do make him a powerful instrument for the salvation of others, executing the divine plan as the brush materializes the dreams of the artist. Here all the limitations to human operations seem to be done away with; here the true boundlessness of work is hinted at, for here, it is God that is working more than man.

Apostolic grace of mind alone -- prophecy

Thus the apostolic grace of prophecy allows a man to know infallibly and to predict with certainty what is unknowable itself to anyone but God, that is, such future contingent things as the free acts of man. Natural gifts are of no help here; there is no preparation or disposition possible, not even the state of grace. This can be done only by supernatural light from God Himself. Man is God's instrument pure and simple.

The prophet may realize his instrumentality or he may be ignorant of it. Prophetic knowledge may come to him in sleep, when he is awake, in ecstasy or without his realizing it at all. This is not something personal but something apostolic, something for the salvation of others. Sometimes such prophetic knowledge is given by a physical apparition, at others by phantasms of the imagination; or, in a higher form, as a purely intellectual vision, Still, it will always be a passing thing, like a note struck from a violin. It is a shaft of divine lightning striking the mind of man, easily seen by all, a certain sign of divine revelation and a confirmation of divine truth. There is a note of human stubbornness and of divine generosity here that must not be missed. It is our hesitancy and our weakness that make such confirmations of prophecy necessary; it is God's generosity that makes such things possible. Generosity is exactly the right word; for it demands a divinely generous heart to give these unutterable truths and then, when they have been so graciously given, to coax us into accepting them.

Apostolic grace of mind and emotion -- rapture

The apostolic state of rapture is a kind of divine violence that plucks a man out of himself, as St. Paul was snatched to the seventh heaven. It is a divine flight as contrasted to the slow crawl to divine things naturally characteristic to man. Here man is abstracted from the sensible world, from the senses, from the imagination; it is as though for a moment he was only a mind, to which the divine secrets are laid bare, and a will enthralled by the joys to those secrets.

This rapture is not to be confused with physical afflictions such as catalepsy or with diabolic possession; it is not the trance of emotion, the overpowering movement of sense love or wild passion. It is a divine scorning of human limitations of the depths of knowledge and a divine outpouring of divine joy. It is primarily intellectual and altogether supernatural; in rapture, mere men, with St. Paul, see the things that are not given to the tongue of man to speak, things, which flood the human heart with an overpowering joy that disrupts all normal channels of communication. Rapture is a species of prophecy with the same divine mark of infallible knowledge of inscrutable things.

Apostolic grace of speech -- the gift of tongues and speech

The men whom Christ sent to convert the world were poor, ignorant, powerless; yet they were sent as teachers of men. That they might get a hearing wherever they went, that they might be able to instruct, that their work might not suffer that fatal slowing down or falsification that comes through the use of interpreters, it was most fitting that God give them the gift that so startled the audiences of the first apostles -- the gift of tongues. By it the apostles spoke and understood the languages of all peoples; an incredible thing in the eyes of men, but child's play to the Author of all speech and the Reader of all hearts.

When, in the wisdom of God, it became necessary to speed up the apostolic work of the Church, this gift has been given, though usually in a form different from that of Peter's first recorded address. In this second form, the preacher speaks his own language but is understood by men of all languages; he understands all men, but understands them in his own language. It is as though a divine translator was busy on the word as it traveled from the mouth of the speaker to the ear of the auditor. It was in this form that the gift of tongues played such a prominent part in the life of Louis Bertrand, the missionary of South America; it surpassed all calculation in the life of Vincent Ferrer to whom this gift was apparently as much a personal characteristic as the shape of his nose. It is always a startling gift, designed not only to bring truth but also to overcome the obstacle of incredulity by its very unusualness.

This gift of tongues was not given as a curious exhibition; it was to be coupled with the gift of speech to attain the ends of divine oratory. The Holy Spirit used the tongue of man to win hearts; men were not only to hear these truths but to love them, to embrace them, to live them. This gift of speech furnished a divine oratorical fire that made a holocaust of the hearts of men.

Apostolic grace of operation -- the gift of miracles

In order that absolutely nothing might be lacking to win men to happiness, the burning words of divine oratory were given the unanswerable confirmation of miracles. In addition, here we have another example of the divine thoughtfulness stooping to human nature. It is natural to man to come to the truth through sensible effects; just as in the natural order he comes to a knowledge of God through natural effects, so in the supernatural order he is led by the hand into the divine presence through unquestionably supernatural effects, which yet can be perceived by the senses. There is no question but that here man is a mere instrument of divinity; indeed, in confirmation of a divine truth, God may make use of an enemy, thus showing even more clearly the unlimited sway of divine power. If, however, the miracle is worked in confirmation of the sanctity of the miracle-worker, it can be done only by a saint; obviously, a miracle is not worked in confirmation of a lie.

These apostolic graces show us just such a combination of divine power and divine thoughtfulness as permeated the life of Christ. They open our eyes to the infinite pains God takes to bring us home, the depths to which He will stoop to accommodate man's nature. Yet looking at the apostles through whom the graces worked, we are breathless at the sight of what a man can do under the power of God: his feeble mind, his wavering will, his stuttering tongue, his weak hands, even the shadow of his garment or the dust of his grave produces results proper only to God.

Modern immodesty: Extreme of immaturity; extreme of senescence

Perhaps we could best sum up this chapter by pointing out that modesty is not a matter of dressing in the dark but of living in the light, in the light of reason's moderation and beauty. Modesty turns the floodlight of reason on the internal and external activities of man; his word, his play, his dress, every detail of his life. From this point of view, it is difficult to escape the conclusion that the twentieth century pagan world is an immodest world. We are, in fact, living in a world of paradoxical extremes: on one hand we see all the sign of immaturity -- giddiness, an unbalanced interest in sex, a restless rush of childish ignorance and activity, a world without poise, without serenity, without that personal graciousness that is the mark of reason; on the other hand, there are unmistakable signs of senescence - - the world is bowed down with hopeless burdens, a world that in its less giddy moments is inclined to be desperately serious, a world chained to knowledge for its own sake, a world as much inclined to shroud itself in blankets of respectability as it is to throw off all slightest pretense of respectability and go entirely animal.

The fruits of immodesty

To say that such a world is an immodest world is to say that it is a world without high hopes or a world doomed to the crash of despair because of its impossible hopes. It means that it is a world, which neglects the knowledge it should have, throws away the possibility of having any knowledge, or puts itself in the absurd position of maintaining that its knowledge is supreme. As immodest, it is a world bereft of the affability, truthfulness and sincerity that go into the making of that serene poise and beauty established by the moderation and proportion of reason. An immodest world means a world that is either so serious that it can find no room for fun, or so giddy that it can see no reason for anything but fun and where eventually fun itself becomes labor. It means a world where the quiet beauty and joy of dress is submerged either in a gloomy ugliness that parades as respectability or an exhibitionism whose tailor is sex.

Modesty, miracles and achievement

Now, our human world, after all, is not the silly world of an adolescent nor the dark, disillusioned world of a grumpy old man. Rather it is a world in which the brilliant spark of reason's order gives beauty, proportion and vitality to all the things that touch on a man's life. It is, briefly, a modest world; a world of vigorous youth and wise serenity that is a reflection of eternal horizons. Modesty, as a matter of fact, is not a matter of hiding. Rather all immodesty is a matter of obscure, narrow places that hide its innate ugliness; it does not, in fact, ever see the world for the world is much too wide for it. Modesty is not an impediment to labor or a phase of life from which we shall probably recover; but, like all the virtues, it is an indispensable condition for supreme labors and progress that end only at contact with the infinite. It is only in proportion to his loyalty to the commands of reason that a man can be said to have achieved.

In the natural order, modesty completes virtue's natural equipment for the attainment of the fullness of human life. When modesty and its companion virtues are lifted to the supernatural order, they are the equipment for that incredible abundance of Christian life, which was the purpose of God's coming amongst us. When we go a step further into the order of the apostolic graces, man's achievements outstrip the bounds of the ordinary both in the natural and supernatural order. It is significant that the supernatural does become ordinary: and that is a tremendous statement of the full play given to the works of man. He has such a wide scope for his powers that he accomplishes the supernatural almost as a matter of course; but under the apostolic graces, even that boundless field of the ordinary supernatural is too narrow. Here the achievements of man are astounding even for the supernatural order, for here, he is the mere instrument of God. To search for any limitations is to attempt to trace the boundaries of the goodness and omnipotence of God.

◫ CHAPTER XX ◫

THE FULLNESS LIFE
(Q. 179-189)

1. Activity and practicality.

2. Thought and human life:
   (a) A human division of human life: active and contemplative.
   (b) The norm of classification.

3. The life of the thinker:
   (a) Conditions of contemplation.
   (b) The field of contemplation.
   (c) Joys and duration of contemplation.

4. The life of the worker:
   (a) Conditions for successful work.
   (b) Its limitations.
   (c) A comparison of the active and contemplative life.

5. States of life:
   (a) Grounds for distinction:
      (1) In general.
      (2) Within the Church.
   (b) Spiritual states of life.

6. States of perfection:
   (a) In general.
   (b) In particular:
      (1) The Episcopal state.
      (2) The religious state:
         a. As a "state of perfection."

b. The essence of religion.

c. The three vows.

d. The labors and support of religious.

7. The field of religious activity:

(a) Basis of differences.

(b) Active orders.

(e) Contemplative orders.

(d) Highest form of religious life -- union of active and contemplative.

8. Entry into religious life.

Conclusion:

1. The common goal -- fullness of life:

(a) Fullness of action.

(b) Fullness of achievement.

2. Contemplation and modern life.

3. Activity and modern life.

4. Religious life as a norm of full life of an age:

(a) In itself.

(b) In the estimate of the age.

CHAPTER XX

THE FULLNESS OF LIFE
(Q. 179-189)

We Americans are an impatient nation. Perhaps it is because we are so close to our beginnings. Obviously, a stockade against Indians could not be built with the leisurely love that went into the Cathedrals. There are so very many things that must be done in all beginnings, things that have to be done in a hurry; and we still smack of that quick, nervous hurry. At any rate, we have developed a philosophy, which we are pleased to call pragmatic; a philosophy that is professedly practical, the central note of which is one of dynamic activity. It is a philosophy careless of principles and intensely interested in problems.

Activity and practicality

Of course, the two, principles and problems, cannot be separated. Nor can activity exist alone. Activity as such can be the most impractical thing in the world, as impractical as twiddled thumbs. It is not the doing of things that is so very important, but the doing of right things; that is, the things that are worth doing because they lead a man to his end. If we forget this, our activity becomes as senseless as a flow of words devoid of meaning; for actions, like words, are important precisely because they have a meaning. To neglect that meaning for love of the action is to destroy the action in itself, to remove from that action its humanity.

In a word, activity is practical insofar as it is human activity, activity with a goal worthy of a man. It is the humanity of that agent, man that is in danger of being overlooked today; and it must not be overlooked under pain of madness.

The life of a plant is a matter of nutrition and generation; but the life of a man cannot be gauged in inches and offspring, for man is not a plant. The life of an animal consists of sensation and movement; but the life of a man is not a matter of speed or smell, because he is not merely an animal. Every living thing can be classified by that which is most proper to it. The proper, the important, thing about man is that he is a man, that is, a thinking animal. His distinctive notes are his thought and love, and the roots of that rational activity. It is on the basis of his thinking and his rational love that a man's life must be judged.

Thought and human life: active and contemplative

How far we have drifted from this obvious, and distinctly human, point of view can be seen in our attitude towards contemplation. It is always something esoteric, mysterious; in particular, cases, it is of doubtful existence. There seems to be something indecent about its practice outside the halls of a cloister. Now, as a matter of fact, contemplation is an activity of the speculative intellect of man searching for truth; external activity is the fruit of the practical intellect of man. Since it is on the basis of his thought that a man's life must be summed up, this double activity is a complete division of human life: every man, living humanly, is either primarily a thinker or primarily a doer.

The norm of classification

Notice that word "primarily." Of course, thinkers must answer alarm clocks, eat meals and put on overcoats; and doers are not automatons or clods with never a thought. This division is not a matter of exclusion, for exclusion of either contemplation or practical action is tragic for a man; in its most extreme terms, it means either starvation or insanity. The division is rather a statement of the principal intention of the individual man and consequently of his greatest pleasure. The man whose efforts are principally directed to getting things done is leading an active life; the man whose efforts are directed principally to the knowledge of truth is leading a contemplative life. Or, to put this on a very human basis, that which we prefer to do in the company of our friends is an indication of the nature of the human life we are living; for the norm of that division, that classification, is the principal intention and the principal pleasure of the individual agent.

It is possible for men to escape both the contemplative and the active life. That is, all of their efforts can be directed to some such thing as sense pleasure which is the life of the voluptuary, or to mere physical development, both being an escape from thought; but then their lives have ceased to be human. They have embraced an animal or plant mode of existence rather than attempt the difficult task of leading a human life.

The life of the thinker: Conditions of contemplation

It is a serious error to identify the contemplative with a dry, dusty, emotionless creature moving in a gray world of cold reason. We come much closer to the truth when we visualize the contemplative as a gallant lover reckless of the cost of his love. Surely, the first condition of contemplation, as of every human action, is love. It may be only the love of knowledge, love like the philosopher's thirst for natural truth; or it may be a love not only of knowledge but also of the thing that is known, the burning love of God, for example, which drives men to search for a glimpse of His beauty in all the world. However, always contemplation must begin in love, endure by love and result in love.

The love of the contemplative is a holy, clean, beautiful love. It must be; for holiness, cleanliness and beauty are conditions for contemplation. In simpler language, the contemplative must possess the moral virtues; there can be no contemplation where the vehemence of passion and the external tumult of the world keep the soul in an uproar. The moral virtues quiet the passions to a whisper and reduce the external tumult to a distant murmur that is almost like a lullaby, enhancing rather than disturbing the peace of the soul. Chastity, above all the other moral virtues, makes a man apt for contemplation. It is true that the brilliant proportion and splendid clarity that go into the making of beauty are essentially things of the intellect; but they are participated by the moral virtues through their participation of reason's order, particularly by that virtue which restrains the passion most likely to upset reason's order and besmirch its splendor. Not that this impure man may not be more powerfully contemplative than this pure man; but the impure man would be an infinitely greater contemplative if the eyes of his soul were not irritated by the dust of the senses.

The field of contemplation

Contemplation is a swift, intuitive knowledge, an instantaneous plunge to the heart of truth. Additionally, we human beings are not intellectual plungers; we are more at home playing for pennies than risking all on one turn of the wheel. We must crawl from depths to heights, from heights to depths; unlike the angels, we approach gradually to the height of contemplation. First, we must get principles of knowledge from others, either by listening, or reading, or appealing to God by prayer. Then we must deduce the truths from these principles by meditation, speculation, mulling over the things we have received, until, finally, we are ready for that insight into sublime truth; a view that strikes the soul like nothing so much as a sunrise seen from an Alpine height.

The nature of contemplation's reward depends upon the nature of the truth that is contemplation's object. The highest truth is the proper and final object of this highest act of man's mind; it is man's highest reward, the reward of heaven itself. Some day we shall have that vision perfectly, directly; but as yet, we are not in heaven. Now we contemplate first the divine effects; they take us by the hand up to the contemplation of divinity itself. It is an imperfect contemplation; but a contemplation that is itself a beginning of heaven.

Thus, from the greatness and excellence of the works of God we are lifted up to an imperfect view of the divine majesty, omnipotence, and wisdom. The consideration of divine judgment opens up the vistas of divine justice; the consideration of His benefits and promises lifts the veil hiding the divine kindness and mercy, and sends us to our knees in praise and gratitude.

These then are the conditions of contemplation: love, the moral virtues, the intellectual acts leading up to contemplation and finally, contemplation itself. True, our contemplation must stop short of the vision of God; short of that rare apostolic grace of rapture, no man in this life sees the face of God. Nevertheless, that vision is the climax, the fitting perfection of our present contemplation.

This hurried view of the conditions of contemplation is more than sufficient to bring home to us the degree to which our age has surrendered its human birthright. Indeed, if we consider no more than two of these conditions -- the moral virtues and the consideration of divine effects and divine truths -- there remains little doubt of the completeness of the surrender by the pagan world of high, human goals. For in a world where virtue is tossed out or respected only as a social instrument, in a world which shunts aside divine causality as unscientific and ignorant, there is no possibility of contemplation; and that means that half, the more important half, of a man's life has been amputated.

As Catholics, we cannot stand aside pitying the modern world from our secure eminence; for these same considerations of the conditions for contemplation make plain a glaring weakness of American Catholic life. It is true that we have the moral virtues and insist upon their practice; it is true that we love God and we do consider, at least from time to time, divine effects and divine truths. Certainly, we do not question God's part in the creation and maintenance of the world. Yet, how about that intermediate process, that series of intellectual acts -- listening, reading, praying, meditating, pondering the divine truths that we might come to the climax of contemplation? Fairly recently in England there has been a determined movement to encourage meditation, spiritual reading and eventually contemplation by laymen. The attempt itself, the effort necessary to put it in motion, is a confession of the great need for such a movement and therefore of the great defect it supplied; here in America the movement has not even been started. Our attitude is, perhaps, that contemplation, meditation, is something for monks and nuns; rather impossible for the layman. All the same, is this true?

It would be much more to the point, instead of abstract speculation on the possibility or impossibility of meditation, to ask ourselves some pertinent questions. How much do we engage in reading that is calculated to give our minds and hearts the food for a consideration of divine things? How much listening do we do to discourses on this same material? How much praying for greater insight into these truths? How much mulling over do they get from us? With these questions answered, we can logically approach the question of the possibility or impossibility of meditation for lay folk; and we do not have to go very far. The first priest we meet can testify from his own experience that meditation and contemplation are by no means impossible to lay folk.

Some years ago, in the course of a retreat, I was approached by a woman in tears. Every morning, after getting her husband off to work and her five children to school, she herself went to work in a factory; she was back to cook the noon meal, and she had to do the rest of the housework in the evening. The children were angels; the husband was kind. In fact, everything was fine, except her prayers. In some completely mysterious fashion, she would find a half-hour during this crowded day to slip into Church; kneeling down, she started the Hail Mary, but she never got it finished. The thought of the goodness of God or His love would come to her mind -- and the half hour was gone. Her point was that this could not go on. After all, her prayers had to be said; what should she do about it? The answer was, of course, to do nothing about it but thank God; for there is no prayer that can compare with such as these.

This is not an isolated experience. In addition, certainly it would seem to indicate that the standard excuse of being too busy for meditation is decidedly thin. If we find little of meditation, very little of contemplation in our lives, some of the immediate causes are not hard to locate: it is because we do not pray enough, we do not give our minds supernatural food to munch on, nor our hearts time for more than a hasty caress. We are too much absorbed by the hurried age in which we live, so busy gathering up knowledge that we starve our minds and our hearts.

Joys and duration of contemplation

Really, this is not a matter of shirking an unpleasant duty; it is a matter of cheating ourselves of a joy that might easily be ours. Remember that contemplation is a beginning, a foretaste of heaven; even in this life, its joy exceeds every other human delight. It is a spiritual joy and so it goes far beyond all carnal pleasure. Moreover, it is the highest act of man, the act most in harmony with his nature, accomplishing that for which he exists; and more and more delightfully, as he develops the intellectual virtues of wisdom and knowledge that make contemplation easier. It is the secret of the scholar's long hours, the philosopher's relentless pursuit of truth; and, far above all these things, the secret of the saint's utter surrender, with its joy of contemplating supreme beauty, supreme love, of contemplating Him Whom we love above all else with a love exceeding all loves.

We do not slip into this joy as easily as we do into a family heritage. There is a bit of a brisk fight to attain it. A fight against the defects and limitations of our own mind, as for instance, against the irritation of reaching to the very edge of truth yet not quite grasping it, like having a word on the tip of our tongue but being unable to say it. It is, too, a fight against the heaviness of our body's bearing us down to lower things. Now, the very fight only makes the triumph the sweeter and the joy the greater.

Yet the necessity of a fight for this thing should not surprise us when we remember that it borders on the divine. It is, after all, the product of that frank likeness of the divine in us, our intellect and our will; like the divinity, contemplation too is spiritual, incorruptible, enduring. It deals with the incorruptible, the eternal truth; there are no contraries to destroy it. Of course, such a thing as this is not to be had lightly. Yet it does not involve straining of muscles, cleverness of hands or quickness of feet. Of course, we get tired working at it; but not as tired as a farmer or a bricklayer doing his work; and we are the more quickly ready to begin again until the time when there will be no call for interruption.

The Catholics attitude towards contemplation has always been one of reverence, while the pagan usually has stood before it puzzled and confused. Additionally, small wonder. To the Catholic, the contemplative is already busy at the work of heaven, occupied with the end and goal of all men. The contemplative brings God closer to the ordinary Catholic and so is a kind of visible intermediary who makes the step to God seem just that much shorter. They are God's favorites, these contemplatives; and because they are friends of ours, they are doing much of our work, throwing a cloak of protection about us, interceding against our own weakness.

Seen in its full significance, this Catholic attitude is nothing less than a recognition of the true values of the contemplative and active life; an acknowledgment of the eternal character of the one and the transient character of the other. This is what stamps Catholic culture with its own peculiar attitude towards active life. It is the radical cause of Catholic culture's refusal to get too excited about active life; of its easy (and to the pagan, shiftless) acceptance of active life and its vicissitudes. It is the thing that enables the Catholic to grin a little amusedly at his success and make his poverty a hothouse for the nurturing of the shoots of sanctity. For the Catholic knows that, the active life does not last; it is a step in a journey. There are things to be done, milestones to be passed, sorrows to be borne, tasks to be accomplished, but all on the way to heaven. In that ultimate home, all activity will be ordered to contemplation and the enjoyment of that eternal truth; not to keeping body and soul together, paying taxes, building up a savings account.

The life of the worker: Conditions for successful work

At the moment, active life is no light thing. Living humanly is never a light thing. For the successful living of the active life, the moral virtues are essential, for it is by these that man gets things done. In addition to the man who maintains that, these are easy, it might be unkindly retorted: "Try it and see." Since prudence is directly ordered to the regulation of the moral virtues, it, too, directly pertains to the active life. There is a serious commentary on the practicality of our modern American philosophy of action in the fact that the proportion of the perfection of prudence and the moral virtues is the proportion of our success in the living of an active life. Obviously, if these are the norms of our ability to live an active life, much of our pagan world has made really practical active living an impossibility for themselves; for prudence gets nowhere without goals to aim at, and there is no room for moral virtue where sense appetite stands alone as the unchallenged driving power of a man's life. Nor is an age that dodges personal responsibility in any sense practical; for the active life (which is practical life) is not a light thing, an easy thing to be faced by a coward. It is a human thing, worthy of the strong efforts of a stout human heart.

It is interesting to note that teaching, for all its airs and grave dignity, belongs next to ditch digging, not next to contemplation. That is, considering not merely the truth conveyed, but rather the conveying of that truth to the student, teaching is a work of the active, not the contemplative life. It is a kind of intellectual hood carrying; and, whether we greet the news with sorrow or with joy, it is a work, which ceases with death. There are no school days in heaven, at least as far as human teachers are concerned. However, this is no slur on teaching. It is frequently necessary for a man to live an active life; in fact, many times in the individual case, it is better for a man to live an active life, never, of course, excluding contemplation. Yet, considered objectively, there is no comparison between activity and contemplation; the contemplative life is far superior, a superiority that is spontaneously, intuitively recognized by the simplest of Catholics.

His family would have every right to their astonishment if the day laborer of no education remarked, over the supper table, that contemplative life is more thoroughly in harmony with the intellectual nature of man as his highest act turning about his highest object. Nevertheless, that same man does grasp something of the full freedom, the approach to divinity of the contemplative life. He recognizes in its serene continuity the beginning of eternity; he sees the reflection of its penetrating joy stamped on the face of the contemplative; he has nothing but admiration for its greater self-sufficiency, freeing man more and more from worldly things. He can agree with Christ that Mary has chosen the best part, a part not ordered to further ends but desirable in itself. He can almost feel the quiet and peace it gives in contrast to the bustling activity of his own life. Perhaps more clearly than anything else, he sees why Mary's part will not be taken away from her; that is, he sees that this is a beginning, a foretaste of heaven. It may well be that some exhausted sweat-shop worker is here and now meriting much more than does this enclosed nun, by reason of the tired girl's more intense charity. Even so, in itself, contemplation is more meritorious than the active life because it directly and immediately pertains to the love of God. Yet we find contemplatives actually praying for a cessation of divine favors that they might engage in active work. Thus, Catherine de Ricci prayed for less of ecstasies that she might more efficiently handle her task of sub-prioress; but this is not a case of the contemplative returning to a better life. Rather it is a sharing of the fruits of contemplation with others, a return to activity in order to direct the active lives of others, to lead these others to the ultimate contemplation of heaven. For active life is really a preparation for contemplation as earth is a preparation for heaven.

Its limitations

Not that the effort and external activity of the active life is not an impediment to the contemplative life. It is. It needs no argument to make evident the fact that the stenographer pounding away at her machine or the electrical worker handling wires of high voltage cannot have their minds free for divine contemplation. On the other hand, the active life humanly lived, with the full perfection of the moral virtues and of prudence, is a positive aid to and preparation for contemplation by the peace and order it instills in the inner life of a man.

A comparison of the active and contemplative life

Are there natural contemplatives? people who are naturally made for contemplation, as there are people who simply cannot sit down and think? This is the old, old question of temperament. It is true that a natural purity and quiet of soul makes one apt for contemplation; it is also true that a naturally passionate nature, a natural drive to action, fits a man for active life. All the same, what is done with these temperaments is quite a different question. Nature is never a sufficient explanation for the destiny of a man. If he is fitted by nature for living the active life well, that means that he is fitted by nature to prepare himself well and quickly for the contemplative life; with that preparation over, he will probably throw himself whole-heartedly into the contemplative life with all the generosity of his passionate nature. However, many a person with a natural aptitude for contemplation is far from a contemplative. In other words, this matter of natural aptitude is rather a question of the amount of preparation necessary before embarking on the daring flight of the contemplative life.

States of life: Grounds for distinction in general

The division of active and contemplative is a division of human life on a basis of human activity, and that activity is exercised by men in different states of life. The very phrase "states of life" calls up pictures of the rich contrasted with the poor, the aristocracy as over against the peasantry, and so on. Actually, all such considerations are too external, too variable, to constitute a man in a state of life. We can see this more readily if we look at the roots of that expression "state of life". A better translation would be "stance of life". The phrase is taken from a comparison with the physical position of a man standing: he stands when he is erect and quiet, not when he is running, walking, lying down or jumping in a pool. Additionally, it is in this position, erect and quiet, that his members are properly disposed, in their natural position -- head above the feet, arms hanging down, and so on.

Thus, a moral state or stance will be an erect and quiet or permanent position of man among his fellows. It implies a certain immobility or quiet and a relation to the obligations affecting the person of a man, to his natural position: that is, according as he stands by himself or by another, according as he is under obligation to another or free from it.

On this basis, there are two general stances or states of life: the state of freedom and the state of slavery. Both are permanent, both have a relation to the obligations affecting the person. The free man, not bound to another, stands erect by himself; the slave, bound to another, is erect only in being bound to another. Thus, the religious is in a different state of life from the secular, for he is a slave to God; the just man is in a different state of life from a sinner, for sinners are slaves to sin.

Within the Church

Under these general states, there will be many more particular ones, according to particular labors and particular goals that men must busy themselves with. Take for example the Church. It reflects the grace of Christ as the universe reflects the perfection of God, demanding almost as great a variety as is to be found in the physical universe; for many facets are necessary for even an inadequate mirroring of that splendor. Then too, we cannot all be nuns, bishops, or country pastors; the Church has a wide task to perform, a task not to be handled by a quick-change artist or variously colored spotlights. In addition, this very variety results in a dignity and beauty of the order found within the Church. In other words, this variety of states of life is necessary in the Church for its perfection, its action and its beauty.

Spiritual states of life

It is in terms of perfection we speak when we distinguish the various states of spiritual life. In spiritual things, there is a double slavery and a double liberty. There is the slavery of sin, which is the state of the habitual sinner; and the slavery of justice, which is the state of the habitually just man. Then there is the freedom from sin, proper to the man who is not overcome by his inclination to sin; and the freedom from justice, which belongs to the man who sins regardless of his inclination to justice. Obviously, the slavery of sin and the freedom from justice go hand in hand and constitute a real state of spiritual slavery; while the freedom from sin and the slavery of justice go together and constitute a state of real spiritual freedom.

It does not take a profound analysis to notice a depressing parallelism here between the "new freedom" and one of these states. That "new freedom" is an exultation in the release from the fetters of justice; it is the youthful sinner's concentration on the freedom involved in the slavery of sin. Apparently, it is only the long school of the years that teaches man that the fetters of sin grow steadily heavier, while the fetters of justice are lightened to the delicate weight of the bonds of love. There is a freedom in the discarding of ethical limitations, the freedom from justice that goes hand in hand with the slavery of sin. Both states, of spiritual slavery and spiritual freedom, are achieved by human efforts. Additionally, that means that they are reached by that slow-motion peculiar to humanity; not all at once, but little by little, with a beginning, an advancement, and a final perfection. In the state of spiritual freedom, these are called the state of the beginners, of those who are progressing and of the perfect; or, in language that is more technical, the purgative, the illuminative and the unitive state.

States of perfection: In general

Notice that all three are subdivisions of the state of spiritual freedom; in other words, the common note that binds all three together is the note of perfection, the note of charity. The point is important to offset the rumor, sponsored by slipshod thinking, to the effect that there is an imperfect charity like an imperfect factory product that can be had somewhat cheaper than the genuine thing. All charity is perfect in the sense that all charity prefers God above all else; there are not several kinds of charity, one good and others not so good. There is only one kind; but there are several degrees of that one kind. Men in all three of these states of spiritual perfection are spiritually free, i.e., they are united to God through charity; a truth that becomes obvious when we remember that these three states include all men in the state of grace.

It should not be hard to see that there are degrees of perfection. It is evident that we are not perfect as God is, loving Him infinitely as He loves Himself. The prosaic necessity of a night sleep is proof enough that we have not the prerogative of the blessed, of loving God to our full capacity and without interruption. There are, as a matter of fact, just two possibilities open to us. We can love God to the extent of avoiding sin; or we can go further and love Him to the extent of directing all our energies to love of Him by abandoning all else that might in any way hold us back from Him. The first is the state common to all the faithful keeping the Commandments; the second is the state common to those who have abandoned the world and entered religious life.

To put the matter in utterly simply language, perfection consists in keeping the Commandments. Christ spoke adequately, beautifully and with divine simplicity when He said: "If you love me, keep my commandments." The counsels of poverty, chastity and obedience are not a bypass to heaven, substitutes or alternates for the Commandments: they are instruments, dispositions for a more perfect observance of those Commandments. They do not set a man on a road different from that followed by the rest of the friends of Christ; they merely remove the obstacles from the common road, doing away with the slightest impediments to charity.

This makes clear a very necessary distinction. A rule of silence and bells that clang in the middle of the night are not essential for the observance of the Commandments; they can be kept in any condition of life, in any place, at any time. Consequently, in any condition of life we can be perfect. However, the public embracing of the counsels, of the fixed, permanent way of life, which we call religious, puts a man in the religious state or state of perfection. Notice that it does not make him perfect; rather it dedicates him to a whole-hearted pursuit of perfection that runs down its quarry only on the other side of death.

In particular: The Episcopal state

As a matter of fact, this state of perfection is not the monopoly of religious; indeed, they have elbowed their way in, by their profession, to a condition that bishops take on by virtue of their office itself. It takes a brave man to accept a bishopric; for it takes a brave man to dedicate himself not only to his own perfection, but to the perfecting of others. His perfection must fill the cup of his own soul and overflow into the souls of others; his love must be a flaming fire, not only sufficient to warm the house of his own soul, but to set fire to the hearts of all of his people.

We are being decidedly petty when we think of a bishopric only in terms of the honor, the administrative planning, the wealth or the power that may go with it; we are forgetting the loneliness of it, the long hours of prayer, the sorrow that escapes all comfort as souls make their way to hell, the agony of a commander whose lieutenants send in such desperate pleas for help from beleaguered fortresses on all sides.

This is an office not to be refused at one's own pleasure, but cheerfully accepted when obedience demands; it is an office lawfully desired, but only by a man who wishes to make a holocaust of himself. Naturally, it is not a state into which one steps lightly.

Immediately upon assuming his office, the bishop becomes the torchbearer for all others, the center of all eyes. He carries the responsibility for the souls of his people and they look to him unquestioningly for leadership. It takes a good man to be a bishop; but not necessarily the absolutely best man. Once he has undertaken his apostolic task, the bishop cannot lightly lay it down; he is dedicated to the souls of others and they must be his first consideration. He cannot desert them for any reasons of personal convenience, safety or even of greater perfection offered by the contemplative life.

The religious state: As a "state of perfection."

Even in religious life, there are grouches, early-morning indispositions, people who find the coffee abominable; for the religious state and sanctity are not synonymous terms. That you can take as absolutely first hand information. There is no halo included in the habit that is given to a postulant. These men and women are called religious because they bind themselves to the service of God with the chains of love; they offer God a holocaust of themselves and that is the work of religion. They die to the world; though not infrequently they have difficulty staying dead. Because by their state they unite themselves to God, it is called a state of perfection.

The postulant is not asked to work miracles as a condition of admittance; for sanctity is not a pre-disposition to the religious life. Rather it is the goal of religious life; indeed, while religious life demands many things, it also offers many helps, gives freedom from many temptations and is, generally, a boon to the weak as well as to the holy. In fact, we might say that one can save one's soul much more easily in the religious life -- but not nearly so comfortably.

The essence of religion

The obligations of the religious are the source of his joy as well as of his discomfort; they embrace, over and above the Ten Commandments, his rule and the three counsels of Christ that make up the essence of the religious life: poverty, chastity and obedience. These latter are embraced under vow and necessarily so: since the state of religion implies an obligation to the things of perfection, an immobility or permanence that is conferred by the vows. There is a graphic statement of the purpose of the vows in the story of the Roman emperor who recovered the true

Cross and, from his piety, determined to shoulder it while he retraced the Way of the Cross; but with all his great strength, he could not move a step along that sacred way until he had taken off his shoes and discarded his royal robes. From another point of view, we might say that the religious, in his vows, has taken to himself a wife that will give him no peace short of perfection, he has put himself under a happy necessity that forever drives him on to better things. Again, the vows enable a man to offer all of his life in an instant; to get the business over with quickly in a kind of spiritual self-destruction, so that he can stand aside in something of the eternity of God, with time stretched out complete before him.

The vows do make up the essence of religious life; and that life can be variously considered. We might look on it as a spiritual gymnasium in which we constantly exercise to perfect charity. It may have the air of a quiet retreat, a state of peace from the uproar of the world and of human appetites; or the emphasis may be on the roaring activity of a holocaust to the Creator. Now, do not let anyone tell you it is a martyrdom; if they attempt it, you may keep a straight face, but in your heart, you have a right to feel amused. What religious life really does is to remove all the impediments to an unrestrained rush to God: the cupidity for external goods, concupiscence, and inordinate self-will.

The three vows

Of the three vows, the greatest -- but not necessarily the most difficult -- is the vow of obedience, simply because it brings the most precious and the most utterly free gift. External things can be extremely valuable; the goods of man's body can hardly be tagged with a price; but the goods of his soul, the utterly sacrosanct faculties that no one or no thing can get at but God and the man himself -- there is a royal gift, the gift of man's own will. This vow of obedience contains the other vows and its acts are closer to the inner acts of religious subjection, the acts by which a man pays his tribute to his Creator in a coin worthy of the Kingdom of God.

From all this it might seem that a religious is teetering on dizzy heights, heights from which it is easy and terrible to fall. In a sense that is true. By reason of his vows, the sin of a religious can be much more serious than the sin of a layman; thus, for instance, a sin of impurity in his case has the added malice of sacrilege. There is too the element of contempt or ingratitude, and the danger of scandal. Yet, on the other hand, the sin of the religious in an individual case, may be lighter by reason of greater weakness or greater ignorance. At the very least, it should be easier for the religious to repent, not only by reason of the habitual direction of his life to God, but also because of the help of his religious brethren.

The labors and support of religious

The young novice who falls into bed at night completely exhausted has long since discovered how false was the rumor of empty, idle days in the convent. Forty years later, she will still be wondering how in the world a story like that ever got around. There are indeed things to be done in religious life; but the general nature of it only indicates that inner spiritual activity that is at the heart of it. As for the external works, well certainly, the religious is not automatically a crusader commissioned to preach, teach, hear confessions and so on; for that, he will need the Sacrament of Orders and authorization of the bishop. Even more certainly, his habit gives him no right to open a pawnshop, operate a coalmine or run a tavern. In fact, secular business is forbidden to religious, unless it is engaged in by reason of charity and then only in moderation and with the permission of his superiors. At any rate, it must not interfere with the essential business of religious life.

Still, after all, these religious must keep alive. How? Well sometimes the very rule of a religious demands manual labor; thus the ancient Benedictines and Carthusians had manual labor as their official work. In other cases, not the rule, but brute necessity demands manual labor. Other religious, as the Carmelites of Wheeling, West Virginia, subsist on alms but they are not allowed to ask for the alms, depending on divine providence to send them sufficient for their needs. Still others live by out and out begging; and among these are the Dominicans and the Franciscans, hence their name of mendicant or begging friars.

The mere fact that so few Dominicans, Franciscans or Carmelites have starved to death is some little indication of the place religious life has in the hearts of Catholic lay folk They understand, of course, that the purpose of the begging is not to insure a lazy leisure for the friars. It is legitimate to receive alms or beg for them when the religious are engaged in works of public benefit, such as contemplation, or when they constantly distribute their own goods to the poor. A lazy or greedy beggar is vicious, whether he wear a religious habit or not; if the solicitation of alms is a medium of humility, of necessity, of penance or of utility, it is virtuous. The particular purpose of Dominican begging is to release the brethren from manual labor that they might more profoundly pursue their work of study, teaching and preaching.

Our astonishment at the cut of a religious habit might be mitigated to some degree if we remember that it was not designed as a pattern for the Beau Brummels of this, or indeed of any, age. It is the garment most fitting to one who has become a fool for Christ as Christ became a fool for us on the Cross. Thomas, in his own day, asked if religious could legitimately wear old or vile clothes; and answered, matter of factually, that of course they could if they had nothing else to wear. The answer might well have been autobiographical. He also noted other reasons such as bringing home to others the religious' contempt of the world, a gesture of penance, or of humility. Of course, if the religious habit is paraded from vanity (God save the mark!), for purposes of greed, or if the clothes are old and shabby through sheer negligence, there is little virtue in the wearing of the habit.

The field of religious activity: Basis of differences

That there is unity in the religious state is evident from the common dedication of all religious to the service of God; that there is variety can be hidden from no man's eyes, least of all from the eyes of a man who has seen the benumbing array of religious habits at a University summer school session. There is, however, a more scientific way of distinguishing religious orders than by the habit; for each order is organized to its last detail with its proximate end in view. Thus, the proximate end of Dominican religious life (to keep the example in the family) is a double one: contemplation in the monastic tradition and the scattering of the fruits of that contemplation by preaching and teaching, particularly in university circles. To attain those ends, the Dominican has very special means: full monastic observance, choral office, cloistered convents, silence and a rigid course of study. The proximate end of the Jesuit Order is the education of youth; and in order that they might be more free for that physically exhausting task which takes up so much of every day, its members are freed from the community monastic observance.

Active orders

Seen in this light, the varieties of religious orders give a panoramic view of the human heart, the wide fields of sacrifice to which the human heart reaches out under the inspiration of divine love. We find military orders with the proximate end of battle, battle in defense of the worship of God, defense of the community or, as St. Thomas suggests -- approving the ideal of a later chivalry -- in defense of the poor or the oppressed.

Then there are the other active orders, less aggressive, who take care of the poor, the aged, beggars, the sick, children, educate youth, indeed, take care of almost everything human that needs caring for. An American needs no examples of this type of religious life. There will be orders dedicated to preaching, the parochial ministry, missions, and so on; in other words caring for the spiritual needs of their neighbor. In addition, there will be orders dedicated to study. In the time of St. Thomas, it was a burning question whether or not a religious order could be dedicated to study. His defense of that ideal was a defense of his own Dominican Order; and he points out, from the experience of his own intense years, that the labor of study is a constant chastisement of the flesh and a curbing of worldly desires. He noticed too, again from his years at the books, that study served contemplative life both directly, by the study of divine truth, and indirectly by removing the intellectual errors, which are an impediment to contemplation.

Contemplative orders

Then there are the purely contemplative orders, which represent a direct approach to the goal, to God Himself. Since the worth of the religious state is measured by its approach to God, these orders are much higher than the purely active orders, higher and harder, for their approach is direct.

Highest form of religious life -- union of active and contemplative

In between the active and the contemplative orders is what is, in practice, the highest form of religious life -- a union of the contemplative with the active, so that both are proximate and principal ends of this type of religious life. It is the type of life represented by the Dominican Order; its superiority is argued by St. Thomas (again in defense of the family) on the obvious grounds that it is much better to have light and give it than merely to have it; it is a greater thing to contemplate and give the fruits of contemplation to others than merely to contemplate. The study, the preaching and the teaching of Dominican life represent one side, the side of the dispersal of the fruits gathered by the other side of Dominican life, the side of contemplation and monastic observance.

Again, in answer to a question of his time, St. Thomas insists that it is not an impediment to religious life for the community to possess goods; the care of such common things is not the care of selfishness but of charity, for each member is seeking not that which is his own, but that which belongs to the community. Abuse is, of course, possible through too much solicitude or too much wealth; but the thing itself is not to be condemned because of a particular abuse of it that may crop up in the course of history.

Strange as it may seem to us, though it is quite logical, solitary religious life is in itself more perfect than community religious life; although it is the most dangerous to all but the perfect. I say this is logical because community life, after all, is a means to perfection; hence, it is unnecessary when perfection is already had. Solitary or hermit life, then, is for the perfect. For anyone else it is extremely dangerous, for it strips a man of the helps he gets from community life: the help to intellect from instruction, and the help to affection from the rebuke of example and correction. It has been said that community life keeps a man from getting old. That may or may not be true. Nevertheless, it is certainly true that community life does all that can humanly be done to keep a man from getting odd. In it, there is as little chance for the development of eccentricities as there is for the seventh child of a family of twelve to become spoiled.

Entry into religious life

An historical or a modern worldwide study of religious life brings to light two practices that meet with small sympathy in our country today: the taking of a vow to enter religious life and the reception of children into monasteries. This coldness is due, to a great extent, to misunderstanding. We forget that a vow is itself an act of virtue, of the virtue of religion; and that just as sin is worse when it proceeds from a will obstinate in evil, so a virtuous act is better if it proceeds from a will firmly fixed in good, as is the case in the vows. What is more important, from the side of misunderstanding, is that we look upon entry into religion as something absolutely irrevocable, like the loss of our second teeth. Granted that having taken such a vow a man must enter the religious life or commit sin; that does not mean that he must stay, nor that he must be kept even if he wants to stay. Nor does it mean that he does not have time, plenty of time, to find out what it is all about before binding himself for life to the religious state.

As for children, much the same limitations must be kept in mind. It is true that children have been taken into monasteries as mere infants; but certainly, they were not bound by irrevocable ties to religious life until they could bind themselves. To St. Thomas, this meant until they reached the age of reason, which, by his computation, was the age of puberty. The practice today, as always, is to guarantee the full freedom of entry into religious life: for it is only by love that this life can be lived, and love cannot be forced.

Perhaps we have adopted too much of the point of view of our pagan age. We wonder if those who enter religious life very young know what they are missing; yet it never dawns on us that they will never finish finding out what they are getting. We concentrate on what they are surrendering, watching them go with a puzzled reluctance. We shy away in distaste from one who induces others to enter religion as we would from a kind of proselytizer; though St. Thomas says rightly that the reward of such is very great. It is the reward given to those who bring others to Christ. No doubt, God, with His infinite patience and comprehensive knowledge of human vagaries, can understand it, but it must be bewildering to the angels to see Catholic parents fighting off their children's attempts to get closer to Christ. Christ Himself had a word to say, a sharp word, to the men who tried to shield Him from children; here it is the children who are being shielded from Christ.

Perhaps some of the modern distaste is inspired by the momentous character of this decision to enter religious life. Such finality of choice comes as a jarring shock; it is such an ultimate disposition of life. Again this is the viewpoint of the pagan; the making of the decision normally does not require much advice-seeking or long deliberation. We should deliberate about things because they are dubious, not because they are final. The entry into religious life is certainly a good; the candidate does not expect to persevere by his own strength but by the power of God. So for the most part, the candidate for religious life enters the novitiate as gaily as a girl goes to her marriage. He might well take counsel about the manner of going, about securing entrance, about the particular order he will choose, the possibility of some impediment that might bar him; but the entry into religious life itself should be as easy as falling in love. That is precisely what it is.

The common goal -- fullness of life: Fullness of action

Now we have come to the end of what is called the moral part of the Summa Theologica of St. Thomas. To sum this up we should really go back to the first chapter of the second volume of this work where we started to talk of the goal of man. If that be difficult, let me point out, just passingly, that in that first chapter we uncovered the key to human life and action, which we said was the goal. Human action is a motion going to some place; and that place, that goal, gives meaning to human life, a goal, which we determined, was the vision of God, the union of man with his last end. From all sides that successful conclusion of human life meant the fullest perfection, the greatest development, the fullness of human life. Therefore, the vision of God is the end of man, and at the same time the fullness of human living.

Fullness of achievement

In all the rest of that second volume, and throughout this one, we have been considering the ways and means by which man wins to that goal: the intellect, the will, the passions: the habits or principles of actions, which when good are virtues, when bad are sins, the one driving men on full speed to the goal, the other dragging him back or shunting him off the road that might lead to the goal. We saw that it was only that which went towards the goal that was worthy of the name of action; that it was only by approach to the goal that we achieve. From the very beginning, then, we have seen the true notion of practicality. Since then we have worked up systematically to its fullest development.

Contemplation and modern life

In this chapter, we have come to the fullness of achievement -- contemplation -- to the most abundant state of human life, the state of perfection -- the religious state. Perhaps this final result of our study would be summed up by the world today in such terms as this: the fullness of action is possessed by the dreamer, the fullness of achievement is found in this thoroughly sterile condition they call the religious life. The statement would be grossly unfair; but it would have the virtue of bringing out clearly by contrast our modern world's notion of action as mere activity and of achievement as the denial of all goals.

We have come to these conclusions with complete intellectual honesty. We have proceeded step by step; not looking at only this or that fact, but insisting on an examination of all the facts. Additionally, all the way through we saw that human fullness and the fullness of virtue marched side by side. Every motion of defense we made for the fullness of virtue was a defense of humanity itself.

Activity and modern life

It is easy, then, to understand how much injury has been done to human life by cutting contemplation out of it. It is as reasonable to cut off a man's head and feet and expect him to run a race as it is to cut off the principles and the goals of human life and their consideration, and expect human life to go somewhere. In other words, we have reached the ultimate in frustration when the modern devotees of activity have destroyed their own idol, when those dedicated to activity have destroyed activity itself, removing from it its human element. Obviously, thought cannot be taken out of human action and have it still remain human; not merely thought, but upward thought, thought of the ultimate goal.

Religious life as a norm of full life of an age: In itself

We might sum up all this in terms of the religious life, by pointing out that the religious life is truly the most practical of human lives because it goes most wholeheartedly to the goal, to the purpose, to the sole reason for all activity. At the same time that it achieves fullness of action, it also achieves fullness of actual accomplishment; for it gets done the things that above all other things must be done.

In the estimate of the age

It is precisely because the Catholic can see this truth that his own active life is so rich in its actions and in its fruits. In fact, we might say that the fullness of the life of any age may be accurately judged by its attitude towards religious life; not towards religious, you understand, but towards the religious state. In an age, that has nothing but contempt for the apparent futility, the impracticality, the inactivity of religious life, there will be little of practicality, little of true activity, nothing of achievement. On the contrary, where religious life is recognized as worthy of the highest of human efforts, you will find men aiming at the right goals and at least trying, trying strenuously, to share in those goals. By that very fact, such an age will share to some extent in that fullness of action, that fullness of achievement. In other words, the men of that age point all their efforts towards the goal that is worthy of men; by those actions they constantly take steps towards the one goal that is worthy of achievement, the one goal that gives reason to human life, the last goal, God.

The End

Visit us at your local bookstore on the web at our web site:

http://Revelationinsight.tripod.com/

E-Mail: Mystic@Orthodox.com

The Spurgeon Library

1st segment

Volumes 1 thru 6

Collected Works   Charles Spurgeon

The Andrew Murray Library

1st segment

Volumes 1 thru 5

Collected Works   Andrew Murray

Women of Faith Series

1st segment

Volumes 1 thru 5

Teresa of Avila   Interior Castle

Selections   Julian of Norwich

Passion of Christ   Anne Catherine Emmerich

Dialogues   Catherine of Sienna

2nd segment

Fundamental Writings   Jessie Penn-Lewis

Works of the "Catholic Classics" Series

1st segment

Volumes 1thru 6

Explanation of the Rule of St Augustine   Hugh of St. Victor

Treatise of the Spiritual Life Books 1 3   Bishop Morozzo O.Cist

Imitation of Christ   Thomas a' Kempis

Note: vol. 2 - 4 are fraternal twins writings

2nd segment

Little Book of Wisdom	Henry Suso
Spiritual Exercises w/ Commentary	Ignatius of Lyola

Works of the "Desert Fathers" Series

Volumes 1 thru 5

1st segment

Wisdom of the Desert	James O' Hanney
Desert Fathers Books 1 & 2	Countess Hahn-Hahn

2nd segment

Evigarius Essentials	Evigarius
Ephrim Essentials	Ephrim of Syria

Ladder to Paradise w/ Commentary by Luis de Garnada   John Climcaus

Works for the Master

"Philosopher's Palate" Series

Vol. 1 thru 4

1st segment

Divine Names	Pseudo Dionysius
First Principle	Duns Scotus
Boethius	Consolation of Philosophy

Pesenes   Paschal

2nd segment

Vol. 5-8

The Greek Thinkers   Theodor Gomperz

The Thomas Aquinas Library

Volumes 1 thru 6

1st segment

The Companion to the Summa   Walter Farrell O.P.

2nd segment

Contra Gentiles   Thomas Aquinas

Works for the Journeyman

"Great Christian Mystical Writings"

Volumes 1 thru 5

1st segment

Ascent of Mount Carmel	St. John of the Cross
Dark Night of the Soul	St. John of the Cross
A Cell of Knowledge	Anonymous
Divine Consolation	Angelina Foligno

2nd segment

A Cloud of Unknowing   Walter Hilton

"The Contemplative" Series

Volumes 1 thru 4

1st segment

Ladder of Perfection   Walter Hilton

Selection of Hugh of St Victor   Hugh of St Victor

Golden Treatise of Mental Prayer   Peter of Alcantra

Third Spiritual Alphabet   Francisco de Osuna

French Enlightenment Series

Volumes 1 thru 4

1st segment

Selections   Francis de Sales

Selections   Francis de Fenelon Vol. 1 & 2

2nd Segment

Selected Works   St. Bernard

Selected Works   Reginald Garrigou-Lagrange, O.P.

Research Essentials" Series

Volumes 1 thru 5

1st segment

Medieval to Modern English Dictionary	R /I Publishing Staff
Contemplative Life	St. Bruno
Ecclesiastical History	Bede
Church Creeds	Various

2nd Segment

Greek to English Dictionary	James Strong

Works for the Apprentice

The Initial Series

"Pilgrim's Pantry"

Volumes 1 thru 5

1st segment

The Kneeling Christian	Anonymous
Passion of Christ	Bro Smith SGS
Way of Perfection	Teresa of Avila
Augustine Essentials	Augustine

2nd segment

Ascent of the Pilgrim   Various Authors

"The Monastic Series "

Volumes 1 thru 6

1st segment

A Short Overview of Monasticism   Alfred Wishart

Monasticism from Egypt to the 4th Cent   W. Mackean

2nd segment

A Monk's Topical Bible in 4 Books.

"Philip Schaff Library "

Church History   Philip Schaff

Spiritual Poetry & Literature Series

Volumes 1-3

1st segment

Liturgical Poetry   Adam of St Victor

The Ante-Nicene Library

Volumes 1 thru 12

All these works may be purchased through us directly or from your local bookstore.

<u>Each series will comprise of 12 volumes each.</u>

Visit us at your local bookstore on the web at our web site

FREE BOOK offer for visiting our website:

"His Daily Bread"

All works <u>always</u> at least 10% off retail, through our store

http://Revelationinsight.tripod.com/

E Books Available in

Amazon's Kindle

Sony E-Reader

B&N Nook E-Reader

PDA

Lightning Source UK Ltd.
Milton Keynes UK
UKHW012149230419
341484UK00001B/165/P